# THEOLOGY, BIBLICAL SCHOLARSHIP AND RABBINICAL STUDIES IN THE SEVENTEENTH CENTURY

*Constantijn L'Empereur (1591-1648)*
*Professor of Hebrew and Theology at Leiden*

BY

PETER T. VAN ROODEN

E.J. BRILL
LEIDEN · NEW YORK · KØBENHAVN · KÖLN
1989

Published with financial support from the Netherlands Organization for Scientific Research (NWO).

This series is the continuation of *Studies over de geschiedenis van de Leidse Universiteit.*

Translated by J. C. Grayson.
Original title: *Constantijn L'Empereur (1591-1648) Professor Hebreeuws en theologie te Leiden. Theologie, bijbelwetenschap en rabbijnse studiën in de zeventiende eeuw.*

**Library of Congress Cataloging-in-Publication Data**

Rooden, Peter T. van.
  Theology, biblical scholarship, and rabbinical studies in the seventeenth century: Constantijn L'Empereur (1591-1648), professor of Hebrew and Theology at Leiden.

  (Studies in the history of Leiden University, ISSN 0169-8362; v. 6)
  Translation of: Constantijn L'Empereur (1591-1648), Professor Hebreeuws en theologie te Leiden.
  Revision of thesis—University of Leiden, 1985.
  Bibliographie: p.
  Includes index.
  1. L'Empereur, Constantijn, 1591-1648.  2. Hebraists, Christian—Netherlands—Leiden—Biography.  3. Old Testament scholars—Netherlands—Leiden—Biography.
  4. Rijksuniversiteit te Leiden—Biography.  5. Leiden (Netherlands)—Biography.  I. Title.  II. Series.
  PJ4534.E47R6613    1989        221'.092 [B]        89-7060
  ISBN 90-04-09035-5

ISSN    0169-8362
ISBN    90 04 09035 5

PRINTED IN THE NETHERLANDS BY E. J. BRILL

*In memory of my father*
*For my mother*

CONTENTS

# FOREWORD

The following work is a revised version of a thesis defended in June 1985 in the Theological Faculty of the State University of Leiden. It aims, in the form of an intellectual biography, to make a contribution to the history of scholarly study of the Old Testament and rabbinical literature in the 17th century. Because great attention is paid to the environment in which this scholarship was carried on, this study moves in several fields. It was thus impossible to avoid explaining things which were self-evident to the various specialists. One should remember, in the author's defence, that the second duty of a historian is to tell a story.

For the transcription of Jewish words and names, the system of the *Encyclopædia Judaica* has been followed. For the not particularly numerous Greek, and a single Syriac word, no scholarly system of transcription has been used. The list of literature cited has no bibliographical pretentions. Hebrew words in the titles have been omitted. For a full description of titles one should consult the bibliographies of Prijs and Fuks & Fuks-Mansfeld. The index includes all the personal names from the main body of the text. It only refers to the notes when a person before 1800 is named, who cannot be found via the text proper. When a correspondent of L'Empereur is referred to, he is distinguished by an asterisk.

My thanks are due to the staff of the library of Leiden University, who handled my many requests without visible reluctance and allowed me access to the stack. I must also thank my two promotors, prof. dr. J. C. H. Lebram and prof. dr. G. H. M. Posthumus Meyjes for the help which they gave me. I am particularly grateful to Jürgen Lebram for his teaching and the countless discussions in which he showed me what history can be, and for the freedom which he left me when I worked for him; and to Hans Posthumus Meyjes for his offer to include this work in the series, *Studies on the History of Leiden University*.

My debt to prof. dr. H. J. de Jonge is too great to be expressed. Fortunately only he knows how many faults he has improved. The discussions which he had with me on some of the theses of this book were, as is his nature, vigorous and lively. They sometimes resulted in a revision of the argument, always in a deeper insight.

# ABBREVIATIONS

## ABBREVIATIONS OF WORKS BY C. L'EMPEREUR

Oratio — *Oratio inauguralis* (...) *de linguae hebraeae dignitate et utilitate*, Lugduni Batavorum 1627.

Middot — *Talmudis Babylonici codex Middoth sive de mensuris Templi*, una cum versione Latina (...) Additis commentariis, Lugduni Batavorum 1630.

ComJes — *D. Isaaci Abrabanielis et R. Mosis Alschechi Comment. in Esaiae prophetiam*, cum additamento eorum quae R. Simeon e veterum dictis collegit. Subiuncta (...) refutatione et textua nova versione ac paraphrasi, Lugduni Batavorum 1631.

MosKim — *Mosis Kimchi HODOIPORIA ad scientiam*, cum expositione Doctoris Eliae, Item Introductio D. Binjamin F.D. Judae Omnia... annotationibus illustrata, Lugduni Batavorum 1631.

ParaDan — *Paraphrasis Iosephi Iachiadae in Danielem* cum versione, et annotationibus, Amstelodami 1633.

ItinBen — *Itinerarium D. Benjaminis*, cum versione et notis, Lugduni Batavorum 1633.

HalOl — *Halichoth Olam* sive Clavis Talmudica, complectens Formulas, Loca Dialectica et Rhetorica priscorum Judaeorum, Lugduni Batavorum 1634.

BavaKamma — *De Legibus Ebraeorum forensibus Liber singularis*. Ex Ebraeorum pandectis versus et commentariis illustratus, Lugduni Batavorum 1637.

RepHeb — C. B. Bertramus, *De Republica Ebraeorum*, rec. commentarioque ill. opera Constantini L'Empereur ab Oppyck, Lugduni Batavorum 1641.

## OTHER ABBREVIATIONS

Aa, van der — A. J. van der Aa, *Biographisch Woordenboek der Nederlanden*, 12 vols., Haarlem [1852]-1878.

*Acta* — *Acta der particuliere Synoden van Zuid-Holland, 1621-1700*, uitgegeven door W. P. C. Knuttel, 6 vols., 's-Gravenhage 1908-1916.

*ADB* — *Allgemeine Deutsche Biographie*, 56 vols., Leipzig 1875-1912.

*AG* — *Archief Gabbema*, berustende in de Provinciale Bibliotheek Friesland.

*ASALB* — *Album studiosorum Academiae Lugduno-Batavae*, ed. W. N. du Rieu, Hagae Comitum 1875.

*ASAF* — *Album studiosorum Academiae Franekerensis* (1585-1811, 1816-1844) I Naamlijst der studenten, onder redactie van S. J. Fockema Andreae en Th. J. Meijer, Franeker [1968].

*BL* — *Biografisch Lexicon voor de geschiedenis van het Nederlandse protestantisme*, onder redactie van D. Nauta e.a., Kampen 1978-...

*BMHG* — *Bijdragen en Mededelingen van het Historisch Genootschap*.

*BNB* — *Biographie Nationale*, publiée par l'Académie royale des sciences, des lettres et des beaux arts de Belgique, 28 vols., Bruxelles 1866-1944.

*BWPGN* — *Biographisch Woordenboek van protestantsche godgeleerden in Nederland*, onder red. van J. P. de Bie en J. Loosjes, 5 vols., 's-Gravenhage [1907]-1949.

*C.I.Rivet/Sarrau* — *Correspondance intégrale d'André Rivet et de Claude Sarrau 1641-1650*, publiée et annotée par H. Bots et P. Leroy, 3 vols., Amsterdam 1978-1982.

*DBDI* — *Dizionairio Biografico degli Italiani*, Roma 1960-...

*DBF* — *Dictionaire de Biographie Française*, Paris 1933-...

*DNB* — *Dictionary of National Biography*, 63 vols., London 1885-1900.

| | |
|---|---|
| *EJ* | *Encyclopaedia Judaica*, 15 vols., Jerusalem 1971-1972. |
| Fuks | L. Fuks/R. G. Fuks-Mansfeld, *Hebrew Typography in the Northern Nether-lands. Historical Evaluation and descriptive Bibliography* I, Leiden 1984. |
| Haag | Eug. et Em. Haag, *La France protestante*, 9 vols., Paris 1846-1859. Id. 2e édit. sous la direction de H. Bordier, 6 vols., Paris 1877-1888 (pas continué). |
| Herzog | *Realenzyklopädie für protestantische Theologie und Kirche*, begründet von J. Herzog, 3. Aufl. herausgeg. von A. Hauck, 24 vols., Leipzig 1896-1913. |
| Jöcher | *Allgemeines Gelehrten-Lexicon*, herausgegeben von C. G. Jöcher, 4 vols., Leipzig 1750-1751. |
| Knuttel | *Catalogus van de Pamfletten-Verzameling berustende in de Koninklijke Bibliotheek*, door W. P. C. Knuttel, 9 vols., herdruk Utrecht 1978. |
| Molh. | P. C. Molhuysen, *Bronnen tot de geschiedenis der Leidsche Universiteit*, 7 vols., 's-Gravenhage 1913-1924. |
| *NBU* | *Nouvelle Biographie Universelle*, depuis les temps les plus reculés jusqu'à nos jours, 46 vols., Paris 1852-1866. |
| *NBW* | *Nationaal Biografisch Woordenboek*, Brussel 1964-... |
| *NDB* | *Neue Deutsche Biographie*, Berlin 1953-... |
| *NNBW* | *Nieuw Nederlandsch Biographisch Woordenboek*, onder redactie van P. C. Molhuysen en P. J. Blok, 10 vols., Leiden 1911-1937. |
| *Prima Scal* | *Prima Scaligerana*, éd. P. des Maizeaux, Amsterdam 1740. |
| Prijs | *Die Basler hebräischen Drucke (1492-1866)*, bearbeitet von J. Prijs, ergänzt und herausgegeben von B. Prijs, Olten/Freiburg i. Br. 1964. |
| *RGG*(2) | *Die Religion in Geschichte und Gegenwart*, 2. Aufl., 5 vols., Tübingen 1927-1932. |
| *RGG*(3) | *Die Religion in Geschichte und Gegenwart*, 3. Aufl., 6 vols., Tübingen 1957-1965. |
| Rotermund | J. C. Adelung/H. W. Rotermund, *Fortsetzung und Ergänzungen zu C. G. Jöchers Gelehrten-Lexicon*, 6 vols., Leipzig 1784-Bremen 1819. |
| *Sec Scal* | *Secunda Scaligerana*, éd. P. des Maizeaux, Amsterdam 1740. |
| *SR* | *Studia Rosenthaliana*. |
| Th | Handschriftenarchief van de *Bibliotheca Thysiana*, berustende in de Universiteitsbibliotheek Leiden. |
| *TvG* | *Tijdschrift voor Geschiedenis*. |
| *TRE* | *Theologische Realenzyklopädie*, Berlin/New York 1976-... |

CHAPTER ONE

# THE HISTORIOGRAPHY
# OF OLD TESTAMENT SCHOLARSHIP

"Idem (the translation and explanation of the Old Testament) quidem ante nos, praesertim sæculo a Christo nato
XVI. & XVII. initio, viri doctissimi, non sine meritis
laudibus, præstiterant; sed si verum dicere liceat, non illis
quidem ingenium, aut diligentia defuit, sed duo præcipue,
quominus posteris diu satisfacere possent, obstiterunt.
Primum est inopia subsidiorum, quibus nunc cincti sumus;
possumus enim de XVII sæculo præfiscini dicere, dum
labitur, amplius esse laboratum in Philologia Sacra exor-
nanda atque expolienda, quam per duo annorum millia antea
factum fuerat. Hinc nata plurima præstantissima opera,
quibus ad intelligendos Scriptores Sacros via nobis munita
est. Hoc & Biblia Polyglotta, Lexica, & Libri omnis generis,
quibus ornatæ sunt nostræ Bibliothecae, eorum antea
indigae, satis superque testantur; & lectio operis nostri, ubi
passim laudantur, ostendet. Alterum est, sæculo XVI propter
controversias recens inter Christianos natas, omnium ingenia
ad theologica, magis quam ad grammatica studia, fuisse conversa; Interpretesque in confutandis erroribus, ut quidem
putabant, magis quam in simplici & critica verborum enarra-
tione, fuisse occupatos."

Jean le Clerc, *Genesis*, Amstelodami 1710, xxvii-iii.

Constantijn L'Empereur, whose intellectual biography is related in the
following pages, is a rightly forgotten scholar. He was professor of
Hebrew at Leiden from 1627 to 1646, during the period of the great
flowering of humanistic and oriental studies at that university, and in his
own time he enjoyed fame as an expert in rabbinical literature.[1] But
although this fame was justified, and he played an important role in
making Jewish literature accessible, he was an ordinary scholar, who
does not deserve a biography on the grounds of his originality or new
concepts developed by him. The form and the content of his work are
traditional: his reasons for studying rabbinica were those he shared with
his age.

Now this very lack of originality has its attractive side. Because
L'Empereur's work possesses a traditional and commonplace character,

---

[1] There is no previous article or book on L'Empereur. The reference works (*NNBW*
8, 1031-2; *BWPGN* II, 35-9; *BL* 2,187-8 refer to the older literature. Katchen's account
of L'Empereur's life (*Christian Hebraists*, 75-95) is better discounted, because of the great
many factual inaccuracies it contains.

it is possible to use him in order to study the current practice in rabbinical and Old Testament studies in the 16th and 17th centuries. That is important, for although there is a literature, albeit not too extensive, on the Christian hebraists, no attempt at synthesis has been made.[2] The history of Old Testament scholarship in the 17th century is a virtually uncultivated and barely surveyed field.[3] This biography of L'Empereur aims to fill both gaps to a certain extent. Through a detailed analysis of his life and work in their various aspects, it appears possible to trace more general characteristics of seventeenth century study of the rabbinical literature and the exegesis of the bible, all the more so since these two projects were linked to each other in a complicated manner. The various aspects which receive our attention in this analysis underlie this book's structure and are derived from the way in which, in our opinion, the history of biblical scholarship must be written. In the first chapter, by way of introduction, an overview is given of the present state and methods of work of research into biblical scholarship in the early modern period, and a new method of describing it is proposed.

In modern handbooks and surveys of the history of biblical scholarship, the seventeenth century is mostly dismissed as an age of transition between the more interesting periods of the reformation and the modern age, in which the only point of importance was the conflict on the orthodox view of the Scriptures.[4] Ludwig Diestel's *Geschichte des Alten Testaments in der christlichen Kirche*, published in 1869, is still the only book to give a description of the period which is anything more than a summary of individuals and episodes. Diestel's work is based on a thorough knowledge of the sources and offers a great mass of material, which is arranged by different periods and problems. The book is of extra-

---

[2] See the extensive bibliography by V. E. Loewe in *EJ* 8, 69ff., to be supplemented by some titles from that in *TRE* 3, 154f.

[3] For works other than those dealt with in this chapter: TRE 6, 360-1. Fraenkel's "Conclusion en guise d'introduction" (in Fatio, *Histoire*, 9-16) reveals the lack of a general framework into which the various detailed findings can be integrated. The recent survey article on the literature which appeared in the period 1948-80 by Karpp, "Zur Geschichte", shows the degree to which interest in these years has centred on hermeneutic questions and the scriptural views of the reformers. For the catholic side, see the works of Baroni, *Contre-Réforme* and *La Bible*. The account of Coppens, *Ontwikkelingsgang* is rightly forgotten. The history of New Testament scholarship has fared little better, apart from the recent works of de Jonge; see his analytical bibliography: de Jonge, *Bestudering*, 85-91.

[4] Thus Kraeling's *Old Testament*, after the reformation, deals in two short chapters with the themes of "The Old Testament from the Reformation to the middle of the 17th century" and "The reaction against the orthodox view of the Old Testament", after which he proceeds to discuss Schleiermacher. The articles in recent encyclopaedias are based on the same periodisation: *RGG* (3) I, 1229-30; *TRE* 6, 348-50.

ordinary interest for various reasons besides its richness of content. In the first place it is a history of scholarship which describes above all the practice of exegesis and linguistic research. Diestel was himself a university Old Testament scholar,[5] who consulted the works of seventeenth century scholars not just from antiquarian interest but also, in part, as still relevant literature. This explains his indifferent attitude towards the greatest problem of every history of biblical scholarship: the emergence of the historico-critical method.

For Diestel, who lived and worked in the age of the great breakthrough of this new scholarly technique, the transition from grammatical and philological to historical criticism, as a whole, did not form a problem. This is most apparent from the structure of his work, which is in three parts. The first book discusses Christian antiquity, the second the middle ages and the third modern times, which Diestel took as extending from 1517 to his own day. In the course of the argument he also expresses his own opinion that the actual beginning of modern biblical scholarship lay in the age of the reformation and humanism.[6] Diestel's feeling of being linked to his predecessors of the 16th and 17th centuries is striking, since more modern historians of Old Testament scholarship are inclined to mark a sharp caesura at the Enlightenment. That Diestel was not alone in this, and that his opinion corresponded with the then current exegetical practice, is evident if one consults at random any work of an exegetical nature from the second half of the 19th century.

But it is also apparent from Diestel's work, how difficult it is to describe the nature of one's own work. His description of the nature of Old Testament research rests on an incorrect concept of his own scholarly activity as a student of the Old Testament, and on a partial misconception of that of the previous centuries. The error is expressed in the title of his work. The scholarly study of the Old Testament in the 19th century did not take place inside the Christian church. Modern historico-critical research is the product of a scholarly community which in the last century had its roots above all in the German universities. The home of research was thus the School and not the Church. Not that modern Old Testament scholars were not believing Christians: on the contrary, historico-critical study of the bible was and is practised predominantly by pious scholars, who belong to the established church order. But a modern biblical scholar lets himself be determined in his scholarly work by his professional colleagues alone. They are the forum before which he tries

---

[5] For L. Diestel (1825-79): *Herzog* 4, 647-50.
[6] Diestel: *Geschichte*, Vorrede; he devotes around a third of his book (pp. 230-555) to the 16th and 17th centuries.

to justify himself and their community and its associated values lend his work its purpose. He lives and works in the university, and the sense of that life and work is determined by the ethos of the university.

This is a way of making it clear that the biblical scholarship of the 19th century occupied an autonomous intellectual and social position and that its activity was in principle independent of the church, in spite of the personal involvement of its practitioners, who were mostly theologians. Diestel's view that he is describing the scholarly study of the Old Testament inside the Christian church is inaccurate, certainly for his own times. We will return below to the concept of a scholarly community, the way in which it is constituted and the values to which it adheres.

H. J. Kraus, who in his *Geschichte der historisch-kritischen Erforschung des Alten Testaments*, was the first since Diestel to give a broad general survey of Old Testament scholarship since the Reformation, makes this independence from the church, which characterises modern biblical scholarship, the starting point of his book. In his opinion, this independence marks the essential distinction between modern times and the reformation, which with its emphasis on *sola scriptura*, is supposed to have set the whole process of biblical scholarship in motion. He describes this development, however, not with the aid of concepts drawn from the sociology of knowledge but in categories drawn from the history of ideas. The rise of modern biblical scholarship must in his view be linked to the fundamental intellectual change which distinguishes the modern period. In the foreword, Kraus remarks that Diestel paid too little attention to these general intellectual and cultural preconditions which determined the development of biblical scholarship, and explains that his aim is precisely to give this fundamental intellectual background the emphasis it deserves.

The first striking difference between his book and that of Diesel is the slight attention which it pays to the period 1500-1750. Diestel thought that this was the period in which the foundations of modern Old Testament scholarship had been laid, and devoted most of his space to it. Kraus discusses the early modern period in less than a fifth of his book, and a good deal of that is devoted to the reformation. This shift of emphasis is the result of the enormous flowering of Old Testament scholarship in the 20th century. Kraus, who was still an Old Testament scholar when he wrote his *Geschichte*, is himself a product of this flowering. His scholarly horizon, which encloses the works which he as an Old Testament scholar regards as important, and with which he discusses, goes back to the second half of the 19th century. In this he reflects the present position of Old Testament scholarship which can only consider works from before 1850 as of merely historical interest.

Yet the early modern period is of essential importance for Kraus' argument. He writes the history of historico-critical research in order to gain a greater insight into the preconditions, motives and tendencies of contemporary research. His main problem is posed by the question, what has become of the reformation's *sola scriptura*, under the influence of the growth of historical criticism[7]. By this standard he measures the history of biblical scholarship, a history which he sees as culminating happily after many vicissitudes in the *heilsgeschichtliche* view of the Old Testament. For Kraus there were in the history of Old Testament scholarship really only two possible viewpoints: to hear the Word of God in the biblical text, or to place man at the centre. These two possibilities were given right from the start in the intellectual attitudes of the reformation and humanism, between which there was an essential gulf. By humanism Kraus understands man's making himself autonomous, exalting himself above the world and the bible in order to rule over both.

This attitude, which Kraus describes above all on the basis of explicitly formulated methods and views on the scriptures, is the decisive factor which motivates historical criticism and which reaches its full development in the Enlightenment. In spite of lip service to the view that the roots of the modern historico-critical investigation are extremely various and diverse, Kraus' conception of the history of biblical scholarship is really of an astonishing simplicity. He describes how in the early modern period the humanistic principle acted like a moorland fire, bursting out every so often in the arminians, socinians, deists and critical philosophers, against orthodoxy which in essence, though in a distorted form, preserved the heritage of the reformation. In this way Kraus manages to turn all the precursors of the Enlightenment into fathers of historico-critical research.[8] His survey of these precursors is consequently rather confused, since he is not so much discussing the development of biblical scholarship as the decline of the orthodox view of the scriptures.

This decline was taken as the theme of his study by K. Scholder. In his *Ursprünge und Probleme der Bibelkritik im 17. Jahrhundert* he gives a survey of the emergence of a new concept of reality and the end of the authority of the bible in the 17th century. This double movement, in his opinion, is decisive for the appearance of historical criticism. Its creators were not the historico-philological criticism of someone like Grotius, but the sceptical and rationalist views of, above all, the precursors of the Enlightenment. Scholder goes on to describe in turn the interconfessional polemic, in which doubt was cast on the reliability of the bible from the catholic

---

[7] Cf. the review by Baumgartner, "Alttestamentliche Forschungsgeschichte".
[8] Kraus, *Geschichte*, 3-4, 27, 37-8, 52, 70.

side, the rationalist view of the scriptures of the socinians, the development of natural science, the new geographical and historical knowledge and the rise of cartesianism. At the end of his book Scholder makes the connection with modern biblical scholarship in a sweeping Hegelian triad, in which the critical views of the 17th century form the thesis, the historical theology of Herder the antithesis and Baur's historico-critical researches the synthesis.[9]

The most recent example of this genre is the comprehensive work of H. Reventlow, *Bibelautorität und Geist der Moderne*. Reventlow too wants his work to make a contribution to a consideration by modern exegesis of its methodic and hermeneutic assumptions, in order to achieve a better understanding of man and the world. The reproach which Kraus made against Diestel is now put to him in his turn by Reventlow. Kraus has neglected the essential roots and provides too much material. Yet in essence one finds Kraus' views reflected in those of Reventlow. As today, so in the 16th and 17th centuries, it was a question of the conflict between the reformation principle and opinions which take man as central. The difference with Kraus is only that Reventlow, besides the bogey man of rationalistic ethical humanism, also knows that of late mediaeval spiritualism. Both tendencies were able, thanks to particular political and social events, to establish themselves in England at the end of the 17th century. They ended in the scriptural opinions of deism, in which the authority of the Old Testament in particular was broken.[10]

Reventlow's book is comprehensive, detailed and learned. But its fundamental weakness appears in the manner in which his thesis on the continued effect of late mediaeval and humanistic traditions suggested to an otherwise not unfriendly critic, the question from where these intellectual tendencies derived their force. The answer that this reviewer went on to give to his own question is a declaration of the bankruptcy of the whole method of research. In his view, resistance to the authority of the bible ultimately derives from the resistance to divine revelation which is present to a greater or lesser degree in human reason at all times. "The timeless conflict of reason and revelation is understood, expressed and confirmed in these traditions".[11] The fundamental and profound explanation of the emergence of historico-critical biblical scholarship, which Kraus, Scholder and Reventlow wish to give, thus ends by affirming that it is not a matter of an historical but of a general human

---

[9] Scholder, *Ursprünge*, 9-10, 171-2.
[10] Reventlow, *Bibelautorität*, 10-5, 672-5.
[11] Karpp, "Zur Geschichte", 155-6.

problem.[12] Essentially they offer a pragmatic history, which looks for examples in the past, to recommend current points of view.

It is not difficult to ridicule this method of writing history, since it appears to be in no way in tune with the practice of modern scholarly biblical research. *Wirklichkeitsverständnisse*, methodologies and hermeneutics at the fundamental level which Kraus and his followers are in search of, play no significant part in the progress of the historical study of the bible. Since the latter established itself as an independent discipline in the 19th century it has been pursued and legitimated by the most various dogmatic trends. Of course it is not difficult to show how personal values led individual scholars to study particular fields, to develop particular questions or to adopt particular views—but individual values, by definition, do not lie at a deep or fundamental level. Moreover, biblical scholarship develops by extending the areas of question and solution, and there is no necessary link between the values which call forth new questions and the further development of these questions. Gunkel came to develop his concept of *Formgeschichte* because he was a neo-romantic, and he could justify the results of his own research theologically, with the aid of an idealistic philosophy of history.[13] Both neo-romanticism and idealistic liberal theology died during Gunkel's lifetime but the questions he developed still to a great extent, thanks to their fertility, determine the progress of research.

It is a scholarly community which supports and maintains the development of historico-critical research, not the values adopted by an individual researcher. Moreover, such a community of scholars does not emerge because its members adopt and follow a set of rules the application of which, for any reason whatever, produces genuine scholarship. A methodology is developed afterwards, as a reflection on practice and is not the basis of that practice. Scholarship is a social activity, not the following of particular rules. A scholarly community is created whenever its members share a technical apparatus and a system of values. The technical apparatus consists of the whole set of questions which are posed

---

[12] Kraus, Scholder and Reventlow all go back for their interpretation to the article of Ebeling, "Bedeutung", which proceeds from a theoretical concept of the historico-critical method, and in which the place of its origin is as it were deductively determined. "Sie (the historico-critical method) ist nicht nur dort, wo sie etwa ihre legitimen Grenzen überschreitet, sondern wesenhaft verbunden mit Sachkritik. Sie kann bei der Beschäftigung mit der Vergangenheit und bei der Interpretation von deren Quellen nicht einfach das Wirklichkeitsverständnis beiseite setzen, wie es der Geist der Neuzeit gewonnen hat. Sie ist darum eng verkoppelt mit dem Fortschritt der Wissenschaften und mit der Entwicklung der Philosophie." (Ebeling, "Bedeutung", 27).

[13] See Klatt, *Gunkel.*

and the whole range of tools and means available to answer these questions. The system of values defines the scholarly community from those
outside it, and regulates the relationships and mutual conduct of the
members. The most important norms are that only those who have
mastered the technical apparatus may be members—in modern times, in
which scholarship has become institutionalised in the universities, those
who have completed a formal education—and that conflicts may only be
decided by an appeal to the technical apparatus. Norms of the freedom
of value-judgements and freedom from prejudice function above all at
this supra-individual level, not at that of the individual scholar. In the
history of historico-critical research there are abundant examples of
scholars who could not be convinced by new developments and offered
a stubborn resistance to new questions and answers. New insights mostly
gained acceptance only when the older generation, which resisted them,
had died out. Because of this irrational character of the individual
researcher, the scholarly virtues are of the greatest importance. They
provide freedom and determine the way in which polemic against opposing views may be conducted. If such an ethos is to be able to function,
then the scholarly community must be recognised by society as more or
less autonomous, for otherwise individual members, who see essential
personal values under threat from the course of research, can appeal to
institutions outside the community to fend off these developments.

All these preconditions were gradually fulfilled in the German universities in the century preceding 1850. In the theological faculties a community arose which concerned itself with the historical study of the bible,
took up an autonomous position and had a technical apparatus and
method of its own. This technical apparatus consisted of philology and
history, and the ethos was founded on a view of protestantism as a
religion which saw conscience and personal freedom of research as para-
mount. This religious self-interpretation attached itself in the course of
the century to the ethos of the German classicists and ancient historians,
who saw it as their task to serve the text alone, without paying any attention to the consequences of the outcome of their research. This ideal of
a *voraussetzungslose Wissenschaft* (scholarship without presuppositions) was
taken over by the theologians who studied the bible as an historical
source.[14]

If one wishes to speak of a general "*Vorverständnis*" which was the foundation of this scholarly undertaking, then it derived from the practice
which in fact prevailed of treating the bible as if it were any other ancient

---

[14] A good description of the ethos of the German philologists and historians in the 19th
century in Fuhrmann, "Sorge", 12.

text. It was this practice which gave biblical scholarship the right to be present in the university. In return, the deep anchoring of biblical scholarship in the universities ensured that the practice of scholarly exegesis was to a great extent independent of external factors.

This description of the practice of present day biblical scholarship was necessary to put the partial correctness of such works as that of Kraus in its proper light. Diestel saw in the early modern period the roots of the research of his contemporaries, and paid most attention to the results gained in the 16th and 17th centuries, which gave historical research an impetus. But there is in fact, as Kraus and his followers saw, a fundamental difference between modern scholarship and that of the earlier period. In the 16th and 17th centuries historical and grammatical study of the bible did not possess an intellectually or socially autonomous position. After the reformation the bible had become the most important element in the ideological struggle which unified the great religious, social and political conflicts of early modern Europe. Thus, to adapt a phrase of Clemenceau, exegesis had become too important to be left to exegetes. The interpretation of the scriptures was closely linked with positions of power in church and state, and served above all the interests and values of the day.

Under these circumstances an autonomous scholarly community could not be formed, and as a result exegesis in the early modern period was far more dependent that it is today on personal values and convictions. Grotius' *Annotationes* are not the result of a conscientious fulfilment of the office of professor, but the fruit of a highly personal ideal, by which he was impelled. In the 17th century, general views of the bible and the authority of the scriptures were not only heuristically important, but also determined whether there should be any literary research into the bible at all, and what technical apparatus should be used for it. The technical apparatus which, seen with hindsight, grew into modern research, developed by fits and starts in which it is easier to show a continuity in the use of particular works, than in fixed traditions which contributed to its development.[15] This lack of autonomy of literary study of the bible in the early modern period justifies us in addressing ourselves also to the cultural and social assumptions which underlay it.

Because traditional interpretations of the bible often played a legitimating role, critical research in this period was often the work of dissidents, or produced results which could be used by heterodox groups. But the various tendencies which set themselves against orthodoxy did

---

[15] An example of a mere description of the progress of technical knowledge in textual criticism in Goshen-Gottstein, "Textual Criticism", 365-76.

not run in a single straight line towards the Enlightenment and the emergence of modern historico-critical research. Resistance to the authority of the bible could also lead to a lack of interest in its explanation. It is remarkable to see the socinians figure prominently in Kraus, while he himself concedes that they wrote scarcely anything on the Old Testament. Because no independent community of biblical scholars was constituted, the continuity of research in the 16th and 17th centuries themselves and the link between the early modern age as a whole and modern scholarship is only formed by the development of the technical apparatus: the manner in which the bible was investigated with more and more highly developed tools and questions, in which the scriptures gradually came, in an ever increasing number of fields, to be treated like an ordinary text. This development of the technical apparatus could be made to serve the most various purposes. Le Brun, in his article "Das Entstehen der historischen Kritik im Bereich der religiösen Wissenschaften im 17. Jahrhundert" rightly draws careful distinctions between various groups.

Le Brun too describes essentially the decline of scriptural authority, rather than the development of biblical scholarship. He begins with the rise of humanism as an intellectual tendency, in which attention was focussed on the words rather than the things, and the goal was the attainment of pure and original texts. In Le Brun's opinion, in which he follows French historiography, this trend was coupled with the emergence of a new type of scholar, free of clerical ties and attached to the universities and the world of the book.[16] It is this marked social emphasis of his approach which makes Le Brun's article important for us. According to Le Brun, it was humanism's striving towards the concept of the original text, the sense of which has been obscured by time, which posed the characteristic problem for the 17th century of the clarity and obscurity of the bible. Protestant orthodoxy—and the official catholic viewpoint was not far removed from it—developed the doctrine of literal inspiration in order to protect this clarity.

Alongside orthodoxy there arose in the Netherlands a philological study of the bible, which in Le Brun's view, was to be continued throughout the century and was supported by the rise of the Republic of Letters, a new social form of scholarship, relatively independent of churches and universities and standing on the fringes of orthodoxy. Professional theologians and defenders of orthodoxy are supposed by Le Brun to have stood outside this international movement of scholars. The philologists did not, it is true, develop any great theories or systems but the

---

[16] Mandrou, *Humanistes*; Chaunu, *Temps des Réformes* II, 297-367.

accumulation of details, the practice of collective work, and the freedom of research, ultimately eroded the traditional positions.

Besides humanist biblical scholarship, Le Brun distinguishes three currents which emphasised the lack of clarity of the scriptures. To a catholic apologetic tendency which goes back ultimately to Erasmus, Le Brun assigns such figures as Andreas Masius, Benito Pereira, Jacob Bonfrerius, and Jean Morin. A second rationalist tendency acknowledged reason as a source of knowledge alongside the scriptures. In it Le Brun includes the socinians and Spinoza. For his knowledge of this tendency Le Brun relies on Kraus and Scholder. As a third tendency he mentions certain groups within French protestantism, which were closely associated with the academy of Saumur. The most important for our subject was Louis Cappel who in his minute textual-critical investigation of the Old Testament showed that Hebrew is by no means a divine, perfect and clear language.

All these trends exercised an influence on Richard Simon, who is described in great and subtle detail in the article, as the exponent of a new historical and critical scholarship. The psychological certainty which Simon needed in order to arrive at his criticism, he derived from his attachment to the ecclesiastical traditions and institutions to which he remained loyal, even after he had been condemned, and from the new legality of the Republic of Letters. Simon's attachment to this community appears from the use of the word "Critique" in the title of his main works. With Jean le Clerc, criticism achieved a methodological self-awareness, and the sacred texts are treated in theory, and to a great extent also in practice, as profane texts.

In his conclusion Le Brun emphasises that criticism and the historico-critical method which were gradually gaining ground at the end of the 17th century, presupposed certain developments in society and the theory of knowledge. The latter can be split into a scientific instrumentarium (which we called a technical apparatus above) and the possession of a philosophy, with which criticism could justify its theory and practice against the certainty of theology.

Le Brun's article, in spite of slight doubts which one may feel about details of interpretation,—it may be that the overstresses the apologetic interest of Richard Simon—is valuable and stimulating. The attention which French historians pay to the social aspect of all human activity makes it possible to gain a vision of historical criticism in the 17th century which is much less purely *ideengeschichtlich* than that of the German scholars referred to above. But the brevity of Le Brun's article prevents a detailed discussion of the distinction and connection between the various factors which contributed to the rise of historical criticism. Thus it is not sufficiently emphasised that catholic exegesis and the work of Cappel, in spite of different motives which underlay them, built on and were incorporated in the philological investigation of the bible as it had been practised by the Republic of Letters. To depict this research as a scholarly practice which slowly destroyed the traditional position, is correct, but too little attention is paid to the shift in the cultural climate in the Republic of Letters around the middle of the 17th century. The philosophy of Descartes and other rationalist tendencies perhaps offered the possibility of an ideological justification of criticism, but the price paid for this was a certain aversion to humanist studies. The collection of ever more philological and historical details, undertaken in order to arrive at a grand synthesis of the values of classical and Christian antiquity, ran into resistance, and the most prestigious places in intellectual endeavour were assumed by philosophy and the natural sciences. The verdict pronounced by the first historian of the Royal Society in 1667, that after a century and a half of research "now the soil of Criticism is quite barren" was widely shared.[17]

This shift—from late humanism to the precursors of the Enlightenment—explains why historico-critical biblical scholarship did not emerge at the end of the 17th century, but only at the end of the 18th. In the end, both Simon and Le Clerc, as far as their influence on the further development of biblical scholarship in their own day was concerned were solitary figures.

Another factor insufficiently emphasised in the article is the close tie between philological research in the north Netherlands in the first half of the 17th century and calvinism. In portraying the Republic of Letters as actually heterodox, Le Brun is the victim of the German scholars who alleged a close tie between historical criticism and the Enlightenment. In the first half of the 17th century, in the Dutch Republic, orthodox calvinists and even theologians could still take part in the humanist programme. Without doubt this was an aspect of a fundamental cultural characteristic which distinguished the Republic from other European countries: the close bond between the young universities and the Republic of Letters.[18] At Franeker and Leiden, calvinism and humanism met face to face and only in the second half of the century were the two tendencies to begin to diverge.

Many of these tendencies can be illustrated from the life and work of Contantijn L'Empereur. He was an orthodox calvinist theologian, who

---

[17] Sprat, *History*, (1667), 23-5.
[18] Frijhoff, *Société*, 23-6; Dibon, "Université", 24-5.

was professor of Hebrew at the most renowned university of the Republic in its most flourishing period. His work and his personal assistance were used by the most prominent philologists of his age, in particular for their work in the field of biblical exegesis. Through his publications in the field of rabbinica, he won himself a place and recognition within the Republic of Letters. But he remained an orthodox theologian. He was responsible for the nonpublication of Cappel's *Critica Sacra* at Leiden, and is thus a spectacular example of the divergence of orthodoxy and the development of biblical scholarship.

What follows attempts to offer an intellectual biography of L'Empereur in which his life and work are described using the concepts derived from the view of the history of biblical scholarship which has been developed above. Its main question is that of his contribution to 17th century biblical exegesis and the study of rabbinical literature. A number of fortuitous aspects of his life make it possible to combine chronological order, which the biographer is obliged to follow, with a thematic structure. The second chapter analyses L'Empereur's descent, family and education and his activities until his appointment as professor of Hebrew at Leiden in 1627. Attention is paid above all to his personal values and to the influences which he underwent during his education. The third chapter describes L'Empereur's appointment at Leiden and the view of his task which he expressed in his inaugural lecture. In this chapter the institutional place of Hebrew at the Dutch universities and the various views of the importance and usefulness of the language among the theologians and hebraists of the Republic are discussed. The fourth chapter is devoted to L'Empereur's life in the years 1627 to 1634, in which almost all his scholarly works appeared. The chapter analyses the actual practice of his work and tries to situate it in the scholarly endeavour of the time. The fifth chapter describes the various circles in which L'Empereur moved during the last fifteen years of his life. It analyses his activities as a teacher, as a member of the Republic of Letters and as a theologian.

Finally the conclusion offers a retrospect.

# CHAPTER TWO

# THE EDUCATION OF A CALVINIST THEOLOGIAN
## (1591-1627)

> "Monstrorum pater est hoc seculum. Nemo non vult haberi
> doctus. Nemo tamen vel labro tenus bonas literas degustavit.
> Iuventus nostra, quae studiis Theologiæ dedicavit sese, a
> Grammaticis ad *meta ta phusika* statim confert se; & in his
> vepretis totam ætatem absumit. Quo fit, ut neque bonarum
> literarum aliquem sensum habeat, neque verba sacrorum
> librorum assequatur."
>
> (Scaliger, *Epistolæ*, no. cccxxxiv)

On the 9 July 1648 the Leiden professor of theology Jacob Trigland gave
the funeral oration on his colleague Constantijn L'Empereur van
Oppyck who had died a week earlier.[1] Following the rules of ancient
rhetoric he first discussed the period which had preceded the subject of
his eulogy. In the case of a man, according to Quintilian, one can set to
work in one of two ways. The speaker can point to the noble family of
the man whom he praises, and then show that his acts fulfilled the
demands made on him by such a glorious origin. If famous ancestors are
lacking, then he relates how the hero, by his own virtue alone and against
every expectation, threw lustre on a humble descent.[2] Trigland followed
the first *topos*. He recalled how L'Empereur in his lifetime had been able
to recount his ancestors from the 12th century. The family was said to
be a well known and noble house from the cities of Brabant and Flanders,
long involved in the government of those provinces.

It was not only their ancient descent and nobility but also their
adherence to true doctrine and religious virtue which characterised
L'Empereur's forefathers. Trigland referred once more to the words of
his deceased colleague when he described the family's conversion to
calvinism. Under the impression of the *constantia*, steadfastness, which
Pierre Brully the first calvinist martyr in the Netherlands displayed
during his execution, L'Empereur's grandfather was said to have begun
to read the bible in order to test the doctrine of Rome and the books of

---

[1] Trigland, *Oratio*. All biographical details in this chapter, unless otherwise stated, are
based on this oration. The name "Van Oppyck", which is spelled in different ways, is
derived from a manor in the neighbourhood of Brussels which the L'Empereurs were
supposed to have owned in the 15th century. (Trigland, *Oratio*, a3). Constantijn and his
brothers only began to adopt this addition to their name in the 1620's. See also below
for this.

[2] Quintilian, *De arte oratoria*, 3, 7, 10-19. Cf. Lausberg, *Handbuch*, §245.

Calvin by its standard. The outcome of this independent investigation was, for Trigland, self-evident. Now such a narrative is a *topos* which says more about the grandson than the grandfather. Rivet believed the same of his mother, Vossius of his father and the exaltation of the religious virtue of one's ancestors can also be found in Drusius and Beeckman.[3] We even know that the essence of this family tradition is not true. Jean L'Empereur from Tournai was already a member of the protestant community there before the burning of Pierre Brully.[4] But this factual inaccuracy and the doubt which one may entertain of the nobility of L'Empereur's ancestors do not impair the pride, reinforced by religion, in his own descent, which these stories handed down within the family express. Trigland attached himself to this sentiment in his speech when he related the marriages of the ancestors of L'Empereur. He based his account on the details supplied by the L'Empereurs, and the oration shows in this way how much they saw the history of their family as embedded in the struggle for the true religion.

Trigland described, inter alia, the marriage of Constantijn's father Anthoine L'Empereur (1552-1615) with Sara van der Meulen, the daughter of a Brabant family which excelled in *nobilitas*, *virtus*, *dignitas* and *auctoritas*. Her brother Andries had been a *schepen* (magistrate) of Antwerp and a councillor of Alençon. Her brother Daniel had also been politically active and moreover extremely skilled in theology (which, as Trigland observed, was a rare accomplishment in a politician). Daniel spoke Greek and read the Old Testament only in Hebrew. Even Scaliger—so Trigland said with reverence—spoke of him with esteem in a letter to Lydius.[5] In fact Daniel van der Meulen had lived in Leiden since 1591, where he had his house rebuilt by Lieven de Key, and moved in the humanist circle associated with the university. Through his marriage to a De La Faille, he had links with important circles in the south Netherlands and was used for this reason by the Brussels government in the later years of the 16th century in one of those half seriously intended peace negotiations which were almost a permanent accompaniment of the Eighty Years' War.[6]

---

[3] Cf. the unpaginated report of Rivet's life in his *Opera Theologica* III, ⟨1⟩-⟨2⟩; Rademaker, *Vossius*, 4; Curiander, *Vitae Drusii*, 22; Van Berkel, *Beeckman*, 11 no. 5.

[4] Moreau, *Histoire*, 112. As early as 1544 Jean L'Empereur belonged to the protestant community in Tournai. In the persecution of that community in 1544-5 he only received a small fine, on the grounds of his respectable position.

[5] Scaliger, *Epistolae*, 583 (no cclxxx); to I. Lydius, 25.7.1600. For the two Van der Meulens, *NBW* 4, 564-9.

[6] A description of his house in Versprille, "Geschiedenis". The report of his diplomatic mission is published in *BHMG* 57 (1936), 240 ff. Descriptions in Kernkamp, "Huwelijk", 282 ff. and Den Tex, *Oldenbarnevelt* II, 294 ff.

Having established the *dignitas* of L'Empereur's father in his description of this marriage, Trigland described his *virtus* by referring to his departure from the Netherlands. Anthoine was particularly religious and after the fall of Antwerp he went into exile. When he realised that the Romish superstition again hung over his city, the ornament of the Netherlands, he broke into tears although he was "otherwise a very hard man, who never wept, as immoveable as Cato". So strong was his love for the Fatherland and above all, for Religion. The emotion which Trigland's sketch of his virtue attempts to arouse is a little modified when one realises that the city where Anthoine settled, Cologne, was not involved in the struggle of the Netherlands, although it did grant freedom of religious worship to protestant immigrants.[7] His departure was probably motivated by more prosaic reasons. To go into exile in the rebellious provinces, under the terms of the surrender of Antwerp, could have led to the confiscation of his property.[8]

It is characteristic of the ethos of the university of Leiden in the middle of the 17th century, that Trigland passed over in silence the occupation of Constantijn's father.[9] In company with Daniel van der Meulen and two other brothers in law[10] and with the aid of an almost endless series of cousins in various cities of Holland, Germany and Italy, Anthoine traded in the products of the textile industry. A great part of his archives has, like that of his son, been preserved in the Bibliotheca Thysiana.[11]

---

[7] For the refugee community in Cologne: Petri/Droege, *Rheinische Geschichte*, 103; for the economic considerations which underlay toleration there, *ibid.* 160 ff. A L'Empereur (Anthoine's uncle?) was even a member of one of the guilds: Schilling, *Exulanten*, 120 n. 170.

[8] In the City Archives of Leiden there is in the archives of Daniel van der Meulen, a letter from Jacques de la Faille to his sister, the wife of Daniel, dated 12.3.1585. He writes to her of the conditions of the surrender of Antwerp and how no one who goes into exile is to suffer any loss of his property, provided that he leaves for a neutral territory. He himself is thinking of going to England, and he has understood that the Van der Meulens are to go into exile in Hamburg (I am grateful to J. W. Spaans who drew this letter to my attention).

[9] A good example of this ethos in Barlaeus, who commented on his departure for Amsterdam as follows (Barlaeus, *Epistolae*, 393-4; to A. Buchelius, 16.4.1631): "ex quieta in turbulentam et negotiosam urbem. Nihil est quod eo me rapiat, praeterquam melioris famae solatium, alioqui plura sunt, quae me hic detinere possint, eruditorum frequentia, Academica studia, loci amoenitas, assuetudo, aliaque. Si Ultrajectinis illud fuisset institutum, quod jam est Amstelodamensibus, maluissem in vestra urbe vivere, quam inter Mercuriales & quaestuosos homines." For the power of the aristocratic ideal in the first half of the 17th century in the Republic: Van Nierop, *Ridders*, 224-231.

[10] Daniel's brother Andries and their brother in law François Pierens who was married to Anna van der Meulen (Van Roijen, "Inleiding"). Daniel was the most important partner in this company. In 1589 he and his brother in law Jacques de la Faille had organised what may have been the first voyage of a Dutch ship to the Levant (De Groot, *Ottoman Empire*, 86-7).

[11] Th. 174-269; the total extent is about 2½ metres.

In looking through these documents it is hard to avoid being reminded of Weber's thesis on the connection between calvinism and capitalism. The letters from Anthoine and his correspondents in the various cities of Europe, all members of inter-related merchant families from the south Netherlands, deal mainly with merchants' news but pass without difficulty into the exchange of family gossip and discussions of political news, both of which regularly give occasion for reflections on the omnipotence of God. The whole network of correspondents was held together by the bonds of family and faith.

Anthoine and his trading partners belonged to the generation which entered adulthood during the beginning of the Revolt while his agents were mostly a generation younger, a difference in age which formed a favourite subject for worried letters from the older men. He was fourteen years old at the time of the Imagebreaking riots in 1566, in which an uncle of his had been closely involved,[12] and as a result of which his father had been executed.[13] At the time of the Spanish Fury, the storming of Antwerp by mutinous troops in 1576, he was twenty-four. One of the eight thousand citizens killed by the troops was a brother of his future wife. At the fall of Antwerp to the triumphant soldiers of Parma, he was thirty-three. As one of his correspondents wrote to him, their generation had been marked by these political vicissitudes.[14]

> "Et comme vous dite de vous meme, que avez perdu vostre pere et passee parmi les feux d'afflictions, Dieu nous monstre, comme aussy a tous les siens, sa grande faveur en nous tirant hors de la bourre et fange pour nous faire passer nostre vie en honneur, dont en devons rendre grace a Dieu. Mais nos enfans lequel n'ont point veu ny conneu les adversitez ceulx la ne savent point que c'est, et pensent que toute chose leur doybt venir a souhait, grace au Seigneur."

For these exiles social reality was determined by faith and family and not by their district, city or nation. Anthoine was a convinced and educated calvinist. In January 1598, he wrote a letter full of good advice to his nephew Hans L'Empereur. He reminded him that man cannot comprehend the ways of Providence, but may trust in God. Hans must realise that if he has done everything with "prudence",[15] the outcome of

---

[12] Cf. the report on the penetration of calvinism among the Antwerp merchants by the spy Philippe Dauxy, from 1566/67, published by van der Essen, "Progrès", 216-17, 221.

[13] Verheyden, *Conseil*, 276: Jean L'Empereur from Tournai was executed. His wife, his brother Anthoine and Anthoine's wife Apollonia Pels were exiled.

[14] Th 203, Paulus Pels to A. L'Empereur, 29.5.1611.

[15] Cf. Appendix I. As well as the recommendation of *prudentia* there are more examples of stoic ethics in Anthoine's letters. In the letter to Isselborgh (Appendix II) he says "la meilleure issue c'est de perseverer, et principalement en vocation publicque comme dit Esaye, 'il fault perseverer d'une constance, estant lumiere aus aultres'." The citation

his actions, be they what they may, is fixed by God for his salvation. Such submission may not lead to fatalism; man has a duty to do what is in him. "Dieu nous a mis notre vie en garde; de la vient le proverbe "God helps those who help themselves",[16] au reste, c'est le Seigneur qui le faict tout en tout". This piety with its stoic traits and dialectic of submission and duty of labour seems to be related to the bourgeois existence of a medium merchant, who does not occupy a dominant position in his market and remains dependent on a number of factors outside his control, but who can still influence his existence by his own efforts.

The letter appears to take its actual content from two citations from the *Institutions* of Calvin, which are freely but adequately rendered by Anthoine without stating his source. It is typical of his piety that they come from book III, chapter 21 and book I, chapter 17, which deal with predestination and the use of the doctrine of providence. In the latter citation, a paraphrase of Proverbs 16:9 it appears that Anthoine associated himself closely with the aspect of Calvin's thought which he emphasised. The Geneva translation of the bible renders this verse, in conformity with other 16th century translations from the Vulgate, as "Le coeur de l'homme delibere de sa voye; mais le Seigneur dresse ses pas." In the margin the translation has a note which gives an excellent explanation of the meaning of the text: Man proposes, God disposes. But Calvin, and Anthoine after him, cite the verse with an obverse meaning: "Le coeur de l'homme doit penser a sa voye, et le Seigneur gouvernera ses pas": Help yourself and God will help you. Such a piety does indeed seem to be "a good consolation in our so miserable age". It is not yet the vulgar ideology of success which Weber depicted as the ultimate link between calvinism and capitalism, and which saw success in the sublunary world as a sign of election. Anthoine's mixture of stoic resignation, the duty of work, and submission, could easily relapse into this. Because his life had been tossed on the storms of history, he understood the danger of an erroneous application of this view, if it were based not as piety on the intent, but as a doctrine on the result of his actions.

---

must be a very free rendering of Isaiah 42:6. For the connection of calvinism and the Stoa in the field of ethics, see Todd, "Seneca".

[16] The Dutch proverb is the first line of one of the more famous sea beggar songs "Helpt u zelf, so helpt u God/uit der tirannen band en strik/ Benauwde Nederlanden". The song probably arose around 1571 in the same circles as those from which the Wilhelmus, the Dutch national anthem, emerged. It was first published in 1601 (Kuiper, *Geuzenliedboek* I, 99-101). The French "aide toi, le ciel t'aidera" is according to dictionaries later (first in La Fontaine), but it is also supposed to have been one of the favourite proverbs of Joan of Arc (Warner, *Joan of Arc*, 83-4). It is possible that both versions are renderings of Ovid's "audentes deus ipse juvat" (*Met.* 10,586; *Ars Amat.* 1, 608, *Fasti*, 2, 782).

From a letter to Henri Isselborgh, a minister at Cologne, it appears that Anthoine saw the signs of his election rather in the faith of his family than in his commercial successes. Isselborgh, well known as a delegate from Bremen to the Synod of Dordt, was one of the students from that city who studied at the expense of a fund, of which Anthoine was one of the administrators.[17] The letter which consists mainly of Old Testament citations applied by Anthoine to himself and his relations, breathes the spirit of a devoted calvinism. Anthoine finds the signs of God's covenant in his family. His father before him, he himself and, God willing, his children after him, confess the true Word of God. By identifying his family with the People of God, he was able to apply the Old Testament directly. The family is this people, and the signs of His covenant are seen by Anthoine in the success of his striving for the growth of the seed of the Word in his children. He was much more independent with regard to the Republic where he was by now living. It is only from love for His name, preserved in such families as that of the L'Empereurs, that God does not punish those countries for their great sins. Anthoine did not yet identify the Republic with Israel, an equation which his son, following a well known seventeenth century *topos*, was to elaborate.[18] His life story confirms this distance with regard to the Republic. In December 1585 Anthoine was married at Antwerp to Sara van der Meulen, and early in 1586 he went into exile at Cologne. There in 1587 his first son Anthoine was born. In 1589 he left for Frankfurt, from 1591 to 1599 he stayed in Bremen, after which he moved to Utrecht. In Bremen his sons Constantijn, (1591) Theodosius (1593) Jean (1594) and Alexander (1596) were born.[19] It is characteristic of his family feeling that he named his sons after himself and his father and, in allusion to the family name, after famous emperors.

During his residence in Utrecht, Anthoine was a prominent member of the Walloon church. Important ministers wrote to him as his "humble et serviable amy"[20] and he arranged a new preacher for the Utrecht Walloons even before he became an elder there. It was the young Charles de Nielles, the later remonstrant, and the son of a family which like the L'Empereurs, originally hailed from Tournai.[21] With his trading part-

---

[17] Cf. Appendix II. Letters from various universities (Leiden, Geneva) from the years 1599-1603 from Isselborgh to Anthoine in Th 231. For him: *ADB* 14, 640-1 and Rotermund, *Lexicon* I, 230-1.

[18] For many examples: Groenhuis, "Calvinism".

[19] Van Roijen, "Inleiding".

[20] In Th 232 four letters from Jean Hochedé, Walloon preacher at Amsterdam from the years 1602-4.

[21] According to the *Livre Synodal* I, 182, 192 Anthoine attended the autumn synods of the Walloons in 1604 and 1605 as an elder with Charles de Nielles. For the latter's com-

ners Anthoine administered the study fund bequeathed by Bertrand de Banos, and used it to allow students to study abroad, such as the above-mentioned Henri Isselborgh and several sons of Nathanael Chytraeus.[22] In 1603 he corresponded with Gomarus[23] about Christoffel Helles. Gomarus was a member of the Leiden University circle in which his brother in law Daniel van der Meulen had been active. The question raised in the letter was whether Helles should study theology at Leiden or Basle. Gomarus recommended Leiden, with the undoubtedly unintended consequence that Helles acquired there the Arminian sympathies which in 1619 were to lead to his deposition.[24] Anthoine also received advice from this Leiden circle, especially from the Walloon professor Luc Trelcat, about the education of his sons. In 1604 Trelcat welcomed Anthoine's intention to let one of his sons study at the recently opened High School in Harderwijk. He praised the good discipline which prevailed there, the excellent tuition in belles lettres, theology and philosophy and the necessary preparation for life at an Academy.[25]

It appears from a letter of Paulus Pels to Anthoine that the latter intended to allow all his children to study.[26] It is in this that one must look for the reason behind his move to Leiden in 1607. All his sons had themselves matriculated at the University there. Anthoine in 1606 as a student of law, Constantijn in 1607, Theodosius and Jean in 1608 and Alexander in 1609, all in letters.[27] The father took a great interest in the education

---

ing from Tournai: Moreau, *Histoire*, 245-6. A letter from him to Anthoine, 15/25.2.1611 in Th 214.

[22] For the Banos scholarship: Pronk-Bosch "Bertrand Theophile de Banos". For the calvinist Chytraei, *ADB* 4,256 and Rotermund, *Lexicon* I, 71-5. Letters from Matthaeus Chytraeus to Anthoine in Th 232. In 1603 he was studying law with Anthoine (the son) at Heidelberg. In a letter of 18.1.1612 he relates how he and his brothers have fared. Very well, except for the youngest, whom he recommends to Anthoine. In fact we find this Christiaan Chytraeus in 1614 as holder of a scholarship bursary from the Hallet fund (Posthumus Meyjes, *Waalse College*, 197 no. 12).

[23] Th 245. Letter of 19.2.1603. Gomarus addresses Anthoine as "Monsieur et trescher Ami". Published by Van Itterzon, "Nog twintig brieven", no. 2.

[24] Letters of Helles in Th 234. For him: *BWPGN* III, 643-5.

[25] Th 206. Letter of 7.4.1604. It is not clear which son is meant. As books used at Harderwijk, Trelcat mentions "le Dialectique Molinaei, Demosthene, le catechisme d'Ursin, la grammaire hebraique, l'Ethique de Picolominaeus".

[26] Th 203. Paulus Pels to Anthoine L'Empereur, 29.5.1611: "J'ay bien entendu la proposition touchant que ditte de vos fils, comment voulles les laisser tous estudier et sy auchuns se donnent a la negoce ce sera Theodose, lequel demeure a present chez Abraham de la Ligne."

[27] *ASALB* 84: 25.9.1606 Anthoine (law) (not the Anthoine L'Empereur, Coloniensis 20, on p. 108, 21.12.1612; he was too young and must be a descendant of the Anthoine who married Apollonia Pels); 87: 19.5.1607 Constantijn, (Bremensis, 15, arts) 90: 23.4.1608 Johannes (Bremensis, 14) and Theodosius (Bremensis, 15, both arts) 96: 2.11.1609 Alexander (Bremensis, 13, arts).

of his sons. A scrap of paper written in his own hand with a daily timetable for Constantijn's study programme has been preserved.[28] Trigland states that Anthoine very early noticed Constantijn's talent for letters and sought a private tutor for him. This was Marcellus Vranckhemius, the later rector of the Latin school at Zutphen. From Anthoine's archives it appears rather that Vranckhemius was not intended specially for Constantijn. A reading of Quintilian explains Trigland's emphasis on Constantijn. In the *De arte oratoria* Quintilian recommends that a eulogist should distinguish according to age.[29] In his description of early youth he must praise the *indoles*, the inclination and genius; at a rather later age, the *disciplinae*, the various subjects which the person eulogised had mastered. In fact Trigland, after describing Constantijn's particular talent, lists the various fields of study which his father chose for him. After the fulfilment of his task, when in 1608 Anthoine's youngest son Alexander had also matriculated at the Academy, Vranckhemius studied at Anthoine's expense at various foreign universities. On the recommendation of his patron he was appointed rector of the Latin school in Zutphen where he was dismissed after a year because of his conversion to catholicism.[30]

On 19 May 1607, Constantijn had matriculated at Leiden as a student of arts. He studied at the university for six years, mainly theology, and on his departure for Franeker in 1614 he received a particularly warm letter of recommendation from Gomarus to Sibrandus Lubbertus. The professor had never had a student whom he could praise so highly.[31] In his student days Constantijn was a witness of the conflict between Gomarus and Arminius. A year after his matriculation, in 1608, this difference of opinion, originally interesting only to a small group of theologians, had become so important that both dogmatists were asked to explain the details of their views concerning the various stages in God's dispensation before the High Council. For the administrators these details were incomprehensible, unimportant and tedious. They were wrong. After the conclusion of the Twelve Years Truce, this abstruse theological point proved capable of rallying groups with various political social and economic grievances, and bringing down the faction which determined the policy of the Republic. In the ten years after 1608

---

[28] In Th 204.
[29] Quintilian, *De arte oratoria* 3,7,15: "Namque alias aetatis gradus gestarumque rerum ordinem sequi speciosius fuit, ut in primis annis laudaretur *indoles*, tum *disciplinae*, post hoc operum (id est factorum dictorumque contextus..."
[30] Letters from this Marcellus Eleutherius or Vranckheim or Francken in Th 238. For his dismissal: Nettesheim, *Geschichte*, 331.
[31] For this letter of Gomarus of 16/26.3.1614: Van Itterzon, *Gomarus*, 206.

the difference of opinion between two professors, grew into a social and political conflict which resulted in virtual civil war.

This theological debate was the continual background of Constantijn's studies. After the death of Arminius in 1609 virulent pamphleteering wars broke out, and the appointment of Vorstius as successor of Arminius in July 1610 led to a further escalation. Gomarus refused to receive this German, regarded as a socinian by orthodox calvinists, as a colleague, and left for Middelburg in April 1611. The contra-remonstrants then unleashed an international campaign against Vorstius and scored a brilliant success. As a result of heavy diplomatic pressure from England, Vorstius had first to purge himself of the accusations of heresy before he could take up his post. The theology faculty at Leiden was thus for a time the focus of the disputes. After the departure of Gomarus it did not have any professors. To provide for this lack, the Mayors and Curators in later 1611 appointed moderate representatives of both parties, after first having assured themselves that both candidates were willing to tolerate each other. The new professors were Jean Polyander and Simon Episcopius. According to Trigland during these troubles L'Empereur was with Cloppenburg and Voetius one of the leaders of the students who were opposed to the coming of Vorstius. Undoubtedly he belonged to the party of Gomarus, but the rest of his life makes such a combative leadership unlikely. He was an orthodox but not a combative nature.[32]

On 8 April 1614 he matriculated as a student of theology at Franeker, followed a month later by his brother Johannes.[33] He deliberately chose this faculty. In contradiction to what is stated in the secondary literature, which reasons backwards from his later appointment, Constantijn did not go to Franeker because of Drusius, the professor of Hebrew, but wished to sit at the feet of the contra-remonstrant leader Sibrandus Lubbertus. Thanks to his letters to his father and mother we can follow closely the course of his studies after his move from Leiden to Franeker. Little evidence of any interest in Hebrew is apparent in this correspondence. Someone who, just arrived in Franeker, after a conversation with Drusius, has to have his Hebrew bible sent on after him, does not arouse the impression that he had changed universities for the sake of the oriental languages.[34] In a letter to his father of 19 April 1614 he

---

[32] The mild temper of L'Empereur has already been observed by Sepp: *Onderwijs* II, 87.

[33] *ASAF* no. 1463 and 1471 (6.5.1614).

[34] Th 178, C.L'E to his father, 29.4.1614. Visits by students to Franeker at this time are almost always regarded in the literature as having been motivated by oriental studies, a view which can already be found in Voetius: "ita olim non pauci studiosi Belgae cursu in academia Leidensi absoluto, primum Franekeram ob florentissimum istic linguae

described his first impression of Franeker. He had found lodgings in a house with some other students, the counts of Goray and their tutor Maccovius, a doctor of theology.[35] The latter made a great impression on Constantijn. He described him as extraordinarily learned in theology and philosophy. At meals he continually debated with him. According to Constantijn, Maccovius was the only theologian who had taken his doctorate at Franeker.[36]

Drusius and Lubbertus were very well disposed to him, thanks to the recommendation of Gomarus. On 6 May Constantijn, together with Johannes visited Count Willem at Leeuwarden. They were to greet their parents from him, "even though he did not know them so well."[37] Three weeks later he had twice opposed and once defended in theological disputes, to the full satisfaction of Lubbertus as he proudly wrote to his father. Lubbertus had even praised him in the presence of other students and the professors. In his enthusiasm he wrote to his father that he had never learned as much—he had then been there only two months. He intended to gain permission to dispute without a president, something which was not even allowed to promoted doctors at Franeker. True, the professors were against it, but Constantijn thought of working via the court of the Stadhouder in Leeuwarden, so that it would not be possible to refuse him,[38] and he had already sent his theses to the Count.[39]

A letter of two weeks later shows Constantijn in more sober mood. Disputing without a president was impossible. At the court he had been disappointed in his request and as a consequence of his ambition his relationship with Lubbertus had cooled. He had been shocked by this, because Lubbertus could do him harm at the German universities, where his opinion was valued. Aggrieved, he wrote that he only wished to show he could dispute without assistance. In reply to a question from Polyander as to who was the author of the theses defended by him, he

---

hebraicae studium se conferebant" (cited in Duker, *Voetius* I, 78 n. 2). The story is also told of Episcopius who, as is well known, spent his time there mainly disputing against Lubbertus. Drusius himself inclined to another opinion in a letter to J. Raphelengius of 15.3.1613 (UB Leiden BPL 1886): "it was to be desired that there were more who had a taste for oriental studies at Leiden. Then it will improve in time, so I hope."

[35] Maccovius and the two barons a Gorai Goraisky had matriculated on 24 October 1613: *ASAF* nos. 1439-1443.

[36] Th 178, C.L'E to his father, 19.4.1614. The statement on Maccovius is correct. He had promoted, the first theologian to do so at Franeker, on 8 March 1614 (Meijer, *Album*, 18).

[37] Th 271, C.L'E to his mother 9.5.1614.

[38] This desire to dispute on one's own authority often arose among students at this time. For a case with the brother of Maccovius: Van der Woude, *Lubbertus*, 346.

[39] Th 178, C.L'E to his father, 12.5.1614.

proudly remarked that he had composed them himself, just as he had done with his philosophy theses at Leiden.[40]

When his father then asked him in a letter whether such independence was not evidence of a mistaken pride, Constantijn was forced to a characteristic defence. His emphasis on his dogmatic skills was not the product of vanity, but was intended to win him recognition as an equal from his fellow students: "for these nobles believe they are of another race and blood". He must be thinking here of Maccovius, who, like every tenth Pole, was of noble birth. It is clear that while Anthoine was still the head of the family his sons had no noble pretentions. But just like the Polyanders they had much more interest in their genealogy than their father.[41] In 1614 Johannes and Constantijn matriculated at Franeker as "L'Empereur Bremensis"; their younger brother in 1631 was "Alexander l'Empereur de Oppyck, nobilis Bremensis".

Constantijn was also able to write to his father that his relationship with Lubbertus had improved and that he had even had the professor's permission to look into the books of Socinus. But Lubbertus had told him to be silent about this object of study.[42] Socinus, according to Constantijn, was the most subtle heretic he had ever seen. In his eyes Socinus was the source of the arguments of the arminians. Just like the arminians he was in a position to sow doubts of the orthodox doctrine, but not to defend his own teachings. He also wrote how two new professors of theology had been appointed, Bogerman and Seppinga. This experience with the appointment practices of the university brought the young ambitious student to realise that "favour", the support of powerful friends, is decisive. Knowledge or orthodoxy alone are not enough.[43] L'Empereur probably returned to Leiden in late July 1614 after a stay of four months in Franeker.[44] He had only been able to follow Drusius' teaching, which was a secondary matter for him, for a short time. When

---

[40] Th 178, C.L'E to his father, 29.5.1614.

[41] *ASAF* no. 2757. For the Polyanders and the differing emphases which father and son laid on their descent, Dibon "Famille". For the strong bourgeois self-confidence of the Antwerp merchants before 1585: Soly, "Verraad".

[42] Lubbertus had been occupied in refuting Socinus since 1600. In 1608 he completed his *De Jesu Christo Servatore*, which only appeared in 1611 (Van der Woude, *Lubbertus*, 131-147).

[43] Th 178, C.L'E to his father, 21.6.1614. The most important friend of Bogerman and Seppinga was Lubbertus. (Van der Woude, *Lubbertus*, 385). Bogerman wanted to come but did not receive permission from the church council and magistracy of Leeuwarden (*BWPGN* I, 466-476). Similar problems also stood in the way of the appointment of Seppinga. While this procedure was still under way, Maccovius was appointed a special professor on 28 January 1615 (Boeles, *Hoogeschool* II, 90).

[44] Th 178, C.L'E to his father 29.5.1614. He asked for money for a stay of a further two months. There is no mention of further requests for money in the letters of June.

he made a second visit to Friesland early in 1617, Drusius had died. After his return to Leiden he studied Arabic with Erpenius in 1614-1615 as can be inferred from his ownership of Arabic textbooks.[45] Sixtinus Amama, who had matriculated in August as a student of Arabic, was one of his fellow students in this.[46]

In 1615 Constantijn made a Grand Tour through France with his brother Anthoine. A letter of 9 October 1615 to his father described the route they had followed and how they had arrived at Saumur on 14 September. They had avoided Paris because of the political troubles and the high prices. After Anthoine had obtained a doctorate in law at Orleans, they went down the Loire valley, past Blois, where they too made the obligatory excursion to see the room in which the Duke of Guise had been murdered, Tours and Saumur. The letter is in direct contradiction of Trigland's oration, which claims to base its report of the journey on an *itinerarium* of Constantijn. According to Trigland the brothers visited Paris, where Constantijn met the professors of the *Collège Royal*, Fredericus Morellus and Gabriel Sionita and spoke to cardinal Perron and Pierre Cotton, the Jesuit confessor of Henri IV. A fantasy of L'Empereur in writing his *itinerarium* or in his conversations? Keeping quiet about an excursion for the sake of conversation with catholics which his father would not have approved? In any case, Trigland also mentions the visit to Paris before the stay at Saumur. From there the brothers returned to Leiden, when they received the news that their father had died on 20 September 1615. In Saumur they had visited Gomarus, Louis Cappel and Du Plessis Mornay because, as Constantijn wrote in his let-

---

[45] AG, C.L'E to Lubbertus, 8.12 ⟨1614⟩: L'Empereur was studying in Leiden and since his departure from Franeker he had not written to Lubbertus. He had heard from Polyander that Lubbertus was to publish his refutation of Bellarmine. He had been busy studying Arabic for two months, which was of great importance for the study of Hebrew. Van der Woude dates this letter to 1620 or 1621 (he is not entirely clear on it; *Lubbertus*, 498). From the Arabic books which L'Empereur possessed before 1622 (see below for this) it appears however that he must have studied Arabic earlier and the only possible time is after his return from his first stay at Franeker. From 1615 Erpenius published a number of Arabic textbooks from his own press (Juynboll, *Beoefenaars*, 81 ff). L'Empereur owned none of these books before 1622. He did possess the Arabic grammar published by Erpenius at Raphelengius' press in Leiden in 1613 (Juynboll, *Beoefenaars*, 72-3) and the Arabic proverbs collected and annotated by Scaliger, and published by Erpenius early in 1614 (Juynboll *Beoefenaars*, 73-4), bound in one volume with Jan Theunisz' edition of the Arabic translation of the Epistle to Titus (1612) and Bedwell's edition of the letters of John (both printed in 1612 by Raphelengius; Juynboll, *Beoefenaars*, 57; auction catalogue, O4o,72). He also owned of the datable books, an Arabic translation of the Psalms (Rome, 1614; O4o,69). Lubbertus' refutation of Bellarmine occupied him all his life, so that the reference to this occupation in L'E's letter is no help in dating (thus Trigland wrote in 1613 to Lubbertus that he was awaiting his book against Bellarmine: Van der Woude, *Lubbertus*, 126).

[46] *ASALB*, 117.

ter to his father, they understood that their father was not paying for the journey for them to see cities and countries, but to speak with important and prominent men.[47] France agreed with Constantijn and he found French students more religious than those from the Republic. In the letter he gave signs of a family feeling which agreed with that of his father.[48] He witnessed his dependence on the family and its vicissitudes and expressed his submission to his father's longing to see his children in a position where they could fulfil their vocation. Anthoine had a good insight into the calling of his sons. Constantijn was to continue to strive for the career chosen by his father—the professorship of theology—for the rest of his life.

After his return to Leiden he provided himself in April 1616 with letters of introduction from Lubbertus and a testimonial of the Leiden church council for a journey to England.[49] On 13 May he landed at Sandwich and travelled via Canterbury and Rochester to London. There he presented himself, with Lubbertus' letter of introduction, to Simon Ruytingius, the minister of the Dutch congregation in London, to Thomas Morton, bishop of Chester and George Abbot, archbishop of Canterbury.[50] L'Empereur was thus introduced to the English network which Lubbertus had built up in his campaign against the appointment of Vorstius to the University of Leiden.

Constantijn decided to visit Oxford because of its good library, and not Cambridge as he had previously planned. Ruytingius and Morton furnished him with letters of introduction and from the beginning of June to August he stayed in Oxford. From the letters to his mother it appears that the brothers had scattered across the various countries of Europe in these years. Johannes was studying theology at Heidelberg and Theodosius, who had been intended at an early age and rather against his will, for commerce,[51] was in England. Oxford appealed to Constan-

---

[47] This remark is followed by a detailed report of a conversation with Du Plessis Mornay on the political situation in France, from which it appears that he gave the brothers a particularly friendly welcome, as he was accustomed to do with Dutch students (Frank-Westrienen, *Groote Tour*, 28).

[48] Th 178, C.L'E to his father, 9.10.1615.

[49] Th 216, testimonial of the Leiden church council, signed by Festus Hommius, 26.4.1616.

[50] Van der Woude, *Lubbertus*, 111, 221, 251-3, 333.

[51] Cf. note 26. Theodosius became a merchant. Cf. the following citation from a letter to his father of 22.5.1610 (Th 178): "Ce que c'est du marchant je l'experimente tous les jours. Mais pour dire la verite, heureux sont ceux a qui Dieu donne le moyen et la commodite d'estudier. Il est bien vray au commencement il est bien amer mais quand on vient en age allors on sente premierement la douceur. Au contraire en considerant la marchandise: il y faut grand travaille et (...) dure touiours. Je voy icy les marchans a l'age de 60 ans aussi 65 qui travaillent comme esclaves pour seulement en ce temple present conserver le leur.''

tijn. He knew no university where they lived so "quietly and modestly". Above all the conduct of the heads of colleges made a great impression on him. In his eyes they lived like great gentry and aristocrats, quite different from the theologians of Leiden and Franeker. Casaubon had made the same observation in 1613 and given the correct explanation of this lifestyle: the particularly high income which the heads of houses enjoyed.[52]

Constantijn was of the opinion that Hebrew and philosophy were taught at a high level in Oxford. From this we can deduce his orientation in both disciplines. The Regius Professor of Hebrew when Constantijn was at Oxford was Richard Kilbye, rector of Lincoln College and one of the translators of the Authorised Version. He was a not particularly meritorious hebraist and had an interest in eastern languages. Casaubon found copies of Raphelengius' Arabic dictionary only in his and Lancelot Andrewes' possession.[53] He had written a commentary on Exodus, which was based largely on extracts from rabbinical commentaries, and which has never been published. He was to have continued the commentary of Mercerus on Genesis, which was of the same nature, but was refused leave to publish it.[54] For his knowledge of the rabbinical commentaries Kilbye was dependent on Jews like the young Jacob Barnet, who in 1613 had disappeared from the university after the tragicomedy of his conversion to Christianity.[55] L'Empereur's remark on the high level of the study of Hebrew at Oxford must refer to biblical Hebrew and not to rabbinica in the narrower sense. Before 1620 no one in Oxford had been in a position to make a catalogue of the hundred and fifty Hebrew books and MSS in the Bodleian Library.[56] Philosophy at Oxford at that period was still taught on strictly aristotelian lines, and L'Empereur's verdict on the philosophical teaching there is a further indication that he had been an aristotelian since his student days.[57]

In August and September 1616 Constantijn stayed in Cambridge, but the university appealed to him less than at Oxford. On 5 October he was

---

[52] Casaubonus, *Epistolae*, 537; to N.N. 17.5.1613.

[53] Casaubonus, *Epistolae*, 537; to Erpenius, June 1613.

[54] *DNB*, XXXI, 101-2.

[55] A report of this affair in Pattison, *Casaubon*, 413 ff., based on letters from Casaubon of July to November 1613.

[56] Cf. *Bodleian Quarterly Record* 2 (1927), 70 note and 3 (1920-22), 144-6. In 1607 (?) Bodley encouraged the librarian to "endevour to gette the help of the Jewe for the Hebrew Catalogue". In 1605 Bodley had asked Drusius' son to make the catalogue (Bachrach, "Foundation", 109). The one hundred and fifty Hebrew books formed only a small part of the five or six thousand books of the Bodleian. The inventory of certain oriental works of the Bibliotheca Palatina was also made by a Jew (*Sec Scal*, 483).

[57] Kearney, *Scholars and Gentlemen*, 63-4, 77-90; Green, *History*, 60; Mallet, *History* II, 147-8.

in London and making plans to return to Holland.[58] In the four months
of his stay in England he had mastered the language of the country. He
was one of the few Dutch travellers in the 17th century who took this
trouble.[59] The explanation for this must be sought in his ambitions. Constantijn believed that important theological works had been written in
English.[60] The books which he had acquired during his visit are discussed
below, but like Amama who had studied with Prideaux during his stay
at Exeter College in 1615,[61] Constantijn was mainly oriented towards the
moderate puritanism that prevailed at the English universities in those
years.[62] From a survey of Constantijn's travels it appears once again
how difficult it is to distinguish between a *peregrinatio academica* and a
''Grand Tour''. We should call Constantijn's travels rather a *peregrinatio*.
He was seeking to deepen his scholarly knowledge as a preparation for
an academic career.[63] But his journeys also had aspects of a Grand Tour,
such as discussions with prominent and important men as a preparation
for service to society. If the recent historian of the Grand Tour states that
the young travellers from various countries and periods all had in common that their descent from respectable families and their careful
upbringing were rounded off by an educational journey as a preparation
for a life of political service,[64] then it proves that what distinguishes Constantijn's travels from this comes down to a question of social status (*pace*
Constantijn's later views on this). Constantijn, the son of an exile from
the south, did not belong to the group which was called on to govern the
Republic. That does not detract from the fact that L'Empereur, followed
by Trigland, could consider such a journey as a training for service to
society, the Church and the Academy.

---

[58]  For this part: Th 271, C.L'E to his mother 3.6. ⟨1616⟩; 20.9.1616; Th 284, C.L'E
to his brother Theodosius, 25.6. ⟨1616⟩; 14.8. ⟨1616⟩; 5.10. ⟨1616⟩. In the letter of June
to his brother there is a reference to a letter to Amama which Theodosius must forward.
Amama had just become the successor of Drusius, after many difficulties.

[59]  Frank-Westrienen, *Groote Tour*, 162. She knows only three exceptions: Pieter de la
Court (1641/2), Constantijn Huygens (1651) and Wicker Pott (1684). Gomarus knew
English, Lubbertus none (Van Itterzon, *Gomarus*, 99; Van der Woude, *Lubbertus*, 215).

[60]  Th 271, C.L'E to his mother 3.6. ⟨1616⟩.

[61]  For Prideaux: *DNB* XLVI, 354-6. For Exeter College under his rule: Platt,
''Amama''. Amama speaks very warmly of him in the foreword of his edition of Drusius'
*De Sectis Judaicis* (Arnhem, 1619).

[62]  Calvinism had already come under attack at Oxford in this period (Laud had
become President of St Johns College in 1611) but was still predominant. Prideaux was
to experience the years of arminian high church supremacy and remain the great champion of a moderate puritanism in Oxford (Curtis, *Oxford*, 222ff; Tyacke, ''Arminianism'', 99).

[63]  Thus Frank-Westrienen defines the peregrinatio: *Groote Tour*, 8. For problems concerning the definition, ibid. 8, 19 ff.

[64]  Frank-Westrienen, *Groote Tour*, 28-9.

On 25 November 1616, L'Empereur was in Franeker for the second time, where on 3 January 1617 he matriculated as a student of theology.[65] In his oration Trigland gave the view of such a step which was customary in L'Empereur's milieu. After his long years of study and academic travels, Constantijn had reached the period at which he "would apply his knowledge of theology and languages to the use of the Church and the Academy". To the benefit of the Academy and the honour of the L'Empereurs. Constantijn came to Franeker with the aim of taking his doctorate and the only goal of this very unusual conclusion to theological studies was to acquire an academic position.[66] In Franeker he was welcomed by his friends. Amama held out the hope of various possible appointments. There were places for a theologian in Franeker and Groningen. Also, a States' College had been set up at Franeker, for which a Regent had to be found.[67] Constantijn's ambition for this last post was slight, perhaps because of his experience of the difficulties which his contra-remonstrant fellow students had managed to cause for Bertius as Regent of the States' College in Leiden.[68] In the hopeful letter, written during his preparation for his promotion, he asked his mother to send him a number of books, among them much English theological literature.[69]

In a long letter to his mother of 25 February 1617 he described the state of affairs concerning his promotion and the extensive academic examinations which would precede it. It annoyed him that once more he was unable to win honour by presiding over the disputation himself. The procedure resembled that which was to be laid down by regulations in 1629,[70] except that Constantijn's examination gives the impression of being harder and his public lecture was not disputed by the professors. After Maccovius, he was the second theologian to take his doctorate at Franeker. His theses, now lost, dealt with *De originis Peccato*, and in them he would, in view of the fact that he promoted under Lubbertus, have defended the infralapsarian standpoint.[71] In an undated letter he invited

---

[65] Th 284, C.L'E to his brother Theodosius, 25.11. ⟨1616⟩. He matriculated again on 3.1.1617 (*ASAF* no. 1634).

[66] Frijhoff, *Société*, 46-7, 264-5. L'Empereur was the third doctor of theology produced by the universities of the Republic, after Arminius and Maccovius. He was certainly ambitious for a university career and saw the promotion as a means towards one.

[67] Cf. Boeles, *Hoogeschool* I, 374. The college was being set up at this time.

[68] The relief with which Bertius resigned his regency in July 1615 is well known. For his difficulties: Kuiper/Rademaker, "Collegium Theologicum", 139-45.

[69] Th 271, C.L'E to his mother 3.1.1617.

[70] See Appendix III. Cf. Boeles, *Hoogeschool* I, 359-61.

[71] Meijer, *Album*, 19. There had been difficulties between Maccovius and Lubbertus as early as 1615 partly of a personal nature, partly based on a theological dispute: Maccovius took a far reaching supralapsarian standpoint. Lubbertus was an infralapsarian.

Theodosius, Anthoine and Alexander to attend the celebration dinner after the promotion.[72] ''Dinner'' is perhaps scarcely the right word: at Franeker it was customary not to remain at table for longer than half an hour and then to go on drinking until midnight or later. Women were not allowed to be present at such parties, especially when theologians were concerned, on pain of heavy injury to their reputation. On 24 March 1617 the ceremony took place. Constantijn earned his title *summa cum laude.*

Constantijn's promotion was the first step on an academic career and the letter to his mother in 1617 described his attempts to win support for the obtaining of a post. In March he received an offer to become professor of theology at a thousand guilders a year, at a theological college to be set up by Janus Radziwill in Lithuania.[73] This post in the east seemed too dangerous to Constantijn.[74] In April he was hoping for the chair of theology of Groningen as colleague of Ravensperger[75] but the position went to Gomarus. Another possibility was a professorship of philosophy at Franeker. He had been advised not to take up the regency of the States' College. It was difficult and disagreeable work, and moreover Acronius had already been chosen by the Friesian States, with the aid of what Constantijn described as exceptionally dirty methods, on which he could not expand in a letter.[76] In June he made several journeys to Leeuwarden to put his case before the Curators of the University of Franeker. He also tried to penetrate to the Stadhouder.[77] A month later he wrote, full of expectation, how he had had an interview with the Count and that some of the Curators were well disposed to him. He hoped for the professorship of physics which had been vacant since the philosopher Joachim Andrea had been appointed to the faculty of law in June 1615.[78] This ambition brought Constantijn into conflict with Maccovius, who was holding the post temporarily,[79] and who feared that his salary would not be supplemented if a successor was appointed. For this

(Van der Woude, *Lubbertus*, 345 ff.) L'Empereur's theses could not be located. Nor do Van der Woude's research notes in the Amsterdam University Library mention them as existing in any European library. The title was usual. Bertius defended theses ''De peccato originis'' in his student days at Leiden (Bosch, *Bertius*, 26).

[72] In Th 271.

[73] For the various 16th and 17th century Radziwills: *RGG* (2) IV, 1679-80, *TRE* 5, 150.

[74] Th 284, C.L'E to his brother Theodosius, 23.3. ⟨1617⟩.

[75] For Ravensperger, Boeles, ''Levensschetsen'', 13.

[76] For Acronius: Boeles, *Hoogeschool* II, 104-8. He was professor from April 1617 to December 1618, mainly appointed in order to counter the state of disorder among the students.

[77] Th 271, C.L'E to his mother, 12.4.1617; 16.5.1617; 2.6.1617.

[78] Boeles, *Hoogeschool* II, 89.

[79] Kuyper, *Maccovius*, 21.

reason he was unwilling to give L'Empereur a testimonial for philosophy, although Constantijn had explained to him that he did not need to earn a high salary, because he only wished to hold the position until a vacancy in the theological or another faculty occurred. Consequently he had to go to Leiden for a reference.[80] This state of affairs explains the curious reference which is preserved in the *Bibliotheca Thysiana*. In this very friendly testimonial, Jacchaeus, the professor of philosophy at Leiden, who was to be dismissed in 1619 for his arminian sympathies, declared, for the benefit of the strictly orthodox L'Empereur, that if some doubt the latter's philosophical ability, he could witness with a good conscience that:[81]

> "five years ago he had made such good progress in philosophy that he could have obtained the title of doctor of philosophy and the highest degree therein, with the greatest dignity. Which would then have happened, if his father (it is not known why) had not guided the outstanding youth into other fields. Yet he has not neglected the important study of philosophy since then: but he has practised it more acutely (as one will observe in his conversation) through linking it closely to theology."

The reference is dated 15 August 1617. But a reference without powerful friends was not sufficient and Constantijn spent the rest of 1617 at Franeker slowly getting used to the idea that he might have to wait years for an appointment.[82] His relationship with the Franeker professors was complicated by a remarkable request from Leiden. Some time after 9 October he received a letter from Polyander who wrote that there was a contra-remonstrant student there who wished to take his doctorate. But because both Polyander and Episcopius had been appointed while the Leiden theological faculty had been vacant after the death of Arminius and the departure of Gomarus, neither of them was in possession of the doctor's degree. Before the promotion could take place, there had to be a doctor of theology at Leiden. In order to maintain the balance between the opposing religious factions the Leiden Curators wished a third party to promote both Episcopius and Polyander. The ceremony

---

[80] Th 271, C.L'E to his mother, 1.7.1617. Cf. the letter of 19.8.1617: "Maccovius m'est en la voye, aussi m'a mandé de venir chez soy, ou me dict la raison pour quoy il s'oppose, a scavoir qu'il vouldroit bien avoir plus de gage des Estats servant a deux vocations."

[81] Th 170, dated 15.8.1617: "fecisse eum ante quinquennium eos in Philosophia progressus, quibus maxima cum dignitate et secundissima nominis fama Doctoris in Philosophia titulum, & supremos in ea honores tueri potuisset. Quod quidem tum factum fuisset, ni pater (quibus de causis incertum) optimum iuvenem ad alia traduxisset, nec tamen gravia ista Sapientiae studia interim neglexit: sed multo acrius (quod ex colloquio disces) propter eorum cum Theologia coniunctionem prosequutus videtur."

[82] Th 271, C.L'E to his mother, 2.9. ⟨1617⟩; 4.10 ⟨1617⟩.

would have to take place quietly. Polyander asked L'Empereur to do this, and tried to tempt him with the statement that he could put the Leiden Curators under an obligation towards himself by granting their request. L'Empereur's reply, which we know from a letter to his mother, was particularly firm and in the later months of 1617 also particularly sensible. It was against his conscience to promote Episcopius. Polyander and Festus Hommius, to whom he had submitted the matter, must give him better reasons. In this way he asked for the fiat of the ecclesiastical leadership of the contra-remonstrant party. He proposed that he should promote Polyander, and that in turn Polyander should then confer the doctor's degree on Episcopius. In his answer, Polyander explained that it was also against his conscience to promote Episcopius and that in any case the Curators of Leiden would not permit such a construction.[83]

The matter had consequences for L'Empereur's position at Franeker.[84] His relationship with Maccovius improved because he had refused to promote Episcopius, but Lubbertus was very cool towards him. He wrote to his mother, that he did not know whether Lubbertus was aware of the request to promote the Leiden professors. In any case Constantijn realised that no more help was to be expected from him in appointments and he prayed that God should help him against the opposition which was to be expected from Lubbertus. It is understandable that Polyander did not ask Lubbertus. After the latter's violent attacks on the appointment of Vorstius the Curators of Leiden university would never have been willing to be under an obligation to him, even if he could have been induced to such a double promotion.

Nevertheless Constantijn's efforts to win support in Franeker had some success. In February 1618 he obtained a reference from the university in which the States of Friesland were advised of his great talents in philosophy.[85] Apparently Maccovius had given up his opposition to

---

[83] See Appendix IV. In his funeral oration on Polyander Spanheim told how the Synod of Dordt had decided, in order to counter heresy, that henceforth all professors of theology must be promoted (Lamping, *Polyander*, 84-6). This could be a consequence of the affair of Polyander and Episcopius of 1617. In 1618 the Senate of the university decided that it would be good to have Polyander promoted by some foreign professors who were present at Dordt. That was done by A. Scultetus and H. Alting on 17 February 1619, as appears from the subsequent approval, drawn up on 9 November 1620 but antedated, of the Mayors and Curators of this action of the Senate (*Molh.* II, 82*). In the course of 1619 Polyander promoted the newly appointed theological staff of the Academy: on 18 October Walaeus, and on 6 December Hommius and Thysius, in a simple ceremony without examination. On 6 December the senate decided to give its approval for such a simple examination: "hac tamen lege, ne cui in posterum in eadem facultate gradus nisi examine et disputatione praemissa conferatur" (*Molh.* II, 82-3).
[84] Th 271, C.L'E to his mother, 4.10.1617; 17.10.1617; 28.10.1617; 15.12.1617.
[85] The reference in Th 172, dated 3.2.1618.

L'Empereur, since this testimonial must refer to the position in physics which he was temporarily occupying. The request had no success and in August 1618 Arnold Verhel was appointed professor.[86] In June 1618 Constantijn's mother died and the letters on his attempts to realise his ambitions cease. He remained in Franeker. As appears from a reference from the rector and Senate he gave tuition in theology "when the professors were absent", because of their participation in the Synod of Dordt. The reference is very warm and must have been intended to facilitate his appointment as successor of Anthonius Thysius as professor of theology and Hebrew at Harderwijk.[87] It is possible that Thysius, who was appointed at Leiden after the purging of the theological faculty there had recommended him. Later Johannes, Constantijn's brother, was to marry a daughter of Thysius.[88]

The High School of Harderwijk, which had been founded in 1600, largely at the insistence of the church in Gelderland, had a high reputation in the first half of the 17th century. It was able to attract good teachers and the school was probably visited by a large number of students. In the first years after its foundation, the High School proper was associated with the Lower School which had been in existence for some time.

The class teaching given to the lower classes included Latin, Greek, logic, rhetoric, Hebrew and above all a great deal of theology. The teaching at the High School followed on from this class education. The same professors gave the lessons, but in a different form—public lectures and private tuition in their homes. Teaching was given in theology, of which Hebrew was a part, law and philosophy. L'Empereur had to give both the basic class teaching and the lectures.[89]

In Harderwijk he married Weyntge Jansdochter de Witt on 19 June 1622. This was a marriage outside the circle of south Netherlands families in which the L'Empereurs moved, but within the same social sphere. Weyntge was the daughter of Jan Pieterszoon de Witt (1558-1621) an Amsterdam merchant and *homo novus*. Jan Pieterszoon had become a member of the *vroedschap*, or city council, in 1609 and belonged

---

[86] Boeles, *Hoogeschool* II, 112.

[87] In Th 172, dated 14.9.1618. The testimonial of the Franeker church council also found there (2.11.1618) already knows of the appointment at Harderwijk.

[88] Bouman, *Hoogeschool* I, 43, raises the possibility that Thysius had a hand in the appointment of L'Empereur at Harderwijk. The marriage of Johannes took place on 19 February 1625: Van Roijen, "Inleiding".

[89] For the teaching at Harderwijk and the significance of the school: Bouman, *Hoogeschool* I, 23ff; Kuyper, *Opleiding*, 551-4; Bots, "Cultuurgeschiedenis", 401-5.

to the faction of Reinier Pauw.[90] He was the son of a timber merchant who had been executed for his religion at Amsterdam on 9 October 1568. The Amsterdam de Witts allied themselves with south Netherlands families in the 17th century. A cousin of Weyntge married a De La Tour, as did Sara, the daughter of the marriage of Constantijn and Weyntge.[91]

Constantijn had been able to marry thanks to his appointment. His professorship in Harderwijk also brought him into contact with members of the political elite and, at some distance, with the closely related Republic of Letters. In complete conformity with the great emphasis on status which typifies his whole oration, Trigland mentions first of all L'Empereur's familiarity with a noble prince of Anhalt. This must have been the brother or son of Christian I of Anhalt-Bernkamp, the governor of the Upper Palatinate. Both men were staying at Harderwijk in the mid-twenties, driven from Germany by the war.[92]

According to Trigland, L'Empereur also formed a friendship at Harderwijk with Hendrik van Essen. Van Essen came of a respectable Gelderland family. Since 1616 he had been a Curator of the High School of Harderwijk, and mayor of that city. He was the delegate of the province of Gelderland at the Synod of Dordt and one of the judges of Oldenbarnevelt. After 1624 he stayed usually in The Hague as representative of his province to the States General. Because Gelderland as a former duchy was the province with the highest status in the Republic, he was naturally employed on a number of important missions. Thus, after the death of Maurice, he was the leader of the delegation of the States General which took the oath from Frederick Henry. In 1624 he left on a diplomatic mission to France together with Adrian Pauw, the protector of L'Empereur's in-laws.[93] Constantijn formed another friendship with Ernst van der Brinck (1581-1649) a son of a Harderwijk mayoral family. Van der Brink was a student at Leiden from 1606-1608. In 1607 he made a journey to England, with letters of introduction from Pontanus. From 1612 to 1615 he was secretary of the Republic's embassy in

---

[90] Elias, *Vroedschap* I, 284 ff. UB Leiden Pap 2 contains a letter from L'Empereur to A. Pauw, 6.7.1646. He asks him for a passport for his foster son, referring to his acquaintance with his in-laws and the many kindnesses which Pauw had already shown him.

[91] A niece of Daniel van der Meulen, the uncle of Constantijn, married in 1618 Daniel Baron du Tour. A son of this marriage married Sara, Constantijn's daughter. (Van Roijen, "Inleiding").

[92] For Christian I: Mann, *Wallenstein*, passim. For Christian II: *ADB* 4, 150-7. For Ludwig of Anhalt: *ADB* 19, 476-83. For the latter's stay at Harderwijk, Ridder van Rappard, *Ernst Brinck*, 18-9. For the history of Anhalt, *TRE* 2, 734-8.

[93] Bouman, *Hoogeschool* I, 31; Van der Aa VI, 229-30; Poelhekke, *Frederik Hendrik*, 79; Schutte, *Repertorium*, 10.

Constantinople. From 1618 he was librarian of the High School at Harderwijk. Lodewijk of Anhalt was godfather of one of his children.[94] The third friend mentioned by Trigland was not an administrator of the High School but a colleague: Johan Isaac Pontanus.[95] Pontanus (1571-1639) was a scion of a Gelderland family and had studied medicine, philosophy and literature. After 1613 he spent three years with Tycho Brahe in Denmark. His *Album Amicorum* is signed by practically all the humanist celebrities of protestant Europe around the year 1600. He was one of the first professors at Harderwijk and taught physics and mathematics, later medicine as well. An early example of the seventeenth century polyhistor, he concerned himself principally with history at the end of his life, and became the official historiographer of Gelderland.

L'Empereur's other colleagues at Harderwijk were not mentioned by Trigland. They were the successive holders of the chair of law, who were mostly appointed on the recommendation of Cunaeus. The latter was not always happy in his choice of proteges. Thus B. Sutholt, a Westphalian appointed in 1625, went over to catholicism in spite of L'Empereur's efforts to dissuade him.[96] His successors only held the chair for a few years.

On 9 February 1627 Anthonius Thysius came from Leiden to summon L'Empereur to the chair of Hebrew as successor of Erpenius.[97] After rather tiresome negotations with the Curators of Harderwijk who were unwilling to let their teacher go,[98] L'Empereur was able to accept his office late in 1627, in a speech on the use and necessity of the study of Hebrew. What qualifications did the theologian in fact have for this task? How useful and necessary had he himself found the study of Hebrew? Where, and with the help of what books had be learned Hebrew?

---

[94] Van der Aa III, 1320-1; De Groot, *Ottoman Empire*, 190-1.

[95] In the *Album Amicorum* of Pontanus, kept during his study journeys until 1601, occur the names of Lipsius, Janus Dousa jr., Sopingius, the brothers Canterus, Scaliger, Thomson, Camden, Piscator, Gruter, Raphelengius sr., Beza and many others (Bodel Nyenhuis, "Levensbijzonderheden"). For his later contacts: *Brieven van Pontanus*, in which there is a brief account of his life, to be supplemented by the *NNBW* I, 1417-20.

[96] For the professor of law in the time of L'Empereur's professorship: Bouman *Hoogeschool* I, 53-9. For Sutholt: *NNBW* II, 1395-6. M. J. A. M. Ashman drew my attention to the presence of a handwritten dedication to L'Empereur in the copy of Sutholt's *Dissertationes undeviginti*, Harderwijk 1623 in the Bibliotheca Thysiana (no. 490). It is noteworthy that in 1624 a certain Johan van Mandeville was given leave to give public and private lessons in Hebrew (Bouman, *Hoogeschool* I, 114).

[97] The letter in Th 172.

[98] Documents of these negotiations in Th 172. The Leiden Curators use towards Harderwijk, among others, the argument that the Leiden academy "is in fact a general university of our fatherland", to which all the other provinces must contribute according to their capacity.

We are fortunate in being able to reconstruct the course of L'Empereur's studies fairly accurately. In the *Bibliotheca Thysiana* a MS inventory of his library has been preserved.[99] This is divided into four rubrics for books (in folio, quarto, octavo and sextodecimo) and one rubric for MSS. L'Empereur listed in this catalogue what books he bought or received as gifts, and how much he paid for acquisition and sometimes for binding. After a while he also began regularly to enter the date on which he acquired a book. The first dated acquisition, in the folios, quartos and octavos is 29 October 1629, but this is not the date of the drawing up of the inventory. In each of the rubrics for books, a first part which comprises one or two pages is written in the same sort of ink. Thereafter, accessions are entered in all the rubrics, in constantly changing sorts of ink. Often the sort of ink varies every three or four books. The first part gives the composition of L'Empereur's library at the moment when he drew up the inventory. The sequence of the books in this first part does not follow the chronology of L'Empereur's purchases but is based on a rough systematic classification. Thus, among the folio volumes the *Opera Omnia* of Bellarmine which L'Empereur had bought, according to a receipt, from Jansonius on 8 August 1619, stand before the *Thesaurus Linguae Latinae* and the *Historia Ecclesiastica Eusebii.* L'Empereur had acquired these volumes at the auctions of the libraries of Mulhemius and Vulcanius, which were held on 4 October 1612 and 15 November 1610.[100] Such anachronisms are not to be found in the 170 books in the inventory between the first change of ink which shows the moment of drawing up the inventory, and the first written date. Apparently, L'Empereur drew up his library inventory some time before 29 October 1629.

To fix the date of the inventory one may first determine a *terminus a quo.* This is given by the last dated book in the first part of the inventory, which must at any rate have been drawn up after the publication of the book in question. Now L'Empereur rarely mentions the year or place of publication of a book, but the year of the appearance of a title named in the inventory can often be found by identifying the work with an entry in the auction catalogue of his library[101] which was less sparing of year and place. Naturally such a reference must be compared, to eliminate the

---

[99] Th 164, 3.

[100] Receipts of L'Empereur's purchases in Th 163.

[101] *Catalogus variorum et insignium praecipue rabbinicorum librorum bibliothecae* (...) *Constantini l'Empereur ab Oppyck* (...) *quorum auctio habebitur in aedibus Gualteri de Haes, Oct 1648*; the catalogue is divided into the various formats (fo, 4o, etc.) and within these into the various rubrics (Theologia, Orientalia, Juridica, Miscellanea etc). Within each of these rubrics each book has a number. Here a book is cited by the rubric, size, number e.g. Th 4o,9 = the ninth book in the theological rubric of the quarto format.

possibility of printers' errors in the catalogue, with the printing history of the book in question. We then find in the quarto section: (1) *Glossarium græcobarbarum meursii.* This is, so it appears from the catalogue (M4o,14) an edition of 1620;[102] (2) *Anatome Arminianismi,* according to the catalogue (Th4o,45), the book of Du Moulin, Leiden edition of 1620.[103] L'Empereur thus drew up the inventory of his library in 1620 at the earliest.

Now it can be made plausible that L'Empereur compiled the inventory of his library in a given year, if one finds works from the same year in the various lists, shortly after the transition. That appears in fact to be the case. In the folio part, one finds as the seventh book after the change of ink, Lessius' *De Justitia et Jure,* according to the auction catalogue (Jfo,4) the Antwerp edition of 1621.[104] In the quarto section we find as the fifth book after the transition *Tileni collatio cum Camerone,* according to the auction catalogue (Th4o,7) the Leiden edition of 1622,[105] and, as the sixth book after the transition: *Exegesis Piscatoris,* also, according to the catalogue, (Th8o,6) a work published in 1622.[106] L'Empereur thus made the inventory of his library not earlier than 1620, and probably around 1622. The last date coincides with his marriage, which took place in June 1622. At that date he began to keep his own household.

We will now investigate with whom and from what books L'Empereur studied, basing our chronology of purchases up to 1622 on external evidence only, such as receipts. We shall then give a brief survey of his purchases in Harderwijk in order to gain an insight into his activities during his first professorate. Of course it is possible that L'Empereur used books in his studies which he did not buy. But the relatively high price of books in the 17th century justifies the use made here of his library to reconstruct his intellectual development and interests.

Trigland states that Constantijn studied philosophy with Snellius and Jacchaeus and also disputed under the latter. He studied literature with Baudius and Heinsius. In theology, his favourite subject according to Trigland, Gomarus was his mentor, while Erpenius taught him the oriental languages. This is a curious survey. A number of the professors named could not have taught L'Empereur during his whole course of

---

[102] In this case one may doubt the correctness of the auction catalogue's statement. Only impressions of 1610 and 1614 are found in the Leiden UB, the Bibliothèque Nationale and the British Library.

[103] Editions of this work at Leiden in 1619, 1620 (J. Marcus) and 1621.

[104] This edition is mentioned in the biographical article "Leys" in *BNB* 12, 79-81.

[105] In the possession of the Bibliothèque Nationale.

[106] Presumably l'Empereur's summary title conceals the *Indices hebraici sex quibus indicantur voces Hebraicae quae in scholiis Johannis Piscatoris in libris Vet. Testam. explicantur* (various editions at Herborn in 1622).

study. Erpenius was only appointed professor in 1613, after years of residence in Paris. Gomarus left in the spring of 1611, Snellius died in early 1613. During L'Empereur's whole student period the professor of Hebrew was Coddaeus, who is not mentioned by Trigland, and who was dismissed for his arminian sympathies in 1619. That may be the reason why Trigland is silent about him. It is true that Jacchaeus was also dismissed in 1619 but he was reinstated in his rights in 1623. Another possible reason is that Trigland preferred to cite the famous Erpenius as L'Empereur's teacher rather than the unknown Coddaeus.

But Trigland was certainly correct in his remark that L'Empereur was above all a theologian. That is the first thing which strikes us on considering his library. On a rough classification into several headings it appears that at the end of his student days, more than half of the books in his possession were concerned with theology.

Table I. Books owned by L'Empereur in 1622.

|  | theology | oriental languages | literature | philosophy |
|---|---|---|---|---|
| folio | 27 | 7 | 8 | 3 |
| quarto | 33 | 13 | 10 | 7 |
| octavo | 41 | 16 | 14 | 10 |
| 16° | 5 | 4 | 8 | 1 |
| Total | 106 | 40 | 40 | 21 |

Total number of books owned: 210 (miscellaneous: 3)

If we look at the list of books in detail, L'Empereur's theological bias comes to the fore.[107] It was, as one would expect of a pupil of Gomarus and Lubbertus, orthodox calvinist. The works of Calvin and his direct followers, such as Beza, Daneau, and Chandieu are prominently represented in L'Empereur's library. He also possessed works of other Romance representatives of calvinism such as Franciscus Junius, Petrus Martyr, Bucanus and Marloratus. The German reformed tradition was absent. L'Empereur owned no works by the reformed theologians of the generation before Calvin, such as Bucer, Zwingli, Melanchthon and à Lasco or of the Genevan reformer's contemporaries such as Bullinger, Musculus, Aretius and Hyperius.[108] Only a single professor of the German reformed academies of Heidelberg, Herborn or Bremen, with whom one would have expected L'Empereur to have been acquainted through Gomarus or Lubbertus, is represented in his library. Famous

---

[107] For the following: Ritschl, *Dogmengeschichte* III; Bizer/Heppe, *Dogmatik*, xvii-xcvi; Andresen, *Handbuch*.
[108] Ritschl, *Dogmengeschichte* III, 243 ff.

names who are missing include Zanchius, Olevianus, Tossanus and Ursinus. In particular, the German ramist and federal-theological tradition is sought in vain. L'Empereur only owned a few lesser polemical works of Alstedt and Piscator. The only well represented German is Pareus, the influential theologian from the Palatinate, but L'Empereur only had his commentaries, not his dogmatic works proper.

L'Empereur had however, presumably as a result of his stay at Oxford, acquired a number of English theological works. He owned the English edition of the collected works of William Perkins (three volumes in folio, London 1612). Further puritan literature is lacking. He possessed a few edifying minor works in English such as a collection of sermons by H. Smith[109] and a commentary by Byfield.[110] But since edifying literature is otherwise completely absent from L'Empereur's library it seems justified to conclude that he had acquired these books to learn English. The second great English theologian in the library is the anglocalvinist Whitaker, but since L'Empereur owned the Latin edition of his works (Geneva, 1610) it is probable that he bought this book in the Republic. Whitaker was popular on the continent as a leading opponent of Bellarmine.[111] L'Empereur's interest in such polemical writings also appears from the presence of the works of Willet. Willet was rather a talented controversialist than a puritan.[112] In addition, L'Empereur, perhaps because of the importance of such works for the remonstrant dispute, had bought the books of the ablest champions of the *Anglicana* against Geneva: Hooker's *Laws of Ecclesiastical Polity* and the *Opera* of the latter's friend Saravia. His interest in polemical literature is evident from other works as well. The literature of the remonstrant dispute is well represented with fifteen books, some of them compendia with more than five works bound in one volume. L'Empereur also possessed the works of catholic controversialists as Bellarmine, Becanus and Cumel, their protestant opponents and the refutations of the socinians by Lubbertus, Grotius and Zarnovechius.

L'Empereur's theological library was that of a follower of orthodox Genevan calvinism of the second generation. The theologians whose work he owned were predominantly characterised by their convinced

---

[109] Henry "silver-tongued Smith" the greatest preacher of his age: *DNB* LIII, 48-9. Gomarus was impressed by his sermons: Gomarus to Walaeus, 1602; Walaeus, *Opera* II, 368.

[110] *DNB* VIII, 112-3. 1579-1622; a puritan who was educated at Exeter College. The work bought by L'Empereur is *An Exposition upon the Epistle of the Colossians (...) being the substance of neare seaven yeeres weekendays sermons*, 1615, fo.

[111] Van Itterzon, *Gomarus*, 28-9. For the characterisation of Whitaker as an anglocalvinist: Broeyer, *Whitaker*, 253.

[112] *DNB* LXI, 288-92.

aristotelianism and the use of scholastic methods in the systematic elaboration of their theology. They laid a great emphasis on the doctrine of predestination. Theologians who resisted the dominance of Aristotle and scholasticism, such as the German reformers who often placed less emphasis on election and were open to Ramus, were not represented.

L'Empereur studied philosophy with Snellius, the most important Dutch ramist,[113] and with Jacchaeus, a subtle Aristotelian.[114] From the reference given him by Jacchaeus, it can be inferred that he was motivated to this study by the importance of philosophy for theology. In view of his theological orientation and the disputation under Jacchaeus one expects from L'Empereur an aristotelian rather than a ramist orientation. His library confirms this suspicion. He owned only four small philosophical works by Ramus and his followers: Snellius' edition of the *Rhetorica* of Talaeus, the arithmetic of Ramus (probably also in Snellius' edition) the *Optica* of Risnerus and the *Astronomica* of Mestlinus, all in octavo. Snellius used these books in his teaching.[115] This ramist teaching material is insignificant compared with the literatue of Aristotle and the neo-aristotelians which L'Empereur owned. His library contained the collected works of the Philosopher, but also the *Summa* of Thomas, the *Metaphysica* of Suarez, works by the neo-aristotelian Spaniards of the university of Coimbra, the edition of the *Organum* by Pacio,[116] theological works of Keckermann, the ethics of Picolominaei, the political writings of Arnisaeus[117] an the edition with commentary of the *De Anima* by Dandini.[118] These are for the most part stout folio volumes, which represent all the most important branches of neo-aristotelian philosophy. It was not without justice that L'Empereur asked Jacchaeus for a reference and obtained it of him. Jacchaeus' teaching since 1607 had been increasingly based on the neo-scholastic Suarez[119] and his pupil L'Empereur was to remain a loyal aristotelian for the rest of his life.

For the classical literatures, which according to Trigland he studied with Baudius and Heinsius we can compare his library with the programme of study which Grotius drew up in 1615 for Aubéry du Maurier, the French ambassador.[120] As a good humanist pedagogue Grotius took into account du Maurier's age, position and busy occupation, but even so the letter gives a good impression of the education given by Leiden

---

[113] For a description of Snellius as a philosopher: Van Berkel, *Beeckman*, 276 ff.
[114] For Jacchaeus: Dibon, *Philosophie*, 69 ff.
[115] Van Berkel, *Beeckman*, 280-1.
[116] Giulio Pace: *NBU* 39, 19.
[117] H. Arnisaeus: *ADB* I, 575.
[118] Girolano Dandini: *NBU* 12, 910-1.
[119] Dibon, *Philosophie*, 70.
[120] Grotius, *Briefwisseling* I, 284-7; to Du Maurier, 13.5.1615.

humanism. Aristotle played a fundamental role in it. Grotius begins with the distinction between practical and theoretical knowledge (*philosophia activa et contemplativa*). Characteristic of the practical Erasmian humanism of Leiden is his warning that theory must only be exercised insofar as it can be of service to practice. The study programme culminates in the law of states and nations and history, because these disciplines are of direct use for service to the community. The structure of the letter is determined by the various preparatory stages of this practical wisdom. Grotius deals successively with logic, physics, metaphysics, ethics and rhetoric. Each time he recommends the relevant work of Aristotle, or in the case of the first three contemplative disciplines, short handbooks with extracts from his doctrines. In ethics, the most important part, he gives besides the inevitable *Nicomachaean Ethics* and *Politics* a long summary of the ancient moralists. For history he does not prescribe any authors, for the sensible reason that one must follow one's personal inclination in reading historical works. Every historical work is useful, and what you read of your own volition will stay with you longer.

If one compares L'Empereur's library with this humanist programme, then one would almost doubt that he had studied at the university of Leiden in its most glorious age. Theoretical philosophy is over represented and of classical literature proper, in 1622, he owned only Caesar, Terence and Sturmius' school edition of the orations of Cicero, Plutarch and Lucian. Even the *De Officiis* of Cicero, which Grotius said to be in everyone's hands, and to be read to shreds by everybody, was not owned by L'Empereur. With some alarm one realises that these were the textbooks from which he learned Greek and Latin. L'Empereur was one of the students of whom Scaliger complained that they passed literature by in order to push on to the summits of theology.[121]

Trigland states that L'Empereur studied Hebrew and oriental languages under Erpenius. That is impossible. As we have seen, L'Empereur at the end of his student days, studied Arabic with Erpenius in 1613, but when L'Empereur was a student Hebrew was taught by Coddaeus, whom Trigland does not mention. The assumption that L'Empereur studied Hebrew with Coddaeus seems to be contradicted by Amama's statement that L'Empereur had learned this language with Snellius using the grammar of Martinius.[122] It is however unlikely that Snellius was still teaching Hebrew in the years after 1607. In the 1580's he had been professor of Hebrew for a short time between Drusius and Raphelengius but Coddaeus who gave the funeral oration for Snellius in

---

[121] For the elementary teaching programme in Greek and Latin: Bot, *Onderwijs*, 152 ff.
[122] Amama, *Grammatica Martino-Buxtorfiana*, praefatio.

1613, only mentions this teaching.[123] Voetius, who was studying at Leiden in the same years as L'Empereur, had learned Hebrew from Gomarus and Coddaeus.[124] L'Empereur also described at the end of the 1630's how he had been initiated into the rudiments of Hebrew in two weeks by Gomarus.[125] Now of course it is possible that Snellius gave private tuition in Hebrew during L'Empereur's student years, but that too is unlikely. The brothers Isaac and Jacob Beeckman, students who were strongly under the influence of Snellius went to Amsterdam in 1608 to study Hebrew with Henry Ainsworth, the minister of the Brownists there.[126] We may thus conclude that L'Empereur had studied Hebrew with Gomarus and probably also with Coddaeus. Amama must have mistaken the name of the teacher, but not that of the instrument. In 1612, Coddaeus republished Martinius' grammar.[127]

L'Empereur's ownership of Hebrew textbooks reflects the Leiden tradition in the teaching of this language. We may assume that he laid the foundations of his knowledge of Hebrew before his departure for Franeker, in the first years of his studies. For a number of works in his possession, one may therefore assume that they played no part in his education because they only appeared in the second decade of the 17th century. Thus he learned his grammar from the ramist work of Martinius, which was probably introduced as a textbook by Drusius[128] and with the more aristotelian inclined book of Bertramus (which may have been recommended to him by Gomarus).[129] The *Thesaurus grammaticae hebraeae linguae* of Buxtorf, which was technically more highly developed, did not appear until 1609. It played no part in the teaching programme at Leiden, because the successive Leiden professors provided their own teaching materials. In 1612 Coddaeus republished the grammar of Mar-

---

[123] Coddaeus, *Oratio funebris*, 15.

[124] Duker, *Voetius* I, 78.

[125] In the "Epikrisis" by him in Gomarus' *Davidis Lyra*. He also names Drusius as his "praeceptor" (*ParaDan*, 256; *MosKim*, 173) but that is based, as shown above, on an exaggeration, which is characteristic of the growing prestige of Drusius in the 17th century.

[126] Van Berkel, *Beeckman*, 26.

[127] Fuks no. 26.

[128] For the Hebrew teaching programme at Leiden to 1620: Lebram, "Studien", in which there is also a survey of the various philosophical inspirations of the grammars. Martinius' grammar in the edition of Drusius, Leiden 1585, was the first Hebrew work printed in the north Netherlands: Fuks no. 1.

[129] For C. B. Bertramus: *DBF* 6, 260; Haag 2, 229-231. His grammar is not present in Dutch libraries but the Bibliothèque Nationale owns his *Comparatio grammaticae hebraicae et aramicae atque adeo dialectorum aramicarum inter se concinnata ex hebraicis Antonii Cevallerii praeceptionibus* ... (in 4o, 1574). The grammar of Chevalier was aristotelian in accordance with the strict Genevan rejection of ramism. In 1602 Gomarus advised Walaeus to use this grammar (Walaeus, *Opera* II, 367).

tinius and in 1619, when Erpenius succeeded after Coddaeus' dismissal, he wrote his own grammar for the teaching of Hebrew, because he found Buxtorf's too complicated.[130]

L'Empereur's library of Hebrew dictionaries was also based on the Leiden tradition. He had probably been using Pagninus' *Thesaurus Linguae Sanctae* since the beginning of his student years. This work which dated from 1523, and played an important part in the revival of Hebrew studies, is a reworking of David Kimḥi's dictionary, the *Sefer ha-Shorashim*.[131] L'Empereur owned the large folio edition published at Lyons in 1577, which had been edited by Bertramus and expanded by works of Mercerus. It is very likely that this book played a role in the teaching at Leiden. In 1570 Raphelengius, who was then active for Plantijn in Antwerp, issued an abbreviated version of Pagninus' dictionary intended as a supplement to the Antwerp polygot. From 1570 to 1578 three editions of this version appeared at Antwerp. After Raphelengius had settled in Leiden and become professor of Hebrew there, he issued a second revision of the work of Pagninus, which was expanded to include Aramaic words.[132] Besides this work by a representative of the first generation of Christian hebraists, L'Empereur also owned a much more modern dictionary, but one which cannot have played any part in his studies: the great *Lexicon Pentaglotton* of Valentin Schindler, posthumously published at Hanau in 1612. This dictionary uses all the aids to Hebrew lexicography, such as the comparison of Hebrew words with those of other semitic languages and with the ancient translations. It remained influential throughout the 17th century, and served as a source of inspiration for the better known dictionary of Edmund Castel, a supplement to the London polygot.[133] L'Empereur also owned the small dictionary of Buxtorf which was based much more on information on Hebrew and Aramaic in rabbinical literature.[134]

---

[130] Erpenius, *Grammatica ebraea generalis*, praefatio.

[131] Sante Pagnino: *NBU* 39, 50-1. His dictionary had a great success. For the various editions see: Steinschneider, *Handbuch*.

[132] The work was very popular: Fuks no. 3, 16, 24, 30.

[133] Schindler: *ADB* 31, 291-2; ?-1604. In 1590 professor at Wittenberg, in 1594 professor of Hebrew at Helmstedt. His dictionary was published after his death and underwent various reissues in the 17th century. The Leiden university library possesses a copy from the library of Isaac Vossius with extensive and erudite annotations of a Dutch orientalist of the mid-17th century.

[134] The various editions of this dictionary bear various titles, thus in 1607 *Epitome radicum hebraicarum et chaldaicarum* ... (Prijs no. 193), in 1615 *Lexicon hebraicum et chaldaicum* (Prijs no. 214). Buxtorf deliberately based himself for preference on the rabbinical scholars: "In subsidium adhibui Chaldaeos & Hebraeos interpretes, priscos & *recentiores*, quotquot mihi illorum copia esse potuit. Ex illorum authoritate quam saepissime lux infertur locis ab interpretibus nostris diversimode redditis." (dedication, Basle edition 1621 (Prijs no. 225), our underlining).

He possessed various Hebrew bibles, such as the sedecimo edition of
Stephanus in seven volumes, the bible which he had had sent to him after
his arrival in Franeker; an edition published at Basle in four octavo
volumes,[135] and Plantijn's edition in quarto, which he bought in 1621.[136]
The work he probably used most in his studies was the edition of the
Hebrew bible edited by Arias Montanus with the interlinear translation
of Pagninus. Heinsius too, like Grotius, used such a bible, in view of the
fact that a copy with his notes is preserved in the library of Leiden university. In the teaching of Hebrew in the French cultural area, this was a
much used work. The edition by Arias originally appeared from the
Plantijn press (Antwerp, 1584) but was soon reissued by Bertramus,
undoubtedly for use in the teaching of Hebrew at Geneva (1587). In the
years 1610-1615 a new edition of the Hebrew text with an interlinear
Latin translation appeared in Leiden.[137] L'Empereur owned the Antwerp folio edition. He also had a number of philological commentaries
by French and Walloon Christian hebraists: the *Biblia cum notis* of
Vatablus (R. Stephanus, 1541, in quarto, bought in 1610[138]), the commentaries of Mercerus[139] on Job and Genesis and the commentary of
Masius[140] on Joshua (Plantijn, 1572 in folio).

So far as rabbinica proper were concerned, we find among the quarto
volumes in his library a title *Rabbini in minores prophetas* and among the
octavos *Seder holam major et minor heb et lat.* It appears from the auction catalogue (O4o,7) that the first is the edition of rabbinical commentaries on
Hosea, Joel and Amos by Mercerus, which appeared anonymously from
Stephanus in 1556. This work gives a Latin translation of the commentaries of Kimḥi, Ibn Ezra and Rashi, without the Hebrew text.[141] The
second book must be the Basle edition of Genebrardus' *Seder olam rabbah
we Seder olam zuta sive Chronicon Hebræorum majus et minus* (1580), an edition

---

[135] Prijs, no. 207; 1611-12.
[136] O4o, 2. Bought at the auction of Mulhemius, 1612. Receipt for this purchase in
Th 163.
[137] For the copy of the Leiden edition of Raphelengius, 1613, which was used by Heinsius: De Jonge "Study", 109, n. 353. For Grotius' copy: Blok, *Contributions* 38 no. 14
and 15. The edition of Raphelengius: Fuks no. 23.
[138] Th4o, 1. Bought at the auction of Vulcanius, 1610. Receipt in Th 163. Vatablus:
*NBU* 45, 989.
[139] Jean Mercier: *NBU* 35, 14 ff.; Haag 7, 328-33.
[140] Andre Maes: *BNB* 13, 120-5.
[141] In 1556 there appeared from Stephanus in Geneva the work "Hosee, cum
Thargum, id est chaldaica paraphrasi Jonathan, et commentariis R. Selomo Iarhi, R.
Abraham Ezra et R. D. Kimchi..." (Moeckli, *Livres Imprimés*, 28). In these years
Mercerus issued a large number of the minor prophets, with targum and sometimes rabbinical commentaries (Haag 7, 329-31). For an analysis of Mercerus' editions of the rabbinical commentaries on the minor prophets and the role which this work played in
teaching, see below, chapter 4.2.

with a parallel translation of this Hebrew chronology.[142] The only untranslated rabbinical work which L'Empereur owned was an edition of the first part of the *Mikhlol* of David Kimḥi published by Bomberg at Venice. This first part, which is also known itself under the name of *Mikhlol*, is David Kimḥi's reworking and popularisation of the grammatical discoveries of his father Josef and his brother Moses, and thus the most important medieval Jewish grammar. The second part of the *Mikhlol* is the dictionary mentioned above, which served as a basis for Pagninus. A work of Buxtorf which he must have acquired after his student years, announces a new development, as it attempts to make rabbinical literature accessible. This is the *De Abreviaturis* of 1613, a survey of the abbreviations used in rabbinical literature.[143] The best represented Christian hebraist, so far as concerns the number of titles, was Drusius. L'Empereur owned sixteen works of this greatest of Dutch hebraists, which for the most part were published by Raphelengius. Mostly these works of Drusius, as is natural given their small size, are bound together, sometimes five at a time.[144]

Jewish works (with the exception of Kimḥi's Mikhlol) were absent from L'Empereur's library of 1622. He possessed only the works and editions of the Christian hebraists. His library corresponds with the teaching of Hebrew at Leiden and also reflects the results of Christian studies of that language in the sixteenth century. The concentration on the French hebraists is typical of Leiden. The scholars who laid the foundations of the study of Hebrew and the oriental languages at Leiden, Drusius, Raphelengius, and Scaliger, had been trained by French masters.[145] All the teaching materials which appeared at Leiden after 1585, the beginning of Hebrew typography in the north Netherlands, were of French origin.[146] The works of German hebraists, especially Münster and Fagius were thus missing from L'Empereur's library. It is true that in the notes by Vatablus on the Old Testament he had access to an extract from the commentary of the two Germans, but that was not known to him. This was the result of a particularly successful deceptive manoeuvre by the

---

[142] Prijs no. 129. Gilbert Genebrard: *DBF* 35, 1003-4.

[143] Prijs no. 212.

[144] L'Empereur owned virtually all the octavo editions of Drusius and four quarto volumes. Gomarus was a great admirer of Drusius. In summing up good Hebrew textbooks for Walaeus he simply concludes: "deinde quicquid Drusius edidit" (Walaeus, *Opera* II, 367).

[145] Drusius by Chevalier, Raphelengius by Genebrard and Mercerus (Juynboll, *Beoefenaars*, 36-7). Scaliger in his *Scaligerana* has the highest praise for such French hebraists as Vatablus, Chevalier and Mercerus. He abuses Münster (*Pr Scal*, 122, 126, 164; *Sec Scal*, 262, 326, 452, 463).

printer Robert Estienne[147] who had published extracts from these protestant commentaries under the name of the catholic professor of Hebrew at the Collège Royal, in order to escape the censorship of the Sorbonne (Paris 1545, in 8vo; Geneva 1547 in folio).

L'Empereur's library also reflects the development of Hebrew studies. These had arisen at the start of the sixteenth century with Germany as their most important centre. Research there stagnated around the middle of the 16th century and the most important publications in Hebrew studies in the latter half of the century were in the French cultural sphere. The results of this tradition of research are found in the library and the education of L'Empereur. The 16th century hebraists had themselves been dependent for their study of biblical Hebrew on rabbinical works and Jewish teachers, but as a result of their efforts by the beginning of the 17th century it was possible to learn biblical Hebrew, as L'Empereur did, purely from works by Christians. Introductions to the rabbinical literature were however scarce and knowledge of it was confined to a few specialists who had to rely on Jewish teachers. The new development of the 17th century was that this literature was made accessible in much the same way as the Old Testament had been before. L'Empereur was to make his contribution to this.

If we now briefly review his purchases after 1622, the most obvious immediate impression is that after a certain date virtually all his new books are concerned with Hebrew and are even intended mainly for a Jewish audience. Thanks to a receipt in the *Bibliotheca Thysiana* it is possible to determine the year in which this sudden change in L'Empereur's interest took place. The sixth folio book after the transition, which he thus bought soon after his new interest emerged, is *Calvinus in V.T.* According to the receipt he bought this work in March 1626.[148] These large scale purchases of mainly Jewish books lasted until 1634. In that year L'Empereur had put together his rabbinical library and won recognition for himself. The change in his interests in 1626 must be connected with the vacancy in Hebrew at Leiden which had occurred after the death of Erpenius on 13 March 1624. L'Empereur was thus already preparing himself for a chair in Hebrew at Leiden in the spring of 1626, though he was not to be invited to take it up until a year later. In the

---

[146] See Fuks, *Typography*.

[147] For Estienne: *DBF* 13, 91-5 and Armstrong, *Robert Estienne*, in which however he fails to note that it was not Vatablus' own work. For this see the article on the latter in *NBU* 45,989. The commentary on the Psalms which is included in the *Critici Sacri* is by him.

[148] Thfo, 27; receipt in Th 163.

following chapter we will describe the state of affairs around his appointment.

The books which he bought in the four years before 1626 correspond in their content to those in his library in 1622. There is no evidence in those years of a special interest in the oriental languages. He bought a number of prestigious humanist works, such as folio editions of Seneca, Tacitus, Xenophon and Dionysius of Halicarnassus, the *Adagia* of Erasmus, the historical works of De Thou, and Quintilian, but the majority of the works he acquired were devoted to theology and mainly of a polemical tendency. Thus he acquired a number of socinian books and expanded his collection of refutations of Bellarmine. Arabic works, such as those Erpenius had been publishing since 1616, were not bought. The only Hebrew works he acquired were publications of Buxtorf: his *Biblia Rabbinica* and *Tiberias*.[149] Other works connected with oriental languages, he received as gifts. He received the *Testamentum Syriacum* of Trostius as a present from Ludwig of Anhalt—it had been published in his principality[150]—and from his old friend Amama the latter's Hebrew grammar of 1625.[151]

What can one say on the basis of the education and library of the thirty-six year old Constantijn L'Empereur who in 1627 became professor of the Sacred Language at the University of Leiden, now half a century old and the most famous in protestant Europe? In the first place, he was in his origin, upbringing and ambition a calvinist and deliberately orthodox theologian. He had been taught to see the faith as agreement to a formalised system of thought, which contained the truth rediscovered in the previous century and now clearly unfolded so that it needed only to be preserved and defended. Formed by neo-scholastic theologians, he saw the greatest threat to christianity in intellectual error. His personal faith, so far as a historian can pass a verdict on it, did not differ from this university view of the essence of Christianity. Devotional works were absent from his library. The opponents of Christianity whom he, in his own view as a university theologian, had to refute, were not the sinners or the representatives of another ideal of life, but the teachers of error.

---

[149] Prijs, no. 222 A + B; 219.

[150] M. Trost: *ADB* 38, 656-7; 1588-1636. Ludwig had the edition of his Syriac New Testament, because that had been published in his territory, at Köthen in Anhalt (in 1621-2; the same edition circulates with both dates). It is a reworking of Widmanstadius' edition of 1555, revised on minor points and with variant readings from the editions of Tremellius (1569) Raphelengius (1574) and Fabricius (1584). This text is the basis of many later editions.

[151] This is the reworking cited in note 122 of the grammar of Martinius, in the foreword to which L'Empereur is mentioned.

In this refutation he saw the social relevance of his function. Trained at the university with the highest scholarly level in Europe, his confidence in the value and the possibility of the secular knowledge of languages and philosophy was unharmed. They could only let the truth shine more brightly. But he regarded literature and philosophy as the ancillaries of theology. During his studies he had not been interested in classical literature and later was only interested insofar as they could contribute to the defence of the truth. It was in the same way that he had been interested in Hebrew before 1626.

# CHAPTER THREE

# ON THE USE OF HEBREW

"O mi Casaubone, rari sunt inter nostros, qui mediocriter
Hebraice sciant, quum tamen rari sint, qui omnino nesciant
Hebraice."

(Scaliger, *Epistolæ*, no. cxxii)

The 18th century saw the start of a development whereby scholarship was definitively institutionalised in the universities. The carrying out of research became the exercise of a profession. Since then the views of an individual scholar on the use and social interest of his subject have been no more than his private opinions, in most cases without consequences for the manner in which he performs his task. In the early modern period, when the place in the university and the intellectual independence of a great many disciplines were far less settled, such scholars' views were of far greater importance for their method of work. In this chapter we shall discuss the most important opinions which were advanced on the place and use of Hebrew in the twenties of the 17th century in the Republic.

To show the significance of such opinions, we first give a brief sketch of the place of the professorship of Hebrew at the University of Leiden. Since Hebrew at that university was above all a propaedeusis to theological studies, we next describe the role which the Leiden theological professors gave to the grammatical and linguistic study of the bible. Then follows a survey of the programme of the professors of Hebrew at the two universities of the Republic, Thomas Erpenius and Sixtinus Amama. Because the latter strove pertinaciously for a social result, and ultimately saw his efforts crowned with success, we shall deal with him in some detail. Finally we shall discuss L'Empereur's call to Leiden, his preparation for this office, his knowledge of Hebrew and his views on the use of his work.

On 8 August 1619 representatives of the South Holland Particular Synod appeared in a meeting of the Mayors and Curators, the administrators of the University of Leiden.[1] That was a unique event, but the meeting was also an extraordinary occasion. The Mayors and Curators, with some representatives of the States of Holland, had been given wide

---

[1] *Molh.* II, 85-7.

powers by that body, to take far-reaching measures at the University of Leiden which were considered necessary after the political and religious upheavals of 1618.[2] The representatives of the Synod thanked the Mayors and Curators for the new appointments undertaken by the committee in the faculty of theology and the reform of the training institution for the ministry, the States' College. They then reminded the administrators of the great necessity to appoint teachers who were sound in doctrine, to positions which were closely related to theology. The representatives naturally had particular individuals in mind in this request, whose continuance as teachers was regarded as undesirable, but the church was most concerned with certain subjects and the structure of the University. It could act itself against individuals.[3] Finally the delegation requested two further appointments to the faculty of theology to give the training a more practical character and to prepare the students better for the ministry. One of these new professors was to teach practical theology. Concerning the second professor, the representatives proposed that he:

> "should read and interpret Vetus Testamentum Hebraice, and that with a short paraphrase, in such a way that it should be possible to get through the whole V.T. in three years, which would be very serviceable, to better to make the students of theology capable for the service of the church."

The representatives suggested a candidate for each post: respectively William Ames, an Englishman whom we shall meet again later, and Anthonius Thysius, the professor of theology at Harderwijk. In a visit of 27 August the deputation repeated this request.[4]

The Mayors and Curators thanked the representatives cordially for their care for the University, pointed to the steps already taken to adapt the institution entrusted to them to the changed times and asked the representatives politely but firmly to mind their own business. Although the Mayors and Curators themselves had been purged and the remonstrant members of this committee replaced by irreproachable adherents of Maurice's faction, the new administrators had no intention of ceding any of the University's autonomy to the church. It is not the place here to relate how the church failed to capitalise on its apparent victory at Dordt, in its demands on the University and elsewhere. For us, this episode is important because of the opinion concerning education in

---

[2] *Molh.* II, 80*-1*; 4 July 1619.

[3] Thus the Synod acted against Cunaeus, without disputing the propriety of his place in the faculty of law (for this affair, see chapter 5.3) and continued to persecute Vossius until the Synod of Delft in 1628, even after he had laid down his function as regent of the States' College.

[4] *Molh.* II, 125*.

Hebrew which is brought to the fore in the request. The representatives
of the Synod considered that the subjects closely related to theology were
the philosophical disciplines and "the knowledge of languages, above all
Hebrew". The Mayors and Curators also began the account of the purge
undertaken by them, the famous "Report of the business of the University of Leiden" with the reflection that "the professors and faculties were
different, such that reason seemed to require that the action taken should
be different."[5] The result of this reflection appeared in the purge. All the
professors who were dismissed came from the faculty of letters.

The University of Leiden was made up of four faculties, of which the
first three, theology, law and medicine, formed the higher faculties. The
faculty of arts or letters, where lectures were given in philosophy and
languages, functioned officially as a propaedeusis for the others. In their
request the representatives of the Synod had the faculty of letters in their
sights. The acceptance of a particular tie between the teaching of Hebrew
and the faculty of theology was in line with a tradition which went back
to the foundation of the University of Leiden. The theologian
Feugeraeus, who in 1575 drew up a programme of study—never
officially accepted—for the university to be founded, began the section
concerning the faculty of theology with the programmatic sentences:[6]

> "So that theology can be taught here (in Leiden), no authors who raise
> endless useless questions will be treated in lectures and no sophists, but the
> two heavenly and divine suns, the one of the Old, the other of the New
> Testament, shall be interpreted from the Hebrew and Greek text."

Such views concerning theological education had the unintended consequence that the role of Hebrew could only be a preparatory one. In
teaching and research in Greek, use could be made of an extensive
literature besides the New Testament, but the professor of Hebrew had
to deal with the same text, the Old Testament, on the basis of which the
theologian, according to Feugeraeus' programme, was to give his
teaching. The influence of this fact is apparent even in self-conscious
hebraists like Drusius, who was unwilling to be satisfied with providing
introductory teaching only. Indignant at the lack of interest in Hebrew
of the administrators of the University, he suggested that the language
should be taught by two professors. The task of the first, according to
Drusius, should be to teach the grammar. The second must, in his eyes,
deal with the text of the Old Testament and the history of God's People.
But Drusius called this second professor a theologian.[7] In practice, the

---

[5] *Molh.* II, 119*.
[6] *Molh.* I, 41*.
[7] Drusius, *Tetragrammaton*, praefatio.

lecturer in Hebrew only carried out the first aspect of Drusius' programme, that of teaching grammar. He provided an introductory course,
which could also be given by others than a professor appointed specially
for the language.[8]

Moreover, in spite of efforts to justify the inclusion of the language in
the humanist programme of study, Hebrew was in fact only regarded as
important for theological students. Feugeraeus' teaching programme,
although it paid lip service to humanist historical ideology and the ideal
of *eruditio trilinguis*, envisaged that the teacher of Hebrew, unlike the
Graecus, should teach only his own and not all students.[9] Thus since the
founding of the University of Leiden, Hebrew had been closely
associated with theology. It causes no surprise that the Mayors and
Curators paid special attention to the Hebrew post in the purge, thus
agreeing with the wish of the Synod.

For a good understanding of the Synod's request for a theologian who
would treat the whole Old Testament in three years, some insight into
the nature of theological teaching is necessary. Around 1600 the teaching
of Hebrew, entrusted to him alongside his proper task, was performed
by the theologian Junius. The lecture roster of 1599[10] distinguished
between teaching based on the Old Testament and the introductory
classes in Hebrew. Junius gave grammatical lessons using Psalms and
Proverbs, while in his capacity as a theologian he dealt with
Deuteronomy and Isaiah. In the same year his colleague Trelcat gave lectures on a *locus communis*, the systematic treatment of a theological subject. No provision had been made for such teaching on the foundation
of the University, but just as in Geneva, life proved stronger than
theory.[11] The Leiden theologians realised very early that some dogmas
lent themselves less well to treatment based on the bible. The teaching
on *loci communes* was to become a permanent part of the curriculum of the
faculty of theology. Now we cannot conclude from the development of
this systematic dogmatic teaching, that the bible-based theological
teaching was literary in its nature. On the contrary, the treatment of a
book of the bible could always provide the occasion for long excurses
in which the lecturer could display his dogmatic talents. These lectures

---

[8] On 27 November 1601 the Rector Magnificus gave a guilder to "a poor Jew who
had taught the students here Hebrew". He declared the money to the university (*Molh.*
I, 402*).

[9] *Molh.* I, 41.*

[10] *Molh.* I, 384-5*. For the various professors of Hebrew at the University of Leiden
before 1620 and the appointment policy, Lebram "Studien".

[11] As early as 1593 Trelcat was giving lectures on a *locus communis* (*Molh.* I, 247*). A
similar development took place at Geneva: Kuyper: *Opleiding*, 168.

were given from the Latin text, with only sporadic references to a Hebrew word.

Thus Rivet, who was professor of Old Testament in the twenties, gave a lecture on Genesis and Exodus in which, as well as an analysis of the separate verses, he also made observations for the benefit of preaching and raised various theoretical and practical points. In this he paid special attention to places which were of importance for interconfessional polemic.[12] On Exodus 16:31 ''And the House of Israel called the name thereof manna, and it was like coriander seed, white; and the taste of it was like wafers made with honey'', for example he must have spent several hours. After some remarks on the analysis of this verse he began a dogmatic excursus. On the basis of 1 Cor. 10:4 where Paul gives a typological explanation of the journey through the wilderness, Rivet claimed that manna was a sacrament and thus a prefiguring of Christ. Since the catholics appealed to Wisdom of Solomon 16:20, where it is said of manna that it adapted itself to the taste of everyone, to show that manna was a figure of the transsubstantiation of the eucharist, Rivet dwelt on this verse, where the taste of manna is mentioned. His thorough and detailed treatment of the difference between the reformed and Roman Catholic views of the sacrament takes up six closely printed folio pages in the printed text of his lectures.[13] One can understand that given such thorough treatment Rivet only dealt with three books of the Old Testament in his thirteen year professorship.[14]

It appears from the request of the Synod in 1619 that the church found the gap between the purely introductory grammatical teaching of Hebrew and such a theological treatment of the Old Testament so wide that an intermediate stage was desired: the cursory reading of the whole text of the bible by a lecturer from the faculty of theology. The Mayors and Curators approved the request and appointed Thysius. It is unlikely that this was enough to satisfy the Synod's request.[15] Thysius too gave

---

[12] A. Rivet, *Commentarii in librum secundum Mosis*. This bulky folio, which is based on his lectures, is dedicated by Rivet to his students. On page (3) of the foreword he describes his method of work: ''Cum enim ea mihi demandata esset provincia, ut veteris Testamenti libros publice explicarem, hunc agendi modum mihi praescripsi, ut nihil intactum relinquerem eorum, quae ab adversariis solent torqueri ad ea stabilienda quae a vero Scripturae sensu sunt aliena, vel quae a nobis ad veritatem confirmandam afferuntur, ab eorum corruptelis & cavillis vindicarem. Addidi, ubi commodum fuit, practicas, ut vocant, quaestiones, & observationes ad mores spectantes.''

[13] Rivet, *Commentarii*, 430-6.

[14] About half of Rivet's three volume *Opera* deal with the bible. In these thousands of pages he discusses a score of Psalms, Genesis, Exodus, Hosea and some detached chapters, such as Isaiah 53.

[15] Two reasons can be given for this suspicion: (1) the son of Walaeus (''Vita Walaei'' in Walaeus, *Opera* I, (28) makes no distinction between Rivet's teaching and that of Thysius. (2) On the departure of Rivet in 1633 Trigland was appointed as his successor.

lectures on the Old Testament in a theological fashion. Thus the position
of Hebrew remained extremely marginal. It was a subject that prepared
for theological study, but was only slightly connected to the method of
teaching which was employed in the higher faculty. What views were
held of the usefulness of this language, which in practice occupied such
a subordinate place?

The twenties of the 17th century were under the shadow of Dordt. Every
decision in politics or theology had to deal immediately with the all-
pervading question of those years, how the decisions of the Synod of
Dordt were to be implemented. That applied also for a subject so closely
allied with theology as Hebrew, and it is no more than fitting to begin
our discussion of the ideals about Hebrew with the views of the professors
in the faculty of theology at Leiden.

The astonishing unity of these four professors, which Heinsius
regarded, with the pleasant situation of Leiden, as one of the great attrac-
tions of the university,[16] makes it easy to determine the view of the
faculty concerning theological study and the part which Hebrew should
play in it. In 1619 and 1620 the new professors gave a number of lectures
which were collected as the programme of the purged faculty and offered
to the Mayors and Curators.[17] The book is a genuine programme and
contains the titles of the fifty-three disputations which the professors
wished to be held, so as to deal with the whole body of reformed dogma
in the spirit of Dordt. This cycle of disputations, undertaken in such
unity, was to result in the dogmatic text book of the post-Dordt period:
the *Synopsis Purioris Theologiæ*.[18] The orations included in it treat the various aspects of theological study. The correct form of this study and the
ideal programme which the professors envisaged for it, formed the subject of the inaugural oration by Walaeus. It begins with a traditional
scholastic definition of theology and a description of the attitude of mind
which befits a theologian. He should separate himself from the world in
order to possess a pure heart. Walaeus then spoke of the various parts
of theological study. First of all the young theologian should know Latin.
It is true that he might possibly be able to dispense with the knowledge
of this language, but that is not to be recommended. Latin is an interna-

---

Rivet's place was considered as the second one. (*Molh.* II, 97* and 186*). Thysius moved
up to this position (this is to be concluded from the precedence which was given to
Thysius above Trigland in 1639: *Molh.* II, 232), so that Trigland took over the work of
Thysius. Even so he only dealt, on his arrival, with Isaiah, thus in a theological fashion.
(*Molh.* II, 190).

[16] AG, Heinsius to Amama, 5.7.1627.
[17] *Orationes inaugurales.*
[18] For the *Synopsis*: Van Itterzon, "Gereformeerd leerboek".

tional language, in which many important dogmatic works are written, and not to have mastered the language would impair the theologian's reputation. In any case he must learn Hebrew and Greek. He ought not to be content with muddy streams but must be able to go to the sources themselves. This image, borrowed from Erasmus, is followed by a metaphor which is of much greater importance for Walaeus' thought. Throughout his oration, he identified the minister with the priest of the Old Testament. He compared the theologian who reads the bible in the original languages with the priest who unlike the common people, might approach the altar. This knowledge however must not be exaggerated.[19]

> "Here I do not approve the studies of those who wear out their whole lives in the learning of these languages, neglecting the other matters which are not less important."

The theologian may not forget that the study of languages is a means and not an end. Minute scholarship is neither necessary nor desirable, and a moderate (*mediocriter*) knowledge of languages is adequate. The other subjects in the faculty of letters also have their usefulness provided that they are pursued in moderation. Some knowledge of history and of certain aspects of philosophy was considered indispensable by Walaeus, who saw Aristotelian logic in particular as necessary for the exposition of the bible, the refutation of confessional opponents and the composition of sermons. It cost Walaeus more trouble to justify the inclusion of metaphysics in the programme of study. He pointed out that the reformers had purified theology of philosophical excrescences and that one must not fall back into the error of the medieval scholastics. But just as the Israelites could marry a heathen woman taken as a prisoner of war, after the required purification, so the theologian too can make a good use of metaphysics.

Theological study proper consists of three parts:[20] catechesis, dogmatics and the exposition of the scriptures. In catechesis, the foundation of theological learning, the most important dogmas are treated, those which must remain beyond discussion in the church. Some were of the opinion that the content of the catechesis might consist only of elements from the scriptures, but Walaeus rejected this view with conviction. He did so not because he agreed with the papists that scripture is not sufficient, but because the church, with her gift of prophecy, can deduce doctrines from the scriptures. Dogmatic theology is more extensive and demands more study. Here the student learns the dogmas which

---

[19] Waleus, "Oratio", 19.
[20] Walaeus says (p. 23) "triplex est ratio".

are derived from the doctrine already treated in the catechism, and the
refutation of the heresies which have attacked the church both in the past
and the present. The exact knowledge of these dogmas and refutations
is the most important and praiseworthy part of theology, since the young
theologian can not refute heretics alone with the aid of the bible. Walaeus
wanted the student first to learn a summary of the most important *loci*.
He can then study treatises on more detailed subjects.

The third element of theology, the study of the Holy Scriptures, must
be linked with the foregoing. Walaeus advised the student to read the
bible each day in the translation of Junius or Piscator, which contain no
commentary but only brief notes. He must make a logical analysis of the
most important epistles and books. Chapters in which important dogmas
are treated, such as some of the Psalms and the epistles of Paul, are to
be learned by heart. Walaeus concluded by describing a method of study
which guaranteed that: "the pious soul can be convinced of the certainty
of the dogmas in this troubled state of the church."[21] In his description
he only worried,—though it seems a little superfluous after the programme which preceded it—about the possibility that reading the bible
might lead the student into heterodox opinions. Some students, according to Walaeus were so afraid of falling into heresy that they only read
commentaries. He considered their fear as real, but "where the danger
is greatest, there the greatest fame is to be won", and moreover there are
ways of reducing the risk substantially. The student must not only read
the bible to gather truth, and furthermore he should follow the traditional
hermeneutic rules. He must pay attention to what precedes and what
follows, to what is expressed more clearly elsewhere and to note the
*analogia fidei*. If he continues to doubt an exposition he can compare the
outcome of his investigation with the opinions of the scholars who have
always been regarded as orthodox by the church.

To the student who followed his advice, Walaeus predicted that his
countenance would shine like that of Moses, so that the people could no
longer look him in the face. The theologian is concerned with the holy,
and that is, according to Walaeus, the Christian doctrine. But since
theology is mainly concerned to preserve the truth of the doctrine,—and
that that was its function, is evident from Walaeus' distinction of the
three parts of theological study—the study of the bible in the original
languages is dangerous and actually superfluous. Of course Walaeus
objected against Roman Catholicism that the Council of Trent had
declared the Vulgate the correct text for dogmatic discussion, asserting
that the knowledge of the original languages is essential for a protestant

---

[21] Walaeus, "Oratio", 25.

theologian. But this objection was pure ideology. Walaeus' survey of the
course of theological study contains not a single positive estimate of
linguistic knowledge. The divergence of humanist biblical scholarship
and orthodoxy, which became more pronounced in the course of the 17th
century, is already heralded in his oration. Around 1640, probably on
the occassion of the appearance of Heinsius' *Exercitationes Sacrae*, Walaeus
expressed his opinion that the humanists in the faculty of letters concerned themselves too much with theology, and that in general the study
of languages and antiquity was not useful to the lecturers in the higher
faculties.[22] Thus the ground which could nourish grammatical and
literary study of the Old Testament among the orthodox grew narrower
and narrower. We shall now investigate whether the hebraists were in a
position, in spite of the changing opinions of the theologians on biblical
study, and their consequent suspicion of the faculty of letters, to demonstrate the usefulness of the literary study of the Old Testament and to
describe it in such a way that it attached itself to developments in church
and state.

To demonstrate the importance of his subject, a 17th century professor
of Hebrew could draw on an arsenal of arguments, which was more than
a century old. Thomas Erpenius, the successor of Coddaeus who had
been purged in 1620, practically exhausted this arsenal when on accep-
ting his new appointment on 27 November 1620,[23] he gave a lecture in
which he set out his view of the importance of Hebrew.

Thomas Erpenius (1584-1624) came from Brabant and studied
literature and theology at the University of Leiden from 1602 to 1608.
Afterwards he made a short journey to England and then stayed in Paris
where he studied oriental languages, especially Arabic. On his return to
Leiden in 1613 he was appointed professor of Oriental Languages
excluding Hebrew.[24] In his oration of 1620 he showed the importance of
the study of Hebrew by pointing to the exalted position (*dignitas*) and the
usefulness (*utilitas*) of the subject. Its *dignitas* appears from the antiquity,
sacredness and beauty of the language. Hebrew excels all other languages

---

[22] "Vita Walaei" in Walaeus, *Opera* I, (29). The remark is made by Walaeus' son
directly after his description of the attitude which his father took during the great dispute
between Heinsius and Salmasius: "Optabat autem litteratores majori circumspectione,
minori licentia in Theologicis versari. Majorum facultatum lumina, qui linguas
negligunt saepe rerum studiosiores inveniuntur, qui peregrinantur minus, minusque
antiqua inquirunt, ea quae Regionis suae sunt melius solent habere comperta." Walaeus
would now be called a "practical theologian".

[23] Erpenius, *Orationes*, 97-132.

[24] For Erpenius: Juynboll, *Beoefenaars*, 59-118. For his appointment: Wijnman,
"Hebraicus".

in these aspects. As a true Leiden humanist Erpenius gave utility by far
the most attention in his speech. Students should not attempt this difficult
study for its dignity alone, without "clear use, and that you do rightly.
I do not wish to be the reason for your using up the flower of your youth
in useless studies."[25]

Hebrew is first of all of great importance for the knowledge of history.
Erpenius showed this by a survey of world history since the creation. He
then described the Old Testament, which, as the source for this history
and thanks to its laws, poetry, wisdom literature and prophecies, is the
most brilliant library ever written. Not only the Old Testament, but the
New also, is founded on Hebrew. The evangelists and the apostles:[26]

> "have, it is true, left us writings with Greek words, but still Hebrew: since
> almost all the stylistic devices, modes of expression and the use of most of
> the words are not Greek but Hebrew, so that for this reason alone it is clear
> that the same Spirit is the author of the scriptures of the Old and the New
> Covenant."

Since Hebrew is thus necessary for a good comprehension of the whole
bible, it forms the basis of all religion and theology. In the following
discussion of the indispensability of Hebrew, Erpenius wished to demonstrate the imperfection of any translations. He hesitated between a
dogmatic and a more aesthetic-personal argument. On the one hand he
stated that the great controversies on doctrine can only be decided by an
appeal to the text in the original language. He illustrated this dogmatic
interest by the example of the Fathers, who expounded the Old Testament so badly because of their lack of knowledge of Hebrew. Much more
warmly, he showed that the beauty and the impressiveness of the bible
can only be appreciated in the original tongues, just as a copy of a great
masterpiece of Lucas van Leyden or Holbein inspires everyone to go and
see the original. Erpenius ended his discussion of the *utilitas* of Hebrew
for biblical study with an impassioned appeal to the students of theology.
They may not be content with reading translations but must be able to
read the scriptures in Hebrew themselves:[27]

> "You, who must be able to be placed in control of Christ's flock, and must
> bring back the lost sheep, should consider that since the fullness of the

---

[25] Erpenius, *Orationes*, 108: "Bene facitis. Neque ego auctor vobis sum, ut juventutis
vestrae florem rebus inutilibus impendatis." Fifty years earlier Junius, in a similar
address, gave by far the greatest weight to the *dignitas*, much less to the *utilitas*. In this
oration (in his *Opera*, I, 1-3) only the last two columns are devoted to the usefulness of
the language. He laid great stress on the beauty of the bible: Van Dorsten, "Sidney",
8 ff.

[26] Erpenius, *Orationes*, 112-3.

[27] Erpenius, *Orationes*, 126-7.

peoples has already come to Christ (permit me to speak Hebrew), the time is almost upon us, in which the Jews, rejected and expelled from the state of grace, and once the true and only people of God, will again come to their senses, as the holy and infallible apostle and prophet Paul foresaw. Then they shall recognise and kiss the Son of God, apart from whom there is no salvation. Consider I say that the time is almost upon us, and that the knowledge of their language is not only useful but even necessary. That is to say of Hebrew. Only through this can they be moved, and in it all the secrets of their religion are preserved.''

Erpenius concluded his oration with a discussion of the importance of Hebrew for others than theologians, in the terms of the traditional renaissance ideology. Hebrew is necessary for all branches of scholarship because the bible is the source of all human wisdom. Also the language gives access to rabbinical literature, which is certainly worth knowing, even though it is not written in completely pure Hebrew. In a final argument he returned to the beginning of his speech. Erpenius argued that because Hebrew is the mother of all languages, every study of languages is benefitted by its study. His master Casaubon had even intended to write a book to prove that Greek was dependent on Hebrew.[28] Erpenius ended by mentioning the great and emulation-worthy scholars who had practised the study of Hebrew, men such as Reuchlin and Scaliger.

It is difficult to use this oration, which has been discussed in some detail because of its great wealth of traditional arguments, to judge Erpenius' actual intention. We can compare it with the oration which he gave on his acceptance of the professorship of Arabic.[29] Then too he began by a reference, intended as an apology, to the beauty and antiquity of the language. After thus establishing the *dignitas* of Arabic, Erpenius illustrated its *utilitas* by four arguments, also highly traditional: (1) the language is widely spread across the east and a knowledge of it is thus useful for commerce; (2) a knowledge of Arabic unlocks a particularly rich literature, which is of importance for a number of disciplines; (3) the language is useful for the knowledge of other languages, especially of Hebrew. The meaning of many Hebrew words "cannot be determined except from this language". Therefore Arabic is also important for a

---

[28] The late humanists were convinced that such a derivation of Greek and Latin from Hebrew was possible. In his excited letters to Amama (AG, 24.3 and 29.11.1629) on the thesis of Pfochen that the Greek of the New Testament did not hebraise, Heinsius says that he has already written a book in which he shows that Homer had read the OT. The posthumously published dictionary of Vossius, *Etymologicon linguae latinae* (1662) is an exemple of the genre. The verdict of Scaliger on such derivations (*Sec Scal*, 477-8) is of his usual sobriety and acuteness.

[29] In *Orationes tres*.

theologian; (4) a knowledge of Arabic makes the conversion of the Muslims possible.

This quartet of arguments has provoked a discussion of Erpenius' actual intention among researchers. According to Juynboll the last, missionary aim was decisive.[30] Brugman considers this last argument and that of the usefulness of Arabic for the study of Hebrew and theology as an argument to fit the occasion, a polite nod to prevailing conventions. Erpenius was no fanatic and personally he saw the greatest interest of Arabic in the use of the language for the sciences, especially for history. Here the influence of Scaliger is thought to reveal itself.[31] Brugman appears to misjudge the times in this argument. In the first place Erpenius, in a letter to the Mayors and Curators not intended for publication, and in which he wished to demonstrate the importance of his subject, employed precisely the same arguments.[32] Secondly, in controversies on anyone's intentions one should bear in mind his conduct, and Erpenius' work served biblical study too. His publications in the field of Arabic can be divided into three groups, the first of which is formed by works of importance for the philological investigation of the bible. He published Arabic translations of the New Testament and the Pentateuch.[33] A more ambitious undertaking in this area failed to proceed for lack of co-operation from the church. In 1619, Erpenius proposed to the Synod of Dordt that a polyglot should be published, an edition of the bible in the original languages with the ancient translations.[34] Such a project, which followed in the tradition of the 16th and 17th century undertakings in biblical scholarship, was not at that time something to be proposed by a man for whom the study and religious tendency of the bible were unimportant. A second element in his scholarly production was the publication of historical works, certainly under the influence of Scaliger's *"omnis historia bona est"*. The third group of writings was formed by publications intended to facilitate the study of Arabic. In the context of these publications Erpenius also intended to publish the Koran, with brief grammatical notes and "where necessary a solid

---

[30] Juynboll, *Beoefenaars*, 75 ff.

[31] Brugman, "Arabic Scholarship", 207-9; Brugman/Schröder, *Arabic Studies*, 9-12.

[32] *Molh.* II, 181*-3*. Erpenius to Mayors and Curators from Thouars, 14.7.1620. In this letter he asked that in the general redistribution of posts after the great purge, he should not be passed over because of his absence. Referring to the high costs of his printing press, he requested an increase in salary, with the solemn promise that he would not use it to buy land. As early as 1613 Erpenius had summarised the usefulness of Arabic in these four points: *Grammatica Arabica*, dedicatio.

[33] In 1616 he published the *Novum Testamentum Arabice:* in 1622 the *Pentateuchus Mosis Arabice.*

[34] On 28 May 1619: Kuyper, *Post-acta*, 284.

refutation of the lies and absurdities in this work".[35] This leads us to a third observation on Brugman's criticism of Juynboll's view.

The conversion motive does indeed play a part in Erpenius' activities, in spite of his "lack of fanaticism". But Brugman fails to see that in Erpenius' lifetime the effort for the conversion and refutation of the Jews and Mohammedans was not a programme point of the hard contra-remonstrant party, but of the more moderate, undogmatic wing of Dutch protestantism. In the years after the Synod of Dordt Grotius occupied his enforced leisure by writing a "proof of the Christian religion", an apology for Christianity with the classic threefold refutation of pagans, Jews and Mohammedans. He used the form of a humanist genre.[36] Grotius undertook these refutations because he strove for a united, undogmatic Christianity, which would find its opponents outside itself, and would not indulge in fratricidal strife. The orthodox party had other matters on its agenda around 1619, than the conversion of Jews and Muslims. The remnants of arminianism had to be cleared up, the doc-trine laid down by the Synod of Dordt had to be worked out and within the church, order had to be restored. Both the *Post-acta* of Dordt and the reports of the South Holland Particular Synods only refer to the "countering of the slanders of the Jews" and not to any efforts for their conversion.[37] A calvinist orientalist such as Boreel decidedly disapproved of an edition of the Koran in 1625, even if it were to be coupled with a refutation.[38]

These considerations on Erpenius' activity as an arabist lead us to put Juynboll's thesis in context. Grotius' and Erpenius' zeal for conversion was based on a wider effort which derived from an ideal picture of Chris-tian society. For Christian humanism the study of languages and thus of

---

[35] Thomas Erpenius, *Rudimenta linguae Arabicae*. This contains a *Consilium* on the best way to learn Arabic, in which Erpenius guides the student to the introductory works he had already published.

[36] For an analysis of the *Bewijs*: Spaans, "Bewijs"; below, 4.4.

[37] Among the Post-acta there is a request of the Synod to the States to take steps against the libels of the Jews (Kuyper, *Post-acta*, 268, 291). It is characteristic that in the gravamen on which it is based, (that of Zeeland; puritan influence?) there is a reference to the conversion of the Jews, but that this point is not taken up by the Synod. For the attitude of the South Holland Synod: *Acta* Gorinchem 1622, a.20; Den Briel 1623, a.15; The Hague 1624, a.15; Woerden 1625, a.15.

[38] Boreel to Walaeus, 3.11.1626; Walaeus, *Opera* II, 440; "Editionem Alcorani quod attinet, si meum esset sententiam dicere, subsisterem. Est vere illud somniorum farrago, saepe etiam cum injuria Historiae Sacrae. Habet Hollandia multos profanos, multos somniorum admiratores, qui facile ex lectione ineptissimi profanissimique scripti, argumenta sibi somniabunt contemnendi illos libros, quos ipsi nunquam attente legerunt, qui continent aeternam invictamque de Filio & Sp.S. doctrinam. Vergit ad senectam Mundus, refrigescit paulatim pietatis & verae illius doctrinae studium. (...) Accessit postea, quod Ecclesia de Praedestinationis doctrina turbata est."

classic and Christian antiquity was of eminent social importance. They were convinced that the purified texts of antiquity would lead to a purified society, in which unity, peace and humanity would be guaranteed. The social importance of their work was quite clear for the humanists, but their defence of their ideal could take on various forms. Thus the wealth of arguments which Erpenius used in his oration on the usefulness of Hebrew can be regarded as an example of the way in which this ideal exceeded his power to articulate it and not as a gesture to prevailing opinions.

The slight theological content of Erpenius' argument is evident from the minor place which he allots to the importance of the original languages for interconfessional polemic. There, and not in a call to missionary endeavour, an adaptation to the spirit of his age would have manifested itself. The eschatological expectation of the imminent conversion of the Jews, in the argument cited above that Hebrew is essential for that conversion, is also found in Grotius,[39] but not in more orthodox circles at that time. This expectation rests on a changed interpretation of Romans 11:25ff, verses to which Erpenius alludes in the passage cited above. Once the exposition of Beza, that these verses refer to the conversion of the real people of the Jews, had been included in the annotations on the Geneva bible, the expectation that this general conversion was imminent came to play an ever greater role.[40] The idea that this conversion would take place soon may have been borrowed by Erpenius and Grotius from the works of Hugo Broughton. This English puritan, described, not entirely without reason, by Scaliger as "furiosus et maledicus", moved in the circles of the religious underworld in the Republic, in which there was also an interest in Hebrew.[41] He had a great interest in the disputes with Jews and their conversion, as is evident from his works.[42] Erpenius may well have made his acquaintance through the abovementioned Johannes Boreel, who carried out the Latin translation of Broughton's commentary on Daniel. Boreel was resident in Grotius' house when the latter lived at The Hague, and was at home in the Leiden humanist environment. Erpenius dedicated his Arabic Pentateuch to him.[43] At any rate, both Grotius and Erpenius were

---

[39] Grotius (Meijer, *Remonstrantie*, 110) uses the argument of the general conversion of the Jews as the first positive reason for the admission of the Jews into the Republic (also referring to Rom. 11:25 ff.).

[40] Toon, *Puritans*, 24.

[41] *See Scal*, 244; for Broughton; *DNB* XLV, 459-62.

[42] Broughton was very interested in the conversion of the Jews and on various occasions he held disputations with them: *EJ* 4, 1410-11; Fuks and Fuks-Mansfeld, *Typography* I, 94-6.

[43] For the contacts of Boreel and Grotius: Meijer, *Remonstrantie*, 69.

familiar with Broughton's work. In Loevestein, Grotius worked with the commentary on Daniel which Boreel had translated and which had been provided for him by Erpenius.[44]

Erpenius' activities as professor of Hebrew were confined to the provision of introductory works, intended as teaching aids. In 1621, he published a simple grammar, dedicated to the four professors of the faculty of theology. The work was a short handbook, to put the student in a position to consult the more complicated grammars of Buxtorf and Pagninus. The dedication gives a sketch, as sad as it is amusing, of the zeal of the theological students in the language taught by Erpenius. Only the most zealous attempt to learn the verb paradigm, but even they, "cum ad Defectiva & Quiescentia ventum est, tempus esse arbitrantur, ut ipsi quoque deficiant & quiescant".[45] In the same year he issued an edition with parallel Latin translation of the books of Samuel. He wanted his students to use this introductory text, because he found the Psalms, the usual entry to the reading of the Old Testament, too troublesome.[46] He published no other works of his own composition in the field of Hebrew, but his liberal humanist attitude is apparent from his arrangement of the publication of Louis Cappel's *Arcanum punctationis revelatum sive de Punctorum Vocalium et Accentuum apud Hebraeos vera et germana antiquitate Diatriba* in 1624. In this work Cappel, professor of Hebrew at the calvinist academy at Saumur, proved that the vocalisation signs in the Hebrew text dated from the talmudic period. This view, which had been generally held among scholars in the 16th century, fell into bad odour with more orthodox protestants, under the influence of interconfessional polemics, in which the catholics used it to impugn the reliability of the Hebrew text of the bible.[47] Cappel, who had completed his work in 1621, asked Buxtorf in Basle, who had chanced to acquire it in manuscript, to arrange for its publication, but Buxtorf thought that it was not opportune to do so. Erpenius, who had also received the manuscript, proceeded to publish it anonymously without the knowledge of the author. Its anonymity was not long preserved. As early as 1624, Schickard mentioned the name of the author.[48] In the foreword to the edition, Erpenius wrote how he had been inclined to Cappel's opinion from his student days. He was thus a true disciple of Scaliger, who had defended the unoriginality of the vocalisation signs in very strong terms against Bux-

---

[44] Grotius, *Briefwisseling* III, 63-4; to W. de Groot, 4.8.1626.

[45] Erpenius, *Grammatica Ebraea generalis*, dedicatio.

[46] Erpenius, *Samuelis libri duo*, praefatio.

[47] For a survey of the influence of this polemic on the study of Hebrew: Lebram, "Streit". See also chapter 5.3.

[48] The first to mention the authorship was W. Schikard, the Tübingen hebraist, in the Errata to p. 39 at the end of his *Jus Regium Hebraeorum* (1624).

torf in 1606. It is not impossible that Cappel took his argument from
Scaliger through Erpenius' mediation.[49] In the second and third quarter
of the 17th century the attitude which an orientalist took towards the
antiquity of the vocalisation signs was to become a touchstone of his
attitude towards the more strictly dogmatic opinions.[50]

Alongside Erpenius' traditional views on the usefulness of Hebrew, the
programme of the other professor of Hebrew in the Republic, Sixtinus
Amama, deserves attention. He was much more successful than
Erpenius in demonstrating the modern and contemporary relevance of
Hebrew studies. Amama, born into a mayoral family in Franeker in
1593, matriculated as a student of oriental languages there in 1610.
Before the end of his first year of study, Drusius had decided to train him
as his successor. As we have seen, he went to Leiden to hear Erpenius
in 1614, and in 1615 to Oxford, where Drusius had contacts.[51] In Exeter
College he studied theology with Prideaux and taught Hebrew from
Ecclesiastes. Amama was still in Oxford when the news of Drusius' death
reached him. He returned at once but discovered how during his absence
a conflict had broken out between Sibrandus Lubbertus and his old
teacher. To his alarm he had to hear how Lubbertus was slandering the
dead Drusius as an atheist.[52] Amama himself was also suspect, as the
chosen successor of Drusius. He had to prove his orthodoxy to Lubbertus
in a detailed examination and although he was appointed to the place of
his old teacher, a year later he was still plagued by intrigues against his
position in the Senate.[53]

---

[49] Scaliger, *Epistolae*, 523v (no. ccxliii); for the contacts of Erpenius and Cappel:
Lebram, "Streit", 30, 59 n. 137.
[50] For this controversy: Schnederman, *Controverse*; Muller "Debate"; below 5.3.
[51] In the dedicatory letter of his *Henoch* (1615) to W. Langton of Magdalen College,
Drusius thanks him for the friendliness and hospitality shown to his son and Sixtinus
Amama. Cf. Platt, "Amama". Drusius had already had contacts with the Bodley family
for some time: Bachrach, "Foundation".
[52] In an extremely emotional letter to Cunaeus of 7 July 1616, Amama describes his
vicissitudes on his return to Franeker. He has often thought of laying aside his office once
again. Cunaeus, *Epistolae*, 133-4: "Ecce enim heri in conventu Academico, cum satis in
me evomuisset, tandem Drusium petebat, eum vocans indoctissimum Asinum, merum
Asinistam, qui tantum apices aliquot Grammaticos callebat, eosque adhuc male, pestem
Academiae, authoremque omnium turbarum, quae in ea unquam, atheum (horresco
refererens) nullius religionis, & si alicujus, eum Arrianis & Samosatenianis annumeran-
dum." For a very partisan account of the conflict between Lubbertus and Drusius: van
der Woude, *Lubbertus*, 309-37.
[53] AG, Amama to Saeckma, 20.7.1616. He thinks that Lubbertus is out to have him
dismissed shortly. If he had known everything in advance, he would never have returned
from England. "Examinatus sum, subscripsi, juravi, praestiti ea quae nullus ante, nullus
post me facturus, et haec omnia ut provisionalis essem, ad menses aliquot, ut ille mihi
objecit." A year later he was still in difficulties: AG, Amama to Saeckma, 18.7.1617.

Amama not only had his own ideas of the usefulness of his subject, like every professor, but also tried to put his ideas into practice. In 1624 he published his "Brief Representation in which all the faithful servants and elders of the reformed congregations of Friesland are bidden to lend a helping hand to the highly necessary awakening of the declining study of the sacred tongues, in which the holy scripture was originally written." In this pamphlet, Amama argued forcefully that students of theology who offered themselves for the ministry should have such a knowledge of the original languages that they could consult the original text of the bible themselves. Amama sent twenty-six copies of his argument to the Friesian Synod. It was impressed and decided that from henceforth students should have to submit a testimonial from the professors of Greek and Hebrew, that they had sufficiently studied the original languages. In addition, the students would have to give the classis where they sought admission a proof of their knowledge, apparently by the oral translation of a chapter from each of the two testaments. In the same year, 1624, Amama approached the South Holland Particular Synod, with the decision of the Friesians and thirty copies of his "Brief Representation". The Synod put the question on the agenda for the meeting of the following year, to give the classes the opportunity to study the matter in depth. In 1625 it decided on the same measure as the Friesians. The decision was sharpened by admonitions from the synodal meetings in the following years. The other provincial synods also must have been approached by Amama. In 1626 Utrecht took the same step, North Holland followed in 1627.[54]

These decisions crowned the views on the importance and use of Hebrew which Amama had been expressing since he took up his office and to which he remained loyal throughout his life. From his letters to Johannes Saeckma, Curator of the University of Franeker,[55] a portrait emerges of a professor who concerned himself not only with the chronic intrigues of Friesian provincial politics, but also with everything which affected his university and thereby subordinated everything to his vision of what was necessary for the church and the republic. Thus for example it is a pleasure to read his letter to Saeckma of 13 May 1625. After pointing to the result of the decision of the synod for the study of languages— the number of students following his lectures had virtually doubled, from scarcely twenty to almost forty—Amama reported with great indignation how three students who wished to become ministers had tried to evade

---

[54] The course of events in Friesland and South Holland in de Jonge "Study", 67-8; the resolutions of Utrecht and North Holland in the *Anti-Barbarus Biblicus*, 239-45.

[55] Johannes Saeckma (1572-1636) was an important Friesian politician, a councillor since 1603, and a Curator from 1626: Boeles, *Hoogeschool* II, 5. See also note 88 below.

the examination of their knowledge of the original languages. His moral indignation passes effortlessly into a very factual discussion of the possibilities for political pressure on the Synod to remain loyal to its decision. Saeckma, whom Amama regarded not only as his patron but also as a friend, played a key role in this campaign, which was carefully explained to him by Amama.[56]

Amama interpreted his vision programmatically and with the intention of achieving international results, in his *Anti-Barbarus Biblicus* of 1628. In this collection he included a number of his earlier publications. Thus his "Brief Representation" reappears as a *Supplex Parænesis ad Synodos, Episcopos et Superintendentes Ecclesiarum protestantium* on pages 196-239.[57] An analysis of this work and the way it is based on earlier publications and activities of Amama shows, just as with Erpenius, how various views on the usefulness of Hebrew could overlap. Amama appears to make use of a number of forms to realise his programme. It is these adaptations which largely explain the success he was able to record with his campaign. The apparent form of the *Anti-Barbarus Biblicus*, which consists of three books, is that of a polemic against Roman Catholicism.

The second and third books of the *Anti-Barbarus Biblicus* discuss errors of translation in the Vulgate text of the Pentateuch and the historical and wisdom literature. These errors of translation, which Amama demonstrates with the aid of his extensive linguistic knowledge, must prove the incorrectness of the decision of the Council of Trent by which the Vulgate had been declared a reliable text. Where appropriate Amama points out the dogmatic consequences of the mistranslations,

---

[56] AG, Amama to Saeckma, 3.3 and 13.5.1625.

[57] The full title reads: *Anti-Barbarus Biblicus in vi libros distributos*; quorum primus ostendit vii fontes omnis Barbariei, quae superioribus seculis sacras literas foedavit: reliqui v non solum exhibent centurias aliquot crassissimorum errorum, qui circa particularium locorum interpretationem ex istis fontibus emanarunt, sed & compluribus locis Scripturae facem allucent. The structure is: dedication/ foreword/ De Barbarie oratio / Speculum SS Ministerii Candidatorum qui minus digne Evangelio vivunt/Oratio de barbarie morum/various testimonials (all unpaginated). In the numbered text various treatises are included: 196-246: Supplex Paraenesis ad Synodos, Episcopos, & Superintendentes Ecclesiarum Protestantium, de excitandis SS Linguarum studiis; 294-365: Sixtini Amama responsio ad excursus eruditissimi Viri D. Marini Marsenni Theologi Parisiensis. Qua defenditur censura vulgatae ad vi priora capita Geneseos ab ipso oppugnata (dedicated to Gomarus and Rivet); 465-558: Sixtini Amama de nomine tetragrammato dissertatio cum responsione ad argumenta Cl. D. Nicolai Fulleri, Angli quibus pro vulgatae lectionis Iehovah certitudine disputavit (dedicated to F. Hommius); 727-751: Sixtini Amama Commentatio de Keri & Chetib (dedicated to Louis de Dieu); 889-924: Sixtini Amama ad celebrem illum locum Proverb viii, 22 *kurios ektise me* commentatiuncula, in qua illud quoque ostenditur, Cl. & celeberrimum virum, D. Joh. Drusium p.m. Arianae impietati non favisse (dedicated to Hachtingius); 966-974: Ad locum Ps 1 vers 5. Pio and *poluistori* Iuveni-Viro D. Johanni Coccejo, meo in Thalmudicis studiis consecraneo.

limiting himself to erroneous views on ceremonies. In such cases he makes use of the polemic scheme which appeals to scholars in the other camp so as to trap the opposing party in internal contradictions. Amama intended to publish three further books which would deal with similar errors in the prophets, the gospels and Acts and the Epistles. Only the fourth part appeared, posthumously. Amama's notes on the various bible verses are certainly not just of a dogmatic-polemical nature, and were not seen as such, as is witnessed by their inclusion in the *Critici Sacri*, the great compendium of humanist philological commentaries. In the argument of the *Anti-Barbarus Biblicus* the second and third books function as illustrations of the first, which is programmatic, and gives an overview of the seven "sources of barbarism". Thus Amama calls the opinions and views concerning the text and study of the bible, which led to the neglect of the study of Hebrew. The first three and the seventh of these are opinions of Tridentine Catholicism; that the translation of the LXX is inspired, that the Vulgate is an authentic text, that the text of the bible has been corrupted by heretics and Jews, that the tradition and authority of the church are necessary, and finally, that every passage in the bible had a literal and a mystical sense. In his first book Amama is at great pains to refute these views fundamentally.

In this polemical character the *Anti-Barbarus Biblicus* is a continuation of Amama's inaugural lecture: *Dissertatiuncula, qua ostenditur præcipuos papismi errores ex ignorantia ebraismi et Vulgata versione partim ortum, partim incrementum sumpsisse* (...).[58] In this oration he had dealt with the Old Testament evidence for catholic views on purgatory, the immaculate conception of Mary, the veneration of saints and the infallibility of the pope. He deliberately used this form to incite his auditors to the study of Hebrew, and not the customary arguments about the antiquity and the usefulness of Hebrew. His first great publication in Franeker, the *Censura Vulgatae* was also based on this method. This form of militant protestantism explains Amama's influence on orthodox dogmatic preachers and his relatively rapid recognition by Lubbertus. Yet one can assert that the actual intention to the *Anti-Barbarus Biblicus* was against his fellow-protestants.

In his short but nevertheless important discussions of the fourth, fifth and sixth sources of barbarism, Amama turned explicitly to the protestants. The *Anti-Barbarus Biblicus* was intended to repeat internationally the success of the "Brief Representation" and to promote the study of

---

[58] Franeker, 1618 (*Knuttel*, no. 2793). For the events accompanying the official approval of the Vulgate text, which made it very easy for Amama: Baroni, *Contre-Réforme*, 218-22.

Hebrew among protestants. The many Germans whom Amama cites
with approval in his works, both calvinists and lutherans like Alting,
Graser, Scultetus, Franzius and Tarnovius and the citations from
Luther, Melanchthon and Flacius Illyricus lead one to suspect that he
was thinking above all of the Empire.[59] The views with which Amama
reproached the protestants and which he regarded as sources of barbarism are respectively: (4) that the study of Hebrew and Greek is by
now superfluous; (5) that the various translations since the 17th century
into Latin and the vernacular languages are reliable; and (6) that one can
be a good theologian without a knowledge of the scriptures. To refute the
fourth opinion, Amama added to his *Anti-Barbarus Biblicus* a Latin
translation of his ''Brief Representation'' but the actual refutation of the
protestant forms of barbarism is found in the dedication, the foreword
and the orations attached to them.

The dedication to the Committee of the States of Holland, the
Curators of the University of Leiden and the Mayors of Leiden, sets the
tone of Amama's exhortation. He reminds them of how fifty-seven years
ago the States of Holland founded the University of Leiden in order to
drive out barbarism, to protect the purified religion and to preserve the
study of literature. They had understood that with a well-ordered educational institution the church and state would never lack pious and learned
servants and courageous and intelligent rulers. In the dedication Amama
makes it clear that he is concerned with a reform of society, which can
only be achieved by a change in education. This effort is in the first place
social, not ecclesiastical. He wants to improve the society of which the
church is one of the most important components. In the foreword
Amama explains the title *Anti-Barbarus Biblicus*. The barbarism which he
is attacking is the neglect of Greek and Hebrew. The barbarians are those
who can learn these languages but do not wish to do so. Amama wants
to show how the neglect of Greek and Hebrew leads to a biblical barbarism and the decline of true religion. Such a depiction is necessary
because even in the evangelical churches there are some who prefer to
allegorise with Origen and Augustine rather than expound the Holy
Scripture purely with Luther, Calvin and Bucer. They are the true barbarians who could do better and against whom the book is actually
directed. Just as in his inaugural lecture Amama tries to incite his protestant public, by means of a polemical work, to study Hebrew. To prevent

---

[59] Alsted between the orations and the actual book; Scultetus 195, 467; Grasserus 238
and *passim* in both orations; W. Franzius 895; Tarnovius 199; Flacius, 25, 230; Melanchthon 230. That the work had no success in Germany is apparent from the letters of Th.
Ebertus to Amama from Frankfurt on the Older, who tried to interest the church of
Brandenburg (e.g. AG, Th. Ebertus to Amama, 5.3.1629).

anyone misunderstanding his intention, Amama added to the foreword two orations which take barbarism as their theme. The first discusses the neglect of languages. The second attacks the degenerate manners of the university of Franeker. According to Amama the two phenomena were closely related.

In the *De Barbarie oratio*, which was given on 22 September 1626, Amama developed a picture of the historical development of barbarism. The approach is brilliant. Eight years ago, so Amama stated, the centenary of the Reformation was celebrated at Franeker. It commemorated how Luther, Melanchthon, Erasmus and Reuchlin had driven away the barbarism which had seized hold of the study of law, medicine and theology. The rising sun of the knowledge of languages and literature had chased away the shadows of ignorance. It had been commemorated, and they had celebrated the Reformation with a scandalous amount of drinking. But, according to Amama, they had forgotten with what giant strides they were on their way back to the same darkness, and how small was the distance which separated the churches from it. The sun can set again and the shadows return. He is convinced that the level of knowledge of languages and thus of culture, is the result of an historical development, from which the individual cannot detach himself.

To make it clear to his hearers, in what historical phase they found themselves, Amama divided his speech into two stages. He began with a generalised survey of history, distinguishing seven successive stages of barbarism since the time of Christ. The nadir was reached in the Middle Ages, when all knowledge of languages had disappeared and theology began to be confused with the pagan and badly translated Aristotle.[60] Thomas and Peter Lombard occupied the place of the Old and New Testaments. The programme of the reformers that put an end to this darkness consisted of four points: (1) the study of languages may not be neglected; (2) the bible must be studied thoroughly; (3) only the bible, no commentaries, translations or human writings, must be read; and (4) scholastic theology may never return to the reformed churches. That was the programme (one can imagine how Amama paused and cast a meaningful eye around the hall, before thundering into the second stage of his

---

[60] Here appears one of the sources used by Amama for his expressions: Flacius Illyricus, who in his *Clavis Scripturae Sacrae* in the praefatio (2a) in book II, gives examples of a mistaken understanding of the Old Testament concepts by the catholics, and continues: "Talia plurima exempla corruptarum sacrae Scripturae vocum sunt in istorum sophistica Theologia: idque in vocabulis, phrasibus ac sententiis longe maximi momenti; tametsi tota Biblia istis hominibus barbarizare, cum ipsorum male verso Aristotele, & corrupta philosophia, corruptioreque Grammatica, coacta sint." In contradiction to Amama, Flacius lays the greatest stress on doctrine (one of the examples he uses concerns—inevitably—*iustitia*).

argument). But what is the situation now? In a very rhetorical sketch of
the state of the protestant universities Amama shows how the heroes of
the Reformation have been succeeded by a new generation, which yearns
for the fleshpots of Egypt and repeats the errors of the Middle Ages.
Once more, theologians are discussing futile and vainly curious specula-
tions. Unnecessary division has been the result, such as that between the
lutherans and the calvinists in their dispute on communion. The protestant professors are wasting rage and zeal on purely theoretical questions,
instead of creating piety from its pure springs and linking thought with
action in order to banish the abuses in the church. The bible is no longer
studied and men swear by translations. Thus, says Amama, in spite of
the earnest warnings of Ramus, scholastic theology is returning. The
return of barbarism and the neglect of the study of languages at the
university takes its revenge in the quality of the ministers trained.
Amama painted a sombre picture of the theological student. He is only
out for financial gain, in his study hours he never reads the bible, he only
learns to dispute and lives like an animal. Such students, when they later
mount the pulpit, can only dispute and have to be silent about piety.
They have no knowledge of the spiritual life from their own experience
(*spiritualis vitae experientiam*), they do not know what practical theology is,
and they are ashamed. Thus the evil spreads from the university to the
whole of society. Amama recommended two remedies against this evil.
The theological student must not neglect the study of languages, but
follow the study programme of Drusius in his training.[61] In addition the
professor of practical theology must play an important role in theological
study.

In the second lecture Amama discussed the barbarism of manners,
which he had already identified at the close of the lecture discussed
above.[62] The tone of his lecture is determined by his alarm at the Thirty
Years' War then raging. The indifference shown by the members of the
University of Franeker to the sufferings of the German protestants only
increases their sin. On the other hand Germany is a frightful example.
The evil in the universities there spread through society and thus caused
the horrors in Germany. It was Amama's deepest conviction that the sins
of the Dutch were not less, and that the punishment which had befallen
Germany would hit the Republic.[63] For there too, the reformation had
become a matter of outward form:[64]

---

[61]  In his *Annotationes in Novum Testamentum*.

[62]  *Oratio Academica de barbariei morum, ubi & de praesenti Academiae Franekerae status disseritur.*

[63]  AG, Amama to Saeckma, 27.12.1626: "si tamen nihil hic fiat, periimus. Ne Moses
quidem & Samuel si starent coram Domino, exorarent eum, quo minus super nos quoque
extendat tandem perpendiculum Germaniae. Ne ipsa quidem salus, si vel maxime velit,
nos servaverit."

"we rest on a correct opinion on theology, and in a naked conformity with formulas and ceremonies, but we think little or not at all on self-denial, on the crucifixion of the flesh and of our desires."

In the *Anti-Barbarus Biblicus* of 1628, all aspects of Amama's individual version of an aggressive protestant humanism come to the fore. In what follows we shall investigate the sources from which he derived this opinion. According to Amama, barbarism grows from a lack of knowledge of languages and is apparent in senseless dogmatic speculation and the neglect of the right life. Thus formulated, Amama's programme, insofar as concerns the symptoms to be attacked, agrees with that of William Ames, a Franeker professor of theology who is frequently cited with approval[65] by Amama in the *Anti-Barbarus Biblicus*, and whom he regarded as an ally.[66]

This convinced puritan, born at Ipswich and educated at Cambridge by Perkins, had been dismissed from his offices for his resistance to the Church of England. From 1611 to 1619 he was in The Hague as chaplain to Horace Vere, the commandant of the English troops in the Republic's army. He became involved in polemics with the remonstrants and was attached as an assistant to the chairman of the Synod of Dordt, Bogerman. From 1610 he had refrained from over-violent attacks on the Anglican church, but the English government continued to distrust him. In spite of his services to the contra-remonstrant cause, the English ambassador effected his dismissal from Vere's service, and hindered the intended appointment of Ames as professor of practical theology at Leiden. Ames was involved for some years in teaching the holders of Amsterdam scholarships at the States' College, and in 1625 became professor of practical theology at Franeker. He considered theology as a *doctrina Deo vivendi*, the teaching of living for God, and set himself against an intellectualist view of the faith. In his description of religion, Ames gave primacy to the will, and not to the intellect. In his opinion, dogmatics was based in morality. On the grounds of this concept of faith as trust and obedience, Ames rejected scholastic aristotelian theology and wished instead to take his stand on Ramus.

Ames too had desired, since his arrival at Franeker, to reform the way of life of the theological students. His *Opera Omnia* include a lecture he

---

[64] "In sano de rebus divinis sensu & nudo assensu in formulis & ceremoniis fere acquiescimus, de abnegatione nostri, de crucifixione carnis & cupidatum nostrarum parum aut nihil cogitamus."

[65] In the *Anti-Barbarus Biblicus: passim* in both orations, further 200, 254, 264, 276, 858.

[66] For the literature on Ames: *BL* 1, 27-31; TRE 2, 450-3. For the problems surrounding his proposed appointment at Leiden and his teaching at the States' College: Sprunger, *Ames*, 65-70.

gave before the students in August 1623, in which he expressed the hope
that academic theology, instead of the "subtle, involved and in fact
unimportant controversies" would deal with "life and practice".[67] The
goal of theology is, while living for God oneself, also to lead others to
God. Ames states that this is not taking place at the university. The
theologians may be studying hard, but not properly:[68]

> "For insofar as theology is a more noble science than all the others, its prin-
> ciples must be more carefully known and more methodically studied.
> Insofar as it has a more direct reference to the practice of life, it must be
> more closely associated with experience."

But most students thought that theology consisted purely of knowing doctrines:[69]

> "and then they do not study all of them but only those dogmas which are
> mostly discussed and which are used for controversy. They only investigate
> those passages of Scripture of which they observe that they have been cited
> by others in one or other dogmatic controversy or argument. They do not
> take the slightest trouble to learn languages. They regard logic as
> superfluous. They rely on apostilles, commentaries, and often even on
> human imagination (...) Keep such impiety, dear youths, far from you. So
> long as you have the opportunity to study the bible zealously, strive to com-
> prehend it logically and clearly, so that you have trained your faculties to
> distinguish right and wrong, Hebrews 5:14. Finally seek in the bible not
> only doctrines and controversies but all the training and teaching in the
> systematic exercise of all piety and virtue."

In the whole lecture Ames tries to exhort the students to the *praxin et
studium pietatis*. The sometimes literal verbal agreement of this lecture
with the programme of Amama goes so far that one may think of a far-
reaching influence of Ames on his friend and neighbour Amama.[70] The
emphasis on the reform of teaching is coupled in Ames with a ramist
philosophical orientation. It is possible that Amama also borrowed his
enthusiasm for Ramus, expressed in his *Anti-Barbarus Biblicus* and also
apparent in his reworking and publication of the ramist Hebrew grammar of Martinius in 1625, from Ames. The latter urged him to publish
this grammar.[71]

The French philosopher and lay theologian Ramus had developed a
practical educational programme, with which he tried to make accessible

---

[67] Amesius, *Opera Omnia* IV, after page 450; "Paraenesis ad studiosos Theologiae,
habita Franekerae Aug. 22 anno 1623".
[68] "Paraenesis", v6b.
[69] "Paraenesis", v7a.
[70] Amama to Cabeljauw, 4.11.1623; Cabeljavius, *Liber Adoptivus*.
[71] *Grammatica Martinio-Buxtorfiana*, praefatio. The ramist character of this grammar is
the guiding thread in Lebram, "Studien".

the results of humanism and which was aimed above all at practice. He was a great opponent of Aristotle and worked out the only educational system of the later 16th century which was not based on that philosopher. His thought was therefore very popular among those reformed who stood apart from the current of the Genevan neo-scholasticism based on Aristotle, such as many German theologians. Those too who were of the opinion that the development of the Reformation had led to a one-sided emphasis on the intellectual aspect of faith, made use of this philosopher with his stress on practical life.[72] Ames was the most outspoken calvinist ramist, right up to his definition of theology. There are other elements in the works of Amama and Ames which coincide. The latter felt himself in sympathy with the efforts of Teellinck, the Middelburg preacher who strove for more precise reformation. Amama was also impressed by the Zeelander's programme. In his *Anti-Barbarus Biblicus* he cited Teellinck's "Necessary Statement" which had appeared a year before.[73]

Nonetheless one would do Amama's programme an injustice if one derived it from the ramist puritanism of Ames. They were both reformers who set themselves against the prevailing tendency of the post-Dordt period scrupulously to protect the gains of the church in the fields of dogma and institutions. In university politics they were sworn allies in the struggle for more discipline and a more moral life for the students and teachers. But this was an alliance of opportunity against common enemies. The roots of Amama's effort for reform and his ultimate goal differed, particularly in the field of linguistic knowledge, from those of the puritan. Amama himself was convinced that his mode of exposition of the bible differed from that of Ames.[74] It is characteristic of Amama's intellectual independence that all the points of his programme are found in works he had written before 1622, the year of Ames's arrival. From the later works it only appears that the formulations used by his colleague made a deep impression on him.

---

[72] For Ramus: Hooykaas, *Humanisme*; Ong, *Ramus*; for the theological use of Ramus: Moltmann, "Bedeutung". Ramism was absorbed by virtually every tendency which set itself against Genevan neo-scholasticism; *ibid.*, 296.

[73] W. Teellinck, *Noodwendigh vertoogh aengaende den tegenwoordige bedroefden staet van Gods Volck*, 1627.

[74] Ames' exposition of the bible was directed much more to practice and edification. One has the impression that he did not possess a profound knowledge of languages. Amama described Ames' method of expounding the bible to Saeckma (AG, 13.3.1625) as: "D. Amesius quidem, sicuti omnis sua ad praxin dirigit, tum in iis quae de Conscientiae cura, inaestimabili labore (ita judicant omnes qui virum audiunt) proponit; tum in Psalmorum explicatione, ita et hoc potissimum agit, non ut inutiles quaestiones ex textu deducat, sed ut ostendat, quomodo Scriptura solide, et cum pietatis incremento coram populo tractari, et applicari debeat."

In 1621 Amama was rector of the University of Franeker. Both in his inaugural and final addresses he preached on the manners of the students.[75] The first lecture is a thunderous sermon, not without merit in its genre, against the abuse of drink, which contains an extended depiction of the hell awaiting the drunken student. His penitential sermon of early 1622 was also directed against the theological students. They were no great lovers of such stinging exhortations.[76] In both sermons we find practically all the elements of the programme of the *Anti-Barbarus Biblicus*. Amama inveighs against *avaritia* and *ambitio* and exhorts the students to the *studium pietatis*, with the argument that one must prepare oneself at university for life as a minister. In true ramist style he points to the practitioners of the *artes mechanicæ* as an example to be emulated.[77] Only the reproach against the theologians for concerning themselves with futile speculation is missing, but this omission is understandable so soon after Amama's difficulties over doubts of his orthodoxy. The puritan aspects of the two sermons can be explained from the influence of Prideaux and the impression which the disciplined and moral life of the members of Exeter College made on Amama. As early as his return from England, his self-confidence had been based on his morally proper life.[78] He was by no means a hypocrite. In a gift of presentation copies to the members of the Friesian States he stipulated that he did not wish to receive any money for them, at the most books.[79] Thus puritanism was one of the roots of Amama's thought. But two elements in his programme are not found to the same degree in puritanism and in Ames. Amama laid a great stress on the whole of society, of which the church is a part. His view of history also points to the erasmian-humanist origin of his programme. As Platt has observed, even the title of the *Anti-Barbarus Biblicus* recalls that of Erasmus' *Antibarbarorum liber*.

Amama played a variation on the erasmian theme that the study of languages and of classical texts purged of later commentaries and overgrowths, will lead to a purified society. He transferred this conviction to the study of the bible and Hebrew. It is not the knowledge of classical literature but that of Hebrew which determines the stage of civilisation. This conviction is at the heart of his periodisation of history.

---

[75] *Oratio de Ebrietate*, Franekerae 1621; *Sermo Academicus, ad locum Ecclesiastiae* 12:1, Holmiae 1625 (in the Bibliotheca Thysiana at Leiden).

[76] Amama to Cabeljauw, 6.1.1623; Cabeljavius, *Liber Adoptivus*.

[77] For Ramus' preference for mechanical arts as examples and teachers: Hooykaas, *Humanisme*, 25, 31-2, 91-5.

[78] AG, Amama to Saeckma, 18.7.1617. For the deep impression which his stay in Oxford made on Amama, cf. Platt "Amama", 243.

[79] AG, Amama to Saeckma, undated, "Iam a septimana".

The course of history from the time of the New Testament to the beginning of the 16th century was characterized by constant decline. Then
thanks to Luther and Melanchthon, Erasmus and Reuchlin, there began
an unprecedented flowering of languages which has by now reached its
zenith. Now civilisation is again in rapid decline. This development is
beyond the control of the individual and therefore the latter is determined
by the age in which he lives. Under the impression of the miseries of war
in Germany and thanks to his conviction that the coming of barbarism
was imminent, this interpretation of history could take on apocalyptic
forms for Amama.[80] The core of his conviction—that the rediscovery of
languages and the reformation belonged together and ought to have led
to an improvement in society, but had failed—goes back to his teacher
Drusius, whom Amama continued to venerate and defend throughout
his life.[81] Drusius adhered to the erasmian conviction that the study of
the bible had to be placed above speculation because the latter led to
senseless strife.[82] He identified the rebirth of language and the reforma-

---

[80] Most strikingly expressed in the letter from Amama to Martinius, at the beginning
of Cocceius, *Sanhedrin et Maccoth*, (\*\*\*2b-\*\*\*3a) in which he praises Cocceius.

[81] Cf. the structure of the *ABB*, as set out in note 57. In the foreword to *De nomine
tetragrammato* he mentions how in his Hebrew lessons at Exeter College he read "Adonai"
and not "Jehovah". When he was questioned on this by a student, he wanted to refer
him to Drusius' work on this subject. When this proved to be sold out, Amama, at
Prideaux' suggestion, wrote this work. It was never published, but now that Fuller is
attacking Drusius on this point, he feels compelled to publish it. The same applies to the
commentary on Proverbs 8:22. Through his exposition of this passage, Druius had fallen
under suspicion of Arianism. In the foreword Amama relates that he had had a defence
of his teacher ready for some time, but had not wished to publish it. Now however, that
doubts have been raised among those who are not experts in the matter, of Drusius'
orthodoxy, he feels himself compelled to issue this work.

[82] Drusius' erasmianism is apparent at various places in his writings. Both in his *Ad
Minerval Serarii Responsio* (p. 9) and in the *De tribus sectis Iudaeorum libri quator* (\*\*2b-\*\*\*3a)
he cites as his programme the letter of Erasmus to Boville of August 1516, (Erasmus,
*Opus Epistolarum*, no. 456). In this letter which corresponds to a great extent with the
*Apologia* which Erasmus published this same year for his New Testament, he defends
himself against attacks from theologians, who in his opinion are too philosophical. The
passage used by Drusius reads: (ll. 130-7): "Sed indignum se iudicant ad istas gram-
maticorum minutias descendere; sic enim vocare solent eos qui bonas didicere literas,
atrox esse convicium existimantes grammatici cognomen; quasi vero laudi vertendum sit
theologo si grammaticen nesciat. Non facit theologum sola grammaticae cognitio. At
multi minus theologum facit ignorata grammatica: certe conducit ad theologiae cognitionem huius disciplinae peritia, officit imperitia." In Drusius 'Annotationes in Novum
Testamentum*, Erasmus is by far the most frequently cited author. Sometimes Drusius
identifies himself with him: on page 129 of the *Annotationum in Novum Testamentum pars
altera*, he relates how Erasmus through his exposition, has involved himself in difficulties
with the theologians "ut lector sciat cum religione non mutata esse ingenia theologorum
quorundam. Nam quis plura passus est ab illis quam ego." In his annotations, references
to Erasmus crop up in the most unexpected places. Thus on Num. 12:10 he notes (in
his *Ad loca difficiliora Pentateuchi*, 413) where the cloud of the presence of the Lord leaves
the tent in which Miriam has become leprous: "Recedebat ergo propter lepram Mariae,

tion and opposed, in the most sarcastic terms, the return of aristotelian philosophy into theology. Thus in his otherwise very grammatical and historical notes on the New Testament he could not resist the temptation to actualise the text of 2 Peter 2:22, "a dog which returns to its vomit" by remarking in passing that it could be applied to his colleagues in the faculty of theology, who after the reformation had attacked the philosophical excrescences, had returned to Aristotle.[83] One can have a certain understanding of Lubbertus' hysterical rage at Drusius.

At first sight it seems strange to regard Amama, who worked so closely with Ames for the good of the church, as a direct follower of Drusius, who in modern study has been suspected of heterodoxy and worse on the grounds of Scaliger's lapidary verdict "Drusius ne sait ce que c'est de religion".[84] A certain distinction appears to be present. Drusius left the judgment of his works to "the catholic church", his pupil to the

---

quae immunda. Quod capiendum de visibili ejus praesentia. Nam alioqui Deus essentialiter est ubique: De quo tamen sobrie disputandum, omissis cloacis & latrinis, cum alia sint in sacris de quibus cum majori fructu disputari possit." This must be a reference to the famous point in the polemics of Luther and Erasmus on free will, in the forewords to which there is a dispute on the omnipresence of God. Erasmus: *De libero arbitrio*, in *Opera Omnia*, IX, 1217C: "Fortasse verum est, quod solent garrire Sophistae, Deum secundum naturam suam non minus esse in antro scarabei, ne quid dicam obscoenius, quod istos tamen non pudet dicere, quam in coelo; et tamen hoc inutiliter disputaretur apud multitudinem."; Luther, *De servo arbitrio*, WA, 18, 622: "Nec tamen recte hoc exemplum tractas, et inutiliter disputari coram multitudine damnas illud, Deum esse in antro vel cloaca ..."

[83] *Annotationum in NT pars altera*, 118: "Canis ad vomitum redit, qui redit ad id quod primi reformatores nunc evomuerunt. Ea est Theologia scholastica quam qui sectantur, veram negligunt, hoc est verbum Dei: Unde omnis veritas christiana & ea ipsa, quam scholasticam appellant, mixta fermento humano, sic ut tam pura & sincera non sit quam esse debeat. Quando tandem haec reformabuntur? Nam ante non erit pax in Ecclesia. Utinam qui ad divina aluntur aliter studia sua instituerent, & spretis his tricis serio se darent ad studium linguarum praecipurarum & ad lectionem textus sacri. Quod si fieret, haberemus Theologos quales optare magis quam sperare debemus."

[84] Scaliger's verdict on Drusius in the *Sec Scal*, 300-2 is negative, including that on his scholarly qualities. The gossip on Drusius' moral degeneracy and negligence, and the remark that he was supposed not to have signed the confession, which lead a persistent life in the secondary literature, rest mainly on the *Scaligerana*. Against this it must be said that (1) Scaliger (it is true in the most amusing way) only relates gossip, as appears from a comparison of the negative remarks on Drusius with the outburst of Lubbertus which Amama recounted to Cunaeus (note 52) e.g. "Le pauvre jugement de Drusius! Il ne sçait rien que sa Grammaire." "An Drusius sit haereticus?" "Drusius ne sçait ce que c'est de Religion: il n'est pas de nostre Confession" "Drusius non est doctus" which all have their parallel in Lubbertus. (2) If Drusius did not sign the confession of faith, which was compulsory for a professor at Franeker (see article 9 of the Statutes, cited in Boeles, *Hoogeschool* I, 436) it is very strange that Lubbertus in his polemic against Drusius let such an opportunity go unused, and nowhere mentioned this fact. Scaliger says that Serarius had heard something of the fact that Drusius had not signed the confession of faith. Although Serarius in his polemic regularly inveighs against Drusius' religious leanings (*Minerval* V, 31; *Trihaeresion* iii, 20), he does not mention this point anywhere.

"reformed churches"[85] but the contradiction is only apparent. Like Drusius, Amama called himself a *grammaticus*, a title which was only apparently based on humility.[86] Drusius and Amama were humanist protestants, who believed that differences on higher aspects of doctrine should not be allowed to lead to disunity. Drusius was a no less convinced protestant than his disciple, proud of the sacrifices which his father had made for the reformation.[87] Amama, almost two generations younger than Drusius, described the object of his dependence more precisely, but could dismiss the differences between lutherans and calvinists as pointless arguments over words. It is characteristic that public utterances of Amama on the conflict between the remonstrants and the contra-remonstrants are not known.

From an important undated letter to Saeckma, of early 1628[88] it is possible to deduce his standpoint in the religious disputes in the Republic. At the end of the twenties, after the appointment of the new Stadhouder Frederick Henry, the problem of the remonstrants appeared more obstinate than it had seemed at first. At the level of the state, it was a question of how the faction excluded in 1619 could be readmitted to political life.[89] The church had to decide what attitude it should take towards the remonstrant laymen, now that the remonstrants had organised themselves into a church. The foci of both questions were Amsterdam and Rotterdam. In Amsterdam the contra-remonstrant party had been forced out of its dominant position in the city government in 1624. Since then conflicts between the city authorities and the preachers had regularly provoked disorder. In 1629 this confrontation reached a climax. In Rotterdam, the city of Oldenbarnevelt and Grotius, where remonstrantism had many adherents among the minor bourgeoisie, the local church was split by the question of the attitude to be taken towards this group. Supported by the magistrates a moderate group on the church council argued for the admission to communion of remonstrant laymen who had continued to take a dissenting stance on the five decisive points, because only so would it be possible to win this con-

---

[85] Drusius, *De Hasidaeis*, 22: "Olim professus sum, quod nunc iterum repeto, me mea omnia subjicere judicio Ecclesiae"; *Henoch*, praefatio: "haec & alia quae in hoc libro continentur, ut & in aliis omnibus a me unquam editis aut edendis subjicio libens Ecclesiae catholicae judicio a cujus recto sensu si dissentio non ero pertinax." Amama, *ABB*, 558: "Omnia Reformatarum Ecclesiarum judicio subjecta sunto."

[86] Cf. Drusius' adoption of the letter of Erasmus to Boville (note 82) and the passages cited in note 119.

[87] Cf. note 3 of chapter 2.

[88] Included as Appendix V. Saeckma too was regarded as an administrator who was not without sympathy for the remonstrants: Grotius, *Briefwisseling* IV, 62-5, 67; from N. van Reigersberch, 27.5.1629; to N. van Reigersberch 9.6.1629.

[89] Poelhekke, *Frederik Hendrik*, 157-65, 206-14.

siderable group back. The matter came before the Particular Synod of
South Holland, which twice decided, in 1627 and 1628, that such a policy
could not be permitted.[90] In his letter to Saeckma, Amama expressed
himself very clearly on both conflicts and condemned the orthodox in
severe terms. Thus he remained faithful to the teaching of Drusius in this
most important ecclesiastical question of the 1620's.

Amama's indifference to the feelings of the orthodox also appears from
the list of his English friends in the foreword of the *Grammatica Ebræa
Martinio-Buxtorfiana*. In it he named Prideaux, William Langton, Edward
Meetkerken and Petrus Baro.[91] The latter was the son of Petrus Baro,
a moderate French calvinist who in the 1590's had become involved at
Cambridge in a conflict with English calvinists over predestination.[92]
The conflict and his name had become known in the Republic as a result
of the publication of the writings generated by this controversy, by
Thysius in 1613.[93] The son was a great defender of the name of his
father. The litmus test using Cappel's *Arcanum* also gives the same result.
Amama came to know this work during the writing of his *Anti-Barbarus
Biblicus*. He immediately revised his opinion on the antiquity of the
vocalisation system, the originality of which he had previously accepted.
He praised the author of the *Arcanum*, who was unknown to him, in the
highest terms.[94]

Amama was a follower of Drusius with a strongly puritan bias, if one
regards the struggle for sanctification of life and a personal living faith
as the most notable characteristics of puritanism. Like Drusius he was a
Christian humanist, who was essentially indifferent to doctrinal disputes.
The most important difference with his mentor is to be found in the
public to which he addressed himself. Drusius wrote for the select circle
of highly educated late humanists and wanted to be recognised by this

---

[90] Cf. *Acta* Dordrecht 1627, art. 14, 20, 22. The strict decision provoked three
gravamina the following year (*Acta* Delft 1628, a. 14). The difficulties in Rotterdam per-
sisted interminably.

[91] In the praefatio to his *Grammatica Martinio-Buxtorfiana*. William Langton, (1573-
1626) was also a friend of Drusius (note 51), studied at Oxford and remained at
Magdalen College where he was president from 1610 to 1626. (Foster, *Alumni Oxonienses*
III, 881). Edward Meetkerke (1590-1657), the son of Adolf van Meetkerken, ambassador
of the States-General to Elizabeth, also studied at Oxford and stayed at Christ Church.
From 1620-1626 he was Regius Professor of Hebrew there. (*DNB* XXXVII, 211-2).

[92] Petrus Baro, the father, (1534-99) was a typical French anglo-calvinist. A jurist, and
later at Geneva; his flight to England took place around 1572. In 1574 he was Lady
Margaret professor of Theology. From 1581 he developed in a heterodox direction. A
conflict with Whitaker in the 1590's led to his resignation. His son Peter studied medicine
and defended arminian viewpoints: *DNB*, III, 265-7.

[93] For the place of this edition of Thysius in the Anglo-Dutch contacts occasioned by
contra-remonstrant disputes, Tyacke, "Arminianism".

[94] Respectively *ABB*, 23-4 and 516. In the last passage he praises the author highly.

group. Amama sought a much wider public. He was not only zealous for the spreading of the knowledge of Hebrew among preachers, but also sought to diffuse this knowledge among the laity, by means of publications in Dutch. He published a grammar, a dictionary and a treatise on the Dutch translation of the bible, all in the vernacular.[95] Those in authority in the church looked at the spread of this knowledge among the people with a certain suspicion. In a letter to Saeckma on the way in which his Dutch Hebrew grammar had been received by the classes in Friesland, Amama gave the reasons for this suspicion:[96]

> "for they dared to express their fear that it might happen that laymen who had acquired some knowledge of Hebrew, could rise up against preachers who knew nothing of it, and insult them and accuse them of ignorance. And I shall certainly not conceal from your honour that this has not been my least goal."

The same lack of tact for the feelings of the reformed churches in the years after Dordt is plain in Amama's campaign for a bible in Dutch. In 1623 he published his "Biblical Comparison in which the Dutch translation of the Bible, which was formerly translated into Dutch from the High German of Dr Luther, is tested chapter by chapter against the Hebrew truth and compared with the best translations..." In this work he subjected the text of the Dutch Deux-Aes translation of Luther's bible to the same criticism as the Vulgate in the *Anti-Barbarus Biblicus*.

He compared the translation with the Hebrew text and, to make his findings credible to a public that knew no Hebrew, with great modern translations: the Latin of Pagninus, Zurich and Junius and Tremellius; the French of Geneva, the German of Piscator, the Spanish of De Valera, the Italian of Diodati and the English of 1611. The dedication to the States General and Maurice, dated 30 November 1623, formulates the programme with which we are by now familiar. Amama stated how the National Synod had resolved that a new translation must be made. That is necessary, because the present version is a poor rendering of the far from perfect translation of Luther. Amama claims that one cannot reproach the church with the poor quality of that earlier translation. At the time in which it appeared, they had only a little linguistic knowledge at their disposal and knew no better. But the making of a new translation can no longer be postponed:

---

[95] *De Hebreusche Grammatica ofte Taalkonst*, Amsterdam 1627; *Ebreusch Woord-boek*, Franeker, 1628.

[96] AG, Amama to Saeckma, undated, "superiore die Domenico": "Audebant nam profiteri metum suum, fore ut Laici aliquam Ebraismi notitiam consecuti, adversus Ministros, qui ejus omnino ignari sunt, insurgescant, illosque aliquando insultent & imperitiam objectent. Et certe apud T.A. non diffitebor, hunc non fuisse postremum meum scopum."

"My Lords, the light of the Tongues is now past its zenith, this sun is sink-
ing to evening; *magnis passibus properamus ad barbariem.* The study of the
languages is everywhere in decline. (...) Many who have devoted themselves to the office of preacher, do not even concern themselves with it. And
although all our Theologians call the knowledge of the Hebrew and Greek
languages a *necessarium Theologiæ instrumentum,* nevertheless no attention is
paid to it in this country in *Examinibus Ministrorum.*"

The aim of the treatise was, by pointing out the countless mistranslations, to call on the States to promote the work. The text is preceded by
a programmatic section, which essentially agrees with the anti-catholic
polemic in the first book of the *Anti-Barbarus Biblicus,* and by a letter of
Gomarus supporting Amama's proposal. Amama had also attempted to
obtain a judgment from the theology faculty of the University of Leiden,
in which the latter should support his efforts for a new translation of the
bible. The correspondence between Amama and the faculty is a symptom
of the already mentioned anxious attitude of certain groups within the
church towards the philological study of the bible.[97]

In letters of 10 July, 26 September and 10 October 1623, each more
insistent than the last, because he had received no reply, Amama
explained the intention of his "Biblical Comparison." He was concerned
to stimulate interest in a translation, and to remove objections among
those who, because of their fear of offence and scandal, were hindering
the work of translation. In the most humble terms, he asked the Leiden
professors for their support in this effort. He explained in detail how the
foreword of his treatise would silence the objections of the papists,
anabaptists and lutherans, who might be in a position to calumniate the
church because of its inadequate translation of the bible. He understood
that the delay was not being caused by the translators appointed by the
Synod, but that there are others:[98]

"some of whom bring forward the scandals, others the enormous costs, still
others I don't know what other pretext. Some of them assert that our
translation must not be so despised that because of some few, perhaps less
correctly translated passages, it must be taken out of the people's hands."

It does in fact seem possible that the proposed new biblical translation
was postponed not only because of practical problems, but that this
delay, as Amama suggests, was also founded on deliberate obstruction.
Certain circles felt that the church had first to be restored to quiet before

---

[97] The correspondence in Eekhof, *Theologische faculteit,* 37-53.
[98] Amama to the theological faculty, 26.10.1623; Eekhof, *Theologische faculteit,* 42.
Amama's request to the faculty was supported by a letter from Gomarus of 5/15
September 1623; (printed in Van Itterzon, *Gomarus* 412-3; a discussion there on pp. 253
ff.).

a new translation could be introduced. Walaeus' son mentions this opinion in so many words in his life of his father.[99] One could conclude that
the Leiden theologians inclined to this opinion, from their answer to
Amama. They distinguished two aspects in his request. In the first place,
the campaign for the carrying out of the resolutions of the Synod of Dordt
concerning the new translation of the bible. That they welcomed cordially. Secondly, the making public of the work for which he was striving.
That they rejected emphatically. They suggested to Amama that he
would do much better not to bring the matter before the public, but to
discuss it with the translators alone (thus indirectly conceding that the latter were at least jointly responsible for the delay). If Amama insists on
publishing his work, he must do so in Latin, to avoid giving offence to
the people and pleasure to the libertines. In any case, the title must be
changed so that it is made clear that he is above all attacking the translation of Luther and not that of the Dutch Reformed Church. In a final
letter characterised by a scarcely concealed sarcasm, Amama tried to
disarm these objections. It appears from the absence of a judgment in the
"Biblical Comparison" that this last effort was also without result. When
the work on translation began in 1629, Amama followed the undertaking
closely and criticised the translators. It is certain that his feeling of being
excluded played some part in this. It is typical of the jealously guarded
autonomy of the church that no professors from the faculties of letters
were asked to join in the translation.[100]

Sixtinus Amama died in 1629. His thirteen year professorate in
Franeker lends itself as a framework for describing various important
characteristics of the study of Hebrew in the Republic during the 17th
century. His most important achievement was without doubt his successful campaign for the compulsory study of Hebrew by ministers. The
publication of a Hebrew grammar and dictionary in Dutch, a symptom
of the approaching end of humanism, found its continuation in the work
of Johannes Leusden, the professor of Hebrew at Utrecht.[101] Amama's
initiative for the publication of the Mishnah tractate *Sanhedrin*, which
appeared under the name of his pupil Cocceius, was, as we shall see in
the next chapter, the beginning of a stream of publications in the field
of rabbinica. The way in which he took care of Cocceius also reveals his

---

[99] "Vita Walaei" in Walaeus, *Opera* I (35): on the delay to the translation: "Dissoluta
Synodo in tuto ponenda Ecclesia erat, nec de ejus ornamento cogitari potuit, antequam
satis firmata videretur. Quod demum anno 1627 evenit." The whole affair raises doubts
on the interpretation of Nauta (in: *De Statenvertaling*, 18-20) and De Bruin, *Statenbijbel*,
282-4, who put all the blame for the delay on the authorities.
[100] This is apparent from his letters to Saeckma in the years 1628-9.
[101] Cost Budde, "Johannes Leusden" and the necessary criticism on this in
Offenberg's edition of Hirschel, "Johannes Leusden".

engaging personality. Not only did Amama train him, he also arranged his first publication, and took an interest in his further career. The publication under Cocceius' name, with translation and notes, of two rabbinical tractates, was due to an initiative of Amama and was probably also in great part his work.[102] Always the talented university politician, he then considered how he could help Cocceius, whom he thought highly of, to a position. Various possibilities were weighed and finally he decided that Bremen offered the most chances.[103] One may wonder whether Amama's influence did not extend to the content of Cocceius' theology. Amama's apocalyptic view of history, together with his great emphasis on biblical theology, are found again in his disciple. It is also possible that Cocceius' Hebrew dictionary, written in the vernacular, goes back to an initiative of Amama. Towards the end of his life the latter had intended to publish Flacius Illyricus' *Clavis Scripturæ Sacræ*. He probably wanted to concentrate on the first book of this work, a biblical dictionary. Amama was prevented by his death from carrying out this intention, but Cocceius' dictionary may, at least in its ultimate form, go back to his memory of his teacher's programme.[104] In the end, Amama's efforts underwent the same twofold division as the programme of Ames. His struggle for more discipline and a stricter way of life was taken over by the voetians, though they coupled this striving for the sanctification of life with a submission to scholastic philosophy and dogma which ran directly counter to the programme of Ames and Amama. Amama's stress on a biblical theology, less marked by the predominant orthodoxy, and his apocalyptic vision of history, influenced Cocceius, but his followers in general showed a great affinity with the philosophy of Descartes, which was an obstacle to the humanistic study of antiquity. The most important characteristic of Amama's work is that this humanist had to forge a link with the church in order to improve the position of Hebrew. There too

---

[102] Amama's programme in the years 1627-9 can be reconstructed from a number of letters in the Gabbema archive. Th. Ebertus to Amama, 20.7.1628, is expecting "Libros Antibarbarorum, Tractatum Sanhedrin, Observationes Sculteti in N.T. ampliores". In the letter of 20.5.1629 a similar summary. V. Grünewald to Amama, 29.6.1628: "Clavis Scripturae S., cuius editionem C.T. jam paravit, a pluribus expetitur." For a discussion of Cocceius' *Sanhedrin et Maccoth*: below 4.2.

[103] Amama to M. Martinius, 30.4.1629, in Cocceius, *Opera ANEKDOTA* II,619; Amama discusses the possibilities of Cocceius' being appoined. The dedication of *Sanhedrin* must be to the Senate of Bremen, the Curators of Franeker, or to Daniel Heinsius. "Et quidem illis, quia ego mortalis sum, & noster Pasor senex est. Posset enim facile ad Graecae linguae & Chald. Syriacaeque professionem promoveri. Huic, quia vir celeberrimus est, & magnae tum apud Curatores Leidenses, tum apud alios extra Belgium authoritatis est. Quia etiam scio, eum a multis etiam extra Belgium consuli de idoneis Professoribus." It was Bremen.

[104] For a discussion of the character of Cocceius' dictionary: Lebram, "Streit", 54.

he was a harbinger of new practices. In the course of the 17th century the language was to be studied and taught mainly by theologians, with far-reaching consequences for the nature of research.

On the death of Erpenius on 13 November 1624 it was immediately clear who should succeed him as professor of Arabic, and the appointment of his pupil Golius was not long delayed. The filling of the chair of Hebrew raised more difficulties. On 12 May 1625 the Mayors and Curators decided to let some professors sound Buxtorf, the most distinguished hebraist in Europe, to see if he would be inclined to accept an invitation to Leiden. One of these intermediaries was Petrus Cunaeus, a professor of law, who had published a creditable book on the political institutions of ancient Israel. Buxtorf politely declined the invitation, but used the opportunity to recommend his son, whose progress in rabbinica he praised highly.[105] For the time being his suggestion had no results. On 13 November 1625, a year after the death of Erpenius, the Mayors and Curators decided to send an invitation to Amama.[106] He was willing to accept the call but was not given leave to do so by the administrators of the university of Franeker. Amama was deeply hurt by this refusal. When he wrote a letter describing the affair, he could not restrain his tears.[107] In the dedication of his *Anti-Barbarus Biblicus* in 1628 to the Mayors and Curators he expressed his thanks for this invitation. In the dedicatory letter he also magnanimously praised the man who had been chosen in his place.[108]

Around February 1626, it must have become clear in Leiden that Franeker's resistance to the invitation to Amama was so great that it was not possible to win him over. Yet all efforts to invite a new lecturer stood still, so that in May and August the Senate felt itself obliged to press the Mayors and Curators to fill the post.[109] The last request appears to have had some success. In September various professors began to work on behalf of certain candidates. Bronchorst put Sinapius' name forward, while Cunaeus renewed contact with the younger Buxtorf.[110] Cunaeus

---

[105] *Molh.* II, 121. Cunaeus, *Epistolae*, 143-52. Letters of 24.6 and 15.9.1624.
[106] *Molh.* II, 124, 128.
[107] Amama to Rivet, June 1626, UB Leiden, BPL 285.
[108] In the foreword he thanks the Curators for the honourable offer and goes further "Exinde vere nobilem, pium & reverendum virum, D. Constantinum l'Empereur de Oppyck SS. Th. Doctorem, meum a multis retro annis consecraneum & amicum comjunctissimum, virum orientalium literarum peritissimum, diligentissimum &, quod supra omnia ista pono, disciplinae amantissimum."
[109] *Molh.* II, 126-7; Bronchorst, *Diarium* 195-98.
[110] Bronchorst, *Diarium*, 198; Cunaeus, *Epistolae*, 152-3. Cunaeus to Buxtorf I, 26.9.1626; he is now working on behalf of his son, "Qua de re licet nihil adhuc constitutum a Curatoribus nostris sit, propterea quod indigenae quidam impense muneris

managed to win Rochus van den Honert, one of the three Curators, for this candidacy. In December 1626 van den Honert contacted his fellow-Curator Adrian Pauw, but could not persuade him to commit himself further than to say that he thought the professorship of Hebrew should be filled, and that young Buxtorf appeared a good candidate. For the rest Pauw carefully kept his hands free.[111] Finally in February 1627 L'Empereur was appointed. After some friction between the University of Leiden and the High School of Harderwijk, which was unwilling to let one of its lecturers go, he was able to register with the Academy on 23 September and present himself to the Senate on 18 October.[112] Three years had passed since the death of Erpenius.

For his appointment L'Empereur must have had the support of one or more Curators. The first who comes to mind is Adrian Pauw, with whom his wife's family had contacts. Pauw could have been familiar with L'Empereur in other ways also. From February to July 1624, Pauw undertook a diplomatic mission to France, in the company of the Curator of the High School of Harderwijk, van der Essen. Trigland mentions the latter in his oration as a friend of L'Empereur. Later L'Empereur was to refer in a letter to Pauw, to kindnesses shown him at the time of his appointment.[113] It is also highly possible that professors in the faculty of theology like Polyander and Thysius were active on behalf of L'Empereur whom they had known for many years. At any rate, in the spring of 1626 L'Empereur knew that he was a possible candidate to succeed Erpenius. For the first time since 1622 he began to buy books in the field of oriental languages and rabbinica.[114] First he acquired, between March and June 1626, a Palestinian Talmud and the dictionary of David

---

hujus honorem ambiunt." In a letter of Buxtorf II to Cunaeus of November 1626 he tells him of his plans: to issue Postel's translation of the Zohar and of Raymundus Martini's *Pugio Fidei*. For the MS of this work, which was with the Buxtorfs at Basle, and was copied from that of Philippe du Plessis-Mornay, see below 4.4.

[111] Cunaeus, *Epistolae*, 196-7; from Rochus van den Honert.

[112] *Molh.* II, 133-4; *ASALB*, 204.

[113] Schutte, *Repertorium*, 9. In the letter of L'Empereur to Pauw referred to in note 90 of chapter II, he writes inter alia, "Sed magis etiam in instituto meo fui confirmatus, ubi recordarer istius favoris, quo Excellentia tua non solum me ad professionem, quam etiamnunc sustineo, vocavit, verum et postea fuit testata quum ulteriori promotioni studeat."

[114] In all the categories in L'Empereur's book list, at a certain moment the acquisition of rabbinica to the exclusion of all else begins. After one or two titles, there follow books which were bought at the auction of the library of Erpenius (see note 115). This auction was held on 2 June 1626. In the folio section, the Palestinian Talmud is directly preceded by "Calvinus in V.T. et Epistolae 4 volum." According to a receipt in Th 163 L'Empereur bought this in March 1626. L'Empereur thus began to acquire his rabbinical library between March and June 1626. The first folio volume which does not refer to rabbinica, was not bought until 1631.

Kimḥi. He then bought a great many rabbinical works at the auction of Erpenius' library, held on 2 June 1626.[115] In the seven years up to 1633 L'Empereur was to build up a respectable rabbinical library. These data strengthen the suspicion that L'Empereur's appointment was the result of recommendations from influential circles in the University of Leiden. He began to prepare himself for the professorship when it had become clear in Leiden that Amama would not be coming. The appointment was made on credit. In 1626 L'Empereur had not given any sign of possessing knowledge in the field of Hebrew. One might even speculate that the year's delay in making the appointment was intended to give L'Empereur the opportunity to prepare himself for a position.

The oration on the dignity and usefulness of Hebrew in which L'Empereur accepted his office in the autumn of 1627, was the first public proof of his knowledge of and views on, the language. The published version of the address, which appeared some months later,[116] includes a dedication to the Mayors and Curators, in which he emphasised the continuity between his work in Harderwijk and his teaching duties at Leiden:[117]

"Hitherto I have led a quiet life, devoted to the study of letters, and which I dedicated wholly to the sacred truth... but my earlier wish has now been fulfilled in another manner, since the same truth can be transmitted in numerous ways. When during the last eight years, I taught the Hebrew of the Old Testament, I expounded the sacred scriptures of the Hebrews. But above all, at the gymnasium of Harderwijk, I have served the method in which the dogmas of the reformed religion are taught with the aid of *loci communes* and disputations (...) Now I expound the same sacred truth, since I must explain the language in which it is written, and the Hebrew text of the books of the Old Testament (which contains the truth necessary for salvation)..."

This foreword sets the tone for the oration which follows. L'Empereur sees the value and usefulness of Hebrew above all in their importance for the teaching of the doctrine of the reformed religion. This aspect determines the structure of his address:

---

[115] According to a receipt in Th 163, the book list in Th 164, 3 and his auction catalogue, L'Empereur bought the following books at the auction of Erpenius' library; in folio the *Aruch* R. Nathan, Lexicon Talm & Chald, Basel (H, fo, 12); the *More Nebuchim* of Maimonides, cum comm. var. Rabbin., Sabionitae (H, fo, 5) and the *Midrash Rabba*, Thessaloniki (H, fo, 33); in quarto the *Thisbites*, hebr. lat. Isny 1541 (O, 4o, 5), the *Sculchan happanim* and the *Calendarium* of Münster, Basle, 1527 (O, 4o, 39); in octavo the *Sepher Alphes* sive Talmudis compendium (H, 8o, 3), and the *Grammatica* Eliae Levitae hebr et lat, Basel, (H, 8o, 24).
[116] On 9 February 1628 the Mayors and Curators decided to give L'Empereur thirty guilders for the dedication of his inaugural oration: *Molh.* II, 139.
[117] L'Empereur, *Oratio*, 5-6.

Introduction (pp. 9-13)

A) The dignity of Hebrew (14-19)
   1) It is the oldest language
   2) It contains the whole doctrine
   3) It contains only literature which is worthy of veneration.
B) The usefulness of Hebrew:
   1) for dogmatic polemic (19-22)
   2) for a good grasp of doctrine (22-25)
   LINKING SECTION: The blinding of the Jews (26-31)
   3) for a good grasp of the New Testament (32-35)
   LINKING SECTION: do not trust translations (36-38)
   4) the use for non-theologians (38-39).
C) Conclusion (40-41).

L'Empereur began with a traditional—and in his case perhaps appropriate—profession of his incapacity and an appeal to the goodwill of the
audience. With a reference to Aristotle he explained the structure of his
address. A prayer to Jesus Christ concludes the introduction. Certainly
for a professor of Hebrew, naming Aristotle indicates a rejection of
Ramus, as the prayer proclaims his close relationship with the
theologians.[118] L'Empereur never shared the explicitly erasmian self-
awareness, expressed by Drusius and Amama as "I know that I am no
prophet nor the son of a prophet".[119]

L'Empereur considered that the dignity of Hebrew was shown by its
antiquity and noble origin. Hebrew is the only language which does not
owe its birth to Babel and thus to sin. Its antiquity is proved in the traditional way with the aid of the etymology of the names in Genesis 1-11.
Appealing to Acts 26:22 L'Empereur shows that Christian doctrine can
be found, in full, in the writings of the Old Covenant.[120]

   "From this it follows that those who learn Hebrew, at the same time learn
   all that which one must know for salvation and the Christian life (for all is

---

[118] The saying of a prayer in an academic oration is a rarity. The only examples known
to us from the years before 1627 are Junius, in his oration on the dignity of Hebrew, also
at the end of his introduction, and Festus Hommius and Sinapius, at the end of their orations in the book named in note 17. These prayers are much narrower in scope.

[119] Drusius, *Quaestionum ebraicarum libri tres* 1: "Quae tracto, pertinent maxime ad
Grammaticam. Nam quae altioris sunt scientiae, mihi non arrogo. Scio illud, Non sum
Propheta, neque filius Prophetae"; *Tetragrammaton*, 81: "ponis questionem alienam a
professione mea (...) quo me loco habeas nescio; certe non sum theologus. An Gram-
matici nomen quod aliquando probrose mihi objectum, tueri possum, nescio ..."
Amama, *ABB*, 238: "Theologus ego non sum, nec Theologi filius." Compare the letter
of Erasmus in note 81. For other examples of Erasmus' apparent humility: Godin,
"Fonction," 32-3, n. 41.

[120] *Oratio*, 16-7.

to be found in the Old Testament), and read only what is true, certain, pure, holy and just ... (..) For everything which is read in Hebrew is directly derived from the true, holy and just God. How sweet it is for a soul, which is eager for truth, only to study true and certain things! How sweet for the pious mind to see and consider only those things which are holy, chaste and just!''

These are traditional arguments for the dignity of Hebrew which L'Empereur had taken from an oration of Franciscus Junius.[121] On the other hand he is a true son of Leiden in the attention which he pays in his address to the usefulness of Hebrew. Here too, however, he remains true to himself. In his transition to his treatment of the usefulness of Hebrew, L'Empereur warns against the confidence which theologians place in translations. This echoes the argument of Amama,[122] but unlike the Franeker professor L'Empereur looks for his examples of the damaging consequences of trusting to translations not in the field of ceremonies, but in that of doctrine.[123] As his first example he takes the doctrine of justification. In his opinion the catholics start from the Latin word *justificare*, translate it as ''to make just'' and explain the concept as ''the giving of the *habitus* of acting justly.'' But, says L'Empereur, the hif'il of *ẓdk* means ''to recognise as just'', and thus supports a forensic doctrine of justification. A second example concerns the concept of ''perfect''. The catholics think that *perfectio* means being without sin, but the Hebrew *tm* only indicates the man who is honourable, whose inward man is in harmony with his outward. L'Empereur triumphantly concluded that:[124]

> ''in the most important articles of the Christian religion, the whole controversy can often be decided with the aid of a single observation by those who have a moderate knowledge of Hebrew.''

The discussion of the usefulness of Hebrew for the determination of the accuracy of doctrine, has the same doctrinal character as this polemical section.

---

[121] L'Empereur took the whole passage on the dignity of Hebrew from Junius' oration. There is even a literal reference: like Junius (*Opera* I, 4) L'Empereur states that Hebrew leaves other languages many ''parasangs'' behind it (*Oratio*, 17).

[122] Above all the second excursus in which L'Empereur shows that one cannot rely on translations, is directly taken from Amama's *Paraenesis*. L'Empereur knew this work from Amama's *Grammatica* in which it is included, and which he had received as a gift. (Th 164, 3).

[123] The difference between L'Empereur and Amama suggests the distinction which Melanchthon makes when he tries to determine the relationship of Erasmus to the reformation, from Erasmus' discussions with Luther. Melanchthon to Erasmus, 1.10.1523 (Erasmus, *Opus Epistolarum*, no. 1500, ll.18-21).: ''Nam cum in summa disputationes Lutheri omnes partim ad liberi arbitrii quaestionem pertineant, partim usum ceremoniarum contineant, de priore iam olim animadverti te dissidere. At de posteriore magna ex parte convenit...''

[124] *Oratio*, 21-2.

L'Empereur then dealt with a possible objection. If the knowledge of
Hebrew provides so much insight into the true doctrine, why do the
Jews, who know the language best, not see the truth? He begins his
answer with the Pauline reference to the blinding of the Jews, and the
Augustinian distinction between the words, which the Jews do know, and
the things which they do not know. He lays the greatest emphasis, however, on the thesis that it is rabbinical literature which hinders the Jews
from understanding the Old Testament. This argument also supplies
him with an opportunity to display his rabbinical knowledge. He cites
three haggadic accounts from the Palestinian Talmud, "where the rabbis
are disputing on the kings who shall inherit the world to come", and lays
great stress on the anthropomorphic and legendary character of these
tales. Two possible defences of the Jews are mentioned in order to be
rejected. A Jewish scholar, to whom L'Empereur had objected the
blasphemous nature of such stories, is said to have replied that these
fables were added to the Talmud by unbelievers. But then, according to
L'Empereur, the Jews ought to remove these tales from the Talmud. The
view of Maimonides, who in the foreword to his commentary on the
Mishnah, regards such stories as esoteric allegories, is rejected by
L'Empereur with the argument that the discussions in the Talmud
excluded such an interpretation. He concludes rhetorically: "are you
astonished that the Jews, given over to this sort of fable, do not know the
fruit of their own language?" After the remark that the neglect of logic
and analysis can also be the cause of the blindness of the Jews, he
returned to his treatment of the use of Hebrew.

The New Testament too cannot be understood without a knowledge
of Hebrew. The idiom of the Greek of the New Testament is Hebrew:
"for the words in the books of the New Testament are Greek, but the
manner of speaking is Hebrew".[125] Here L'Empereur gives not only
examples which concern the meaning of words, but also sees hebraisms
in the syntax. He makes it very easy for himself in doing so. Unlike
Greek and Latin the Hebrew verb has only two paradigms to indicate
aspects of time and mood. Thus, what is expressed in Greek and Latin
with the aid of the different moods and tenses, and in the modern
languages by auxiliaries, is expressed by the same forms in Hebrew.
L'Empereur used this characteristic of Hebrew to neutralise some New
Testament passages which were rather troublesome for the calvinists. For
example he interprets Hebrews 10:29, which speaks of the punishment
deserved by someone who "thinks impure the blood of the covenant by

---

[125] *Oratio*, 32: "nam voces quidem Graecae in N.T. libris, sed loquendi modus est
Hebraeus".

which he was consecrated" as a hebraism. This text was one of the proofs employed by the remonstrants in their polemic against the *perseverantia sanctorum*, the dogma that the elect cannot lose grace, a consequence of the doctrine of predestination. This point at issue, one of the five articles of the Remonstrance, was thought so important that the medal struck at the conclusion of the Synod of Dordt symbolically defined this dogma.[126] According to L'Empereur there is no question here of the blood by which the person involved *is* consecrated—then the remonstrants would be correct in their opinion that the elect too could fall—but of the blood by which he would be consecrated. If he here regards an indicative as an unreal, in I Tim. 3:15, where the church is called a pillar and the foundation of the truth (a favourite passage of the catholics in their attack on the protestant dogma of the *sufficientia scripturae*), he explains "is" as "ought to be". In 1620 Bronckhorst had taken great pleasure in this passage in his opposition during a disputation on the sufficiency of the scriptures under the presidency of Walaeus.[127]

A second excursus discusses in terms reminiscent of Amama the impossibility of trusting to translations such as the Vulgate. Finally L'Empereur mentioned some general and non-theological advantages of the language. Many Greek and Latin words are of Hebrew origin and because Hebrew is the original language, it reflects the essence of things. He concluded that everyone must learn Hebrew. Everyone wishes to know the word of God, and:[128]

> "the Hebrew idiom is demanded so that we can draw the salvation-bringing truth from the Old and New Testaments with certainty and remove objections and doubts root and branch from our consciences."

According to L'Empereur everyone could devote a few hours to Hebrew in order to undergo this wholesome effect. How many languages do the Dutch merchants not learn in order to make a profit? L'Empereur concluded with the traditional reference to his famous predecessors in the study of Hebrew.

We have discussed this address in such detail because although its form corresponds to the traditional humanist scheme, its concentration on doc-

---

[126] Cf. Sellin, "Medal", 181, 185 and the notorious work of P. Bertius, of which James I remarked that the title alone was enough to burn the author: *Hymenaeus desertor sive de Sanctorum Perseverantia et Apostasia*, LB 1601 and the work of R. Thomson brought back from England by Grotius, *De amissione et intercissione Gratiae et Justificationis*, Leidae 1616. For the contacts between England and the Republic on this point: Tyacke, "Arminianism", 96.

[127] Bronchorst, *Diarum*, 147 f. The rather self-important Bronchorst describes with evident Schadenfreude the contortions in which he forced Walaeus to involve himself.

[128] *Oratio*, 40.

trine and its presentation give a good impression of L'Empereur's own
interests. In fact, as he states in the dedication of his address, he had
remained the same in spite of his new appointment. A theologian in
Harderwijk, he remained a theologian as professor of Hebrew at Leiden.
Elements from previous orations, such as those of Junius, Erpenius and
Amama are recognisable, but they only play a subordinate part in his
argument.

Some of the central ideas which had been important for them, such as
the importance of Hebrew for the personal life of faith, and that of the
bible as a correction of an over-emphasis on doctrine have disappeared
from L'Empereur's oration. Its orthodox character also appears from the
lack of a reference to a possible conversion of the Jews. They function
in the oration only as a possible objection.

The excursus on the blindness of the Jews was borrowed from a
lutheran tradition. In the orations on the study of Hebrew which are
included in the works of Melanchthon and in a lecture in Flacius
Illyricus' *Clavis Scripturae Sacrae* (a book which L'Empereur acquired in
the early twenties), the problem of the Jews who know Hebrew but do
not accept Christian doctrine is a recurring theme.[129] The explanation
which L'Empereur gives for their blindness, the Jewish attachment to
rabbinical literature, derives from mediaeval catholic polemic against
Judaism. As we shall see below he took this argument from Buxtorf.
L'Empereur also owed Flacius Illyricus the idea of the importance of a
knowledge of Hebrew for polemic against catholicism. Flacius' *Clavis* is
intended as an aid to put every protestant in a position to polemicise
against the papacy on the basis of the bible alone. Even his examples are
borrowed from Flacius. The biblical-theological dictionary which forms
the first part of the *Clavis*, gives under *justificatio* and *perfectio* the
references to the Hebrew words which we find in L'Empereur.[130] The
use of Hebrew in the polemic on justification was in any case so popular
that *ẓdk* is one of the few Hebrew words in the *Synopsis purioris theologiæ*.[131]
In L'Empereur's oration however these arguments are elaborated in a
way which points to a further development in the knowledge of Hebrew.
Around 1600, following 16th century study of the bible, there began a
new approach behind which the unlocking of rabbinical literature was a

---

[129] Melanchthon, *Opera* XI, 708-15: "De lingua Hebraea", 866-77: "De studio
linguae Hebraeae"; XII, 386-92: "Declamatio de lingua Hebraea discenda" (respectively 713, 873-4, 388); Flacius, *Clavis* II, 661-76: "Adhortatio ad studium linguae
Hebraeae", 668. L'Empereur had possessed Flacius' work since the early 1620's. Unlike
Melanchthon and Flacius who point to the neglect of the belles lettres by the Jews,
L'Empereur mentions their neglect of logic and analysis.
[130] Flacius, *Clavis* I, 498-502 (*justificare*) and 878-82 (*perfectio*)
[131] *Synopsis purioris theologiae*, 331.

driving force. In L'Empereur's oration we find the first signs of this. Thus he cites a definition of *tm*—without quoting the passage—from Salomon Iarchi, the famous mediaeval Jewish exegete Rashi.

The way in which L'Empereur acquired his knowledge of rabbinical literature is relatively simple to trace. In Buxtorf's *Lexicon*, a Hebrew dictionary which had been in his possession since 1623, the definition "honourable" is given for *tm*, with Gen. 25:27 as the only reference. In the *Biblia Rabbinica* published by Buxtorf, an edition of the Hebrew text of the Old Testament with the Targumim and commentaries of various mediaeval rabbis, which had also been in L'Empereur's library since the beginning of the twenties, we find in Rashi's marginal commentary on this verse the definition given by L'Empereur. We can conclude from this that L'Empereur was in a position to follow references to the *Biblia Rabbinica* and to consult it independently. In so doing he followed the reading of the Christian hebraists. It is also possible to explain in this way a quotation he makes from Ibn Ezra on the antiquity of Hebrew. That too is given in Hebrew and borrowed from Buxtorf's *Biblia Rabbinica*. The quotation is a commentary on Gen. 11:1 "the whole earth was of one language", the introductory verse of the story of the tower of Babel. This is the classical passage for the treatment of the antiquity of Hebrew. Thus Mercerus, in his commentary on Genesis (which L'Empereur already owned before 1622)[132] observes on this verse that the oldest language of humanity was Hebrew. The third reference by L'Empereur to a rabbinical commentary, a haggadic treatise of Salomon Iarchi on Gen. 1:21, is not quoted in Hebrew and he probably did not consult the *Biblia Rabbinica* for it. He quotes Rashi's commentary as an example of the absurdity to which rabbinical exegesis can lead. It is the story how God, when he had created the Leviathan in two sexes at the Creation, realised that their descendants would overwhelm the earth and then castrated the male creature and slaughtered the female to preserve it as a banquet for those who should inherit the world to come. This tale formed a permanent part of the mediaeval polemic against Judaism and had also penetrated into Latin literature. All the elements cited by L'Empereur can be found in a bulky treatise of Rainoldus against Bellarmine. Rainoldus may have taken the story from Münster.[133]

The view of Maimonides, quoted by L'Empereur, on the esoteric character of the haggadic parts of rabbinical literature, is to be found in Paulus Ricius' summary of Maimonides' foreword to his commentary on

---

[132] Mercerus, *In Genesin Commentarius.*
[133] Rainoldus, *Censura librorum apocryphorum*, I, 228. Münster in his commentary on Gen. 1:21. Buxtorf repeatedly recurs to the story in his *Synagoga Judaica*: 29, 74, 366, 536.
[134] Pistorius, *Artis Cabalisticae*, 258-87, esp. 261.

the Mishnah, included in his "De Thalmudica doctrina Epitome".[134]
The only rabbinical quotations which cannot be found in secondary
literature are thus the three haggadic stories from the Palestinian Talmud
which L'Empereur presented as examples of the absurdity of rabbinical
exegesis. In the 17th century quotation from the Palestinian Talmud was
unusual. It is plausible that L'Empereur wanted to put off acquiring the
much more comprehensive and expensive Babylonian Talmud until he
was sure of his appointment. At the end of 1629 he paid Erpenius' widow
225 guilders for the sixteen volumes of the Babylonian Talmud in the edition of Bomberg, Venice—almost half of his annual salary.[135] In 1626 he
had bought a Palestinian Talmud for twenty guilders.

Even the choice of the passages cited above allows us to see that
L'Empereur was a beginner in rabbinical studies. The three citations he
gives can all be found in *JSanhedrin* 10,2. The Talmud, as a commentary
on the Mishnah, follows the arrangement of this work. Sanhedrin is one
of the sixty-three tractates of the Mishnah and is itself sub-divided into
thirteen chapters. Each of the chapters is divided into verses, which are
themselves called mishnah. All of L'Empereur's citations derive from the
commentary in the Palestinian Talmud on one of these verses. That he
read these particular passages—undoubtedly with a Jewish teacher—can
be explained from the Christian secondary literature. As early as the
great survey of the Talmud in Galatinus' *De Arcanis* Sanhedrin 10, which
deals with who shall have a part in the world to come, and the Messiah,
was regarded as the most important part of the Talmud for Christians.[136]
L'Empereur only bought Galatinus' work in 1628, after he had given his
inaugural address, but he could find the same verdict in Buxtorf's *De
Abreviaturis*[137] if he needed such a reference in the literature. The importance of the chapter was generally known. When Gomarus began reading
the Talmud in the company of a rabbi in 1602, he started with Sanhedrin
10.[138]

Thus we find ourselves once again confronted with the question of the
origin of the first excursus in L'Empereur's oration. The most important
reason why the Jews reject Christ is, in L'Empereur's opinion, their
attachment to rabbinical literature. L'Empereur took this mediaeval

---

[135] Th 164, 3. L'Empereur was invited at a salary of six hundred guilders a year (*Molh.*
II, 134).

[136] In the Babylonian Talmud the tractate in question is the eleventh chapter of
Sanhedrin. The recommendation: Galatinus, *De Arcanis*, 12. For Galatinus and this
work: below chap. 4.4.

[137] *De Abreviaturis*, 211.

[138] Gomarus to Walaeus, 1602; Walaeus *Opera* II, 367.

anti-Jewish topos from Buxtorf.[139] But in the latter's *Synagoga Judaica* and *De Abreviaturis* one also finds another interpretation of the Talmud. It is the view that it contains hidden secrets which confirm the truth of Christianity.[140] As we shall see in the next chapter, L'Empereur was in his later work to share this opinion, which also goes back to mediaeval catholic controversialists. The absence of this view from his oration, is a further indication that at the time of his acceptance of the chair, he had only concerned himself with rabbinical literature for a short time.

Even more markedly than is the case with Buxtorf, his verdict on rabbinical Judaism in his inaugural lecture is in complete contradiction to the attention which he had paid and would later pay to this literature. His preparation for the professorship had in fact consisted precisely of acquainting himself with rabbinical literature, to which his oration was unable to grant any value. Both the conversion motif and the view, also found in Buxtorf, that Christians might become more aware of the grace by which they live, by looking at the blindness of the Jews and the divine wrath which rests upon them, are absent in L'Empereur.[141] On the basis of his inaugural address alone, one would even expect L'Empereur, like the Wittenberg professor Forster, to reject the use of the rabbis for the linguistic interpretation of the Old Testament. The actual reasons for L'Empereur's involvement with rabbinical literature can thus only be reconstructed from an analysis of his work. It is to this analysis that we shall now turn.

---

[139] Buxtorf, *De Abreviaturis*, 199: "Vides, Lector, obstinatissimae & obcaecatissimae gentis, de suo Talmud & ejus compilatoribus impudentissima & impia elogia. An ergo mirum, quo Dei verbum reliquerunt, & Patrum traditiones secuti sunt? Haec causa est, quod in omnibus suis scriptis nil nisi Talmud suum, Sapientes & Rabbinos suos perpetuo crepent, et subinde lectori ipsorum sententias & edicata obtrudant." Cf. also *Synagoga Judaica*, 47, 60-1, 70, 461.

[140] Buxtorf, *De Abreviaturis*, 191-2; "Talmud est Opus doctrinale, sive Corpus doctrinae magnum, a variis ac doctissimis quibusque Rabbinis compilatum, multiplicem omnium Scientiarum doctrinam continens, & potissimum Jus civile ac canonicum Judaeorum plenissime ac perfectissime proponens, ut secundum illud universa gens & Synagoga Israelitica optime feliciterque vivet. Multiplex etiam ipsi historia inserta est, quae quia profundos, arcanos & mysticos sensus plerumque comprehendit, ideo a paucis intelligitur & juxta externam literam puditissimarum fabularum nomen potius occupat." We find the same verdict in Galatinus, *De Arcanis*, 114-5.

[141] Buxtorf, *Synagoga Judaica*, 549-50.

CHAPTER FOUR

THE ACCESS TO THE RABBIS (1627-1634)

"Rabbini sunt difficiles"
(*Secunda Scaligerana*, 526)

In the winter of 1631-1632 Frederick Henry asked the Leiden theologian André Rivet to become tutor of his son William, the continuer of the dynasty. This was a shrewd political choice. The scholar was of irreproachable orthodoxy, but not rigid or fanatical and certainly in a position to "furnish the princely little brain of young William with whatever scholarship belonged in it".[1] Rivet, who had not been unknown at the Court since his arrival in Leiden in 1620, placed his service to a prince above that to church and university. At the end of January 1632, the Mayors and Curators were informed of his departure, and for the first time since the troubes of 1618-19 they were faced with the task of choosing a new professor in the theological faculty.[2] Mindful of earlier, catastrophic appointments, they went very carefully about the work. So carefully that it was only a year later, in February 1633, that they were able to choose between four candidates, each of them of undisputed orthodoxy. They were Festus Hommius, the regent of the States' College, who had drawn the attention of the administrators on himself;[3] Hendrik Alting, who had gone into exile in the Republic after the fall of Heidelberg in 1622 and had been a professor at Groningen since 1627; Gijsbertus Voetius, the preacher of Vianen who had been the youngest member of the Synod of Dordt, and Constantijn L'Empereur, who did not let this chance to achieve his ambition go by. After a detailed report on the candidates and their qualities had been received from the faculty of theology, the Mayors and Curators decided to invite Alting.[4] The negotiations with Groningen were tiresome. Alting, who hoped to be able to return to the Palatinate, was unwilling to respond to the invitation immediately. Finally there was some division within the college of Mayors and Curators over the choice.[5]

When in the winter of 1633 it finally appeared that Alting would not

[1] Poelhekke, *Frederik Hendrik*, 351.
[2] *Molh.* II, 163. The Mayors and Curators were informed on 26 January 1632.
[3] *Molh.* II, 170. 9 February 1632.
[4] *Molh.* II, 182. 21 February 1633.
[5] Polyander to Alting, 29.8.1633; Lamping, *Polyander*, 162.

be coming, an appeal was made almost at once to Jacob Trigland, preacher at Amsterdam. The sudden haste in this appointment is understandable. Since 1 July two of the three remaining Leiden theology professors had been involved in the revision of the translation of the Old Testament.[6] In the minutes of the Mayors and Curators, the decision on the appointment of Trigland is followed by a remarkable passage:[7]

> the request D. Constantini L'Empereur, S.S. Theologiæ Doctoris ac Linguæ Sanctæ Professoris, to be honoured with authorisation to treat in writing the controversies between the Christians and the Jews, and the refutation of the said Jews, being examined, it is after deliberation, understood and resolved thereon, that D. L'Empereur aforesaid, continuing in the performance of his present professorship Hebræae et Chaldææ Linguæ, shall in addition have to write adversus Judaeos, and that he shall be honoured for that writing with a fee of 400 guilders yearly, of which the first year shall have begun to run from the 8th Novembris last, and that he shall be able to borrow the books, necessary to him for the aforesaid refutation of the Jews and lacking to him, from the public library of the University and should any such books be missing therefrom, they shall be bought at the expense of the said University.

On 7 August 1634 the Mayors and Curators gave L'Empereur an honorarium of one hundred guilders, for the dedication of the first work which he published by virtue of his new function, of writing against the Jews.[8]

The appearance of this work, *Halikhot Olam*, the only book in which L'Empereur describes himself on the title page as *Professor Controversiarum Judaicarum*, marks the close of a period in his life. Virtually all his published works were produced in the seven years between his appointment as professor of Hebrew in 1627 and that of professor for Jewish controversies at the end of 1633. Around 1634, thanks to this scholarly work, he had become an honoured citizen of the Republic of Letters. In this chapter his oeuvre will be discussed and analysed, excluding his edition of Moses Kimḥi's Hebrew grammar and the reissue of Bertramus' *De Republica Hebrœorum*, which we shall deal with in the next chapter in the context of a discussion of his teachng. A survey of L'Empereur's life in these seven years, in the first section, is followed by one setting his work in the framework of the 17th century scholarly effort to make rabbinical literature accessible. The third and fourth sections describe the use which could be made of rabbinical literature: the exposition of the bible and the refutation of the Jews.

---

[6] *De Statenvertaling*, 35.
[7] *Molh.* II, 185-6, 29 December 1633.
[8] *Molh.* II, 190.

## 4.1 *Life. The winning of recognition*

In this section we shall confine ourselves to a few aspects of L'Empereur's life in the years 1627-34. We shall discuss his interest in rabbinica, as it appears from the composition of his library, his theological and political attitudes and positions, and finally his place and ambitions within the university and the international community of scholars.

The importance of the period 1627-34 for L'Empereur's scholarly development appears from the fact that in this period he built up his library in the field of Hebrew and rabbinica. Only fifteen of the fifty-eight folio volumes he acquired did not have a direct connexion with his appointment as professor of Hebrew, while in the fourteen years after 1634 the balance was reversed. The nature of L'Empereur's interests is evident from the important place which Jewish books, that is books by Jewish authors, written and published for a Jewish public, occupied among his purchases. Unlike during his student years, the works of the Christian hebraists were much less numerous.

Table II. L'Empereur's books in folio and quarto 1627-34.

|        | Jewish works | Christian hebraists | Others |
|--------|--------------|---------------------|--------|
| folio  | 34           | 9                   | 15     |
| quarto | 37           | 41                  | 35     |
| Total  | 71           | 50                  | 50     |

During these seven years L'Empereur, who had been appointed at an annual salary of six hundred guilders, spent about nine hundred guilders on the acquisition of these books. The majority of the Jewish literature which he acquired consisted of commentaries, partly on the Mishna and the Talmud, but above all on the Old Testament. The last category counts the greatest number of titles. Thus he owned about twenty-five biblical commentaries by 15th and 16th century, mostly Spanish Jews like Moses Alshekh, Moses Albelda, Isaac Arama, Isaac Caro, Bahya ben Asher and Isaac Abrabanel.[9] The commentaries of the classical mediaeval Jewish biblical scholars, such as Rashi, Abraham ibn Ezra, David Kimhi and others, were accessible to L'Empereur through his purchase of Buxtorf's *Biblia Rabbinica*.[10] Older paraphrasing works, such as the various Midrashim, the *Tanhuma* and *Pesikta Zutarta*, and

---

[9] Alshekh, 16th century, Adrianople: *EJ* 2,758; Albelda, 16th century, Spain: *EJ* 2, 529; Arama, 16th century, Spain: *EJ*, 3, 256; Caro, late 15th century, Spain; *EJ* 5, 193; Bahya, 13th century, Spain; *EJ* 4, 104; Abrabanel: see note 20.

[10] Published in 1618-9. Prijs no. 219. For a detailed bibliographical description: Prijs, *Hebräische Drucke*, 331-43.

anthologies from such works as the *Yalkut Shimoni*, can also be included among biblical expositions.

A second group is formed by the characteristic works of Judaism. In the first place, naturally, the Babylonian Talmud. As we have seen L'Empereur had acquired this quite soon after his appointment. Because the Talmudic literature is virtually inaccessible without aids, he also bought a number of books which were necessary in order to understand it. In the case of the Mishna he possessed the classic commentaries on this work by Maimonides and Obadiah of Bertinoro. In his edition of the Talmud, printed by Daniel Bomberg at Venice, the commentaries of Rashi and the work of the Tosafists were included. He owned Jewish dictionaries which could be used for the study of the Talmud, especially the *Arukh* of Rabbi Nathan, and various indices and extracts from the Talmud, such as the *Zikhron Torath Moshe, Ein Yisre'el* and *Ein Ya'akov*.[11] He also had Maimonides *Mishneh Torah*, with commentaries, and Moses of Coucy's *Sefer Mitzvot Gadol*, a survey of the applicable *halakhah* in the form of a summary of the 613 commands and prohibitions in which references to the Talmud and the Midrash are included as source references. All these works occur in the survey of aids to the study of the Talmud which J. C. Wolfius gave in his *Bibliotheca Hebræa* in the early 18th century.[12] Wolfius stood at the end of a long scholarly tradition in the field of the study of rabbinical literature, as appears from his five-thousand page survey of all the literature in the field of Judaism. Wolfius' list of aids to study gives a few titles which were not in L'Empereur's possession, but shows the same characteristic interest in just a few aspects of the Talmud which can be reconstructed from L'Empereur's library and his works.

The Mishna and the Gemara are in essence judicial works although the Gemara of the Babylonian Talmud in particular contains many haggadic sections, in which the most various subjects can be discussed. The Talmud does not give legal decisions in a codified or systematic form, but is the reflection of discussions among legal scholars, in which it is not always stated which opinion is the correct or valid one. This unsystematic character was the reason for the appearance of commentaries, which attempted to construct underlying principles behind the legal rulings, and tried to adapt the law to changed social circumstances. The greatest example of this is the commentary of Rashi. His work gave rise to an

---

[11] These three works are named in the survey by Wolfius, cited in note 12, respectively as an index to both Talmudim by Moses ben Joseph Pig, as an index to the haggada in the Talmud by Eliezer ben Isaac, and as a haggadic anthology by Jacob ben Habib.

[12] Wolfius, *Bibliotheca hebraea* II, 988-93: ''De subsidiis quae ad Talmud rectius intelligendam vel tractandam a Christianis aut Judaeis prolecta sunt''.

extensive literature of socalled *Tosafot*, supplements and improvements to
his commentary. A second large group of works which are based on the
Talmud as legal literature is formed by the codes. Because he regarded
the Talmud as too comprehensive and difficult to grasp as a whole, for
practical legal use, Maimonides wrote at the end of the 12th century, his
*Mishneh Torah*, a systematic codification of the valid law, in which
deviating opinions were no longer mentioned. In spite of strong
resistance from other legal scholars, who feared that Maimonides'
codification would be the end of Talmudic study, because he did not give
the sources on which he based his decisions, the work rapidly gained
great popularity and became the model for a new genre. Later editions
of the *Mishneh Torah* were provided with commentaries in which source
references were given, and as a result other works with the same goal
were produced, such as the *Sefer ha-Turim* of Jacob ben Asher, from the
beginning of the 14th century, and Joseph Caro's *Shulhan Arukh*, published in 1565.

In his survey Wolfius mentioned the work of the Tosafists, but considered it as superfluous and too involved, and advised against its use.
He discussed the various codes together with works which contain indices
to the haggadic sections of both Talmudim or to the biblical passages
cited in them. He regarded the codes—in accordance with the use which
the Christian hebraists made of them—as entries into the Talmud. In
1627-34 L'Empereur bought only the *Mishneh Torah* of Maimonides, and
he too did not consider this work as a legal codification. In his opinion
it was an excellent survey of the customs, usages and institutions of
biblical times.[13] He saw rabbinical literature as biblical exposition, either
as a theology in the form of a doctrinal system, or as a description of the
history and customs of the Jewish people. He shared this opinion with
almost all the Christian hebraists of the 17th century. They all considered
rabbinical literature as an exposition of the Old Testament. Of course
this does not say much. As we shall see in the course of this chapter, rabbinical literature could be used for the most varied forms of bible exposition. But an interest in Judaism as a way of life which was mainly determined by practical rules and which derived its unity from them, or an
interest in living Jewish law, is only to be found incidentally.[14]

---

[13] Cf. L'Empereur's verdict in the letter to Barbio, Appendix VI, and in *MosKim*, *6b:
"Sane unus ille Maimonides liber, cui titulum fecit Jad Chazaka, tantam antiquitatis
descriptione Sacris Literis facem accendit..."

[14] This lack of interest is also remarked by Baron, *History* XIII, 413, n. 43:
"Remarkably, even humanists with good juridical training paid little attention to Jewish
Law." He expresses his astonishment at this, because it was only thus that it was possible
to acquire a genuine knowledge of Jewish culture. Naturally, as will be argued in what
follows, the interest in Jewish literature was not motivated by a desire to become
acquainted with contemporary Judaism.

L'Empereur's interest explains the occurrence of virtually all the Jewish historical works—they were not so numerous—in his library. He used them for his understanding of the bible and for his knowledge of the lives of the mediaeval rabbis and the history of Jewish literature. He possessed *Seder Olam Rabbah* and *Zuta, Yuḥasin*, the *Sefer ha-Kabbalah*, the *Zemaḥ David* of David Gans and the *Me' or Einayim* of Azariah di Rossi.[15] His preference for biblical exposition and doctrinal theology explains the almost complete absence of cabbalistic, mystical works from his library, while it was precisely this literature which became the most important and extensive within Judaism in the 17th century.[16] The Christian hebraists of the 16th century had still had a great interest in the Cabbala, but this interest went into a severe decline in the first half of the 17th century.[17] What L'Empereur sought in Judaism is best illustrated from the work of Don Isaac Abrabanel, virtually all of whose writings he acquired. That he was deliberately collecting them is evident not only from his library but also from a letter to his relative and friend David de Wilhem, of October 1632, in which he elegantly requested de Wilhem not to bid against him for works of Abrabanel at the auction of the library of the deceased Zeeland orientalist Boreel.[18] L'Empereur regarded Abrabanel as the "most learned of the Jews" and in this praise he was the first of a long line of Christian hebraists in the 17th century.[19]

The life of Isaac Abrabanel (1437-1508) is inextricably interwoven with the tragedy of Spanish Jewry. Born at Lisbon into a respected Jewish family, the exceptionally gifted Abrabanel reached a high position at the court of the Portuguese king Alfonso V. He was a great financier and moved in court circles, with which he was linked not only by political

---

[15] Description of these works, the most important representatives of the not very extensive genre of Jewish historical literature in Waxman, *History* II, 461-9, 476-81, 517-22.

[16] Scholem, *Sabbatai Sevi*, 66-76.

[17] In his bibliography, which ran to more than fifteen hundred pages, Wolfius could be satisfied with fifty pages for a survey of the literature on the Cabbala: Wolfius, *Bibliotheca hebraea* II, 1191-247. Cf. the extremely meagre survey of the 17th century in Secret, *Zohar* and in Scholem et al., *Kabbalistes*. In the time of L'Empereur only the translation of the *Sefer Yetsira* by J. S. Rittangelius, Amsterdam 1642 appeared (cf. Van Rooden/Wesselius, "J. S. Rittangel"), and a work by du Voisin at Paris. Most 17th century knowledge of the Cabbala was derived from the works of Pico, Reuchlin and Postel (Blau, *Christian Interpretation*, 95-102).

[18] Appendix IX: Boreel (1577-1629), pupil and friend of Scaliger (*Sec Scal*, 241), friend of Erpenius (who dedicated his Arabic version of the Pentateuch to Boreel), in his youth travelled in the Middle East, translated Broughton's commentary on Daniel into Latin, and later became *raadpensionaris* of Zeeland: Juynboll, *Beoefenaars*, 9-10.

[19] Already in *ParaDan*, 188: *Middot*, 174; see also the letter to Ussher cited below (note 44). For an overview of such favourable opinions of hebraists, Majus: *Vita Abrabanelis*, 20-35.

alliances, but also by a shared enthusiasm for humanism. As a member of the faction of the Braganzas he shared in the fall of this most powerful of Portugal's noble families after the accession in 1481 of the new king João II. In 1483 he fled to Spain where he almost immediately won a high position in the service of Ferdinand and Isabella, and became one of the most important leaders of Spanish Jewry. In 1492, in spite of effort by the royal house to retain him, he shared the fate of the Spanish Jews and went into exile with them when they were expelled. For a third time he made a career at a court, this time in the kingdom of Naples. There dynastic troubles and the French invasion made life impossible for him. He died in Venice. Abrabanel was one of the first Jews to be influenced by the renaissance and was very well acquainted with Christian theology. His writings were mainly commentaries on the bible, in which he presented Judaism as an all embracing religion of revelation. The commentaries are theological and anti-rational in character and opposed to the allegorising interpretations of Maimonides. Abrabanel based himself on the literal sense, without being particularly interested in language or grammar. Polemic against Christianity is a permanent feature of all his works.[20] As L'Empereur claims, it was thus difficult for a Christian to acquire them.[21] The attraction which Abrabanel exercised on L'Empereur is not hard to explain. Abrabanel's theological method of exegesis, directed towards doctrine, systems of thought and polemic, was related to that of L'Empereur's own upbringing.

Thanks to the inventory of his library which L'Empereur kept up, it is also possible to answer the question of the origin of his Hebrew books. In the early years of the 17th century it had been very difficult to buy Jewish works in the Republic. On the liquidation of the publishing business and university bookshop of Raphelengius in 1619, the catalogue of works remaining contained a large number of grammars by Christian hebraists, but no rabbinical works.[22] The great humanists of the early years of the 17th century had to have them sent from abroad. Drusius bought Jewish books from a rabbi in Emden, Moses ben Jacob Halevi;[23]

---

[20] Netanyahu, *Abravanel.*

[21] *ComJes*, ( + 7a): "ille tam avide a Iudaeis passim conquiritur ut vix tandem ejus compos fieri potuerim." Cf. also his letter to de Wilhem (Appendix IX), and the trouble which Mueller had in acquiring Abrabanel's commentary on Daniel (note 300). From Cocceius' "PROTHEORIA, de ratione interpretandi" it appears that he had heard of Abrabanel, but did not know his works (*Opera ANEKDOTA* I, 67).

[22] According to the *Catalogus librorum residorum Tabernae Raphelengianae* in: Van Gulik/Vervliet, *Gedenksteen*, 18-9. On his death in 1599 Marnix of St. Aldegonde, a leading hebraist, only owned two rabbinical works: a "grammatica Hebraea Kimchi Venetiis" and "Preces Rabbinorum literis rabbinicis": Marnix, *Catalogue.*

[23] Fuks, "Brievenboek", 9-10.

Scaliger, thanks to his French contacts, directly from Venice.[24] Of course one could also complete one's library at the auction sales of deceased hebraists. L'Empereur bought many rabbinical works at the auction of the library of Erpenius and later too, through the mediation of Thysius,[25] he acquired from Erpenius' widow, some works which had been left over at the auction. At the auction by Perduyn in 1632, of the library of the Zeeland orientalist Boreel, he acquired the writings of Abrabanel which he was still lacking. But the greater part of his library he must have bought from the Jews of Amsterdam. The growth of the Jewish community there created new possibilities for the study of rabbinical literature. The Amsterdam Jewish presses which were to replace Venice as the world centre of the Jewish book trade in the course of the 17th century, were still in their infancy at the end of the 1620's, but the Jews of Amsterdam kept up close links with other Jewish communities. The origin of many Jewish works in L'Empereur's book list is not given. But with a single exception, all the books whose origin he did make a note of, were acquired from Amsterdam Jews. Between January and April 1631 L'Empereur bought eight folio works for about fifty guilders, from Menasseh ben Israel. That is years earlier than the beginning of the known activities of Menasseh as a bookseller and also before he earned wider fame through the publication of his *Conciliador* in 1632.[26] On 4 September 1631 L'Empereur bought two books from one Fonseca, who can very probably be identified with the rabbi Isaac Aboab. It is tempting to assume that the name "Matera" on one title just after October 1632 is a corruption of the name of a third Amsterdam rabbi: the venerable and strict Saul Levi Morteira.[27] Other Jews from whom he bought books in these years were Isaac Palache, and one Jacob Justo.[28] After 1634 we become acquainted with the name of one Moses Levi. It appears likely that the origin of L'Empereur's works, even where it is not stated, must be sought in Amsterdam.

---

[24] Cf. the correspondence of Scaliger with Fabry, De Harley Darlot, Velserus and Thomson in *Epistolae*, 272-6, 378-81, 627-30, and in *Epistres Françoises*, 243-4, 412-3.

[25] Thysius acted on behalf of Erpenius' widow with the Mayors and Curators, in the sale of the deceased's library to the University of Leiden (*Molh.* II, 124). As late as 1632 L'Empereur paid money to Thysius, for Erpenius' widow, for a book by Isaac ben Arama.

[26] Fuks, "Menasseh ben Israel", 34. In 1634 Menasseh visited a book fair at Frankfurt for the first time. His first sales elsewhere are known from 1635.

[27] Cf. the titles of the quarto volumes in L'Empereur's list, after October 1632: "Caphtor or Pesach, bought from Matera and paid for it ... 5/ the conciliator is bound with it, worth... 2". Katchen, *Christian Hebraists*, 310 n. 25 for Morteira's contacts with Christians.

[28] Respectively in the spring of 1630 and on 30 June 1634.

The Jewish works acquired by L'Empereur reveal a theologian's interest in Judaism. He acquired above all those works which display Judaism as a rival theological system of doctrine, appealing to the bible for its legitimation. He did not see Judaism as another way of life or as a pattern of another kind of piety. In this chapter it will become clear that the nature of his scholarly work confirms the interpretation indicated here.

In the case of L'Empereur, this view was undoubtedly the result of his theological training. His interpretation of his subject, as he explained it in his inaugural lecture, showed the same concentration on doctrine and the theological exposition of the bible. In the years 1627-34 his interest, besides rabbinica, only extended to the most important dogmatic and political dispute of his age. Between September 1631 and September 1632 L'Empereur bought twenty works by socinians. The interest of the church party in this sect, regarded as the gravest of all heresies, had again increased since the end of the twenties, occasioned by a violent round of polemics against the remonstrants. This offensive had been undertaken when the fear arose that through the appointment of Frederick Henry as Stadhouder in 1625 the political and ecclesiastical decisions of 1618-9 might be revised. In 1626 the professors of the Leiden theology faculty issued an attack on the remonstrant confession, published four years earlier, in which they attempted to prove that the doctrine of the recently founded sectarian brotherhood paved the way for socinian heresies.[29] A lengthy paper warfare was provoked by this work, and in the years 1629-30 became inextricably intertwined with the debate on the "great matter", the peace offer from Spain which had the support of Frederick Henry, Amsterdam and three of the provinces. The attitude which the government had to take against the remonstrants, who were manifesting themselves ever more emphatically and striving for recognition, and the question whether the war was to be continued, were closely involved in this, the greatest debate within the political elite of the Republic since the Truce. Leiden, one of the cities which was most forceful in its support of the 1618 solution, provided its delegation to the States of Holland in September 1629 with explicit instructions to block discussion of the peace proposal as long as Leiden's demands for a stricter observance of the decrees against the remonstrants were not granted.[30]

In his first publication L'Empereur took up a position in this debate. His edition of the Mishna tractate *Middot* which deals with the dimen-

---

[29] *Censura in Confessionem.* Other examples: Kühler, *Socinianisme*, 199-201.
[30] Israel, *Dutch Republic*, 228 ff. The attitude of Leiden, *ibid.*, 231-2.

sions of the Temple, was dedicated to the States of Holland and reminded their Great Mightinesses of their duty to protect the church. The dedication emphasised that now the church was threatened by people who were trying in an underhand way to introduce socinian and arian heresies, the care of the government was more than ever necessary. In an impressive argument L'Empereur described the history of the Ark and the Temple as a prefiguring of the vicissitudes of the reformed church in the 16th and 17th centuries. Like the Ark, it had moved from place to place, through Germany, France and other countries until, like the Temple of old, it had been established in a fixed place, under the protection of the States of Holland. "O fortunate Republic, where religion is the highest care!" Such a care is necessary and useful, for the history of the state of Israel teaches that a community only flourishes when the government is zealous for true religion. True, there are people who do not share this opinion, but their view is emphatically dismissed by L'Empereur:[31]

> "I know that there are many who are of the opinion that the decision on religion must be left to the conscience of each individual. But if every father of a household counts the religion of his household members among his cares, then so does the magistrate in the government ... There are even people who are out to win a freedom which removes every hindrance for any error whatever. Thus a breach is made, in contradiction of the perfectly clear Word of God, in the required obedience of the magistracy in the matter of the just fulfilment of the divine worship, yea, it is even rejected. As if the government was only bound by God to raise armies, to extend the frontiers of its rule, and to care for such matters; but left religion free for each individual."

Fortunately L'Empereur could count on the States to carry out their task. Had they not, just as once the kings of Israel purified the cult in the Temple, at the time of Dordt set up again the tottering church, God's Temple? L'Empereur's remarks are only noteworthy for the high degree of abstraction with which he describes the struggle between two views of the state. So far as the content is concerned, his view is entirely at one with that of the church.[32] In virtually all his published works he was to restate this view.

He was not content merely to adopt a position in the discussion. In 1630 an Amsterdam printer who also printed works for the remonstrants, published an anonymous socinian work, the *Dissertatio de pace et concordia Ecclesiæ*. Shortly afterwards, it was rumoured by Rivet at Court and by Walaeus in Zeeland that this was the work of a remonstrant, probably Episcopius himself, and that the socinian tendencies of the remonstrants

---

[31] *Middot*, *3c-**2a.
[32] Van Gelder, *Getemperde Vrijheid*, 84-8, 238-40.

had finally come out into the open. Wtenbogaert, according to a letter to Grotius, was particularly alarmed at this accusation. In view of the situation, so tense for the remonstrants, that need cause no surprise.[33] The source of this rumour, so a particularly indignant Barlaeus wrote to Episcopius on 1 July 1630, was L'Empereur. He had disseminated the treatise among influential circles at The Hague. Barlaeus made fun of L'Empereur in his letter, calling him a professor of Hebrew who, after describing the Temple, had now taken on himself the role of high priest. "He is not frightful, but he wants to give that impression. The professor has more columns in his lecture room than students."[34] (If Barlaeus is not exaggerating, L'Empereur had no more than three students in these years). L'Empereur's interest in sociniana, as it appears from the affair and his purchases in the autumn and winter of 1631, was shared by the faculty of theology. On 22 December of that year the four Leiden theologians, on their own initiative, requested the States of Holland to act against the printing and sale of socinian works. The content of their request shows such an agreement with L'Empereur's arguments and interests that there can be no doubt of a close bond between him and the faculty.[35]

In spite of this link, L'Empereur, as we have seen, was passed over on Rivet's succession, in favour of Alting. In the course of 1633 it seemed as if he might have a second chance and he managed to manoeuvre himself into a favourable starting position for an appointment. Alting had been invited in February 1633, but did not come at once. The University of Groningen at first did not give him permission to accept the invitation, and Alting himself, who vainly hoped that the war situation in Germany had decisively changed after the intervention of Sweden, wished first to make a journey to Heidelberg to see if he could resume his professorship there.[36] The delay in the appointment was particularly inopportune, since Thysius had become Rector Magnificus in February and in July the revision of the Old Testament books of the States' Translation began. Thysius and Polyander were involved in this very time-consuming work. In August Thysius asked the permission of

---

[33] Grotius, *Briefwisseling* IV, 223-4; from Wtenbogaert, 10.6.1630. In reality the work was by S. Przipcovius. For the affair: Rogge, *Wtenbogaert* III, 233-43. As early as 21 June Grotius knew that Episcopius was regarded as the author: *Briefwisseling* IV, 230-1; to W. de Groot.

[34] Barlaeus, *Epistolae*, 335-9; to Episcopius, 1.7.1630; 359-61; to Wtenbogaert, 19.12.1630.

[35] Eekhof, *Theologische Faculteit*, 132-5: the professors, like L'Empereur, stated with distaste that the remonstrants believed that the sale of socinian books must be left free. The examples of socinian books which they gave, were all bought by L'Empereur in these years.

[36] *BWPGN* I, 115.

the Mayors and Curators to have L'Empereur substitute for him in his teaching, because of the pressure of his activities. It appears from a letter of Polyander that this request was one of the attempts to bring about L'Empereur's appointment after all. Polyander wrote how attempts had also been made, without his knowledge, to have a substitute appointed for him, and advised Alting to settle the question with Groningen quickly and to abandon his planned visit to Germany.[37] Thysius' support for L'Empereur need not surprise us. L'Empereur's brother was Thysius' son-in-law and L'Empereur himself had married one of the professor's numerous nieces, Catherine Thys, on 25 July 1628.[38] According to a cryptic remark in the dedication of the *Halikhot Olam*, L'Empereur did indeed deputise for Thysius until September 1634, when the revision of the translation of the Old Testament was completed.[39]

L'Empereur contributed to the attempts to bring about his appointment as Rivet's successor by dedicating to François van Aerssen his edition of the travel narrative of Benjamin of Tudela, which appeared in the course of 1633. Van Aerssen was a Curator of the University and a very powerful man. L'Empereur took no half measures, and more than half of the fairly extensive dedication consists of a detailed description of the extraordinary qualities of the object of the dedication.[40] Another work which he published in 1633 was used for the same purpose. L'Empereur dedicated it to the Mayors of Leiden. The efforts had no success and in December 1633 Trigland was appointed, but there can be no doubt that the appointment of L'Empereur as professor to write *adversus Judaeos* which was decided in the same session, was intended as a compensation for the fact that he had been passed over twice. The appointment and the large increase in salary of four hundred guilders (very generous for the not so open-handed Mayors and Curators) are an indication of the strength of the forces which had worked for L'Empereur.[41] The appoint-

---

[37] Polyander to Alting, 29.8.1633; Lamping, *Polyander*, 162.

[38] On 25 July 1628: van Roijen, "Inleiding".

[39] In this foreword, dated 7 August 1634, L'Empereur thanks the Mayors and Curators for his appointment to write against the Jews and points out that it is a perfect gift, in all its aspects, including that of the time: "etenim cum varios tractatus, partim publici juris fecissem, partim paratos saltem haberem: tum demum id mihi oneris impositum fuit, quod animum vacuum requirit, *cum etiam alter iste labor, cujus nec lucrum, nec laudem capto, de quo exantlato nec glorior (licet & publico prosit, nec viros multos cordatos lateat) ad finem jam decurreret*..." (our underlining: *HalOl*, **1b).

[40] *ItinBen*, *7-**4. The praise of van Aerssen's talent as a diplomat is timely in view of his contacts with France. It was in these very months that important diplomatic negotiations with France were in progress, in which van Aerssen was not involved: Poelhekke, *Frederik Hendrik*, 416 ff.

[41] On 15 May 1629 the M. & C. gave him an extraordinary salary increase of f.100 for three years (*Molh.* II, 146). In 1631 they raised his salary by f.200 a year with effect from August (*Molh.* II, 162).

ment was a personal matter without social consequences or motives, intended only to meet L'Empereur's theological ambitions as far as was possible.

L'Empereur made the acquaintance of or renewed his friendship with a great many of the theologians who came to Leiden for the revision of the States' Translation of the bible—the Old Testament between July 1633 and September 1634, the New from November 1634 to August 1635. It appears from his inventory that he received gifts of books from Gomarus, Revius, Baudartius, Diestius and Van Renesse as he had already received them from his Leiden colleagues Rivet, Thysius and Polyander (Walaeus is conspicuously absent). His involvement in the States' Translation went further than this however. As professor of Hebrew he was called in to give technical assistance, as had originally been desired by the Synod of Dordt.[42] In a letter of 16 November 1633 to Ussher, the learned bishop of Armagh with whom he had probably become acquainted through the latter's contacts with Louis de Dieu in the field of Syriac,[43] this becomes clear:[44]

> "I have been asked by those who are translating the Old Testament into Dutch to make observations on the more difficult passages. If it is permitted, then I would request leave to use that Syriac commentary on the hagiographa and the prophets for a time. For so far as the Pentateuch and the other historical books are concerned, the revisors (as they are called) have already investigated them and are now proceeding with the hagiographa. In doubtful passages I am accustomed to consult my Abrabanel (the best of all commentators) but even he is not always adequate."

This contact with Ussher is not alone. Besides his efforts to become a theologian, L'Empereur wanted to be recognised by the members of the international community of philologists, jurists and some theologians which is known as the Republic of Letters. His place in it will be discussed in the next chapter, but here we have to describe how he won recognition in these years.

One earned recognition through publication. In 1633 the strictly orthodox L'Empereur sent three of his works to that Hollander in exile,

---

[42] The Synod of Dordt had resolved that the translators should be able to consult the professors of Greek and Hebrew (Nauta, in *De Statenvertaling*, 16). The letter answers the question of de Bruin, whether this part of the decisions of Dordt was being implemented (De Bruin, *Statenbijbel*, 296-7).

[43] See the letter of Ussher to de Dieu, 9.6.1632; Ussher, *Works* XV, 550-4 in which Ussher speaks of "eruditissimi Constantini tui". Heinsius too came into contact with Ussher through de Dieu's mediation (Sellin, *Heinsius*, 34).

[44] Ussher, *Works* XV, 577. L'Empereur to Ussher, 16.11.1633.

who was regarded as the representative par excellence of the *respublica litterarum*, Hugo Grotius.[45] His publications consisted mainly of textual editions of rabbinical works with a parallel Latin translation. Such editions unlocked a literature, which had hitherto only been accessible to specialists. All of L'Empereur's works were produced in the years 1628-33. Of the publications which appeared later we know that his editions of *Halikhot Olam* (1634) and *Bava Kamma* (1637) were written or conceived around 1632. L'Empereur's republication in 1641 of Bertramus' *De Republica Hebræorum*, to which he himself only added notes, is the only work the existence of which before 1633 cannot be demonstrated. In these years he was even concerned with several works which were ultimately never to be published.[46] We shall have occasion later to discuss the causes of this sudden decline in publications after 1633, but a personal reason was certainly the fact that L'Empereur's ambitions were then fulfilled, so far as this was possible. At the end of 1633 he had become, through his appointment as professor in the *controversiæ judaicæ* an important university teacher, as close to the faculty of theology as possible, and at the same time he also became a recognised member of the Republic of Letters.

That is aptly shown in a letter of Ussher to de Dieu.[47] Around 1630 a change of generations had taken place in the little world of the Christian hebraists. In the second half of the twenties, Johann Buxtorf I of Basle and Sixtinus Amama of Franeker were considered as the leading hebraists in Europe. The first died in September 1629, the second, who was regarded after Buxtorf's death as the most important champion of Hebrew studies,[48] four months later. In 1632 Ussher could state with satisfaction that the Republic of Letters had surmounted this loss. Leiden had compensated for the loss of Amama by the appointments of de Dieu, L'Empereur and Golius. Buxtorf had left a son, who, so Ussher had

---

[45] Grotius, *Briefwisseling*, V, 133; to J. de Cordes. 1.6.1633. L'Empereur sent him *ParaDan, ItinBen, ComJes*. He also sent these three works in one packet to Cocceius: Cocceius to L'Empereur 25.9.1633; Cocceius, *Opera ANEKDOTA* II, 631-3.

[46] In *ItinBen*, ***1a L'Empereur surveys what he has done and continues "cui codices Talmudicos, Berachoth, Zebachim, Bava Kamma, Bava Metsia & Bava Batra, quod jam paratos habeo subjiciam". In Thysiana 164,2 there is a translation (not publishable in this form) of the Gemara on the first chapter of *Berakhot*. Cf. also the letter cited in note 141 from L'Empereur to C. Schraderus, in which this same survey is given. The annotations did exist. Bochart mentions in his *Hierozoicon* (*Opera Omnia* I, 676) annotations by an anonymous hand on Bava Batra, which appear from the index to be those of L'Empereur. Juynboll, *Beoefenaars*, mentions on the basis of the older secondary literature a *Grammatica chaldaea et syra* by Erpenius, of which L'Empereur is said to have arranged the publication in 1628. We have been unable to find any reference to such a work in libraries or in the letters of L'Empereur.

[47] Ussher, *Works* XV, 553; Ussher to de Dieu, 9.6.1632.

[48] AG, Heinsius to Amama, 29.11.1629.

heard, appeared to justify great expectations. In fact Johann Buxtorf II had to wait a few years longer than L'Empereur for recognition. The reason for this was his less rapid tempo of publication in the years immediately after 1630. The growth of L'Empereur's prestige, which was well under way around 1632 appears from the presentation copies of the books which he received. Such gifts of books by their authors formed to a great extent rewards for services given and L'Empereur began his career by giving away large numbers of books. Thus, for his first work, the edition of *Middot*, an account has been preserved in the Bibliotheca Thysiana of his publisher, Elzevier, for fifty copies which he ordered himself apparently to use as presentation copies to serve as introductions.[49]

The development of the extent of his contacts can be followed closely. Besides those with the theologians who were involved in the States Translation, he received works from Cloppenburg and Caspar Streso.[50] But as well as these names, to be expected from his studies and previous appointment, we also find traces of familiarity with a large group of non-theologians. The earliest are contacts with other orientalists in the Republic. He had already formed a friendship with Amama in his time at Franeker, and it is not surprising that he received Cocceius' *Sanhedrin et Maccot* in 1629. They had been personal friends since a visit of Cocceius to Leiden.[51] Directly after his arrival he studied oriental languages with his colleagues in the faculty of letters, Syriac with Louis de Dieu,[52] and Arabic with Jakob Golius.[53] He received teaching materials partly as gifts. Other teachers in the Leiden faculty of letters also gave him presentation copies of their books, like the philologists Daniel Heinsius and Gerard Johannes Vossius, and the philosopher Burgersdijk. M. C. Boxhorn who became lecturer in eloquence in 1632, and professor in 1633; Dionysius Vossius, the son of Gerard Johannes and interested in orientalia and Antonius Thysius jr. the son of the theologian, all young and

[49] Th 164,4.

[50] 1603-64, born in Anhalt. Streso had contacts with Gomarus (Van Itterzon, *Gomarus*, index s.v.), and with the circle around Hartlib (Blekastad, *Comenius*, 216, 335.) In 1639 he became a minister at The Hague. The contacts with L'Empereur date from the years 1632-4.

[51] Cocceius, *Opera Omnia* I, praefatio, **2b; as early as *Middot*, 188 L'Empereur had called him his friend.

[52] In the spring of 1628 he received de Dieu's Syriac grammar and edition of the Syriac version of the Revelation of John. He also acquired Buxtorf's Aramaic-Syriac dictionary. De Dieu was an acquaintance of David de Wilhem (*BL* 2, 167).

[53] In October 1629 he bought Erpenius' Arabic grammar and around the turn of the year 1603-1 he also purchased his *Saracenica Historia*. He followed the teaching in the company of some other arabists: Juynboll, *Beoefenaars*, 191 ff. L'Empereur also received some MSS. from Golius: *Moskim*, 94; *ItinBen*, **7a-b.

very promising students and teachers, belonged to his circle of friends. The last named helped him in collecting passages from the classical authors, in which L'Empereur, as we have seen, had a rather inadequate education.[54] Other members of his circle included outsiders interested in oriental languages, non-members of the Academy who led a life on the borders of church and court, David de Wilhem,[55] Johannes de Laet[56] and Lodewijk a Renesse.[57] They gave him books and were of assistance to him in his scholarly work. The growth of his international contacts appears from his relationship with other hebraists. In the autumn of 1629 he bought the *Reges Persiæ* of Wilhelm Schikard, professor of Hebrew at Tübingen; in 1634 he like Grotius[58] received a presentation copy of Schikard's *Phurim*, after having first sent him a book.[59] The same development characterises his relationship with Johann Buxtorf II. He bought Buxtorf's translation of Maimonides' *Moreh Nevukhim* in 1629, the year of its publication; he received a copy of the concordance, compiled by Buxtorf senior and published by his son in 1632, as a gift. In these years he also made his previously mentioned contacts with Ussher and Grotius. Thus the years 1627-34 formed a decisive period in the life of L'Empereur. From a theologian in a provincial town, he became a generally recognised member of the European scholarly community. In the years after 1634, the great majority of his library acquisitions consisted of presentation copies. He only acquired the entree to this community by his rare specialism, the knowledge of rabbinical literature. Theologians with a background like that of L'Empereur only rarely occupied an important place in the Republic of Letters, which deliberately tried to be interconfessional. Only theologians with rich international contacts, a high personal reputation and an influential position or publication in a field other than theology, belonged to it. Of the four Leiden theologians of the *Synopsis*, only the Frenchman Rivet had a prominent place in the scholarly community. But Rivet, who had been sought out in 1620 by the Mayors and Curators in order to provide their newly erected and purged theology faculty with the vitally necessary

---

[54] For the help of A. Thysius jr.; *ItinBen*, 161-2.

[55] See Appendix IX. *MosKim*, 229. He also received the *Vikku'ah Hadath* from de Wilhem (*Bava Kamma*, 70). For this see note 297, below. For de Wilhem's residence in the east: de Groot, *Ottoman Empire*, 223 ff, 334; "Betekenis", 33; Juynboll, *Beoefenaars*, 185 ff.

[56] For his involvement in *ItinBen* (\*\*\*1a) see below 4.3. For him: Bekkers, *Correspondence*, xv-xvii.

[57] *NNBW* II, 1193-5; Frijhoff, *Société*, 91. L'Empereur received an old MS. from him: *ItinBen*, 155; *Bava Kamma*, 128.

[58] Grotius, *Briefwisseling* V, 250; from Vossius, 28.5.1634.

[59] According to *HalOl*, \*\*\*\*\*3b. For him: Seck, *Schikard*.

prestige, could draw on the Franco-Walloon intellectual tradition at the University of Leiden, and his outstanding contacts with French protestant and catholic scholars. After his appointment at Court, he was even able, thanks to the influence attached to it, to fulfil the same function as the Dupuys in Paris.[60] L'Empereur, who saw himself as a theologian rather than a linguistic scholar,[61] and was regarded as such within the Republic of Letters,[62] was in his origin, self-awareness and education, closer to the other three Leiden theologians than to Rivet. Even so he was named far more often than Walaeus, Polyander or Thysius in the international correspondence of leading scholars.

### 4.2  The aids to scholarship

L'Empereur's scholarly work, as will become apparent in the following section, shows three important aspects: didactic, exegetical and polemic. Almost all his works are editions of texts in the field of rabbinica with a parallel Latin translation. Such editions were intended as aids to the teaching of rabbinical literature. The knowledge gained with the aid of these works could be put at the service of biblical exegesis and theological polemic. In this section L'Empereur's scholarly work will be described as the unlocking of rabbinical literature, and we will concentrate on three works in more detail: his editions of *Middot*, *Bava Kamma* and *Halikhot Olam*.

L'Empereur's first published work was the edition of the Mishna tractate *Middot*, which deals with the dimensions of the Temple. The work, an edition of the Hebrew text with a Latin translation and notes, has the character of a teaching and practice book. Its publication was a sign of a new development in Hebrew studies. L'Empereur's editions of *Middot* (1630) and *Bava Kamma* (1637) were, with Cocceius' *Sanhedrin* and *Makkot* (1629) the first editions of this sort published by Christian scholars in the 17th century.[63] The genre was much imitated in the course of the century, and when Willem Surenhuys published the whole *Mishna* with a Latin translation between 1698 and 1703, he was able to make use of

---

[60] Cf. Bots, "Rivet".

[61] On the flyleaf of all his books he refers to himself in the first place as "SS Theologiae Doctor" and only afterwards as "professor sacrae linguae".

[62] When Vossius writes to Grotius (Grotius, *Briefwisseling*, IX, 20-1, 6.1.1638): "Haec cum scripsissem, intervenit Constantinus L'Empereur, Hebraearum apud Leidenses literarum professor, vir tui amans et aestimans supra *sui ordinis* complures" (our underlining), then it must be the "ordo" of the theologians which is meant.

[63] Cf. Bischoff, *Geschichte*. Only Philip Aquinas, a baptised Jew published a new translation of *Pirkei Avot* in the vernacular in 1620. (Bischoff, 46).

earlier published versions for twenty-five of the sixty-one tractates.[64] Cocceius, or rather, as we saw in the previous section, Amama and L'Empereur, stood at the beginning of the development of the new genre in the study of Hebrew. The edition of the *Pirkei Avot* by Paul Fagius in 1541 does not detract from the originality of their work. His edition had a quite different character.

Fagius (1504-49),[65] a pupil of Capito, was a hebraist of the second generation. He considered his edition as an aid to the learning of Hebrew without making any distinction between the various stages of the language. *Pirkei Avot* is a collection of proverbial wisdom ascribed to various rabbis, and occupies an exceptional position in the Mishna. Fagius was interested in this tractate because of its particular content. He saw the work as an expression of a general human wisdom such as is also to be found in classical literature. Such an interest also appears in his other works. In the foreword to his edition of a Hebrew version of Ben Sirach, he described it as his task:[66]

> "that I should collect and bring to light from the writings of the Hebrews, not so much that which is necessary for learning the language, as that which is helpful in promoting piety, forming life and improving manners, which certainly must be the goal of all our studies."

In conformity with this erasmian programme, transferred to Hebrew studies, the explanations given in brief notes, which he added to the text of the *Pirkei Avot*, are not explanatory but of an expressly moralising and educational character. The explanations refrain from all dogmatic polemic and stress the practical wisdom. Naturally the work was intended, in its bilingual form, with Hebrew text, Latin translation and notes, to be of service to linguistic study. But Fagius was thinking of general practice in Hebrew and not of access to a particular genre in Hebrew literature.[67] The relationship of the *Pirkei Avot* and the *Adagia* of Erasmus cannot be overlooked. For later imitators of this work of Fagius, one must think of Drusius' editions of Hebrew proverbs, in which we find the same combination of biblical and rabbinical literature,[68] and the

---

[64] Surenhuys: *NNBW* 9, 1084. A discussion of his edition and borrowings from previous editions: Bischoff, *Geschichte*, 20-3. For the nature of his edition: Van Rooden, "Surenhuis".

[65] *Herzog* 5, 733-4; Willi, "Christliche Hebraisten", 121 ff. For his contacts with Elias Levita: Weil, *Levita*, 133-51.

[66] Fagius, *Sententiae morales*, epistola nuncupatoria.

[67] Both in the foreword to his edition of the *Pirkei Avot* and in that of his *Ben Sirach* and *Tobit* he mentions the usefulness of these works for practice in the study of Hebrew without drawing any further distinction.

[68] Drusius, *Proverbia, Alphabetum, Proverbiorum, Apophtegmata*.

edition by Erpenius of Scaliger's translation of Arabic proverbs.[69] These early 17th century works, besides their erasmian function of simultaneously passing on a knowledge of the Hebrew language and moral wisdom, also had a place in the scholarly study of the New Testament.[70]

Compared with them, the works of L'Empereur and Cocceius belong to a new genre. To understand its nature and the rapid recognition which L'Empereur won through his publications, we must pay some attention to the teaching aids which were at the disposal of the student of Hebrew and rabbinica at the start of the second quarter of the 17th century. A good survey of these materials is offered by Amama's *Consilium de studio Ebraica feliciter instituendo*, a short handbook to the study of Hebrew which he added to his edition of Buxtorf's revision of Martinius' grammar.[71]

The *Consilium* was a part of Amama's campaign for the knowledge of Hebrew among preachers, and the public he had in mind consisted of theologians. The first part of the work is a guide to the use of the grammar he had republished. It offers an outline of a programme for learning Hebrew in three months. The *Consilium* lays great stress on the thorough learning of the rules and all the exceptions to them, of the grammar of biblical Hebrew. Like Erpenius, Amama advised the student to begin by reading prose works, and not with the Psalms. The ultimate goal of the programme is the ideal situation, in which a minister reads each day a chapter of both Testaments in the original language. Amama advised the use of a short commentary, such as that of Junius, Beza, Piscator or Vatablus. The reader must always have a grammar or dictionary to hand, preferably that of Pagninus or the *Lexicon Pentaglotton* of Schindler. Should the high cost of these two works stand in the way of their purchase, the student could be content with the *Dictionarium* of Buxtorf.[72] Amama emphatically rejected the use of interlinear translations in the learning of Hebrew, but it did in his eyes, play an important part in the daily cursory reading.

In this survey of the study of biblical Hebrew, which clearly goes back to the teaching practice of the universities (in the summary we recognise L'Empereur's textbooks of fifteen years earlier), Amama described the fruit of Hebrew studies since their flowering at the start of the 16th century. The early history of this flowering has often been related, but literature on the study of Hebrew since the middle of the century is lack-

---

[69] *Proverbiorum Arabicorum centuriae duae*. These annotations too have a partly moralistic character, explaining the morality of proverbs.

[70] De Jonge, *Bestudering*, 40-7; "Study", 78.

[71] An analysis of this grammar in Lebram, "Studien".

[72] Prijs no. 193; *Epitome radicum hebraicarum* or *Lexicon hebraicum et chaldaicum* (1607).

ing.[73] The South German and French hebraists of the first half of the 16th century wanted to make Hebrew accessible. For them Hebrew was above all the tongue of the Old Testament and the teaching aids which they produced were intended to put Christians in a position to consult the Old Testament without being dependent on Jews to do so. Their works consisted mainly of aids such as Amama summarised: grammars, dictionaries and interlinear translations. A great variety of motives impelled these 16th century hebraists, who belonged to various confessions. The influence on them of neo-platonist, humanist and polemical tendencies can be demonstrated, but the most important result of their work was a body of aids to the study of biblical Hebrew and the Old Testament. The works of the 16th century hebraists which could be of service for the study of rabbinical literature, stood apart and were only to be rediscovered in the course of the 17th century when the knowledge of rabbinica among Christians became more general. Only through this development were they taken up into the scholarly tradition, thus losing their individual and eccentric character.

The continuation of Amama's *Consilium*, which gives a survey of the aids available for a deeper study of the bible, illustrates this development. In this survey Amama distinguished between various forms of further study. First he mentioned the *"notitia Ebraismi et sacræ Philologiæ"*. Sacred philology consists of an historical and not directly theological understanding of the text of the Old Testament, laying the stress on history and institutions. He advised the use of Münster, Fagius, Galatinus, Mercerus, Drusius, Fullerus, Helwicus, Graserus, Buxtorf, Cunaeus, Bertramus, Caninius, Scaliger (his chronological works and polemic with Serarius) Sigonius and Casaubon (the *anti-Baroniana*). The summary is worth reflection. The authors named by Amama and their works can be divided into a number of groups. A first category is formed by the philological commentaries and annotations on the Old Testament (the works of Münster, Fagius, Mercerus, Drusius, Fuller and Caninius, which are all included in the *Critici Sacri*).[74] A second group of works deals

---

[73] The German hebraists of the beginning of the 16th century have been quite well researched. There are modern biographies of Reuchlin, Münster and Fagius. We are much worse served for studies of the French hebraists associated with the Collège Royal, such as Vatablus, Mercerus and Genebrardus (to name only the most important). Their tradition continued to the end of the 16th century, and it was in it that Scaliger and Drusius, the fathers of the study of Hebrew in the Dutch Republic, were educated. Numerous articles have appeared on Christian hebraists but a more general scheme or interpretation is lacking.

[74] For Caninius: *DBDI* 18, 101-2. Italian humanist who pointed out the Hebrew character of passages in the NT. In the 1550's he published at Paris grammatical works in the field of oriental languages, parts of which were republished in the *Critici Sacri*.

with the history of the state institutions of Israel (Bertramus, Sigonius, Cunaeus) and the chronology of Old Testament history (Scaliger, Helwicus).[75] These two categories make up sacred philology in the stricter sense: the exposition of, and the study of the history behind the sacred text. The polemic of Scaliger and Drusius with Serarius, and Casaubon's attack on Baronius on the other hand refer largely to the history of the Jewish people in New Testament times and later.[76] The continuation of this history until the emergence of the Mishna and the Talmud and the rabbinical commentaries must be the reason why Amama also names the works of Galatinus and Buxtorf. In their writings they give a survey of the Jewish literature after the Old Testament.[77] This later Jewish history and literature were of importance for what Amama called "Ebraismus". Originally, a hebraism was the use of a Hebrew turn of phrase or meaning in the New Testament, which can be illustrated by a reference to the Old Testament or rabbinical literature. For Amama the concept seems to have acquired a wider meaning, and to refer to all aspects of Judaism and rabbinical literature which could be useful for the study of the bible. The close connection which he makes between "Ebraismus" and "sacred philology" is understandable when one realises that the works which serve sacred philology are based mainly on the knowledge of rabbinical literature and Jewish biblical scholarship. For a good grasp of the output of these Christian scholars, a survey of Jewish literature and history was necessary.

The independent consultation of rabbinical literature which was thus regarded as a means and not as an end, did however demand a knowledge of the idiom and the method of reasoning of the rabbis. In the continuation of his *Consilium*, Amama described the teaching aids which were available for such studies. After a brief summary of the introductory works and textbooks for the Masora and the Syriac language,[78] he discussed the way in which a student can master Aramaic and the rabbinical mode of expression. For the Aramaic of the Old Testament and that of the Targumim, he named three kinds of aids, which also played a part in the study of Hebrew: first of all the grammar of Buxtorf I[79] and

---

[75] C. Helvicius (Jöcher II, 1477) 1581-1617, studied at Marburg, professor of theology, oriental languages, Greek at Giessen. Wrote polemical works against the Jews and everything which differed from lutheranism and also works on chronology. C. Graserus (Jöcher II, 1132-3) 1557-1613, taught Hebrew at the gymnasium of Thoren. He published an exposition of Daniel 9 and a history of the great anti-christ.

[76] Lebram, "De Hasidaeis".

[77] See chapter 3.

[78] The *Biblia Regia* and Buxtorf I's works in this field.

[79] Prijs no. 215; *Grammatica Chaldaica* & *Syriaca* (1615).

secondly the dictionaries of Buxtorf II[80] and Schindler. Also important for teaching were editions of an Aramaic text with a parallel translation. Amama advised the student to begin with the Aramaic sections of the Old Testament and then to study the Targumim. He can make use of the bilingual editions by Arias Montanus in the *Biblia Regia*[81] and that by Fagius of the Targum on the Pentateuch.[82] After this survey the *Consilium* proceeds to sketch a programme for the *studium Rabbinicum* and the reading of unvocalised Hebrew.

Amama thought it necessary to begin with the assurance that the reading of the rabbis and of unvocalised Hebrew, contrary to general assumption, is not so difficult. Only a good knowledge of the grammar of Hebrew and a moderate one of Aramaic is necessary. The problems which appear to have been encountered, in view of the small number of aids which Amama could recommend for this study, are understandable. He mentioned Buxtorf's *Introductio ad lectionem Rabbinicam*, an introduction of thirty-five pages, which is included in his Hebrew grammar,[83] and the ninety page *Lexicon Rabbinico-Philosophicum*, which was added to the last edition of Buxtorf's dictionary.[84] Amama also knew of the existence of an Aramaic and rabbinical dictionary by Münster,[85] but had never had a copy in his hands, and in his view Schindler's *Lexicon Pentaglotton* could offer some assistance. The only text edition which Amama was able to name was Mercerus' commentary on the first five minor prophets, which included a translation of the commentaries of David Kimḥi, Ibn Ezra and Rashi.[86] The student had to provide himself with a *Biblia Rabbinica*, since Mercerus' commentary only contained the Latin translation of the commentaries of the three rabbis. Amama advised the student to begin with Kimḥi, then to study Ibn Ezra, and to end with the difficult commentary of Rashi. He concluded this meagre survey with the pro-

---

[80] Prijs no. 226: *Lexicon Chaldaicum* & *Syriacum* (1622).

[81] For a description of this work: Rekers, *Arias Montanus*, 109-10.

[82] The Latin translation of the Targum Onkelos, 1546.

[83] Prijs no. 199; pp. 612-48.

[84] Prijs no. 214; pp. 865-953.

[85] Burmeister, *Münster*, no. 187; *Dictionarium Chaldaicum*, Basle, 1527.

[86] For this edition: Moeckli, *Livres imprimés*, 153. The first edition was printed by Estienne, Geneva, 1583. It appears not to have been a success and was later bound in with the edition of Mercerus' commentary on Genesis (Geneva, 1598). At least the copy in the Leiden University Library (shelf no. 512 A2) contains both works, but is not a privately bound combination. L'Empereur had possessed this commentary from his student days but it cannot be established from his library catalogue, whether the edition of the rabbis on the minor prophets was also included in it. At any rate, it appears from Chevallier's foreword that Mercerus' work was intended for a teaching book: "Rabbinorum autem scholia (...) integrum & ad verbum interpretata exhibuit, viam ad intelligenda alia eorum scripta ejusdem generis sternens".

mise that if God should grant him life and time, he would publish works for this part of Hebrew studies.

It appears from the survey in the *Consilium* that Amama, when he spoke of rabbinical studies, was thinking above all of the commentaries of the mediaeval rabbis on the Old Testament. Yet the work which Cocceius published on Amama's initiative, the edition and translation of *Sanhedrin* and *Makkot*, helped to unlock a far wider tract of Jewish literature, the Talmudic literature of the Mishna and Gemara. This expansion of Hebrew studies to cover the whole of Jewish literature, is a characteristic of 17th century research. Although Amama's survey of 1625 would suggest otherwise, the following century, until the decline of rabbinical studies around 1725, was to experience a flowering of interest in rabbinical literature. Amama's summary of the possible aids was incomplete. When in 1702 Adriaan Reeland published his *Analecta Rabbinica*, he was able, from the self-consciousness of a long scholarly tradition, to mention various technical aids and parallel translations, to which Amama could have had access,[87] and even this survey was not complete.[88] But the books which Reeland named had been rediscovered in the course of the flowering of rabbinical studies and because of their rarity or their obscurity they had played no part in its beginning. Rabbinica probably did not form a part of Amama's university teaching programme. In looking for teaching material he would in that case have chanced upon Coddaeus' bilingual edition of Mercerus' translation of the commentaries of the three rabbis on Hosea, of 1621.[89]

Amama's survey illustrates the dominant position which was held in Hebrew studies by the Buxtorfs of Basle.[90] Johann Buxtorf I, the father (1564-1629) was born at Basle, studied under Olevanius and Piscator at Herborn, and learned Hebrew from the latter. After a period at

---

[87] In his *Analecta*, which were intended for teaching rabbinica, Reeland reissued Genebrardus' *Isagoge ad legenda & intelligenda Hebraeorum & Orientalium sine punctis scripta*, Parisiis 1587, and his *Meditationes et tabulae rabbinicae*. In his extensive foreword Reeland also gave a survey of all the translated works (**5ff.) which were useful for the study. He names Fagius' translation of the commentary of David Kimḥi on ten psalms (which he also republished), Genebrardus' translation of rabbinical commentaries on Joel and the Song of Songs, and other useful works by him. He would have been thinking of his translation of *Seder Olam Rabbah* and *Zuta*, Parisiis 1578. He also names A. Pontanus and the works of Mercerus. Cf. Wolfius, *Bibliotheca hebraea* II, 591-3; "Index eorum, qui ad Rabbinorum lectionem expeditius instituendam vel praeceptis, vel aliis praesidiis viam muniverunt", in which mainly teaching works are listed.

[88] L'Empereur owned Giggeo's translation of three rabbinical commentaries on Proverbs, Milan 1620, which is not mentioned in any of the surveys.

[89] Fuks, no. 32.

[90] There is no good biography of the Buxtorfs. For Buxtorf I: Tossanus, "Oratio"; Buxtorf-Falkeissen, *Johannes Buxtorf Vater*; Kautzsch, *Buxtorf der Aeltere*. For Buxtorf II: Schnederman, *Controverse*; Staehelin, "Briefwechsel"; Muller, "Debate".

Heidelberg and a tour of the universities of Switzerland, where he became acquainted with Beza and Grynaeus, he was appointed professor of Hebrew at Basle in 1591. He perfected his knowledge of Hebrew by following the teaching of Jews, whom he received in his house. His good personal relationship with these teachers was a source of amazement to Scaliger who did not understand that the Jews so appreciated Buxtorf, who had sharply attacked them in his *Synagoga Judaica*.[91] Just as with Elias Levita and Menasseh Ben Israel the recognition which the distinguished scholar gave them will have played some part here. In any case, Buxtorf's relationship to his Jewish informants was so close that in the summer of 1619 a circumcision took place in his house. Buxtorf was given a fine for this, the Jews received a few days imprisonment.[92] His works brought the knowledge of Hebrew on to a higher level and expanded it to the whole of Jewish literature. He described the Masora, provided a survey of rabbinical literature, published some introductory works for its study and arranged the publication of a *Biblia Rabbinica*, an edition of the Hebrew text of the Old Testament, with commentaries by mediaeval rabbis and targumim, which was intended both for a Jewish and a Christian public.[93] His son, Johann Buxtorf II, taught Hebrew by his father, and a university trained theologian, succeeded him in 1629. He arranged the edition of various works left in MS. by his father such as a concordance and a great dictionary to the Talmud.[94]

Remarkably enough the Buxtorfs, who made available so many aids to the study of rabbinica, did not publish any bilingual editions of rabbinical texts. In 1629 Buxtorf II issued a translation of Maimonides' philosophical defence of Judaism, the *Moreh Nevukhim*. In spite of the profession in the title and the foreword that this edition was intended to serve the study of the Hebrew language, he omitted a parallel Hebrew text, to the great displeasure of a number of correspondents.[95] The work gives the impression that he was interested above all in Maimonides' elegant manner of explaining the anthropomorphisms and other apparent

---

[91] *Sec Scal*, 248-9.

[92] Buxtorf-Falkeissen, *Johannes Buxtorf Vater,* 32.

[93] Prijs no. 219; *Biblia rabbinica* 1618-9. For the characteristics which were the result of the two-fold public to which they were addressed, see Prijs, *Hebräische Drucke*, 336.

[94] Prijs no. 237; *Lexicon Chaldaicum, Talmudicum et Rabbinicum* (1639).

[95] Prijs no. 231. E.g. Heinsius to Buxtorf II, 17.10.1629; J. J. Buxtorf, *Catalecta*, 467-70. See also note 96. The work shows a great interest in Maimonides' approach to the bible. Besides the translation Buxtorf's main work on the edition was to furnish a very detailed index to biblical passages. As he states in the foreword, he saw Maimonides' exposition and its nature, as the greatest attraction of the book: *Doctor Perplexorum*, (2) ff. So far as the method of argument is concerned, Buxtorf remarks that Maimonides does not dispute in the talmudic fashion but "ex Scriptura ipsa, Philosophia, & sana ratione".

imperfections of the Old Testament. Buxtorf II continued to take an interest in such Jewish defences of the revelatory character of the Old Testament. His edition of Jehuda ha-Levi's *Kuzari*, another apologetic work produced by Spanish Judaism also derived from this interest.[96] Although the Buxtorfs themselves did not publish any, bilingual editions of rabbinical works were important in the teaching of rabbinica at Basle. In a fascinating *Epistola de recte instituendo studio Rabbinico*, written about 1635, Johann Buxtorf II offered a survey of the teaching he gave.[97]

Like Amama, Buxtorf emphasised thorough previous knowledge of the grammar and texts of biblical Hebrew. The student of rabbinical literature must begin with a simple unvocalised text, such as a commentary of Kimḥi, of which he has a Latin translation at his disposal. With the aid of the translation he must vocalise the Hebrew text. Each day he is to submit three or four lines to his teacher, who improves his vocalisation and provides it with a commentary. Once he has thus enlarged his vocabulary, his knowledge of abbreviations and grammar, the following phase of teaching begins. The pupil must read aloud and clearly, a passage from an unvocalised text prepared by him, during which he may consult the Latin translation. The following phases consist of successively leaving out the preparation and the reference to the translation during the reading aloud. Buxtorf also mentioned Mercerus' translation of the rabbis and the minor prophets, as the only students' book which can be used for this teaching. At the end of the teaching of rabbinical commentaries on the Old Testament Buxtorf marked a clear caesura. For a theologian it is, in his eyes, enough to have acquired this ability. He can even be content with a lower level, and only needs to be in a position to consult the Jewish commentaries published by Buxtorf I in the *Biblia Rabbinica*.

Only when the student himself expresses a desire can the teaching be extended to the "more hidden books of the Jews" and the Talmud itself. In that case, the pupil must first attain a good knowledge of the dialects of Aramaic. Here Buxtorf listed the aids to study which we know from Amama's *Consilium*. But his summary continues:[98]

---

[96] Prijs no. 266. *Liber Cosri* (Basileae 1660). This edition does give a Hebrew text with parallel translation and brief notes. In the praefatio Buxtorf II mentions that many had regretted that he had not given a Hebrew text in the *Doctor Perplexorum*.

[97] Published in *Museum Helveticum ad juvandas literas in publicos usus apertum* VIII, Turici 1748, 122-7. It can be approximately dated because there are references to the dictionary to the Talmud which is to appear shortly (see note 94).

[98] "Deinde magnum sunt subsidium, omnes illi libri, qui ex Hebraea in Latinam Linguam sunt translati: ex illorum enim collatione mirum quantum quis proficiat. Hos diligenter sibi comparare debet studiosus Rabbinismi".

"Further, all the books translated from Hebrew into Latin are of great assistance. For through the comparison of them (i.e. of the Hebrew with the Latin text) one makes great progress. The student of Rabbinica must collect such books eagerly."

Amama could not have made such a remark in 1625. Insofar as earlier translations of rabbinical literature were known at that time, they were difficult to obtain.[99] Only after 1630 did there appear, especially in the Republic, translations of Mishna tractates, of Jewish historical works and of treatises by Maimonides and Abrabanel. Many of these translations were the work of authors who had been L'Empereur's pupils for a time, and they will be discussed in the following chapter, in which his teaching will be described. But almost all the works of L'Empereur belong to the aids to the study of rabbinica, so highly praised by Buxtorf. Even so, he was not the first scholar from the Republic to issue such a work. The edition of *Sanhedrin* and *Makkot* by Cocceius in 1629 preceded his edition of *Middot* by a year. Because this edition offers the possibility of a comparison with L'Empereur's work, we shall first discuss this work of Cocceius.

The edition is a remarkable one, with a complicated variety of intentions expressed in the forewords and a much more sober practice in the book itself. It begins with a dedication to the city magistracy of Bremen, Cocceius' native town. In this dedication, the young, twenty-six year old Coch explained how he had come to study rabbinical literature better to understand the Word of God. For Cocceius, the disciple of Ames and Amama, this study is in the service of the practice of the church. A thorough knowledge of the bible is in his opinion necessary for the preacher who wishes to build up the living personal faith and piety of his congregation. His edition is intended to be of assistance to others who wish to study rabbinical literature. The city magistracy of Bremen, which had earlier for the sake of Cocceius' studies made an exception to the rule that Jews might not enter the city, were already aware of Cocceius' rabbinical studies.[100] The choice of the recipient of this dedication had been, as we have already seen,[101] carefully considered by Amama and Martinius, Cocceius' previous teacher at Bremen, with an eye to the future appointment of the young student. The same goal was served by a letter

---

[99] What Reeland says in his *Analecta Rabbinica* ***2 about his copy of Fagius' edition, published at Isny, of the text and translation of Kimhi's commentary on the Psalms, is characteristic: the copy had belonged to Gomarus, Cocceius and Leidekker, and was now in his possession. He received Genebrardus' works from van Til.
[100] Cf. the life of Cocceius by his son: Cocceius, *Opera Omnia* I, praefatio **2b.
[101] Chap. 3, note 103.

from Amama to Martinius, published in the book, in which he described
the importance of the edition and Cocceius' achievements. The letter
which is dated 3 August 1629, is the last public statement by Amama and
shows his humanist eschatology in a completed form:[102]

> "On his ( = Cocceius's) study I can briefly observe that he has been aroused
> by God to bring the knowledge of the eastern tongues to a higher level, and
> to pave our way to the secret holy places of the Jews. Not one Christian has
> ever publicly achieved so much in the field of the Talmud as he has in this
> most learned work, of which only the best scholars can judge. Through his
> example, he will arouse others to apply themselves to the same sort of
> research. Perhaps the time has already dawned, which God has determined
> for the conversion of the Jews. I dare to pledge myself, that an honourable
> appointment at one or other Academy will not be denied him, once this
> erudite study comes into the hands of the learned world.
> But if Barbarism and unbridled licence gain the upper hand in these ter-
> ritories, then I hope that God will rouse pious and great souls (and verily,
> He has already begun) which will set up new schools and colleges in the far-
> thest west and the New World, more inclined to this sort of study and spirit.
> I myself prostrate myself humbly before God, when I consider the
> marvellous and unceasing guidance of the just God over the study of letters,
> since the Gospel was again preached and study was re-established. I pray
> Him that the light which has been lit among us shall not only not dwindle
> but even increase. But this is part of another argument."

This is typical Amama. The remarkable mention of the already centuries
old idea of a *translatio imperii et studii*, an ever westward shift of world
domination and culture,[103] will have been suggested to him by Ames'
intended departure for New England. Others too in this time were aware
of the importance of the colonisation of North America.[104] The exceptionally generous praise of Cocceius is intended to assure his appointment. For the same reason, Amama is careful to say nothing of his own
initiative behind the edition, but it is obvious that his eschatological
expectation of the conversion of the Jews was responsible for the choice
of the tractate *Sanhedrin*. His *Consilium*, in which he announced the
publication of a work in the field of rabbinica, ended with the same
expectation, which was even described there as the most important
reason for the study of Aramaic and rabbinica. With the help of rabbinical literature the Jews could be refuted and converted, and:[105]

---

[102] Chap. 3, note 80.

[103] Chenu, *La théologie au douzième siècle*, 79-80.

[104] E.g. Polyander who in his *Grondt onser salicheyt* (Leiden 1630), 326, says that servants of the Word "are now about to proclaim the Evangelium Christi in America, the
fourth and last part of the world" (cited in de Jonge, *Bestudering*, 17, note 21).

[105] Amama, *Coronis*: "Ex omnibus ultimi judicii prognosticis solam & unam
Iudaeorum conversionem restare, constans & fere unanimis Theologorum opinio est. Et
certe fundamentum habet in cap. ad Romanos xi."

"that the conversion of the Jews is the sole and only one still lacking, of the signs which presage the Last Judgment is the constant and almost general opinion of the theologians. And this idea can certainly appeal to Romans 11 for support."

Now it is remarkable that Cocceius, who in the course of his life was to adhere to much more elaborate millennarian views—as early as 1633 he regarded the intended publication by Johann Buxtorf II of his father's dictionary to the Talmud, as a possible sign of the end of the world, in terms which recall the letter of Amama cited above[106]—neither in the foreword nor in the notes to his edition gave any sign of expecting the imminent conversion of the Jews. In the foreword he described in traditional terms the usefulness of rabbinical literature for a better knowledge of Hebrew and a good understanding of the law of Moses. Equally traditionally, he referred to the necessity to refute the Jews from their own writings. But he saw the insight into the blinding of the Jews, the result of such a refutation, in terms which recall Buxtorf, as a warning to, and an arousing of the Christians. How terrible is the judgment of God which is expressed in this blindness:[107]

"I could go into much more detail here, if I should wish to show in how many ways we must fear such shadows, if they had not long covered our eyes in very many important matters."

Naturally Cocceius also emphasised the importance of rabbinical literature for the exposition of the background to the New Testament. But the greatest part of his foreword is taken up by what he presents, with some considerable enthusiasm, as a new argument for the use of rabbinical literature. The argument consists of a linguistic treatment of the nature of New Testament Greek. This Greek is, according to Cocceius, characterised by a profusion of semitisms. It is influenced by Hebrew. Now this aspect of the argument is not new—we have met it above as a rather worn weapon from the arsenal of arguments for the usefulness of Hebrew—but what is original is the great stress which Cocceius places on the fact that the Hebrew spoken in the synagogue at the time of Christ was not biblical Hebrew, but the language preserved in the Mishna. The long discussion of this thesis in the foreword was highly relevant. Cocceius took up a position diametrically opposed to the book, published in the same year, of Sebastian Pfochen, his fellow-student and competitor from Franeker, in which the latter had argued that the Greek of the New

---

[106] Cocceius to Buxtorf II, 26.8.1633; Cocceius, *Opera* VIII, 79.
[107] Cocceius, *Sanhedrin*, ****a.

Testament was a pure classical Greek.[108] This thesis, which was to introduce a scholarly debate lasting more than a century, was for the hebraists
and humanists of the Republic, who saw it as a threat to a venerable
scholarly tradition, a reason for unusual excitement.[109] As we shall see
below, L'Empereur also took up a position in this debate. Of course the
very elaborate argument of Cocceius was not responsible for his undertaking the edition. Probably he had already begun to print the work when
Pfochen's publication appeared. In the edition itself one can find nothing
of the linguistic use of Mishna Hebrew advised by Cocceius, unlike the
traditonal explanation of the background of the New Testament.

The book, published in quarto, consists of two parts. The first 125
pages give the complete Mishna of *Sanhedrin* and *Makkot*. Each separate
mishna is printed in Hebrew with a parallel Latin translation in the next
column. The translations are separated by notes. A remarkable feature
of the edition is that Cocceius has used small circles in the Hebrew text
to indicate those views in the Mishna (which sometimes include reports
of discussions without a decision between the conflicting opinions) which
are valid *halakhah*. For this he used a Jewish work which gave such a
survey, the *Kaf Naḥat*.[110] Although L'Empereur also published a rabbinical work which could be used, inter alia, for such a purpose, such an
interest in Judaism as a living legal system was rather uncommon among
Christian hebraists. In his notes Cocceius made no use of the *Kaf Naḥat*.
Pages 126-436 give extracts from the Gemara on both tractates, in the
same form as the edition of the Mishna text. The selection which was
made points, as does the choice of the tractates themselves, to Amama's
original interest in the refutation and conversion of the Jews. Almost half
of the chosen fragments, extending over about 125 pages, derive from the
Gemara on Sanhedrin 11, and the majority of the citations deal with the
Messiah.

Yet Cocceius' notes are largely of a linguistic and explanatory nature.
There is no reason to doubt his own verdict on the intention behind the
edition, as he expressed it in a letter to Heringius in March 1630:[111]

> "Now I had only this as my intention, that an example of the Talmudic
> tractates with a Latin translation should exist, and that, if there were any
> problem in the field of language or history in the text, which was not easily
> solved with the aid of the usual dictionaries and the authors I have read,
> that should be illustrated from the rabbis."

---

[108] S. Pfochen, *Diatribe de linguae Graecae puritate*, Amsterdam 1629. For this debate cf.
Ros, *Bijbelgrieksch*, 12 ff.; de Jonge, *Bestudering*, 35-7; further literature, *ibid.*, note 35.
[109] AG, Heinsius to Amama, 24.3.1629.
[110] Cocceius, *Sanhedrin*, ****4b.
[111] Cocceius to J. Heringius, March 1630; Cocceius, *Opera ANEKDOTA* II, 621-2. For
Cocceius' technical knowledge; Katchen, *Christian Hebraists* 70-4.

For such explanations Cocceius made use above all of Maimonides, both his commentary on the Mishna and his *Mishneh Torah*. There are two longer notes which deserve separate treatment, because they to some extent deviate from the simple and explanatory character which typifies the others.

At *BSanh* 38b, Cocceius inserted as a note a long excursus which probably derived largely from a theological disputation.[112] The excursus refers to a pronouncement in the Talmud that every verse of scripture which the heretics misuse has in its near vicinity an answer to their incorrect interpretation. As examples, some Old Testament texts are cited, which seem to suggest a plurality in God. In the note Cocceius argued that such a method of disputing against the Christians is futile because they recognise that God is in a certain sense one. He continued by stating that there are also some so-called Christians who deny the Trinity: the socinians. The fifteen-page note contains a largely philosophical, systematic theological refutation of this heresy. Cocceius also attacks Socinus' exegesis of Gen. 1:26 and 11:7, in which the latter had denied, in a rather unfortunate way, that these verses spoke of plurality in God. But a refutation of the Jews, except for one passing remark,[113] is not attempted. The relevance of the polemic against the socinians at the end of the 1620's has been discussed above. In L'Empereur too, one can find such attacks on the socinians occasioned by Jewish texts.

Cocceius paused to go into detail in a group of shorter notes on *BSanh* 98a-99a.[114] The discussions in this section of the Gemara deal with the Messiah, but Cocceius consciously discussed these views in his notes as a hebraist. Thus he concluded a survey of the various names of the Messiah with the words: "how much can be done with these proof passages against the Jews, is something we leave to the theologians."[115] Polemic is virtually absent from the notes and a discussion with Judaism can only be found on two points. Cocceius places great emphasis on the fact that the Jews do not distinguish between the coming of the Messiah in humility and that in glory. The second point demands some explanation. At Franeker, Cocceius had had access to the Basle edition of the Talmud. This edition was rather injudiciously censored, because the printer had been eager to obtain a papal approval and an imperial

---

[112] *Sanhedrin*, 216-31 gives long citations from Socinus; and cf. for example the characteristic "Resp." (page 230).

[113] For this he used the cabbalistic work *Scepha Tal* (p. 219), recently published by Sheftel Horowitz, and cited its foreword to show that the Jews too recognise a plurality in God.

[114] *Sanhedrin*, 363-87.

[115] "Quantum his testimoniis adversus Judaeos effici possit, Theologi viderint" (*Sanhedrin*, 379).

privilege.[116] All passages which were considered to concern Christ or Christianity, were omitted. Cocceius, who deplored this censorship, and wished to have a Bomberg edition at his disposal, had recourse to Galatinus' *De arcanis catholicæ veritatis* in order to avoid it. Galatinus, who in this work adopted a stance in the conflict round Reuchlin and the Talmud, cited some passages which the opponents of the Talmud believed to slander Christ. He argued that they do not refer to Christ, but to another Jesus.[117] Cocceius did not follow Galatinus in this interpretation. He regarded the texts as anti-Christian polemic and provided them with a refutation, rather moderate in its tone. The debate on the question whether Christ appeared in the Talmud was to last throughout the whole of the 17th century.[118] Thus Cocceius in his method of publishing the two Mishna tractates appears not to have answered Amama's express intention to refute and convert the Jews. The theological parts of his commentary concern internal Christian disputes and a single refutation, which, in view of his efforts to print the complete text, was necessary.

We have discussed this edition in such detail in order to show the problems which arise in investigating the motives behind these editions of rabbinical texts. Even in the first such edition we are dealing with motives of several persons, of various natures, as they appear in the choice of the subject of the edition, the reaction expected from the readers, and the notes in the text. Similar problems meet us in dealing with the works of L'Empereur.

L'Empereur's first publication was his edition of the tractate *Middot*. This work occupies a special place in the Mishna. It does not contain any legal rules, but is a description of the form and dimensions of the Temple. Since as such it could not form an occasion for further discussion, a Gemara on it is absent from both the Palestinian and the Babylonian Talmud. In the dedication to the States of Holland, L'Empereur expressed his pride that he was the first to bring this work to light. After the long theological-political argument which we have discussed in the first section of this chapter, he stated the reason which had led him to publish the tractate:[119]

---

[116] Prijs, no. 124; (1578-80). For a detailed description of this censorship: Prijs, *Hebräische Drucke*, 175-82.

[117] Galatinus, *De Arcanis*, 14 ff.

[118] This was an extensive debate in the 17th century as is still the case today.

[119] *Middot*, \*\*2b. Cocceius was expecting this work as early as October 1629. Cocceius, *Opera Omnia* XI, 620.

"to which the most brilliant lights of your Academy often encouraged and aroused me, among them the noble and exalted Daniel Heinsius. For several centuries there has been no one with a greater intellect, a sharper judgment, a more passionate zeal for piety and virtue, and a more abundant learning. I still recall that while I was living in the outer provinces, I heard that your University was much frequented for his sake. As I said, he has never ceased to urge me to publish certain tractates from the Talmud in Latin and to provide them with notes and commentaries. Since he himself is master of all sciences and disciplines, and therefore the best knows what is and what is not useful to publish, (for who knows that except the man who is in a position to compare all disciplines among themselves?) I have heartily agreed to publish an example from that work."

The second light of the Academy who had stimulated him to publication, Gerardus Johannes Vossius, was praised in rather less exaggerated terms. The late humanists were professional flatterers, and exploited all the wealth of possibilities which Latin offers for this activity. But even by the standards of the time, L'Empereur's eulogy is somewhat exceptional. It may be repaying the debt in which L'Empereur thought that he stood to Heinsius because of his appointment. It is also possible that he thought he would need him in the future. At any rate, it is a tribute to the position which Heinsius occupied in the University of Leiden.

Daniel Heinsius, the son of immigrants from Ghent, was at the zenith of his fame in these years, immediately before the arrival in Leiden of his great rival Salmasius.[120] A pupil of Scaliger, he had been attached to the University of Leiden since his youth, and saw himself as the successor of his teacher. There is no reason to doubt Heinsius' involvement in the edition of *Middot*, because of the *topos*-like character of L'Empereur's reference to his encouragement by friends. His all-pervading interest extended to the philological exegesis of the New Testament, a tradition of scholarship in the Republic which went back to Scaliger and Drusius. Heinsius was in a position to put into practice his ideas on which developments in the study of literature could be of service to such an exegesis of the bible. Thus he stimulated de Dieu in his study of Syriac and was involved, in his capacity as a scholarly advisor to the Elzeviers, in the publication of works in the field of biblical exegesis.[121] One of the characteristics of this humanist biblical scholarship was the use of rabbinical literature to clarify the background to the New Testament.[122]

---

[120] Sellin, *Heinsius*, 38. After his appointment as historiographer to the States of Holland, he had the same salary as Scaliger. Salmasius was appointed in 1631.

[121] *BL* 2, 167 ff. His involvement with Elzevier: Sellin, *Heinsius*, 34. The involvement was generally known at the time: de Jonge, "Study", 80; n. 302, n. 330.

[122] *Sec Scal*, 453: "lisez les bons Auteurs, la Metamorphose d'Ovide, le Thalmud, illa sunt necessaria ad Biblia." More generally: de Jonge, *Bestudering*, 41-7.

Heinsius was convinced of the usefulness of a good knowledge of this literature. Since, as we have seen, such knowledge could only be acquired with difficulty, he sought contact with and help from specialists and encouraged bilingual editions. He was one of the correspondents of the young Buxtorf, who lamented the absence of Hebrew texts in the latter's translation of Maimonides' *Moreh Nevukhim*. While there was still talk of an appointment of Amama as successor to Erpenius, he saw one of the great advantages of Amama's coming to Leiden in the aid which he would be able to give him in his work on the exegesis of the New Testament.[123] As we shall see in the next section, Heinsius in the thirties was to make such a use of L'Empereur's talents in the edition of his great commentary on the New Testament, the *Exercitationes Sacræ*. We know that L'Empereur and Heinsius were in close contact around 1630[124] and the method of publication of *Middot* suggests the interest which Heinsius took in rabbinical literature.

L'Empereur's edition is intended to be of service to biblical exegesis and the study of rabbinical literature. The form of the work is that of Cocceius' edition of *Sanhedrin* and *Makkot*, but L'Empereur's edition is also provided with an extensive apparatus of indices. The last fifteen pages of the almost two hundred which make up the work, contain indices to subjects, biblical passages and Hebrew words. The notes to the edition are largely of an explanatory nature and regularly include references to, or explanations of, passages in the Old and New Testaments. For the notes L'Empereur used the four commentaries on the tractate which he found in his editions of the Talmud and the Mishna. These were Rashi, his pupil Shemaiah, Maimonides and Obadiah of Bertinoro. He also referred to the dictionary *Arukh*, of Rabbi Nathan.[125] All in all, the work is an impressive witness of the vigour of humanism at the University of Leiden. In only a few places did L'Empereur follow his own bent and education, and begin a theological discussion. But these deviations are incidental. *Middot* is not one of the Mishna tractates which lends itself to classical polemic against Judaism. The work with which L'Empereur had first concerned himself, the commentary of Joseph ibn Yaḥya on Daniel, was suited to this, and had been chosen by him for this very reason. But this commentary was only to be published in 1633, at the insistence of a printer, as we shall see.[126] It is

---

[123] AG, Heinsius to Amama, 5.7.1627.

[124] L'Empereur had received a book each year from Heinsus since his arrival.

[125] Cf. *Middot*, 66 where he gives a summary of all the literature he had consulted on a knotty problem. Shemayah of Troyes (11th century) was one of the most faithful disciples of Rashi. Only his commentaries on Middot and Tamid have been preserved, but they have been included in all the editions of the Talmud since 1522 (*EJ*, 14, 1374-5).

[126] See the analysis of this work below (5.3).

more than probable that L'Empereur's choice of the form and content of his edition was based on the inspiration of Heinsius.

L'Empereur's edition of *Bava Kamma*, which appeared in 1637, is of the same character. *Bava Kamma* is the first of a trio of Mishna tractates which deal with civil law. The first discusses the compensation which must be given for various forms of damage. Since it is a purely legal work, there is a Gemara on it in each of the Talmudim. L'Empereur's edition takes the same form as his edition of *Middot* and also has copious indices. In the foreword, a dedication to Caspar Vosbergen, L'Empereur describes the work as an explanation of the Law of Moses. The basis of the development of the Law in the Mishna is formed by the Pentateuch. For that reason, according to L'Empereur, the tractate is of great importance for Old Testament exegesis. He lays by far the greatest emphasis, in a long excursus, on its interest for the exegesis of the New Testament. In this excursus he took up a position in the debate on the purity of the Greek of the New Testament. Like Cocceius and Heinsius he accepted that this Greek was not pure, and was characterised by semitisms. A knowledge of the idiom of the Talmud was therefore necessary for a knowledge of New Testament Greek.[127] He has an interesting sociological-historical theory to offer on the origin of this type of Greek. After the conquests of Alexander, the new rulers forced their subjects in the east to speak Greek. But the subject peoples penetrated the language with their own ways of speech and meanings.[128]

As with Cocceius, the exegetical practice in the notes on the text corresponds little with the declaration on the usefulness of rabbinica. The notes are of the same nature as those on *Middot*. They explain the rabbinical idiom and mode of argument and contain few remarks which concern the exegesis of the bible. Since *Bava Kamma* was the last and largest work of L'Empereur,[129] we can use it to determine the degree of knowledge of rabbinical literature which he attained. The translation of the Mishna text is excellent.[130] In the notes he cites, on almost all the mishnayot, the relevant Gemara of the Babylonian Talmud. For the understanding of these talmudic passages he used Rashi's commentary, which is mentioned twenty-seven times. He also cites from about fifteen other Talmud tractates, and sometimes from the Palestinian Talmud. In addition he frequently mentions the commentaries of Maimonides and

---

[127] *Bava Kamma*, praefatio.

[128] For a discussion of the place which L'Empereur here holds in the debate on the purity of Greek: de Jonge, *Bestudering*, 36-7.

[129] He had already been working on this in 1633; thus he cites in *ItinBen* (**8a) Maimonides' commentary on *Bava Kamma*.

[130] Only a single error is to be found, in the translation of BK iv, 5 (*Bava Kamma*, 80).

Bertinoro on the Mishna, twenty-two and fourteen times respectively. Besides this use of his editions of Talmud and Mishna and the aids to study included in them, he also worked with the systematic codifications of the Jewish Law which he possessed. By far the most frequently cited work in *Bava Kamma*, with more than fifty references, is the *Mishneh Torah* of Maimonides. The emphasis is on the section which deals with the civil laws.[131] He made use also of the *Ḥoshen Mishpat*, the fourth part of Jacob ben Asher's *Sefer ha-Turim*, which had been put at his disposal by Abraham Heidanus,[132] and of Moses of Coucy's *Sefer Mitzvot Gadol*. Like Selden L'Empereur will have found his references to other Talmud tractates by working back from the commentaries on Maimonides' *Mishneh Torah*, which attempt to give the sources for his decisions, and by consulting the other codes in a similar way.[133] L'Empereur also used the rabbinical commentaries on the biblical texts to which *Bava Kamma* refers. In the context of his comparison of the justice of the Jewish law with that of the Roman, which he undertook in his edition and which forms the subject of the fourth section of this chapter, he mentioned the *Kaf Naḥat*. All in all, even when one takes into account that he was probably assisted by a Jewish teacher in the study of the work, it is a proof that so far as concerned his capacity to use the Jewish aids which were available for an understanding of talmudic literature, L'Empereur had reached the level of the best hebraists of his time.

The most truly introductory work to the talmudic literature which L'Empereur published was his edition of *Halikhot Olam*. This rabbinical work, on which he was already occupied in 1632,[134] is a genuine introduction to the Talmud. It gives a survey of the content and the various rabbis in the Gemara, explains the formulas used in the Mishna and Gemara and the various methods of interpreting the bible, and contains a summary of the ways of determining the outcome of unresolved discussions in the Talmud.[135] L'Empereur's edition consists of a translation only without notes, but it has the most copious indices, especially of rabbinical modes of expression, of all his works. It is provided with a dedication and an introduction, in which he sets out his opinion on the importance of the knowledge of rabbinical literature. The typographical quality of the edition is the highest of all his works. Until the end of the 17th cen-

---

[131] *Mishneh Torah*, book XI: "Sefer Nezikin", esp. pp. 1-3.
[132] *Bava Kamma*, 166.
[133] Cf. Herzog, "Selden", 242-4.
[134] He already cites it in *ComJes*, 53.
[135] A good survey of *HalOl*: Wolfius, *Bibliotheca hebraea* II, 700-2. Wolfius points out that paragraph 4.4 is missing from L'Empereur's edition. This part deals with the allegorical exposition of the bible. For its author, Jeshua ben Joseph ha-Levi (a 15th century Spanish Jew): *EJ* 10, 3.

tury, his edition of *Halikhot Olam* was to remain the only introductory work for the study of the Talmud.[136]

The pride and the highly developed self-consciousness manifested in the dedication to the Mayors and Curators of the University of Leiden are therefore understandable. In the dedication L'Empereur thanked the college for his appointment as *Professor Controversiarum Judaicarum*. As in his edition of *Middot*, he linked this foreword with a paternalistic, anti-liberal concept of the state, in order to defend the true doctrine.[137] He stressed the usefulness of the publication of such a work as *Halikhot Olam*, by describing the importance of talmudic literature for the polemic against Judaism. The older Jewish authors, who are to be found in works which had hitherto been inaccessible, are according to L'Empereur fully in agreement with the Christians against the modern Jews. This view, which rests on mediaeval catholic apologetic, was in fact at the heart of L'Empereur's polemic, as will be shown in the fourth section of this chapter.

In the foreword L'Empereur also described the usefulness of a knowledge of rabbinical literature in another way. It can be helpful for the exegesis of the bible. As his elaboration of this argument makes clear, L'Empereur is here referring to a theological method of exegesis. Rabbinical literature must be used for the exegesis of those passages which are crucial for theological attack on Judaism, especially the Old Testament citations in the New Testament and the christologically interpreted passages in the Old. L'Empereur goes on to summarise a number of Christian dogmas, such as original sin, and the necessity of divine reconciliation, which play a role in this polemic. Finally, rabbinical literature can be useful in what L'Empereur regards as an important duty of the exegete, the removal of apparent contradictions in the Old Testament, above all in the field of chronology. The use of rabbinical literature for an understanding of customs and institutions of biblical times is of only slight importance in this survey. This self-conscious introduction to *Halikhot Olam* gives the impression that it reflects L'Empereur's own views on the use of rabbinical literature. He had in mind above all the theological exegesis of the bible and the refutation of the doctrine of Judaism. In the last two sections of this chapter, both these aspects of the use of rabbinica will be analysed. In doing so we will describe L'Empereur's involvement in the humanistic biblical exegesis of his own

---

[136] Carpzov calls it the only introductory work in his introduction to Martini's *Pugio Fidei* of 1687 (p. 79). Wolfius, *Bibliotheca hebraea* II, 991 gives some similar works but they all date from around 1700.

[137] *HalOl*, *4a. For his self-awareness: *HalOl*, *****3a: "Hactenus ad Talmudica studia defuit introductio: eam ut haberes allaboror".

day and his own exposition, and investigate the derivation and originality of his polemic against Judaism.

The scope of the following description of the various ways in which one could make use of rabbinical literature, must not cause us to forget that L'Empereur's work consisted mainly of making accessible the means to these ends. That is evident above all from the characteristic bilingual form of his editions. In his editon of *Halikhot Olam*, he took care that his translation corresponded exactly with the Hebrew text.[138] This form goes a long way to explain the moderation which L'Empereur practised and the literary character of the editions. L'Empereur himself regarded his work first and foremost as the provision of practice material for study in the rabbinica, as he wrote in a letter to Barbio:[139]

> ''Finally he (the student) ought to read accurately translated authors, such as those of whom I have published many with the requisite notes (...) Since not so many rabbinica have been translated and even fewer talmudica, the student must acquire all the editions to arrive at a better knowledge. Mercerus translated the rabbis on the minor prophets. Cocceius translated Sanhedrin and Makkot. Gerson, a converted Jew, has earlier translated the Babylonian Gemara of Sanhedrin into German. I myself have translated Yaḥya on Daniel, Benjamin's Travel Narrative, the Halikhot Olam, the codex Middot and the first codex of Nezikim. I have also translated many other works and furnished them with a commentary, but they have not yet been published.''

L'Empereur's self-esteem in this letter accords with the further 17th century scholarly development of rabbinica, which was to reach its greatest flowering in the second half of the century. Bilingual editions were a characteristic genre in this scholarly tradition, and L'Empereur was the first Christian scholar to produce them in large numbers. But that did not mean that he was the initiator or the dominant figure in this development. In our discussion of these works in this section we have already seen how complicated is the question of the motives of just a few Christian hebraists, who lived in the same country at the same time. The roots of the study of rabbinica were very various, and when this tradition attained an awareness of itself in the work of some of the Christian hebraists at the end of the century, they could find their precursors as early as the 16th century, and the beginning of the flowering of the *eruditio hebraica*. The unity of this tradition was based on its characteristic works and the public that was interested in it.

---

[138] *HalOl*, *****1b, ''Id operam dedi, ut omnia perspecue redderem: qua de causa, licet ubique vocibus religiose adhaererem''.
[139] See Appendix VI.

L'Empereur's oeuvre had features which caused it to meet the taste of this public in the second half of the century, and which were responsible for various republications of parts of his work. These characteristics were not those which had won him recognition within the Republic of Letters. The survey in this section explains the short time which was necessary for this recognition. The majority of editions of rabbinical texts which appeared in the 1630's, came from L'Empereur, and a man like Grotius was so interested in such works that he did not wait for a presentation copy of a new book by L'Empereur, but bought it as soon as it arrived in Paris, read it and recommended it to others.[140] Nevertheless the market for such works was small. After 1637 the great Leiden publishers like Elzevier and Maire refused to print works by L'Empereur.[141] This is a general reason for the decline in L'Empereur's scholarly output after 1634. The limited extent of the market for the works which attempted to open up rabbinical literature, as opposed to the much larger market for

---

[140] Grotius, *Briefwisseling* IX, 335; to Vossius, 28.5.1638.

[141] In 1636 Elzevier was occupied in the printing of *Bava Kamma*. De Dieu expected that the other Bavas would rapidly follow (de Dieu to Ussher, 22.8.1636; Ussher, *Works* XVI, 15-6). L'Empereur himself also thought that both the other tractates would follow shortly (L'Empereur to Cocceius, 10.8.1637; Cocceius, *Opera ANEKDOTA* II, 641-2). In 1641 Lemaire was supposed to be going to print the works. L'Empereur to Cocceius, 11.10.1641 (Cocceius, *Opera ANEKDOTA* II, 649): "Ubi Lemairius excuderit secundum & tertium librum de legibus (quod hac futurum hyeme spero) dabo operam ut inter primos nanciscaris." It is understandable that L'Empereur in a letter to Grotius could complain of the greed of the printers (L'Empereur to Grotius, 27.2.1641; *Epistolae celeberrimorum virorum*, 163-5), but the Elzeviers, who were already in difficulty with their oriental publishing, in which as university printers they were bound to print a certain quantity of text (*Molh.* III, 75*) could probably simply not afford it, because there was only a tiny market for it (Juynboll, *Beoefenaars*, 157-8). L'Empereur himself understood this too as appears from a letter to C. Schraderus, 31.8.1641 (Bashuysen, *Clavis talmudica maxima*, 361-2): "Quam pauci hodie tui similes! quae causa est cur typographi adeo sint segnes, & tardi in id genus scriptis typo vulgandis; quod emptores rari sint. Hinc labores mei, in codices nonnulli Mishnajot versi & illustrati jacent, nec lucem aspiciunt. Nihilominus id mecum fatebuntur, credo, qui linguarum istarum sunt gnari, post tantos virorum doctorum in sacris illustrandis labores, nihil excogitari posse, unde porro plus lucis affulgeat sacris literis, quam si quales quive fuerint olim Ecclesiae Judaicae mores, rites atque jura, proponantur ex Mischnajoth & adjunctis Gemaris. Nam passim in V & N. testamento ad ejusmodi respiciunt scriptores sacri. Neque mirum: quandoquidem in istorum temporibus, istiusmodi in Ecclesiae obtinebant. Perge itaque, mi Schradere, studiis istis nonnihil temporis impendere. Jam diu vidisti meam Clavem Talmudicam, quae viam monstrare poterit. Post editum codicem primum de legibus, nihil feci publicum. Parati tamen sunt Codex Berachoth cum Gemara primi capitis; item Zebachim. Deinde secundus, & tertius codex de legibus forensibus, i. Nesikim (nam primus jam diu factus est juri publicis), Vikuah Hadath, aliaque affecta, non perfecta. Sed quid agas, si typographi lucro semper inhient; & grammaticas ac autores vulgares edere magis cupiant." L'Empereur was still trying to publish rabbinica in 1644: Hoornbeek to Cocceius, 16.8.1644; Cocceius *Opera ANEKDOTA* II, no. xcv. The bibliography of Fuks and Fuks shows that only a limited number of rabbinical works with translation appeared in the 17th and 18th centuries.

works which reported on the results of consulting it, is a constant theme in the 17th century. Buxtorf's great dictionary to the Talmud had only one impression through the whole century.[142] This phenomenon makes the question of the use which could be made of rabbinical literature all the more important. To that question we now turn.

### 4.3  The exegesis of the bible

We have seen how inaugural lectures on the usefulness of Hebrew and the forewords to L'Empereur's introductory works for the study of rabbinica, emphasised the study of the bible. In this section we shall analyse exegetical practice and the actual use which it made of rabbinical literature. First, L'Empereur's involvement in the exegetical activities of Daniel Heinsius and Hugo Grotius will be described, and then the nature of the exegesis in his own works. Finally two of his works which refer directly to biblical exegesis are discussed, his editions of the travel narrative of Benjamin of Tudela and the commentary on Daniel of Joseph ibn Yaḥya.

The nature of 17th century exegesis of the New Testament has been investigated in recent years in a series of publications by H. J. de Jonge.[143] He has convincingly demonstrated that two literary genres, produced by two different groups, were important in exegesis. One can distinguish theological commentary and *annotationes* commentary. Theological commentary was the product of university theological teaching. As we have seen, it originally took the form of lectures on the text of the bible, and even though dogmatic teaching on the basis of *loci communes* was reintroduced at the majority of protestant universities, theological teaching from the bible maintained its position. The professor expounded the dogmatic system of his day, by means of long excursuses and an intensive conceptual apparatus, from the text of the bible. Such teaching was the basis of theological commentary, which has three characteristics. First of all it proceeds from the idea that the message of the bible is addressed not only to its readers at the time of the emergence of the Old and New Testaments but also, and above all, to the contemporaries of the exegete. The present day meaning of the text receives far more attention than its significance for the original public, and the deter-

---

[142] Prijs' *Hebräische Drucke* also gives an excellent impression of the market which existed in the 17th century for the various works in the field of Hebrew studies. Buxtorf's lexicon to the Talmud saw only one impression, but his grammar and dictionary of biblical Hebrew were reprinted roughly every ten years.

[143] De Jonge, *Bestudering*; "Study"; "Hugo Grotius".

mination of the meaning for his own contemporaries is seen as the most important task of the exegete. Secondly, the bible was considered, not as a source of information on the history and theological views of Israel and the early church, but as an arsenal of *dicta probantia*, of texts which proved the accuracy of a dogmatic system. Thirdly, this exegesis is not descriptive but normative. The calvinist theologian did not say "in ancient Israel the church was in principle independent of the king", but "this history shows that the church order of Dordt is the right one".[144] All these characteristics are founded on the idea that the bible is a book unlike all other literature, and occupies a completely unique position. The theoretical elaboration of this starting point, self-evident in theological exegetical practice, can be found in the first chapters of many a protestant dogmatic work.[145]

The second genre was that of *annotationes*, that is philological notes and comments on the text of the bible. This form had been created by Lorenzo Valla (c. 1406-57), the Italian humanist, who in his notes on the New Testament had improved inaccurate translations in the Vulgate. Erasmus, who discovered and published the work of Valla, had in his turn written similar annotations on the New Testament. In imitation of his work the genre was widely practised in the 16th and 17th century. Unlike the theologian, the writer of *annotationes* is not mainly interested in the unity of the text or its present day meaning. The observations of a linguistic or historical nature which he makes on a particular verse are founded on comparison with other ancient literature and are intended to understand the text in its historic context. The annotator is therefore free to pass over verses or sometimes whole chapters, on which he has no remarks to make. The practice of this exegesis was that of the student of classical literature, in which a text is understood as an historical document. The fragmentary nature of *annotationes* commentary ensured that the principle of equality, by which the bible is treated like any other text, did not need to be explicitly formulated or consistently applied. The writers of *annotationes* recognised the special nature of the bible, and only asked for room to practise their research into subordinate details. The form of this apologetic argument goes back to Erasmus' introduction to his edition of the New Testament.[146] The systematic practice of historical exegesis was not the result of the putting into effect of a principled programme, but grew gradually through the development of scholarly ques-

---

[144] For the dogmatic dispute on the history of Israel: Polman, *Elément historique*, 506-8.
[145] Cf. for example *Synopsis Purioris Theologiae*, disputatio ii-iv; Heppe/Bizer, *Dogmatik*, which adopts the customary form of the dogmatics of the 17th century, also begins (locus 2-3) with a discussion of the scriptures.
[146] Erasmus, "Apologia", in *Opera* V, **2b.

tioning and the accumulation of detailed knowledge, the result of the tradition of philological *annotationes*. Individual exegetes could pass over dogmatically sensitive passages, or, in the case of a less traditional exegesis, present their interpretation as merely incidental.[147]

Of course, *annotationes* commentary also had dogmatic implications. Beza wrote his annotations on the New Testament with the intention of superseding those of Erasmus in the protestant world by a reference work of unimpeachably reformed character.[148] This dogmatically motivated attack on Erasmus earned Beza the verdict by which Scaliger was accustomed to express his greatest disdain for a person: 'Il n'estoit pas docte en Hebreu''.[149] Scaliger's pupil Heinsius, as we shall see below, shared this negative opinion of Beza's commentary. In spite of such dogmatic differences, *annotationes* commentary was founded on a literary and thus in principle historical exposition of the bible. The distinction in genre between the two sorts of commentaries had little to do with the personal convictions of the writer. Among the authors of *annotationes* and theological commentaries, one finds orthodox and heterodox, and the most important difference was formulated as early as the 17th century by John Selden: "Laymen have best interpreted the hard places in the Bible, such as Johannes Picus, Scaliger, Grotius, Salmasius, Heinsius".[150] The *annotationes* genre was only rarely practised by theologians. Most writers stood outside the university or belonged to the faculties of letters.

This is one of the reasons why the universities of the Dutch Republic, where the genre of *annotationes* attained its greatest flowering in the first half of the 17th century, produced so few of such commentaries on the Old Testament. The teaching staff in the faculties of letters who were active in the field of Greek, were less closely connected with the faculties of theology than the Hebraist.[151] Only Drusius, with his completely independent character, and the regent of the Walloon College, Louis de

---

[147] The observation of J. Chomarat, "Les *Annotations* de Valla, celles d'Erasme et la grammaire" in Fatio, *Histoire*, 227-8: "Il faut expliquer l'Ecriture comme on explique Virgile, Cicéron ou Suetone, voila ce qui signifie l'exégèse grammarienne", thus goes further than is desirable, because it suggests a conscious programme. This was only the consequence of the slow growth of practice, in which such a consistent application of this principle only developed gradually.

[148] Roussel, "Histoire", 183 n. 6. De Jonge, "Study", 78, states that for Scaliger, the *Annotationes* of Beza, which he thought very poor, were the chief stimulus which made him think of providing his own annotations to the N.T.

[149] *Sec Scal*, 231.

[150] Selden, *Opera* III, 2010.

[151] For the teaching of the graecus: de Jonge, "Hoelzlin".

Dieu, who spent his life mainly in the circle of the Leiden Faculty of letters, wrote *annotationes* on the Old Testament.[152]

L'Empereur, who saw himself as a theologian, did not write any *annotationes*, but he did contribute to the development of this type of commentary. As a source of information on rabbinical literature, he was used by Daniel Heinsius and Hugo Grotius. These two philologists, trained at the University of Leiden by Scaliger, had been on bad terms since the troubles during the Truce, in which they had ended in opposing camps. From Paris, Grotius kept himself carefully informed on the scholarly and other activities of the friend of his youth whom he had come to dislike, and who unlike himself had succeeded in acquiring a distinguished position in the Republic. In January 1638 he heard from G. J. Vossius that the printing of Heinsius' commentary on the New Testament had got as far as the Epistle to the Romans, and that Heinsius had made use during the printing of L'Empereur's services as a specialist in the field of rabbinical literature, and as a kind of censor, to warn him of giving offence to orthodox feelings.[153] Vossius was very well informed. In an old missal, a former notebook of his father Antoine, in which the latter had transcribed parts of Calvin's *Institutions*, there are seventeen closely written folio pages with notes by L'Empereur on a work, which appears to correspond to Heinsius' *Exercitationes Sacrae*.[154] Each note is preceded by a reference to the page and line, e.g. 198,47... A careful comparison shows that some of these annotations were included in the printed version of the book. This implies that L'Empereur, as Grotius had heard, was involved in the publication of Heinsius' commentary. To understand the nature of his co-operation properly, we must pay some attention to a technical aspect of printing in the 17th century.

The printing process was a time-consuming activity. A large printing shop had several presses, but one press printed each sheet separately, during which process several operations had to be performed, so that printing the entire impression of a folio sheet could take several hours. To print a large book took months, sometimes more than a year. Since

---

[152] De Jonge ("Study", 69) also sees an exception in de Dieu, because as a theologian his interest was chiefly literary. On him: Posthumus Meyjes, *Waalse College*, 80-2. His scholarly work: Lebram, "Streit", 32-3; de Jonge, "Study", 72-6; *Bestudering*, 47-51. Like Heinsius and Scaliger he was very critical of Beza. Lebram cites from the foreword of the posthumously published *Animadversiones* of de Dieu on the OT, how his work was seen to be in the tradition of Fagius, Münster and Mercerus. De Dieu was at any rate a very open calvinist. In 1642 he organised, with Heerebord and Heidanus, a meeting between Descartes and Comenius at the castle of Endegeest (Thijssen-Schoute, *Cartesianisme*, 615).
[153] Grotius, *Briefwisseling*, IX, 21: from Vossius, 6.1.1638.
[154] An evaluation of the scholarly content of this work: de Jonge, "Study", 93-100.

the highest fixed costs for the printer were his investments in type, it was not possible to make the first setting of the whole work and run off a proof of it to be checked by the author. Such a method of working would have required too much type and thus too much capital. It was therefore customary to make a limited proof of a few pages, and to have them corrected by the author, or if he could not be present during the whole time occupied by the printing process, by a corrector. While the corrected pages were being printed, new pages were set up, and in their turn corrected. The correction of the proofs therefore took as long as the printing of the book itself.[155] For the publication of Heinsius' *Exercitationes Sacrae*, a folio volume of about one thousand pages, the Elzeviers must have been occupied for about a year and a half.[156]

L'Empereur's involvement in Heinsius' edition went much further than simply correcting the proofs. He suggested improvements and additions to the content. This means that every few days for a year or more, he received a few pages and made notes on them. He sent the notes and the proof to Heinsius, who adopted a number of this suggestions and returned the proof to the printer to print the revised text. A comparison of L'Empereur's comments with the definitive text gives a fascinating insight into the way in which an orthodox theologian experienced the development of the *annotationes* genre and the extent to which a philologist like Heinsius was willing to confine himself within ecclesiastical boundaries. No one could suspect Heinsius, who had translated the *Acta* of Dordt into Latin and had been the secretary of the deputies of the States General at the Synod, of heterodox sympathies. In a solemn declaration at the end of the foreword to his book, he left the verdict on his exegesis to the orthodox theologians. Yet it is evident from L'Empereur's comments, how far the development of exegetical practice had outstripped the ability of orthodoxy to incorporate the results of scholarly exegesis of the bible. An analysis of the roughly three hundred and fifty observations which L'Empereur made confirms Grotius' information on the nature of his involvement in the edition.

In the first place L'Empereur was used by Heinsius as a specialist in rabbinica. Thus he remarked on page 61, line 38, that "Rabbah" was not the title of Nachman, but of his son, with a reference to his own edition of *Halikhot Olam*. Heinsius looked up the reference and in his com-

---

[155] For the time taken in correction and publication: Voet, *Golden Compasses* II, 174-93, 302-9. For Plantin the costs of type were so heavy, that he sometimes preferred to print a smaller number of pages than he required immediately and had the page reset later (Voet, *Golden Compasses*, II, 101).

[156] In January 1638 they were up to Romans (note 153); the work itself did not appear until 1639.

mentary on Matth. 17:20 we now read: "So too says Rabbi bar Nachman, who is called Rabbah". The number of such improvements suggested by L'Empereur is considerable, and Heinsius followed almost all of them, even where they concerned a fairly major change. On page 79, 26-9, L'Empereur made the following comment:[157]

> "If *kbd* is used for a costly thing, then it is a rarity. I do not recall it. Would it not much rather be a Syricism? so that for *kbd jqr* must be read. *Jqr* is used by the Aramaeans and Syrians, it means firstly, "to be heavy, weighty" and then "to be valuable" to which this *barutimon* refers."

This refers to the ointment with which Jesus was anointed, according to Matth. 26:7. The Greek adjective used to describe this ointment (''*barutimon*'') is rare, and apparently Heinsius wanted to derive it in the original version of his commentary from the Hebrew *kavod*. He replaced this etymology by the suggestion of L'Empereur. His printed text now reads:[158]

> "That the ointment was called barutimon, is a pure Syricism: for it is well known how the word *jqr* was used among them in a transferred sense for a valuable thing."

Such observations were especially valuable for Heinsius, who in his *Exercitationes Sacrae* consistently tried to derive the meaning of a great many Greek words in the New Testament from Hebrew and other oriental languages.[159] His use of L'Empereur as a theological censor, on the other hand, led to hardly any alterations. The theological observations fall into several groups. In the first place L'Empereur rejected Heinsius' view in rather a large number of passages, where the latter had suggested more possible interpretations for the understanding of a passage than merely the orthodox calvinist one.

On Luke 24:32, the close of the account of the man on the road to Emmaus, Heinsius remarked: "this passage, although elegant, has troubled us not a little; since various expositors of this place doubt it (and that not because they wish to do so, which is easily possible)".[160] The first half of this observation provoked L'Empereur to the irritated reaction: "The expositors ought not to have doubted, for the Evangelist explains himself". For L'Empereur the fire in the hearts of the men on the road

---

[157] "KBD si de re praetiosa dicatur, raro saltem, ego non memini. Nonne potius est Syriasmus? ut pro KBD ponatur JQR. Sane JQR Chaldaeis et Syris usitatum, primo significat *gravem esse et ponderum* deinde *preciosum esse* quo spectat illud BARUTIMON."
[158] *Exercitationes Sacrae*, 79: "Cum unguentum dicitur BARUTIMON, purus Syriasmus est: apud quos notum quomodo TO JQR etiam de re preciosa usurpetur ..."
[159] De Jonge, *Bestudering*, 33.
[160] *Exercitationes Sacrae*, 198.

to Emmaus was without doubt the work of the Holy Ghost, and in his eyes it was superfluous to suggest other possibilities.[161] At other and much more sensitive passages, Heinsius would not give way an inch. On page 236,38 where Heinsius dealt with John 14:28, the passage which is so troublesome for the classical dogma of the Trinity, "for the Father is more than I am", L'Empereur noted:[162]

> "Not so far as concerns the logical order, by which the Father precedes, and not as if the Father is earlier – not al all! but this is said only with reference to the office of the Redeemer."

In spite of this remark, Heinsius maintained in his commentary the summary of a number of different interpretations, which suggest a certain subordination of the Son, referring to the exegesis of some of the Greek Fathers. He expressed no preference for any explanation, but concluded his survey with "let us proceed".

The discussion between L'Empereur and Heinsius on Acts 7:15-6 reveals very aptly the different ways in which a philologist and a theologian approached the text of the bible. The passage is part of Stephen's speech in his defence before the Sanhedrin. An important part of this speech is made up by a survey of the history of Israel. The verses concerned state how Jacob and the fathers died in Egypt, and that "they were removed to Shechem and buried in the tomb which Abraham had bought for a sum of money from the sons of Emmor at Shechem". Here the story of Abraham, who bought a grave at Hebron, has been confused with that of Jacob, who acquired the grave at Shechem. The text of Acts is thus a direct contradiction of the account in Genesis. Heinsius suspected a textual corruption here, and proposed another reading.[163] Such a use of textual criticism in order to remove discrepancies need not only be the fruit of an effort at harmonisation. Suggestions for textual emendation in passages which, in the sober opinion of a philologist, were not to be reconciled with other texts, are also found in Scaliger and Grotius.[164] Such suggestions are based not so much on a conservative strategy of rescuing the unity of the bible, but are rather to be seen as the result of a lack of scholarly technique. They were still unable to visualise the gradual emergence of a text within several social groups and

---

[161] On 198, 47: "Interpretes non debuerent dubitare: quia Evangelista se explicat".

[162] "Non ad ordinem quo Pater praeit, nec quasi esset antior, absit, sed hoc dicitur respectu officii mediatoris."

[163] *Exercitationes Sacrae*, 227.

[164] Scaliger suggested a textual emendation in order to resolve the discrepancy which he saw between Mark 15:25 and John 19:14 (de Jonge, "Study", 82-3); Grotius did the same for a contradiction between Gal. 2:1 and Acts 15:24 (de Jonge, "Hugo Grotius", 111).

the results which this entails, or the possibility that contradictions can exist within a single text. Fifteenth century Italian humanists applied textual criticism in a similar way in their editions of classical authors.[165] Heinsius' textual emendation was rejected by L'Empereur because it was founded on taking seriously the contradictions in the text handed down. He preferred the centuries-old method of harmonisation, in which the words of the text were not altered, but the things described in them were reconstructed, with some imagination and without paying any attention to historical probability, so that they were in accordance with the various texts. He referred Heinsius to Junius' solution, which he thought a successful one, for this problem verse.[166] Heinsius adopted nothing from this suggestion.

Heinsius was certainly not a champion of textual criticism. He had been intimately involved in the publication of the Greek text of the New Testament which was to become the *textus receptus*, and in his own exegesis he took a conservative standpoint insofar as textual emendation was concerned.[167] Yet he understood that the Greek text was far from reliable. On II Tim. 1:3 he made the following programmatic observation:[168]

"Although we reject those who want to see themselves permitted to use the freedom which they are glad to seize on in the profane authors, in casting doubt on the sacred authors, who would be amazed if, in such a great variation between the manuscripts (of which the Fathers of the church themselves continually speak) here originally for *suneidèsei hōs, suneidèseōs* had been written? (...) For no one can doubt that the Greek and Latin Fathers of the church, depending on the various MSS. which they used, often deviated considerably from the usual reading. It would be possible for scholars to compile a large collection of variant readings on many passages from their writings."

The occasion for this remark is slight and Heinsius' suggestion for emendation did not rest on a variant reading in a MS. But the comment is an illuminating one, and permits us to see how Heinsius understood the variety in the textual transmission of the New Testament.[169] It is

---

[165] For the 15th century humanists: Grafton, *Scaliger* I, 25. Humanist jurists also had recourse to textual criticism, when all other aids had been exhausted: Troje, *Graeca leguntur*, 130-1, 136 ff.

[166] To be found in Junius, *Opera* I, 1077, a part of the work *Sacrum Parallelorum*, which is entirely devoted to the removal of such contradictions (*Opera* I, 982-1266).

[167] De Jonge, *Bestudering*, 23: "Study", 94.

[168] *Exercitationes Sacrae*, 523.

[169] In this Heinsius followed Scaliger, who had more confidence in the citations in the Fathers, than in the MSS. of the NT. *Sec Scal*, 589: "Quant au vieux livres du Nouveau Testament à la main, je ne m'y voudrois tenir, tant vieux soient-ils, car ils sont tres corrompus; il vaut mieux se rapporter au Peres qui citent l'Escriture, et qui se sont servis de meilleurs exemplaires."

characteristic that Heinsius coupled his proposal to compile a collection of variant readings from patristic literature with the obligatory recognition of the special nature of the bible. In spite of this verbal rejection of the principle of equality, theologians regarded this development with suspicion and alarm. L'Empereur's reaction is characteristic:[170]

> If it were once allowed, that because of a deviation which occurs elsewhere, we should create it, even where there is not one variant, and even with such a difference of letters, what will then be certain in the Holy Scriptures? Moreover there is (in this case) no need at all..."

Heinsius did not bow to such theological sensibilities in his edition. This is most strikingly shown in an aspect of the *Exercitationes Sacrae* which has only been remarked upon by de Jonge.[171]

In his commentary Heinsius continually attacked the exegesis of Beza without naming him except as *recens interpres, vir doctus* and so on. A trained calvinist theologian such as L'Empereur could not of course be deceived by such a tactic. On countless occasions L'Empereur pointed out to Heinsius the imprudence and superfluity of such explicit reference to differences of opinion, and in the course of the work he becomes increasingly peevish at the constant criticism of Beza. Halfway through, at page 337, he bursts out in rather guarded terms which say a great deal about his relationship with Heinsius:[172]

> "Without wishing to offend you, I must say that I am afraid that all the things which are urged so accurately against Beza's translation, will make the otherwise so brilliant discoveries less welcome. For if someone in a spirit of contradiction, should wish to defend the comments of Beza, then it seems he would be able to find the material here to do so."

On the following pages L'Empereur carefully observes several times where Heinsius agrees with Beza, with the tactful suggestion that he would do well to mention such an agreement in the text. L'Empereur's warning that Heinsius' attacks on Beza could embroil him in a polemic, was not unfounded. Soon after the publication of the *Exercitationes Sacrae*, Rivet attempted to rouse Heinsius' great antagonist Salmasius to defend the honour of Beza.[173]

---

[170] "Si id semel admittatur, ut propter varietatum, quae alibi occurrit, etiam ubi nulla varietas est, eam faciamus, et quidem tot vocibus mutatis; quid erit certi in sacris? Deinde nulla plane necessitas..."

[171] De Jonge, "Study", 95.

[172] On 337, 18: "Pace viri N. dicam vereor ne ista quae passim contra Bezae versionem tam accurate disputantur, caetera praeclarissima inventa quodammodo ingratiora reddant. Nam si quis animo contradicendi ista Bezae defendere vellet, aliquando materiam invenire posse videretur..."

[173] Zuber, "De Scaliger à Saumaise", 476-7.

A third group of annotations concerned an aspect of the exegesis of the New Testament with which L'Empereur was particularly concerned, and in which he could use his specialist knowledge, but where Heinsius also refused to follow him. This refers to the Old Testament citations in the New Testament, a very sensitive subject, which was involved in many ways with dogmatic discussion. Every annotator of the New Testament was almost immediately confronted with the problem, because the Gospel of Matthew is to a great extent written as a fulfilment of Old Testament texts. Heinsius discussed it at Matth. 2:15 where Hosea 11:1 "I have called my son from Egypt", is cited as a prophecy of the return of Jesus from Egypt, where Joseph and Mary had fled. Heinsius stated that according to Jerome, Julian the Apostate had used this verse against the Christians, and had quoted it as an example of their distortion of the Old Testament. The full text of Hosea 11:1 reads: "When Israel was a child, then I loved him, and called my son out of Egypt" and from this it appeared, according to Julian, that the verse was not a prophecy of the Messiah, but a looking back to the Exodus. Heinsius gave a survey of the content of Matth. 2 and concluded that:[174]

> "The Evangelist has used this verse excellently. Not because he believed that it was originally a prophecy about the person of Christ, but because this passage is very appropriate here. Indeed, it agrees even better with Christ (...) For Julian's argument on the grounds of the name Israel is inept (...) Everyone who is even slightly acquainted with this subject, knows that Israel often means the son of God. The Apostate understands this as if it was Matthew's meaning, that God had promised through Hosea that he would call his son Christ out of Egypt, and that this was then fulfilled. While the Evangelist in fact used this verse from the prophet elegantly and stylishly, of which he says that it can be properly applied here (...) It is thus not a matter of the promise of God, but of the application of a verse of scripture."

This explanation is not entirely clear. Against Julian, Heinsius appears to wish to maintain that Hos. 11:1 can be interpreted messianically, but in continuing his exposition he stresses the fact that Matthew applies and does not expound the biblical text. This injury to the inter-connection of the two Testaments led L'Empereur to write a complicated note, which may explain the ambiguity of Heinsius' annotation, and which gives an insight into the way in which a theologian could use rabbinical literature.[175]

---

[174] *Exercitationes Sacrae*, 14-5.

[175] "Atqui nihil est quod eo nos descendere cogat. Imo stylus hoseae suadet ut de messia intelligatur. (..) Neque Rabbini in Midrash ad Ps 2,7 longe discedunt: nam cum D.K. ad Hoseae locum de filio agi dicat, cujus mentio ex 4,22: illi in Midrasch testantur cum dicitur *filius meus es*, confirmari illo loco exod. 4,22. Ergo cum veteres ps 2 de Messia etiam ibidem exponent, hoseae testimonium Messiam respicit."

But there is nothing which compels us to take refuge in this. On the contrary the style of Hosea shows that the verse must be understood of the Messiah (...) And the rabbis in the Midrash on Ps. 2:7 do not differ much from this. For although D.K. says on this passage of Hosea, that it refers to the son who is spoken of in Ex. 4:22, they state in the Midrash that when it is said "thou art my son", that this is confirmed by the passage Ex. 4:22. Thus since the elders also explain Ps. 2 in the same place as referring to the Messiah, the witness of Hosea refers to the Messiah."

This is a curious chain of reasoning. David Kimḥi linked Hosea 11:1 with Ex. 4:22, in which there is a clear reference to the People of Israel as God's Son, but he did not expound the verse in a messianic sense. Psalm 2 is expounded messianically in the Midrash and reference is also made there to Ex. 4:22. With the aid of Kimḥi, Ps. 2 and Hosea 11:1 can thus be linked and the latter verse, in contradiction of Kimḥi's view, regarded as an allusion to the Messiah. Such a use of rabbinica was to become an important part of the theological apology for the revelatory character of the Scriptures. L'Empereur also tried to defend the traditional interpretation of other Old Testament citations, which Heinsius had understood in accordance with their own character and therefore as applications.[176]

In the theological annotations on the *Exercitationes Sacrae* L'Empereur's view on the Scriptures and his own method of dealing with the bible, come to the fore, as they do not in the technical information on rabbinica. The thanks which Heinsius expressed at the end of his prolegomena, for L'Empereur's contribution were, in view of the nature and extent of this assistance, appropriate.[177] He compared his collaboration with L'Empereur with that between the four theologians of the *Synopsis*, who had agreed immediately after their appointment to submit their work to each other before publication, in order to avoid dogmatic disputes.

That it was the exegetical practice of the annotators, and not the methodical or theological concepts behind it, or the justification of it, which was unwelcome to the theologians, is shown for example in the reaction of the remonstrant theologian Episcopius to the works of the calvinist Heinsius. He found the *Exercitationes Sacrae* insufficiently edifying.[178] It can also be illustrated from a comparison of the exegetical work

---

[176] Cf. the use of Ps. 2 in the Epistle to the Hebrews. L'Empereur remarks on this (546, 20): "ille psalmus totus de Christo, nullo modo de Davide".

[177] *Exercitationes Sacrae*, (40). The passage follows a homage to the Leiden professors of theology.

[178] Episcopius to Grotius, 25.11.1641; *Praestantium ac Eruditorum virorum Epistolae*, 813-4.

of Grotius with that of L'Empereur. For the purpose of this comparison, we give first a general survey of Grotius' exegesis.

In his exile Grotius wrote *annotationes* on the Old and New Testaments, in which he consciously tried to attain an historical understanding of these texts.[179] Exegesis was at the service of his ideal of a reunification of the competing confessions. This ideal gave him the strength to write his extensive commentaries in spite of his diplomatic activities, in the service of foreign powers, since the Republic would not and could not allow him to return, as the symbol of the party defeated in 1618. This highly personal ideal reinforced the historicising tendency which typified humanist *annotationes* commentary. In his exegesis Grotius deliberately remained within the horizon of the culture of the classical, mediterranean world. He attempted to understand the Bible historically. In this way he hoped to make the abuse of texts for contemporary dogmatic polemics which kept the churches divided, impossible. He took the standpoint of a reader in the age when the texts had been written, not that of the public of his own day. His means to attain such a goal was, in the case of the New Testament, the use of classical literature. The numerous and mostly well chosen citations from classical authors had to place the New Testament in the world in which it had arisen. The references to rabbinical literature of the Targumim, the Mishna and the Talmud also try to reconstruct the way of life and thought of the readers of the New Testament writings. He was therefore especially interested in the research of Christian hebraists into the customs of the Jews at the time of the composition of the New Testament.[180]

Grotius' less extensive commentary on the Old Testament has the same character. It starts from the Vulgate, but continually recurs to the Hebrew text. More than his commentary on the New Testament, it is a true example of *annotationes*, in which Grotius passes over numerous verses and often pays little attention to the unity of sections of text. The work was intended above all to stimulate and simplify cursory reading.[181] Here too the citations from classical literature serve to make the text comprehensible from the cultural and religious assumptions of the age for which it was originally intended. Thus on II Sam. 24:8 Grotius gives a brilliantly chosen quotation from Hesiod. The chapter is the story of the sin which David committed by holding a census, and for which the people were punished by a plague. The citation from Hesiod expresses the idea that a city is often punished with a general evil by the gods, for

---

[179] De Jonge, "Hugo Grotius".

[180] Cf. his interest mentioned above, in the work of L'Empereur and his encouragement to Wilhelm Schikard, e.g. *Briefwisseling*, V, 269.

[181] Diestel's characterisation, *Geschichte*, 430.

the offences of one of its inhabitants. Grotius uses this quotation to place II Sam. 24 in the context in which it belongs, the assumption of collective responsibility of a community for its members.

Rabbinical literature played quite an important part in Grotius' exegesis of the New Testament, in which he was able to attach himself to an older exegetical tradition. The nature of his use of rabbinical literature in the exegesis of the Old Testament has never been investigated, but it seems likely that it served inter alia, to promote historical understanding in the same way as the classical erudition displayed in his commentaries. In his annotations on the Pentateuch, he prefers to cite rationalising explanations of laws and customs from Buxtorf's edition of Maimonides' *Moreh Nevukhim*.[182] He also quotes from rabbinical literature to define the meanings of words. For his knowledge of the rabbis he used the works and text editions of the Christian hebraists who have been discussed in the previous section. Thus on Lev. 7:16, a verse which deals with the sacrifice which someone brings as a promised or voluntary offering:[183]

> "*if someone offers because of a promise or voluntarily*. Either on the grounds of the previous obligation of a promise, or from pure generosity. The first is called *neder*, the second *nedaba* from the verb *nadab* which means to give. Thus *nedaba* (sc. in the LXX) is translated as *doma:* Dt. xxiii, 24; II. Chron. xxxi, 14. And so Maimonides distinguishes in *Maasse Karbanoth...*"

The reference to *Ma'asseh Karbanot*, a part of Maimonides' *Mishneh Torah*, creates a very learned impression. But Grotius followed Selden's adage: "To quote a modern Dutchman where I may use a classic author, is as if I were to justify my reputation, and I neglect all persons of note and quality that know me, and bring the testimonials of the scullion in the kitchen."[184] Grotius borrowed Maimonides' opinion from L'Empereur's *Bava Kamma*.[185] Meijer's opinion, that Grotius knew biblical Hebrew, but was dependent on others for his knowledge of rabbinical literature, is very likely, in spite of later attempts to salvage Grotius' *eruditio rabbinica*.[186] L'Empereur was prominent among the Christian

---

[182] Cf. his praefatio, in which he rightly observes: "In Lege sensum & causas praeceptorum & mores eo pertinentes, ab antiquis Judaeorum magistris maxime sumpta, addidi."

[183] "*Si voto vel sponte quispiam obtulerit hostiam* (..) sive praecedente voti obligatione, sive ex mera liberalitate. Illud NDR vocatur, hoc NDBH a verbo NDB, quod est donare. Itaque NDBH DOMA vertitur Dt xxiii.24 ii Paral xxxi.14 Et sic distinguit Maimonides in Maase Karbanoth, qui & hoc notat, ubi nullo NDBH dicitur intelligi holocaustum."

[184] Selden, *Opera* III, 2017.

[185] *Bava Kamma*, 263.

[186] Meijer, *Remonstrantie*, 58-67. Further literature: Baron, *History*, XV, 390, n. 31 to be supplemented by Lachs, "Hugo Grotius", who shows that Grotius was mainly depen-

hebraists whom Grotius plundered. Grotius made detailed marginal notes on his works.[187]

The whole of Grotius' exegetical oeuvre is a proof of the high level that the technique of humanistic textual exegesis had attained. It was only the consistent application of this technique, trained in classical literature, to the bible, which was long neglected.[188] The critical, historical exposition of the bible was not, as is often assumed, the result of the emergence of a new mechanised world-view under the influence of the natural sciences. This can be illustrated in several ways from the work of Grotius. To begin with, one may wonder whether a world-view drawn from the natural sciences could have had much influence on a trained humanist. There is a letter from Grotius to his friend G. J. Vossius of 1635,[189] in which he gives his opinion on Galileo's recent condemnation by the Inquisition. In one sentence he mentions the controversy between the copernican and ptolemaic world-views, states that the scholars are divided on the question, and expresses the expectation that it will become clear in the end. He gives the impression of being about as concerned over the problem as a modern historian would be by the question, not altogether devoid of importance, whether the universe will continue to expand or collapse in on itself again.

The limited influence of a world-view on exegesis appears above all from the most famous characteristic of Grotius' exegesis of the Old Testament. Grotius was convinced of the possibility of miracles and prophecy, but his humanistically trained mind refused to believe in prophecies with a fulfilment which would have meant nothing to the public originally intended. This capacity for historical imagination is the basis

---

dent for the rabbinical citations in his *De jure Belli ac Pacis* on the works of L'Empereur. Rosenberg, ''Hugo Grotius'', who tries to save Grotius' rabbinical knowledge, does not succeed in his undertaking, because he does not investigate the possibility of Grotius' dependence on secondary literature. In a rather superficial investigation of the use of rabbinical citations in Grotius' annotations on Genesis, Exodus and Leviticus, more than eighty per cent could be immediately located in the works of Fagius, Münster, Vatablus, Drusius, Amama, Buxtorf II (whose *Doctor Perplexorum* supplies virtually all the quotations from Maimonides), the *Conciliator* of Menasseh ben Israel and the works of L'Empereur.

[187] Blok, *Contributions*, 34-43, n. 11.

[188] Cf. the highly developed historical technique used by Causaubon to demonstrate the spuriousness of the *Corpus Hermeticum* (Grafton, ''Protestant versus Prophet''), and the way in which Scaliger proved the non-apostolic character of the *LXXXV Canones Apostolorum* (de Jonge, ''Scaliger's Diatribe''). Scaliger doubted—albeit not in his published works—the genuineness of Revelation and of all the catholic epistles except I Peter (de Jonge, ''Study'', 84). For the reluctance to apply this criticism to the bible, cf. for example *Sec Scal*, 398-9: ''Il y a plus de cinquante additions ou mutations au nouveau Testament & aux Evangiles; c'est chose estrange, je n'ose la dire; si c'estoit un Auteur profane, j'en parlerois autrement.''

of the most striking tendency in Grotius' Old Testament commentaries, his refusal to explain as such those prophecies which were traditionally considered to refer to Christ.[190] He looked for the fulfilment of such texts in the history of Israel. Thus he regarded Isaiah 53 as a prophecy of the suffering of Jeremiah. Naturally such an approach created theological, and in the case of the New Testament, exegetical problems. We find the reflection of these problems in Grotius' commentaries, especially in those on the New Testament, because his exegesis of the Old Testament remained consistently within the history of Israel. It appears from a systematic investigation of Grotius' exegesis of all the Old Testament passages cited in the New, that he only exceptionally mentioned such a use in his *annotationes* on the Old Testament.[191]

Grotius gave four different solutions for the problems which his historical exegesis of the Old Testament threw up. They were partly theological and partly exegetical. The consistency of these answers is problematical. Grotius' most important solution is based on the use of the concept of typology[192] which, so far as concerns its classical formulation, goes back to Thomas Aquinas,[193] and formed the foundation of Calvin's exegesis of the Old Testament.[194] According to this conception, the words of the Old Testament indicate things, such as events in the history of Israel. These things have been so structured by God, the almighty author of history, that they point to other things, such as events in the life of Christ. It is clear that such a theological view gives the exegete the freedom also to investigate the first, direct meaning. In his commentary on the psalms, Calvin mostly deals first with the significance of a psalm in the history of Israel, and then goes on to show how this history was fulfilled in Christ. In Grotius' Old Testament commentary, however, the typology hardly corresponds any longer with an exegetical practice and has been reduced to a purely theological justification of his exegesis.

---

[189] Grotius, *Briefwisseling*, V, 269-70; to G. J. Vossius, 12.8.1634.

[190] Grotius' 'judaizare' has often been remarked on. There is a fine characterisation in Kuenen, "Hugo de Groot", 318-22. There is no occasion to doubt his explanation in the foreword to the *Annotationes in V.T.*: "Feci autem hoc, quod, ni id fieret, viderem male cohaerere verborum rerumque apud Prophetas seriem, quae caeteroqui pulcherrima est."

[191] Only on very well known passages such as Ps. 2, Ps. 45, Is. 53.

[192] A good survey of the various solutions is given in his note on Luke 24:27.

[193] Thomas, *Summa*, Ia,q.1, a.10. Cf. Lubac, *Exégèse*, 2/2, 272-302. The protestant theologians adopted Thomas' formulation without change: Junius, *Opera* I, 632: "Allegoria, imago rerum (ut ita loquamur) expressa verbis alienis sive aliud significantibus; aut (si placet brevius) verbalis imago rei alicujus: Typus vero est realis imago, hoc est, imago rerum, in qua res una per aliam adumbratur."

[194] Wolf, *Einheit des Bundes*, 123-33, 150 ff.

Moreover he linked the concept of typology with a second, more exegetical solution of the problem of the relationship of Old and New Testaments. Like Heinsius, Grotius was confronted right at the start of his New Testament commentaries, by the citations from the Old Testament. On Matth. 1:22 he described in a long annotation the purpose and the nature of the way in which the evangelists used the Old Testament. In essence, Grotius follows the socinian argument that the evangelists and the apostles did not use the Old Testament passages to prove the truth of their message, which was already firmly established by the miracles and the teaching of Christ, but to illustrate it.[195] Whoever has recognised the truth of Christianity, understands from the citations that God has so ordained the history of the Old Testament that it foreshadows Christ. Thus for Grotius the typological, indirect meaning becomes a mystical, esoteric sense. A third solution, which goes back to Origen, is connected with this esoteric character.[196]

According to this conception, some Old Testament passages possess a secret, mystical significance which was revealed by Christ to his disciples and has been preserved in the church. This higher sense is esoteric, but sometimes Grotius used citations from rabbinical literature to confirm its existence.[197] In this way this use is allied to his fourth, historicising solution. In certain cases, Grotius tries to show that the Old Testament passages involved were understood in a messianic sense by everyone at the time when the New Testament was compiled, and could therefore be properly cited as proofs by the evangelists and the apostles.[198] He demonstrates the existence of such an explanation by making use of older rabbinical literature.

None of these opinions is original. Grotius used the existing literature on the relationship of Old and New Testaments to find solutions for the theological problems with which his exegetical practice confronted him. The variety of the answers which he gave shows that this practice was independent of theological conceptions. They could influence the exegesis of a passage incidentally,[199] but it would not be correct to state that Grotius' historicising exegesis was founded on a theological view of both Covenants. His exegetical practice created the problems, for which

---

[195] Socinus, *De auctoritate S. Scripturae*, 267; Diestel, *Geschichte*, 391; Grotius on Matth. 1:22.

[196] Von Harnack, *Dogmengeschichte* I, 664. This solution is also found in Cunaeus, *De Republica* iii, 8.

[197] E.g. on Ps. 22:19; Ps. 45:7-8; Zach. 9:9. See above note 192. Cocceius thought it necessary to attack such a view in his "Praefatio apologetica pro meditatione Scripturarum" (*3a) (in his *Opera Omnia* II).

[198] On Matth. 1:22; I Cor. 10:1; Gal. 4:24.

[199] De Jonge, "Hugo Grotius', 112-3.

he then sought theological solutions. Nor was it the nature of these solutions which alarmed the orthodox theologians: as we shall see below, L'Empereur was willing to use the same arguments, whenever he was faced with a problem that could not be solved in any other way. Yet L'Empereur wrote to Cocceius that he could not understand what spirit had moved Grotius to write such a work.[200] The nature and the degree of the theologians' alarm is clearly shown in a correspondence between Rivet and Buxtorf II.[201] In their eyes, Grotius' consistent and needless application of historical exposition created theological problems instead of removing them. In rejecting such a procedure, catholics and calvinists could agree. Rivet cited with approval the verdict of a catholic theologian on Grotius' exegesis.[202] How an orthodox calvinistically trained theologian explained the bible, and to what extent he was willing to make use of humanist exegesis, appears in the exegetical remarks in L'Empereur's works.

L'Empereur saw biblical exegesis as one of the most important purposes for which rabbinical literature could be used,[203] and all his works are provided with extensive indices to biblical passages. Yet the scope and quantity of the actual exegesis in his work is rather disappointing. In the last part of this section we shall discuss the biblical exegesis practised in his works, and examine his view of the mystical sense, and the use of the Old Testament by the writers of the New Testament. Finally some works which mainly concern biblical exegesis will be dealt with. L'Empereur sometimes followed the current practice of *annotationes* commentary and used rabbinical literature to explain turns of phrase, assumptions and customs in the Old and New Testaments. Thus he cited the *Midrash Tehillim* on Ps. 87:1 to clarify Rev. 21:21. In both texts it is said of the New Temple that God will make its gates from a single pearl.[204]

---

[200] L'Empereur to Cocceius, 23.5.1644, Cocceius, *Opera ANEKDOTA* II, 657.

[201] University Library Leiden, BPL 285. Grotius' works led Buxtorf II to pass the following characteristic general verdict on the development of humanist biblical exegesis: Buxtorf II to Rivet, 1.9.1644: "Tuam autem, Vir Venerande, subscribo sententiam, Liberiorem Criticem in sacris esse suspectam et periculosam. Nihil istiusmodi homines mihi videntur quaerere, quam acuminis alicujus singularis gloriam, nihil facere, quam contentiones favere, atque adeo latiorem ac liberiorem adversariis nobiscum congrediendi campum aperire. Prudentia hic opus, pietate, adde etiam doctrina et eruditione, nec facile quoque in istam Criticem irrumpere debet, nisi probe ab omnibus necessariis subsidiis instructus."

[202] Cf. also the verdict of Rivet which can be reconstructed from the letter in which Sarrau replied to him: *C.I. Rivet/Sarrau* II, 429; from Sarrau, 12.11.1644. Cf. also how Rivet cites with approval the opinion of a jesuit professor, "que cela n'est point tolerable dans la Chrestienté" (*C. I. Rivet/Sarrau* I, 129).

[203] Cf. the letter cited above, note 141, to Schrader.

[204] *Middot*, 141.

"through which we see that the New Testament writings have everywhere been adapted to the assumptions which were already common among the Jews; which, if the present argument were to require it, could be shown without any difficulty from the comparison of the Talmud and the Targumim with the writings of the New Testament."

Such observations, however, form only a small part of his exegetic comments. In the exegesis of the Old Testament he used the rabbis to clarify turns of phrase and anthropomorphic assumptions. For example, he explained Gen. 5:24 "and Enoch walked with God" by appealing to the rabbis, as "Enoch honoured God in the proper way".[205] L'Empereur also used the rabbis to understand the things mentioned in the Old Testament such as the Urim and Tummim.[206] He thereby stood at the head of a long series of 17th century scholars. The Italian baptised Jew Ugolino was able in the middle of the 18th century to fill thirty-three large folios with hundreds of tractates describing such *realia* with the help of rabbinical literature.[207] The most important group of connected exegetical remarks in L'Empereur's work concerns the harmonisation of contradictions. He regarded the rabbis' solutions to such problems as one of the most attractive features of their work.[208] Following Abrabanel he explained for example the difference between the number of cavalry of Hadadezer, king of Zoba captured by David according to II Sam. 8:4 (1700) and I Chron. 18:4 (7000) by assuming that Samuel was only counting the leaders, Chronicles all the cavalry.[209] He also applied similar methods in a number of longer exegetical passages.[210]

The idea that no contradictions could occur in the Old Testament formed the starting point for L'Empereur's thoughts on the mystical sense. The foreword to his edition of *Middot* contains a long exposition of the way in which the existence of a higher sense in the Old Testament can be demonstrated. The starting point of this argument, to which he recurred many times in later works,[211] is given by several rabbinical texts,[212] and the principle, usual in protestant hermeneutics, that allegory is permissible where a text is in conflict with right reason.[213] In this passage L'Empereur discusses the last chapters of Ezekiel, which include

---

[205] *MosKim*, 120-1.
[206] *MosKim*, 206-9. Other examples: the altar and the idolatry of Peor (*Middot*, 99-103, 116-7).
[207] Ugolino, *Thesaurus*.
[208] E.g. *HalOl*, ****1a; *ParaDan*, 10-11; *Bava Kamma*, 169.
[209] *Bava Kamma*, 169.
[210] Cf. the long passage on the Ark in the foreword to *Middot*, **4b-***3a.
[211] *Middot*, ***4b-****2b.
[212] He already cites the texts in *ParaDan*, 188.
[213] Cf. e.g. *Synopsis*, 48; Rivet, *Isagoge*, XV, 14.

a plan for a new temple, which differs from the first temple and was not realised in the second. According to L'Empereur this difference shows that the temple described in Ezekiel was not a real building, but a spiritual one, the Christian church, in which the old ceremonies will no longer be observed. The thesis that the temple can indicate a spiritual phenomenon, was supported by Alshekh's exegesis of Hag. 2:10. According to L'Empereur the principle was to be extended to large parts of the Old Testament:[214]

> "The same method (sc. of exegesis) of the temple of Ezekiel also has its application to the old rites and ceremonies by which the state of the Christian church is represented and prefigured in the Old Testament. For whenever these ceremonies do not agree with the commandments of God as handed down by Moses, then it is natural to deduce from this that it was God's intention to show us, by this difference and contradiction, that these ceremonies and what is concerned with them, must not be understood literally but contain a spiritual sense (on which more from Abrabanel on another occasion)."

L'Empereur was thinking here of such prefigurings as Mal. 1:1 and Isaiah 19:19, where there is mention of altars outside Jerusalem, a prophecy which is in conflict with the commandment for centralisation of worship in Dtn. 12:14. He extended the possibility of a mystical sense even further by making use of the anti-eschatological traits in the work of Maimonides. Maimonides forcefully defended the view that the nature of reality would not change in the messianic period,[215] and was of the opinion that those texts in the Old Testament which seem to predict such a change must be explained allegorically. L'Empereur made grateful use of this rationalist interpretation of the bible, by adopting Maimonides' thesis for the period after the first coming of the Messiah. Thus he was able to explain Isaiah 11:6, which speaks of the panther lying down with the hind, as a prophecy of the Christian church, which was called forth from among Jews and heathens. Following Maimonides' spiritual understanding of the passages which concern the future wonderful state of the land of Canaan, L'Empereur also remarked:[216]

---

[214] *Middot*, \*\*\*\*1b.

[215] For Maimonides' anti-utopian eschatology: Scholem, *Sabbatai Sevi*, 12-5. L'Empereur also used Abrabanel as an authority for such an exegesis; *Middot*, 132-3.

[216] *Middot*, 133. He also approaches Haggai 2:10 in this same way. There it is stated that the second Temple is better than the first. Nevertheless the Jews too concede that certain things were lacking in the second Temple. L'Empereur concludes (*Middot*, 103-4): "Unde consequitur aliquid in secundo templo fuisse quod illa non tantum aequaverit, sed etiam superaverit: nimirum Messiam Deum & hominem, ubi erat ipsa divinitas (in secunda persona S.S. Trinitatis subsistens) modo longe praestantiori quam olim in priori templo, una cum Spiritu qui absque mensura in ipso habitat."

"Thus we see that Paul in the Epistle to the Hebrews 11:10 is completely correct to say that Abraham with Isaac and Jacob accepted the promises about the land of Canaan in such a way that they expected a heavenly inheritance because of them, even though that was hidden in shadow."

In this view we find an indication of one of the reasons why rabbinical literature held such an attraction for L'Empereur. He felt himself in harmony with the essentially theological way of reasoning of the rabbis. Use of the rabbis for a theological exegesis in the service of the defence of the unity of the scriptures as championed by L'Empereur, was to become an important part of the work of the Christian hebraists in the second half of the 17th century.[217] By then the traditions of humanist biblical exegesis and Christian study of rabbinica had already grown apart. L'Empereur, Grotius and Heinsius still formed part of a single intellectual community. They could make use of each other's arguments and works, and L'Empereur could also adduce other, much more historical arguments in defence of the bible.

The foreword to his edition of *Halikhot Olam* contains a noteworthy passage. In the form of an apology for the knowledge of rabbinical literature, L'Empereur raises the problem of the citations from the Old Testament by the evangelists and apostles.[218]

"The authors of the New Testament apply many witnesses from the Old to Christ. In this they followed the guidance of the Holy Ghost, and because it went before them they were free from error. But the enemies of the Gospel never leave off ridiculing their work. Here it must be observed that the holy men of God, whenever they discussed Christ and His teachings, used many texts of the Old Testament, because there was no doubt among their public, that the texts referred to this, that is, that they must be applied to the Messiah, although this is not always to be clearly deduced from their context. But since they were generally understood in that sense, as really referring to it, they were rightly cited to confirm the case to be proved! If these passages are now brought into doubt after so many centuries, the historical texts must be consulted, from the authority of which those, with whom we are in conflict, do not dare to withdraw themselves. For although what we want to prove with the aid of these texts can be demonstrated more than adequately by the resurrection of Christ, His miracles and those of the apostles, by other similar proofs, as also by the holiness and success of the doctrine, and also by those parts of the O.T., which not infrequently prove

---

[217] Cf. Diestel, *Geschichte*, 338; Van Rooden, "Surenhuis", In all the reissues of L'Empereur's works in the second half of the 17th century, this motive played a very important part. Compare Bashuysen, *Clavis Talmudica maxima*; id. *Observationum sacrarum liber*; Surenhuis, *Mischna*, id. *BIBLOS KATALLAGES*. Cf. the apologetic use of L'Empereur by Reimarus in his youthful work *Vindicatio*, 101, 126-7, 149, 157, 160, 162, 172, 176, 187.
[218] *HalOl*, ***3b-*****1a. The citation ***3b-c.

this very thing, yet it is marvellous how much strength the authority of the ancient Jews, on which they so pride themselves, has to refute the enemies of the Gospel and to stop their mouths.''

This is a far-reaching acknowledgement of the historically determined character of the New Testament. L'Empereur adopts the socinian argument for the truth of Christianity that we have also found in Grotius. But the example which he gives of this use, and the way in which he reacted to Heinsius' *annotationes* make it clear how far he differed from Grotius.

The example chosen by L'Empereur is the use of Ps. 2 in Hebrews (1:5; 5:5) to prove the divinity of Christ. He mentions how Rashi literally explained Ps. 2 of David, but had to admit that older Jewish exegetes interpreted it mystically of the Messiah. He then cites some passages from the targumim and Talmud to show that the older Jews, like Paul, also understood it literally as referring to the Messiah, but he does not go beyond this survey. It is not clear if L'Empereur wanted to show by his analysis that Ps. 2 is cited in the New Testament because it was (1) generally, but wrongly, understood messianically at the time, or (2) because it deals, not literally of course, but in a certain spiritual sense, with Christ, a spiritual sense for which the older rabbis stand sureties; or (3) because it is literally concerned with Christ, but that this meaning has been falsified by the modern Jews. This unclarity arises because L'Empereur's interpretation of these texts is founded on a polemical approach, intent on refuting the interpretation of his opponent without worrying too much about his own consistency. L'Empereur could use any one of the interpretations named above, depending on how it suited him. He was not interested in a real understanding of the use of the Old Testament citations in the New Testament, but only in defending them.[219] The polemical context of his argument is evident from the continuation of the discussion of the usefulness of the rabbis in the introduction to *Halikhot Olam*. L'Empereur argues that the most important Christian dogmas, such as the passion of the Messiah, original sin, and the necessity of a divine mediator to be redeemed from it, can be confirmed from rabbinical literature.

---

[219] Very clearly in a passage in *ComJes*, 44-6. Abrabanel argues that Is. 53:12 (he shall divide the spoil) cannot refer to Christ. L'Empereur advances some mutually contradictory arguments against this: (1) that the Christian authorities do in fact do this and (2) that this can be explained spiritually, as the bringing of souls to the true faith and thus capturing them from the Devil. And why should Abrabanel not explain this passage spiritually, when the Jews themselves do so in so many places? In *ComJes*, 106-9 he refutes Abrabanel's identification of the suffering servant in Is. 53 with the people of Israel, referring to Benjamin of Tudela's report of Jewish kingdoms (in which L'Empereur himself did not believe). Simon (*Histoire critique du Nouveau Testament*, 245) gives a full historical solution.

This theological interest in the exegesis of the bible, of which the refutation of heterodox opponents is an important part, is also found in those works by L'Empereur more particularly concerned with exegesis. The first of these is the travel narrative of Benjamin of Tudela. This 12th century Spanish rabbi undertook a journey through the lands round the Mediterranean from Spain to Baghdad, spending some time in Palestine. He left an account of this travels, which became especially popular among the Jews. After it had been translated by Arias Montanus, the Spanish hebraist who was involved in the publication of the *Biblia Regia* by Plantin,[220] it also came to be valued in humanist circles, because it contained a mine of information on the customs and manners of the 12th century Jews and other groups, and a detailed description of the Holy Land. In their commentaries Grotius and de Dieu regularly make use of it as a source of information on the geography of Palestina. This popularity, the fact that Arias' translation was known to be poor,[221] and the relatively simple Hebrew of the text, explain the intention of a number of hebraists to produce a new translation.[222] L'Empereur, encouraged by Rivet, was the first to realise this intention. He was already occupied in translating the work in 1631, and it appeared two years later.[223] The edition was a commercial success, probably the only one among all L'Empereur's works. It went into a second impression the same year, without a parallel Hebrew text.

The first impression took the form of a bilingual edition, with notes, as typified by the works described in the previous section. In the notes L'Empereur made use above all of Zacuto's *Yuḥasin* and the *Zemaḥ David* of David Gans, for historical information. In the foreword he states that he has used two Hebrew texts for his edition, one printed at Constantinople, put at his disposal by Heinsius, and the copy of a rare edition from Breisgau that Buxtorf had sent to Scaliger.[224] He also mentions in the foreword some *"notae marginales"* of Scaliger, made available to him by Johan de Laet, the historian of the West India Company.[225] De Laet was a pupil of Scaliger, and it is possible that he was one of those friends who were allowed to select books from Scaliger's library before they were auc-

---

[220] See Rekers, *Arias Montano*.

[221] *Elenchus Trihaeresii*, 99: Cf. *Sec. Scal*, 227. Such accounts of travels were very popular at that time: Diestel, *Geschichte*, 465, n. 10-11.

[222] E.g. Drusius' son: Drusius, *Annotationes*, "lectori amico"; someone in the circle of Grotius: Grotius, *Briefwisseling*, V, 151-2.

[223] *IbinBen*, *5. He was working on the translation as early as 1631. (cf. *MosKim*, 21; *ComJes*, 86, 99).

[224] *ItinBen*, **5.

[225] *ItinBen*, ***1b.

tioned or presented to the library of Leiden University.[226] The notes
must derive from Scaliger's copy of Montanus' edition, for although the
copy of the Breisgau edition, which is still in the possession of Leiden
University Library,[227] does contain some annotations in the
characteristic handwriting of Scaliger, they are not those which
L'Empereur mentioned in his notes.[228] De Laet himself must have
owned the copy of Montanus' edition, or have transcribed the notes.
L'Empereur's own annotations contain some linguistic and historical
remarks on the text, but by far the greatest attention is paid, in foreword
and notes, to a theological argument. In his account of his travels, Benjamin mentions the existence of Jewish communities in the east, which
enjoyed a great degree of political autonomy. He also repeats tales which
he had heard of the kingdom of the Ten Tribes. L'Empereur regarded
these references as the most important aspect of the work. He believed
that Benjamin had tried in this way to deprive of its evidential force an
Old Testament prophecy which shows that Christ has already come.
Genesis 49:10 "the sceptre shall not pass from Judah until Shiloh
comes", had been interpreted since the middle ages as a prophecy of the
loss of political independence by the Jews after the coming of the
Messiah. In his notes L'Empereur took great pains to refute Benjamin's
reports of autonomous Jewish communities.[229]

A polemical interest is also the leading characteristic of L'Empereur's
edition of a commentary on Daniel. In 1633 he published a translation
of Joseph ibn Yaḥya's paraphrase of this book of the bible. This was
L'Empereur's first work in the field of rabbinica, which he had probably
completed as early as the end of the 1620's. In the dedication to the
Mayors of Leiden L'Empereur again expressed his political and
ecclesiastical standpoint. Referring to the siege he praised the zeal of the
city magistracy of Leiden for the true religion. Indeed, Leiden was one
of the cities which most vigorously upheld the settlement of 1618.
L'Empereur stressed that the city remained so loyal to its own traditions,
and was an example for other cities.

In the foreword he also described how the work had come into
being.[230] He had acquired Ibn Yaḥya's paraphrase from the library of
Erpenius and studied and translated the work in order to be able to use

---

[226] For Scaliger's will: de Jonge, "Latin Testament".
[227] Shelf number 875 F 43/2. Montanus' edition was not listed in Scaliger's auction
catalogue.
[228] L'Empereur cites notes of Scaliger on pp. 161, 162, 164 of *ItinBen*.
[229] Menasseh ben Israel cites Benjamin of Tudela with approval in his discussion of
Gen. 49:10: *Conciliator*, 92.
[230] *ParaDan*, *****4.

it for teaching rabbinical literature. He thought the work very suitable for this purpose, because of its brevity and above all because of its content. It contained many Jewish doctrines, so that according to L'Empereur it was possible to construct a Jewish dogmatic system from it. In addition the text included many typical formulae and modes of expression, which made it suitable for the study of rabbinical language and literature. Finally L'Empereur remarked that Ibn Yaḥya sometimes succeeded in making clear the prophet's intention. For these reasons L'Empereur found it very suitable for students of theology and rabbinica. L'Empereur's translation and annotations were put into order and written out in fair copy by J. H. Engelerus, a student of oriental languages who lodged in his house,[231] in order to gain practice in rabbinica. On his departure Engelerus left this MS. with his teacher. When the printer Wilhelm Christiani asked L'Empereur for a work by him so that he could use his new Hebrew and Arabic types,[232] this was the only work which he had ready. Although he understood that in fact there was much in it that ought to be altered, L'Empereur parted with the MS. at the printer's insistence.

The form of the edition corresponds with L'Empereur's summary of the attractive features of the work. It is a bilingual edition, with two kinds of notes, the shorter ones clarifying the idiom of Ibn Yaḥya, and longer notes in which L'Empereur attacked the author's theological opinions. L'Empereur's own interest was mainly in the theological interpretation. He would have preferred, so he wrote in the foreword, to publish Abrabanel's commentary on Daniel, which he had not yet known when he was translating Ibn Yaḥya. As we shall see in the next section, this work of Abrabanel was regarded by Christian hebraists as one of the great Jewish anti-Christian writings. In the edition of Ibn Yaḥya's paraphrase, L'Empereur's attention was fixed mainly on the passages which concern Jewish-Christian polemic. The most important of them is Dan 9:24-7, the prophecy of the seventy weeks which will pass until the coming of an anointed one.

This prophecy was generally regarded as one of the clearest predictions of the coming of Christ in the Old Testament. Yet the heart of the prophecy—that sixty nine weeks shall pass between the order to rebuild

---

[231] *ASALB*, 205. J. H. Engelerus, Tigurino-Helveticus, 23, matriculated as a student of theology on 3 November 1627.

[232] Wilhelmus Christianus van der Boxe (Briels, *Boekdrukkers*, 184-5). This explains the strange combination of the statements on the title page (Apud Ioannem Janssonium, Typis Wilhelmi Christiani. Anno. 1633) and the last page (Lugduni Batavorum; impressa in officine Typographica Wilhelmi Christiani, 1633). Cf. Fuks and Fuks, *Typography*, 141.

Jerusalem and the coming of an anointed one—is not so clear, so that virtually every Christian exegete of Daniel could offer his own solution. This diversity had led Scaliger to make the sarcastic remark that the best argument that Porphyry could have wished for his attack on Christianity was the abundance of ridiculous interpretations of the seventy weeks.[233] L'Empereur too presented a new solution, and although Cocceius could judge it a simple one in comparison with other suggestions,[234] his interpretation is a sample of all the methods which were at the disposal of a harmonising exegete. He assumes interruptions in the series of years counted, counts lunar and solar years, and accepts lifetimes of hundreds of years for the Jews who had experienced the exile. In these theological interpretations one can assume a certain playful element, and L'Empereur too presents his suggestions with the necessary reserve as a possible solution. In his interpretation of the book as a whole, he followed the calvinist tradition of Piscator, Tossanus and Junius, praising the last named in particular.[235] Following Junius he identified the fourth monarchy with that of the Seleucids. Lutheran exegesis, which adhered to a mediaeval tradition that considered the fourth monarchy as still persisting, was rejected by the calvinists, who had no ties to the Empire.[236] Other aspects of L'Empereur's exegesis of Daniel are mainly concerned with harmonisation.

His treatment of the problem of Darius the Mede may serve as an example. This Darius, who occurs in Dan. 6:1-2 and 9:1 had long been a problem for exegetes. In Daniel everything seems clear. Darius is king of the Medes, succeeds Belshazzar as king of Babylon, and divides his empire into 120 satrapies. He ruled over Medes, Persians and Babylonians. The problem is that he does not appear in secular historical literature and that this literature does not even know of a Median empire between that of Babylon and that of the Persians. Solutions to this problem mostly hinge on a remark of Josephus that this Darius was known to the Greeks under another name. The problem was thus reduced to identifying this person. L'Empereur paused for a long time on this problem, discussed and rejected various solutions and finally arrived at an interpretation of his own with the aid of Ibn Yaḥya's comment on Dan. 6:28,[237] that Cyrus was the son in law of Darius the Mede.

---

[233] *De Emendatione Temporum*, e4a-b.

[234] He did not however agree with this; Cocceius to L'Empereur, 25.9.1633; Cocceius, *Opera ANEKDOTA* I, 632.

[235] *ParaDan*, 53. Cf. *MosKim*, 121.

[236] Marsch, *Biblische Prophetie*, 154-7 shows how German lutherans and catholics joined fraternally in opposing Bodin's dismissal of the identification of the fourth monarchy, which guaranteed the continuance of the world, with the German Empire.

[237] *ParaDan*, **1-***2, 112-3.

Cyrus was king of the Persians, and, according to Greek historical literature, the conqueror of Babylon. L'Empereur linked this remark with the statement in Xenophon's *Cyropaideia* that Cyrus was the son in law of Cyaxares, a Median prince, and then identified Darius the Mede with this Cyaxares. Finally he assumed, appealing to Joseph ben Gorion's Hebrew history, that Cyrus had made Cyaxares governor of Babylon.

This solution is only interesting because it gives us an insight into the way in which L'Empereur practised exegesis and shows his very defective humanist training. To begin with the latter, it had been known as early as Cicero's time that the historical value of Xenophon's *Cyropaideia* was extremely slight, and Scaliger had repeated this verdict in his *De Emendatione Temporum*.[238] In his polemic with Serarius Scaliger had also adequately demonstrated that Joseph Ben Gorion was not a Hebrew work of the Jewish historian Josephus, but a historically unreliable product of the middle ages.[239] Although Scaliger is cited in the *Paraphrasis*,[240] L'Empereur had not properly studied his works, of which he had not bought the *De Emendatione* until 1629. At the time when he was writing his notes on Ibn Yaḥya, he still considered Joseph ben Gorion as a reliable historian, although as early as the foreword of *Middot* (1630) he repeated the evidence of Scaliger and showed the unreliability of ben Gorion.

It is characteristic that L'Empereur used rabbinical literature in his effort to harmonise the problem of Darius the Mede. He starts his attempt to find a solution from Ibn Yaḥya, whom he always describes elsewhere as wholly unreliable in the field of history and chronology. A harmonising interpretation of the bible does not need to prove the probability of a solution, but only its possibility. The procedure is based on the assumption that the bible has a unique position. Such an interpretation is therefore typically theological. Also theological in its nature was L'Empereur's further exegesis of Daniel, in which he used the text as a source of proof passages for Christian doctrine, starting from Ibn Yaḥya's exegesis. His own exposition is so closely related to Ibn Yaḥya's paraphrase that the index of subjects, which includes mainly references to the treatment of parts of doctrine, can also point with approval to Jewish exegesis. The entries "the kingdom of Christ is eternal" and "it is pretended that God's providence only concerns the Israelites" both

---

[238] Cicero, *Ad Q. Frat.* I, i, 8; Scaliger, *De Emendatione Temporum*, d3b; "Nam Xenophontem tam constat historiam noluisse scribere, sed exemplum bene educti principis proponere, quam certum est, nihil in tota Cyripaedia verum esse".
[239] Scaliger, *Elenchus Trihaeresii*, 41-5, cf. *Sec. Scal*, 352-3.
[240] *ParaDan*, 166.

refer to Ibn Yaḥya's text.[241] As a calvinist theologian L'Empereur was above all interested in a doctrinally oriented exposition of the bible. Such an exposition he found in the rabbis' exegesis, and he could use it to confirm his own system of doctrine or to refute a rival, but related system. We shall now turn to L'Empereur's attitude with regard to Judaism and its refutation.

## 4.4  *The refutation of Judaism*

At the same time as Hebrew studies were developing in the universities of the Dutch Republic, a sizeable Jewish community came into being there. Around 1580 there were probably only a few Jewish families in the northern provinces, but the last decades of the 16th century saw the beginning of the growth of an originally modest Jewish community in several cities of the Republic. Its origin is wrapped in obscurity.[242] It is only clear that the arrival of marranoes, mostly directly from the Iberian peninsula or via the marrano communities in the south of France, formed the most important factor in this immigration. The marranoes were by their own account the descendants of baptised Jews, who had confessed catholicism in Spain and Portugal. In the Republic they were converted to Judaism, although many of the immigrants had scarcely had any acquaintance with Jewish customs and assumptions in their youth. The reason for their return to Judaism in the Republic is a great enigma in the history of this group. Elsewhere they gave preference to catholicism or the reformation, and the explanations offered vary from purely religious to predominantly socio-economic. One which can even appeal to one of the Amsterdam rabbis claims that the marranoes could only maintain their own way of life in the Republic by constituting themselves as a religious community, since they were not permitted to form their own Portuguese nation with their own magistrates and economic privileges.[243]

In any case, the history and the character of the Jewish community which settled mainly at Amsterdam, were fundamentally determined by their descent from converts, who had not been imbued with a religious

---

[241] "Regnum Christi aeternum" and "Providentia Dei in solos Israelitas fingitur".
[242] Nahon, "Marranes", 344-5.
[243] The relations between French and Amsterdam Jewish communities: Nahon, "Rapports". For Morteira's unfavourable estimate of the marranoes: Salomon, "Morteira", 137-9. Boyayin, "New Christians", denies the persistence of a Jewish tradition for certain groups. A good example of such an ambiguous transition in Salomon, "Manuscript". Kaplan, "Portuguese Jews" contains a general description. For a survey of the literature on the Amsterdam community: Nahon, "Marranes".

tradition in their youth. In the first half of the 17th century, numerous conflicts broke out within the community. After 1603, three different synagogues were set up within fifteen years, and divided between them the small group of Jews, probably only a thousand, who lived in Amsterdam.[244] In spite of the fact that the three congregations kept up and jointly administered some essential communal provisions such as a cemetery, a poor fund and their contacts with the authorities,[245] the creation of the different synagogues was certainly connected with differences in opinion on the way in which they wanted to adopt Judaism. Conflicts on the *halakhah* revealed the resistance of leading laymen, such as David Pharar, to the authority of the religious leadership of the rabbis.[246] The rabbis themselves were divided between a more philosophical-rationalist approach to their faith, which followed Maimonides, and a mystical-cabbalistic tendency. Rabbi Saul Levi Morteira, who became chief rabbi of the three congregations, when they were united after great efforts in 1639, was the most important representative of the first tendency.[247] Against him stood the adherents of the Cabbala, such men as Abraham Kohen de Herrera, Isaac Aboab da Fonseca and Menasseh ben Israel.[248] In the thirties this gave rise to a serious conflict between Aboab and Morteira.[249] After Morteira's death in 1660 the former took over the religious leadership of the Amsterdam congregation. The changing of the guard was a radical one. Within half a year of Morteira's death, the decision was taken that from henceforth no Italian, Pole or German should be allowed to give instruction in the *Talmud Torah*, the congregation's educational institution.[250] It is possible that this decision was directed against the memory of Morteira, who passed—wrongly—for an Italian.[251] Under Aboab's leadership the Amsterdam community participated enthusiastically in the excitement over Shabbetai Zevi.[252] As well as these conflicts, which all took place within the confines of Judaism, there was an undercurrent of religious scepticism within the Sephardic community in the first half of the 17th century. This tradition is known from the problems it created for such of its representatives as Delmedigo, Uriel da Costa, Juan de Prado and, the most famous of them

---

[244] Israel, "Economic Contribution", 513.
[245] Brugmans, *Geschiedenis*, 244 ff.
[246] Brugmans, *Geschiedenis*, 229.
[247] Salomon, "Morteira".
[248] Melnick, *Polemics*, 34-40, 43-54.
[249] Altmann, "Eternality of Punishment", 10-6.
[250] Brugmans, *Geschiedenis*, 283.
[251] Salomon, "Morteira".
[252] Scholem, *Sabbatai Sevi*, 520-2.

all, Spinoza.[253] In this group traditionally sceptical elements from
Spanish Jewish religious philosophy and the ambivalent religious attitude
of the marranoes combined with the fluid and not yet authoritatively
established religious character of the Amsterdam Jewish community.
Thus the marrano origin of the community led to a great cultural diversity. The most important task for the rabbis was the education and
assimilation into Judaism of the new arrivals. In this process, polemic
with Christianity, carried on by manuscript, of which traces have been
preserved, played an important part.[254]

The attitude of the authorities in the Republic towards the Jews was
distinguished from an early stage by great tolerance. The famous lines
of Marvell:[255]

> "Hence Amsterdam Turk-Christian-Pagan-Jew,
> Staple of Sects and Mint of Schisme grew;
> That Bank of Conscience, where not one so Strange
> Opinion but finds Credit, and Exchange"

refer to the fifties, but the Jewish community had won a high degree of
acceptance much earlier. On the occasion of a discussion in the States of
Holland during the Truce on the drawing up of regulations for the
residence of the Jews in the province of Holland, Grotius presented a
draft for such a regulation, his *Remonstrantie*, mentioned above. This was
a fairly liberal advice, but even so Grotius set quite strict conditions for
the residence of the Jews. The draft probably says more about his personal attitude towards Judaism than about the considerations which
determined the policy of the city magistracies towards the Jews.[256]
Ultimately the States took no decision and left it to the individual cities
to adopt their own policies. The patriciates of the cities of Holland,
especially Amsterdam, left the Jews more freedoms than those provided
in Grotius' draft. As the lines quoted from Marvell suggest, economic
considerations played a significant role in this.

The contribution of the Jewish community to the economy of the
Republic in the first half of the 17th century should not be exaggerated.
In the levy of the 200th penny tax in 1631 there were only twenty-one
Jews among the fifteen hundred wealthiest Amsterdammers.[257] But the
contribution of the Jewish merchants was unique. In its commerce and
industry the community was quite as distinctive as in its religion and way

---

[253] Revah, *Spinoza*, 13-20.
[254] See the inventory of Ets Haim: Fuks & Fuks, *Hebrew Manuscripts* II, 91-133.
[255] The Character of Holland, ll. 71-74.
[256] Meijer, *Remonstrantie*, 95.
[257] Van Dillen, "Vreemdelingen".

of life.[258] In the traditional branches of Holland's trade, the Jews could not penetrate because of the vigorous competition, but in the trade with Portugal and the Portuguese colonies, they had a virtual monopoly. The Brazilian sugar trade in the thirties and forties for example was mainly in the hands of the Jews, which led, when the colony was conquered by the West India Company, to one of the few outbursts of an economically motivated anti-semitism in the Republic.[259] In the course of the 17th century a sizeable class of Jewish artisans was to emerge in Amsterdam for the first time in Western Europe. They were employed in the industries which processed the products of this colonial trade—sugar, diamonds, tobacco, silk and perfume. This industry was the basis on which the Amsterdam Jewish community was able to grow into the largest in Western Europe. Since the Jews did not usually offer economic competition, because of the special nature of their commerce, the city patriciate was able to take a very liberal attitude to them. More eloquent than any declaration of tolerance is the fact the Republic in 1632-3 was willing to let the peace negotiations with Spain founder on the condition put forward by the Dutch, that their Jewish subjects should enjoy the same rights in trade with Spain and Portugal as their other citizens, so that they should be protected against the Inquisition. This demand, more than any other, roused the Spanish government to fury. Although it is possible that this condition was chiefly defended by those groups in the Republic which were supporters of the continuation of the war, and who therefore tried to put unacceptable demands to Spain, the condition was only credible because from 1619 a clearly formulated and consistent policy with regard to the Jews, had been part of the foreign policy of the Republic.[260]

The care of the government made a deep impression on the Jewish community of Amsterdam. The story of the *Curiel Mekhila* symbolises their amazement and joy at this toleration. David Curiel, a prominent member of the Jewish community, was attacked by a robber, an unknown German, who seriously wounded him with a knife. Curiel pursued his attacker through the city, helped by his Christian neighbours. The man was arrested, tried and executed. Curiel then received a letter from the States of Holland in which they expressed their regret at the

---

[258] Israel, "Economic Contribution", 506: "In effect, the Portuguese speaking Jews of Holland and Zeeland constituted an exceptionally tightly-knit economic grouping, as wholly distinctive in trade and industry as in Religion and lifestyle."

[259] In 1637-38 Brazilian merchants and the Brazilian classis undertook a joint campaign against the Jews, with clear economic motives: van den Berg, *Joden en Christenen*, 20-2.

[260] Israel, "Spain", 15, 26-7.

incident and invited him to be present at the anatomical lesson on the corpse of his attacker in their own University at Leiden. This story which is handed down in five different MSS., preserved in Jewish libraries, was probably read on the feast of Purim as the *Curiel Mekhila*, directly after the reading of Esther, the book which relates an earlier attack on the Jews and the painful destruction of their enemy.[261] The fullest recognition was the visit of Fredrik Hendrik to the restored synagogue of the united communities on 22 May 1642, accompanied by his son and the Queen of England.[262]

Numerous contacts with the Jews arose in intellectual circles in the Republic. Within the medical world, a profession in which the Jews were traditionally active, mutual contact was customary. Joseph Bueno, a Jewish physician, was called to the deathbed of Maurice, while the list of acquaintances of Abraham Zacuto is a catalogue of the most important physicians of the Republic: the Leiden professors Heurnius and van der Linden, the Amsterdam physicians Nicolaus and Bernardus Fontanus, Isaac Pontanus from Harderwijk and Johan van Beverwijck from Dordrecht.[263] In March 1633 the first Jew took his doctorate at the University of Leiden in medicine,[264] and according to a—late—report of G. J. Vossius his religion played hardly any role in the consideration of whether he could be admitted to promotion.[265] In the circles of the humanists, such contacts were above all directed to the acquisition of information about Judaism and rabbinical literature. The best known are the contacts of Menasseh ben Israel, who through the mediation of Vossius made the acquaintance of numerous Christian scholars, including Barlaeus, Grotius, Salmasius and de Wilhem.[266] Vossius got to know Menasseh after he had moved to Amsterdam in May 1631 to become professor at the newly founded Athenaeum there. In a letter of November 1632 he described Menasseh in a way which makes it clear that he had known him for some time. This is the earliest Christian source on Menasseh's contacts with Christians. From Jewish sources we know that he had been consulted by Christians as early as 1629.[267]

---

[261] Fuks & Fuks, "Historiography", 436-8.
[262] Méchoulan, "Visite".
[263] Blok, "Barlaeus", 188 ff.
[264] *Molh.* II, 179; see Frijhoff, *Société*, 55.
[265] Vossius, *Epistolae*, 452; to A. v.d. Linden, 29.3.1647. He writes that Vorstius had told him "haud in considerationem venire, quae fidei sunt, sed quae Medicae artis".
[266] Méchoulan, "Saumaise"; "Problème"; "Menasseh"; Ter Horst, *Isaac Vossius*, 11; see note 262.
[267] Vossius, *Epistolae*, 208; to S. Bellimontus, 14.11.1632. Katchen, *Christian Hebraists*, 127-8.

As we have seen, L'Empereur bought a number of books from
Menasseh in the spring of 1631. It is possible that he had been introduced
to him through Vossius' mediation. L'Empereur had an excellent personal relationship with Gerardus Johannes Vossius, whose son Dionysius
was one of his pupils.[268] But it is also possible that his contacts with
Menasseh dated from some time before. In the foreword to his edition
of *Halikhot Olam* L'Empereur mentions that he had visited Jews in
Amsterdam in their homes and in the synagogue, and that his teacher in
rabbinica got into difficulties with the Parnassim, the leaders of the community, because L'Empereur made no secret of the fact that he studied
rabbinica with the intention of using his knowledge against Judaism.[269]
Such teaching from a Jewish master was indispensable in order to learn
to understand the Mishna and the Talmud. "On ne sçauroit l'entendre
sans la vive voix d'un Juif", said Scaliger, who might well know and who
welcomed the proposed settlement of a Jewish community in Haarlem
because he would be able to find a new teacher there.[270] It is known that
virtually all the Christian hebraists who were active in the field of rabbinica, made use of Jewish masters.[271] L'Empereur's schooling at
Amsterdam must be dated around 1627 when he was preparing himself
for a professorship at the University of Leiden. In his inaugural lecture
he made reference to a dispute with a Jew in a conversation.[272] It is possible that L'Empereur's Jewish teacher must be identified with Menasseh
ben Israel. Menasseh is the only rabbi for whom such teaching is
documented, and Vossius' description of his attitude towards Christian
scholars gives the impression that his desire to be of use to Christians

---

[268] L'Empereur received all Dionysius' works as presents. In a letter to Salmasius of
3.12.1633, soon after the death of Dionysius, Gerard Johannes includes L'Empereur
among his "amicissimi": Vossius, *Epistolae*, 229-30.

[269] *HalOl*, ***1a.

[270] *Sec Scal*, 590-1. Cf. also Scaliger to Drusius, 21.12.1595, Scaliger, *Epistolae*, 594
(no. ccxciii). This is the (seldom cited) last part of the famous letter on the death of
Philippus Ferdinandus: "Mira tamen ejus, & quanta non nisi hominem Iudaeum, eum-
que a puero informatum, potest cadere, in Thalmudicis exercitatio erat. Quae certe
frustra Christiani nostri conantur: qui nihil illarum literarum sine praesidio hominis
Judaei, & Iudaice instituti, perfecte tenere possunt. Hoc ego & mihi simper persuasi; &
verum esse, reipsa sum expertus. Hoc serio affirmare possum, me ab eo didicisse, quod
praeter Iudaeos nemo me docere poterat."

[271] E.g. Erpenius (Grotius, *Briefwisseling* I, 547). Grotius also consulted rabbis in
Amsterdam before 1619: *Briefwisseling* V, 151. For Gomarus: Gomarus to Walaeus,
1602; Walaeus, *Opera* II, 367: "Ego orbatus jam sum meo Rabbino; quia obiit peste. Hic
secundus Iudaeus post quartum fere mensem adventus sui sublatus est: ut alter"; for
Cocceius see note 100; Johannes Leusden: Hirschel, "Leusden", 25. The comparative
ease with which it was possible to find a Jewish teacher was the result of a relative
weakening of the internal cohesion of the Jewish communities: Zimmer, "Collaboration". Golius made a similar use of Persians: Juynboll, *Beoefenaars*, 162 ff.

[272] *Oratio*, 26-31.

predated his meeting with Vossius. There is even a certain degree of agreement in the terms in which Vossius and L'Empereur describe the attitude of the Jewish community towards such teaching.[273]

No public statements by L'Empereur or Menasseh on their mutual relationship are known. In his *Esperanza d'Israel* Menasseh took the trouble to correct a small error in L'Empereur's translation of Benjamin's *Itinerarium*,[274] but this need not be a sign of a poor relationship. In the thirties Menasseh gave L'Empereur a number of the works he published.[275] Public contacts between a theologian like L'Empereur and Menasseh were not exactly to be expected. In fact the publication of Menasseh's works gave offence to several orthodox theologians. Following a poem of Barlaeus' in Menasseh's *De Creatione Problemata XXX* of 1635, a polemic arose between Barlaeus and some theologians from the school of Voetius, in which Barlaeus was accused of socinianism. Voetius himself was moved by this affair to begin a course of lectures on Judaism, in which he deplored the freedom granted to the Jews in the Republic.[276] L'Empereur himself must have been well aware of an earlier clash between Menasseh and the Leiden theologians over his *Conciliator*. This work, originally written in Spanish, and translated into Latin by Dionysius Vossius, contains a number of solutions to contradictions in the Pentateuch. In each case, two bible verses are cited and the apparent contradiction between them is described in a commentary and resolved. The rationalistic nature of the objections makes one suspect that these were questions raised by marranoes who had just gone over to Judaism, so that the book will originally have been written for internal use in order to consolidate the Jewish community intellectually. Incited by Vossius and Barlaeus, Menasseh had the work translated into Latin and attempted to gain official recognition by requesting the States of Holland for permission to dedicate his work to them. On 15 September 1633 the States sent the *Conciliator* to the theology faculty at Leiden for their verdict. By 28 September the faculty had already returned an advice which, although it recognised that the book offered some useful observations, urged the rejection of Menasseh's request. The book, it said, contained Jewish fables and other matters which were not in accordance with orthodox doctrine. The States followed the negative advice and declined the dedication, which so alarmed Menasseh that in part of the edition of

---

[273] The "invidia" and the attitude of the Jewish community towards such contacts. Menasseh first appears in the accounts of Newe Shalom in 1627-8: Brugmans, *Geschiedenis*, 256.

[274] Méchoulan & Nahon, *Esperance*, 144; see *ItinBen*, 207.

[275] *De resurrectione mortuorum* (1636), *De Creatione* (1635), *De fragilitate humana* (1642).

[276] Prins, "Drukpersvrijheid", 158-65; Blok, "Barlaeus", 200-2.

the *Conciliator* which he printed himself, he altered the supposed place of publication to Frankfurt. The book was not banned, but the affair led to alarm within the Jewish community. Because of the danger that such publications might change the tolerant attitude of the authorities, the Jewish leadership instituted its own preventive censorship.[277]

It is also possible that L'Empereur's teacher must be identified with another Amsterdam rabbi with whom he was personally acquainted. That was Isaac Aboab da Fonesca (1605-93) from whom, as we saw above, he bought some Jewish books in September 1631. Aboab became rabbi of the Beth Israel community in 1626 and in 1636 became embroiled in a conflict with Morteira on the universality of salvation. He used cabbalistic opinions on the transmigration of souls to defend the idea that ultimately everyone would be saved. In 1639, on the unification of the three communities, he became assistant to Morteira. In 1641 he left for Brazil to become rabbi of the large Jewish community in Recife. After the death of Morteira, he succeeded him as chief rabbi.[278] L'Empereur used him in 1632 as a teacher, to explain some works he had published. In his account book for 1632 we find the entry: "to Fonseca for Halichot Olam to explain, 2 June f.30/It. Mishnayoth to the same the 23 July f.10".[279] That this Fonseca can be identified with Isaac Aboab is probable on the grounds of a letter of L'Empereur to Rivet of January 1639.[280] In this letter he writes how he had intended to write to the "most learned Fonseca" about a question of Rivet's concerning modern Jewish marriage customs, but that this was not necessary because Fonseca paid him a visit. The incident and the tone of the letter create the impression that L'Empereur's relationship to Fonseca was quite close and that he esteemed him as a prominent person. Besides these intellectual contacts he also had relations with Jews in a rather unexpected area. In the second half of the thirties he was involved, with some relatives, in the sugar trade from Brazil. As well as substantial profits, which in some years were twice as much as his not inconsiderable professor's salary, this commerce provided him with contacts with Jewish merchants.[281]

All these personal contacts left no trace in his work. His verdict on and characterisation of Judaism were determined purely by his knowledge of some Jewish writings and a long polemical tradition about the way in which these writings were to be read. Nowhere in his work does he appear to be aware of the different tendencies in the Amsterdam Jewish

---

[277] Prins, "Drukpersvrijheid", 165.
[278] The conflict with Morteira: Altmann, "Eternality of Punishment".
[279] Th 164, 4.
[280] Appendix VII.
[281] See the following chapter.

community, or of any variety within Judaism. His attitude was that of
an intellectually orthodox theologian, who saw Judaism as a timeless and
monolithic dogmatic doctrine. As such it was one of the many deviant
doctrines, which must be attacked and refuted and against which the
truth of the orthodox doctrine must be vindicated. This intellectual
refutation was not associated in L'Empereur's mind with any special
emotion. Judaism was not for him, as it had been for Luther and
Erasmus, a threat to the freedom of the life of the spirit. It was not a symbol of a possible existential choice for Christians too with which they
could forfeit *die Freiheit eines Christenmenschen.*[282] It was simply intellectually wrong, like the doctrines of the catholics, remonstrants, socinians
and other dissident groups. L'Empereur's refutation of Judaism and
defence of orthodox teaching are, it is true, characterised by the usual
accusations which flourished in interconfessional polemic—the charge of
intellectual bad faith against the opponent and of the deliberate choice of
untruth which lies at the heart of his deviant opinion—but they are otherwise free from any special tone, which might have arisen from any special
place of the Jews in his intellectual world.

In his theological thinking too, L'Empereur did not allocate any
special place to Judaism. Nowhere in his work does he refer to Romans
11, the text which had been used since Beza's exegesis to justify the
expectation of the imminent conversion of the Jews. Judaism played no
part whatever in his eschatology. In this he was exceptional in the 1630's.
Even the marginal notes in the States' Translation comment on Romans
11, that this chapter refers to the conversion of all the Jews.
L'Empereur's rejection of the expectation of a mass conversion was only
shared by a few theologians, like Maresius and Vedelius.[283] In his further
theological work L'Empereur, as befitted an orthodox thinker, attached
himself entirely to the general opinion. It is likely that the absence of
future expectations in which the Jews were involved, can be explained
from the lack of interest, mentioned in chapter 2, which L'Empereur
showed in the German federal-theological and the English puritan
traditions.[284]

In the dedication to his edition of *Halikhot Olam* we find L'Empereur's
most outspoken explanation of his view concerning his task as a hebraist,
so far as it affected the Jews. According to L'Empereur, by commission-

---

[282] Cf. Oberman, *Wurzeln.*
[283] General influence of Romans 11: van den Berg, *Joden en Christenen*, 25-35; Vedelius:
Blok, "Barlaeus", 94; Maresius: Nauta, *Maresius*, 334.
[284] Van den Berg, "Eschatological Expectations," 148 gives three roots of the expectation of the general conversion of the Jews: (1) the exegesis of Rom. 11; the German
federal-theological tradition; (3) a moderate English millennarianism.

ing him to write against the Jews, the Mayors and Curators had wished:[285]

> "that I should set the truth of Christianity in writing against the errors of the Jews, as the light against the shadow; and with this intention and purpose 'that it may happen that God will grant them a change of heart and show them the truth, and thus they may come to their senses and escape from the devil's snare' (II Tim. 2:25-6), or, if their obstinacy should prevent that in this age, that the Christians should at least be able to show the fame of the Saviour more clearly to them, and better defend their dogmas, and thus establish the faith more and more firmly."

If anywhere, then it was here that the citation from Romans 11, which Amama had given at the end of his survey of the aids for the study of Hebrew, would not have been out of place. L'Empereur chose the close of a passage from the second Epistle to Timothy, which does not refer to Jews but to the heterodox in general. He gives the impression of thinking a conversion of the Jews very unlikely, and sees his most important duty as vindicating the rightness of the Christian faith and refuting Jewish dogmas. His knowledge of this doctrine and opinion was not taken from his contacts with his Jewish contemporaries.

His personal friendship with Jews probably does explain his relatively tolerant view of the attitude which was to be taken towards them. In the dedication to his edition of *Bava Kamma*, he praised the Zeeland politician Casper van Vosbergen, to whom the dedication is addressed, because as a councillor of Maurice in the principality of Orange, he had abolished a number of antisemitic customs. The Jews must be treated as human beings.[286] Thus his social attitude towards the Jews appears moderate. Intellectually, he had a great deal of respect for some Jewish exegetes, and we are led to believe that in the course of his rabbinical studies, he gained a certain understanding of the character of rabbinical literature, and its customary mode of reasoning, which went further than the mere glorying in the absurdities of the Talmud, and the imperfections of rabbinical logic, which had marked his inaugural lecture and his first works.[287] It will hardly be a coincidence that the most negative characterisation of the Jews to appear in his work, the quotation from Terence, "*monstra hominum, non homines*" is to be found in the edition of Ibn Yahya's paraphrase of Daniel, his first work.[288] But these moderate

---

[285] *HalOl*, *3a-b.

[286] *Bava Kamma*, ***2b.

[287] Cf. the difference between "Saepius miram nobis Logicam exhibere depreaehenduntur Rabbini, cum quidlibet e quolibet deducunt" (*ParaDan*, 200, before 1629) and "id ex Judaeorum mente acceptum nihil absurdi continet" (*Bava Kamma*, 133, between 1633 and 1637).

[288] *ParaDan*, praefatio, Terence, *Eunuchus*, 4, 4, 29.

traits are by no means enough to make L'Empereur a philosemite. For that he lacked the necessary emotional involvement with Judaism.[289]

L'Empereur saw it as his task to refute the doctrine of Judaism, to support that of the Church and to rebuff attacks on it. His interest was purely intellectual. In the following pages we shall describe his scholarly work under this aspect of the refutation of Judaism. In the first place we shall analyse the form of a work directed specifically against the Jews. Then we shall show that the content and method of argument are traditional and, as was the case with almost all the Christian hebraists, dependent on mediaeval anti-Jewish polemic. Finally we shall investigate a new argument, which he developed in his edition of *Bava Kamma*.

L'Empereur's edition of the *Commentarii in Esaiae Prophetiam* of 1631 is a curious work. In the dedication to the States-General, in which the importance of the work is explained, he stated that the truth of the Christian religion is entirely to be found in the doctrine of Christ's redeeming death. This dogma is described in Isaiah 52 and 53. When, years ago, as a theologian at Harderwijk, he had argued against the Jews, he had wished above all to prove the truth of the Christian exegesis of these two chapters. In Leiden he had not changed his opinions and had investigated Jewish works to find whether they contained anything that was in conflict with Christian doctrine. Such research was particularly timely:[290]

> "because many, who themselves confess Christianity, do not shrink from wholly approving the error of the Jews; since they entirely deny the redemption by Christ of our sins."

After this dig at the socinians, he set out the aim of his work. It comprises the publication of a number of Jewish interpretations of Isaiah 52-3: two by Abrabanel, one by Moses Alshekh and fragments from the *Yalkut* which refer to both chapters. L'Empereur added to the edition a refutation of the Jewish exegetes, a new Latin translation of both chapters and a paraphrase. This is indeed all to be found in the work. But in this the form of the edition differs from that of L'Empereur's other work: the Jewish commentaries in the edition are not provided with a parallel translation. This omission is not the result of L'Empereur's lack of ability, but a sign of the insecurity he felt in this first example of a new genre: the publication of anti-Christian Jewish texts. Abrabanel's exegesis is a conscious attack on the Christian understanding of Isaiah

---

[289] Schoeps, *Philosemitismus*; recent literature on philosemitsm: *TRE* 3, 154-5.
[290] *ComJes*, ( + 4b). *Bava Kamma*, 239.

53. Through this commentary and works like it, he came to be regarded later in the century by the lutheran theologian Carpzov as the greatest Jewish antagonist of Christianity.[291] In this sense L'Empereur's edition and refutation of these commentaries is his only work to be concerned wholly with Jewish-Christian polemic.[292]

A brief survey of the way in which Christian hebraists in the 17th century approached Jewish polemic against Christianity makes it clear that L'Empereur's omission of a parallel translation was the result of the deep concern which works of this sort aroused among the orthodox.

A fairly extensive Jewish anti-Christian literature existed, but naturally circulated in MS.[293] The existence of such works had not remained hidden from the Christian hebraists. Münster had already referred in his works to a *Sefer Nizzaḥon*, a specimen of this genre.[294] In spite of the fact that the Jews attempted to keep such writings secret, the Christian hebraists succeeded in acquiring them. Thus L'Empereur owned three or four Jewish polemics, which he translated and considered publishing with a translation and refutation. In December 1633, he wrote to Ussher how he was working on the translation and refutation of a dearly bought MS., that he had earlier acquired, and in which a Jew had included everything he could urge against Christianity.[295] At around this time he was also occupied on a similar translation and refutation of the *Sefer Nizzaḥon*, which had been put at his disposal by Buxtorf II at Basle.[296] In 1637 he mentioned his ownership of a work *Vikku'aḥ Hadath*, a work which he believed was unknown to the Christians, by Abraham Peritsolidae, presented to him by David de Wilhem. It is possible that this is to be identified with the book mentioned in his letter to Ussher.[297]

---

[291] Carpzov, "introductio" to Martini's *Pugio*, 80-1.

[292] In his list of "scriptores Christiani Anti-Judaici recentiores", (*Bibliotheca hebraea* II, 1013-48) Wolfius mentions only the *ComJes* (p. 1031) of L'Empereur's works.

[293] Waxman, *History* II, 527-61.

[294] Hackspan, *Liber Nizachon*, 215 ff gives a detailed survey of the Christian hebraists who had seen the work, with references to passages: Münster, Fagius, Urbanus Regius, Buxtorf, L'Empereur, Schikard, Graserus. For the MS. of Buxtorf: Horbury "Basle Nizzahon".

[295] L'Empereur to Ussher, 16.11.1633; Ussher, *Works* XV, 576.

[296] Buxtorf II to Ussher, 26.8.1633; Ussher, *Works* XV, 569.

[297] In *Bava Kamma*, 70-1 he speaks of the anti-Christian work "Vichuah Hadath" which he ascribed to Abraham Peritsolidae, and which had been given him by David de Wilhem. At the end of his list of books he also names the MSS. he owned; they include only two Jewish polemics: "Vichuah hadath contra christianos, authore Abrahamo Judaeo", and "Montaltus Judaeus de satisfactione Christi". The latter work is the one mentioned in note 298. For the *Vikk'uaḥ Hadath* see de Rossi, *Bibliotheca Judaica anti-christiana*, 7, no. 3, identified by the author, following Wolfius in his appeal to Abrabanel, as by Abraham ben Chasdai. The name "Vikku'aḥ" was a popular one for such

The most curious MS. of this genre is now preserved in the Bibliotheca
Thysiana. It is a Dutch translation of the beginning of Elyah Montalto's
*Tratado Sobre El Capitulo 53 de Ezayes.* L'Empereur must have acquired
this MS. from a Jew in Amsterdam. Elyah Montalto (? -1615) was a marrano, born in Portugal. He studied medicine at the University of
Salamanca and was converted to Judaism in later life. He lived in Italy
and after previous contacts became court physician to Maria de Medici,
having stipulated as a condition that he should be permitted to confess
his Jewish faith openly. Saul Levi Morteira was his pupil, followed his
master to Paris and later transported Montalto's body to Amsterdam to
have it interred there. The numerous MSS. of Montalto's *Tratado* preserved in the libraries of Amsterdam's Jewish community, go back to
him.[298] The most remarkable feature of L'Empereur's MS. is the
language in which it is written. Other Dutch translations are not known
and it is obvious that he had it translated. But why into Dutch?

It was not personal circumstances which induced L'Empereur not to
publish any of these works. In 1641 the Hamburg minister Johan
Mueller[299] wrote a letter to Johann Buxtorf II of Basle, in which he
requested a favour of him:[300]

> "The rabbis of the Spanish synagogues here, R. Abraham de Fonseca and
> R. David Cohen de Lara, have very often spoken with me about the Chris-
> tian religion, and urged against me, when I spoke of the abolition of
> sacrifices, the authority of a Jew who is called Isaac Abarbanel. They boast
> of him excessively, and say that in his commentary on Daniel he has an
> answer to all the Christian arguments separately. When I searched every-
> where in Germany and Holland, even in Spain, for this author with letters
> and money, but was unable to get hold of the commentary on Daniel, I
> found in the book of Menasseh ben Israel, *de termino vitae,* as I understood
> from a statement of Constantijn L'Empereur, that you have translated the
> book of Abarbanel into Latin."

Mueller's information was correct and Buxtorf sent him his translation
which Mueller then used in a work directed against the Jews. The Hamburg preacher had also had access to a MS., of which he had had a
translation made, of the *Ḥizzuk Emunah* of Isaac ben Abraham of

---

polemics: Waxman, *History* II, 536 ff. In December 1643 L'Empereur paid one "Sigis-
mund, Jewish Christian" for transcribing Niẓẓaḥon: Th, 164, 4.

[298] Fuks and Fuks, *Hebrew Manuscripts* I, no. 277 (with literature); II, nos. 198, 214,
225, 226.

[299] For Mueller: Jöcher III, 731; Rotermund, V, 67-73; Müller, "Religionsgespräch".

[300] J. Mueller to J. Buxtorf II, 12.10.1641; J. J. Buxtorf, *Catalecta,* 441-2. Cf.
Menasseh ben Israel, *De termino vitae* 3, 6.

Troki.[301] In the previous section we have seen how L'Empereur had considered, instead of the commentary of Ibn Yaḥya, publishing that of Abrabanel on Daniel. Buxtorf II, who appears from the correspondence with Mueller to have already translated the work, was also considering an edition with translation and refutation in 1646. In a letter to L'Empereur he asked his opinion on the appropriateness of such an edition, in view of the troubled state of the church.[302] L'Empereur's reply is not known, but not surprisingly given his own decision not to proceed to publish such tractates, it was negative. Buxtorf's edition never appeared nor did that of the *Toledot Yeshu*, the MS. of which had been made available to him by Diestius.[303]

The only complete edition of a Jewish anti-Christian work which appeared during L'Empereur's lifetime was that of a version of the *Sefer Niẓẓaḥon* by Theodore Hackspan, professor of Hebrew at the University of Altdorf.[304] Hackspan (1607-59), was a lutheran theologian, who had studied with Calixtus and in 1636 became professor of Hebrew at Altdorf. In 1645 he exchanged his chair for an appointment in the faculty of theology.[305] His edition has two features which were characteristic of editions of such works in the first half of the 17th century. Firstly, he had only been able to acquire the MS. of the work with difficulty. He had, as he says in the foreword, stolen it from a Jewish acquaintance. Secondly, and more important, his edition, like L'Empereur's *Commentarii in Jesajam*, only offers a Hebrew text and no Latin translation. The first to publish Jewish anti-Christian works in translation was a pupil of Hackspan, J. C. Wagenseil (1633-1705). The analysis of his *Tela Ignea Satanae*, a compendium of various Jewish polemics, also throws light on the reluctance of earlier Christian hebraists to undertake such editions.

Wagenseil was not a theologian but an historian and philologist, who after his studies at Altdorf from 1649-55 had travelled around Europe and was later excessively proud of the many scholars whom he had met on his travels. In 1667 he became professor of history and law at Altdorf. In 1674 his teaching duties in history were altered to those of oriental languages. He had many contacts with members of the Austrian nobility and was involved in the city government of Nuremberg. In 1693 he

---

[301] *Judaismus ex Rabbinorum scriptis detectus et verbi divini oraculis refutatus*, Hamburg 1644. For the ownership of the work of Isaac ben Abraham: Müller, "Religionsgespräch".
[302] Appendix IX.
[303] Vossius, *Epistolae*, 260-1; from H. à Diest, 8.4.1644.
[304] A survey of the various Niẓẓaḥons: Wolfius, *Bibliotheca hebraea* I, 734-43; Horbury, "Basle Nizzahon". For the partial publication of a similar work by Schikard; Seck, *Schikard*, 76-8.
[305] *ADB* 10, 299-300.

declined an invitation to come to Leiden.[306] In the exceptionally prolix foreword to his *Tela Ignea Satanae* published in 1681, he attempted to justify his publication of anti-Christian treatises.[307] In good late 17th century style, his apologia contains a survey of the history of the censorship of books since the beginning of humanity, and of the reasons which underlay such censorship. In his survey Wagenseil appears as a convinced adherent of an absolutist theory of the state, which only acknowledges the right to exercise censorship to the sovereign authority, and not to lower organs of the state, or bodies with their own jurisdiction, such as the church. The state should, and is entitled to, prohibit books which lead to social troubles. Other books, which do not entail any danger to public order, can be tolerated. Among this group belong the anti-Christian writings of the Jews. Only a few Christians had ever been converted to Judaism, and these works are therefore not a danger to Christianity, and might be published. Such publications are even useful, since these works can make Christians mindful of their own fortunate position. Thus they will be encouraged to zeal for the conversion of the Jews, which in this way might even come about in the lifetime of Wagenseil, so that the latter days might dawn. The pietist tendency of this work ought not to be overlooked.[308] Wagenseil dedicated it to none less than Jesus Himself, and ended this prayer, written in the classical form of a letter of dedication, with a passionate "JESU, JESU, JESU have mercy on me".

Wagenseil was an enlightened pietist, whose thoughts revolved around Christ, the state and a general Christianity, which finds its expression in the faith of individuals. In the whole dedication, which runs to more than a hundred pages, there is not one reference to the church. Wagenseil, who was not a theologian, did not see in the publication of Jewish anti-Christian works, any danger to the piety and faith of individual Christians. The orthodox theologians, L'Empereur, Hackspan and Buxtorf II on the other hand, considered such books as a threat to the established churches of which they were members. They were not interested in defending Christianity in general, but the dogmas of their own particular churches.[309] They feared that Jewish polemics might give support to

---

[306] *ADB* 40, 481-3.

[307] It is very possible that Wagenseil borrowed the title of his work from his teacher Hackspan, who had described his edition as the unveiling of a work from which "tela" were shot at Christianity. (*Liber Nizachon*, 215). The foreword: *Tela ignea Satanae*, (7)-(104).

[308] Spener is cited in very laudatory terms: *Tela*, (88). The pietist bias of Wagenseil's work is overlooked by Dickmann, "Judenmissionsprogramm", 90.

[309] Grotius hoped to be able to publish Porphyry's work against the Christians: *Briefwisseling*, V, 26.

dissident Christian groups, who could borrow arguments from them.

Naturally, the representatives of such groups noticed and deplored the fact that orthodox hebraists preferred to defend the doctrines of their churches rather than refute the Jews. In 1638 and 1640 G. H. Vorstius, a pupil of L'Empereur,[310] published two translations of rabbinical works. This Vorstius was the son of Conradus Vorstius, the professor of theology appointed at Leiden during the Truce, who had become the symbol of all those forms of heterodoxy with which the contra-remonstrants reproached their opponents. The son, who refused to disown his father in any way (on the title pages of both editions, he presented himself as "C. filius"), and who could therefore be described by Rivet in a letter to a friend as "le filz du feu Vorstius l'Heretique", moved in mennonite and socinian circles.[311] His editions of rabbinical works were intended to attack Judaism and thus work for a reunited Christianity. In his *Constitutiones de fundamentis legis Rabbi Moses F. Maiiemon* of 1638 he published a bilingual edition of the first chapter of the *Mishneh Torah*, in which the basis of Jewish belief is described, together with a similar work by Abrabanel. In the foreword he announced that he had published the two editions to show that the Jews are a combative and disputatious people:[312]

> "if any, then this sort of people should be regarded as excessively disputatious; one often sees in the Chaos of the Talmud, a great many scholars disputing over a subordinate point, and everywhere one sees them making uproar and tumult. I know very well that many lament that a lack of the holy religion of Christ gives rise to similar reproaches, and that even they, who strive with the greatest praise and ingenuity to investigate thoroughly the secrets of the Talmud, do so. But these same people, as if they had wholly forgotten the tears which they had shed on the threshold of their work, prefer, when they are advanced in their work, after changing the person of their opponent, to carry on a war of words against those who confess the same Messiah, rather than open the door to those who have gone astray, to community with the king, a community which has been awaited in vain for so many ages. Truly the knowledge of truth would be spread with more success and more fruit if they would devote their tongues and pens to the honour of their leader and head, and not set so much store by an immoderate zeal for the faith."

The specialist in the field of rabbinica whom Vorstius accuses of preferring to attack his fellow Christians rather than the Jews, can only be

---

[310] *ASALB*, 225: on 22 April 1630 G. H. Vorstius, Steinfurtensis, matriculated as a student of philosophy.

[311] *NNBW* X, 1136. His marginal position is evident from the fact that his edition of *Żemach David* bears no dedication. His edition of Maimonides is dedicated to G. Anslo. For him see chapter 5.1. The characteristion by Rivet: *C. I. Rivet/Sarrau* II, 328-9.

[312] *Constitutiones*, (a3b).

L'Empereur, who as we saw, called on the authorities in several of his works to take action against remonstrants and socinians. This suspicion is confirmed in the foreword to Vorstius' translation of the *Ẓemaḥ David* of David Gans. In it he makes his excuses for the inclusion of some passages from the Talmud which slander Christ and assures the reader that his intention was only to strengthen him in his own faith and to teach him to despise Jewish fantasies. The refutation of the Jewish attack on Christianity serves this purpose and Vorstius expressed the wish that L'Empereur, who was so learned in rabbinica, would complete the publication of R. Lippmann's *Niẓẓaḥon*, which he had translated and refuted. "The Christian world has suffered under enough disputes, let us finally turn our weapons on the enemies of our Messiah."[313]

L'Empereur however did not proceed to publication, and his polemic with Judaism consequently retained its traditional character. The structure of his *Commentarii in Jesajam* illustrates this. L'Empereur regarded Abrabanel's commentary as an example of the approach of the modern Jews, who had turned away from the true interpretation of the bible. In the foreword he also praised the commentary included in his edition of Moses Alshekh, another modern Jewish biblical scholar, because he would often differ from the opinions of more recent Jewish commentators and revert to the older Jewish biblical exegesis. In L'Empereur's opinion this older exegesis vindicated the Christians against the more modern Jews. For that reason he also included some parts of the *Yalkut*, a compendium of such older commentaries. The basis of L'Empereur's only publication to have the refutation of Judaism as its most important goal, is thus a polemic scheme which distinguishes between older and more recent Jews. This procedure, in which the mediaeval rabbis are attacked with the aid of the Talmud, Midrashim and Targumim, is characteristic of 17th century anti-Jewish polemic. Cartwright, an English puritan hebraist, refers in the foreword to his *Electa Thargumico-Rabbinica* to the possibility of attacking Judaism using this polemical scheme, and describes it as the most important fruit of the study of rabbinical literature. He refers to the works of Galatinus, Porchetus, Mornaeus and Grotius.[314] This summary reveals the roots of the polemical scheme. All these authors were directly or indirectly dependent on the *Pugio Fidei* of Raymundus Martini.

Raymundus Martini was a Spanish dominican (c. 1210-c.1285) who completed his *Pugio Fidei adversus Mauros et Judaeos* in 1278.[315] This is the

---

[313] *Chronologia sacra-profana*, 4a. The passages on Jesus in the Talmud: 257 ff.
[314] Cartwright, *Electa Thargumico-Rabbinica*.
[315] For Martini: Cohen, *Friars*, 129ff; Willi-Plein, *Glaubensdolch*.

greatest anti-Jewish work of the middle ages, and although as such it was important in legitimating the development which was to lead to the expulsion of the Jews from Spain, it is difficult not to feel some admiration for Raymundus' intellectual achievement. This admiration concerns the extent of his knowledge of rabbinical literature and the consistent application of the scheme which he used to justify his appeal to it and to arrange his knowledge logically. Raymundus was a product of the dominican school of Raymundus de Pennaforte, who had drawn up a detailed programme for the refutation of the heathen. Pennaforte stimulated Thomas Aquinas to write his *Summa contra Gentiles*, and set up teaching institutions where Hebrew and Arabic were taught for the benefit of missionary endeavour.[316] The use of rabbinical literature for the refutation of the Jews was customary in this school. Raymundus Martini distinguished himself from the other dominican anti-Jewish writers, such as Pablo Christiani who held a public dispute with Nachmanides in 1263, by his greater rabbinical knowledge and his elaborate methodological reflection on its usefulness.

In the foreword to the *Pugio*, Raymundus makes a distinction between the modern Jews, who lived after Christ, and the ancient Jews of the time before the split between church and synagogue. These latter agree with the Christians and traces of their views are to be found in rabbinical literature, above all in the Talmud, Midrashim and Targumim.[317] On the basis of this methodological consideration he deployed his immense reading to support the following chain of reasoning by rabbinical citations: (1) the Messiah has already come; (2) God is triune; (3) because of his original sin, man must be reconciled with God; (4) this reconciliation can only be accomplished by a God-man; (5) the Messiah has already come and can be identified with Jesus Christ.[318]

The scheme and this method of reasoning proved exceptionally influential. They could be used in all manner of variants in works of the most various tendency. Only in the second half of the 17th century did printed editions of the *Pugio* appear, produced by a catholic scholar in Paris and an orthodox lutheran in Leipzig.[319] But as early as the late mid-

---

[316] For Pennaforte: Cohen, *Friars*, 106 ff.

[317] Martini, *Pugio*, prooemium, v-ix. Cf. (ix): "Non ergo respuamus traditiones ejusmodi, sed potius amplectamur, tum propter ea quae dicta sunt, tum quod nihil tam validum ad confutandam Judaeorum impudentiam reperitur, nihil ad eorum convincendam nequitiam tam efficax invenitur. Denique quid jucundius Christiano quam si distorquere facillime possit de manu hostium gladium, & eorum deinde mucrone proprio caput praecidere infidele, aut instar Judith ipsius arrepto pugione truncare?"

[318] Respectively book II (1), book III A (2), book III B (3), book III C (4 & 5). For a detailed analysis: Willi-Plein, *Glaubensdolch*, 38-9.

[319] Paris edition by du Voisin, Jöcher, IV, 1697-8. In a way which typifies the changed

dle ages, Raymundus was exercising an influence through other
works.[320] The method, the argument and a good deal of the rabbinical
knowledge of the *Pugio* became known in the 16th and 17th centuries
through a variety of works which were dependent on Raymundus. The
first of them was the work of Petrus Galatinus, already mentioned several
times above, his *De Arcanis Catholicae Veritatis* of 1518.

Petrus Galatinus, or Pietro Colonna (c.1460-c.1539) was an Italian
franciscan, who had studied Hebrew with Elias Levita.[321] As Scaliger,
who had consulted Raymundus' work in MS.,[322] was the first to point
out, the *De Arcanis* is a fairly shameless piece of plagiarism. Besides a
number of citations[323] Galatinus also took over Martini's scheme and his
mode of argument.

The work begins with a survey of the Talmud, in which Galatinus
unfolds the distinction between the ancient and the modern Jews.[324] He
varies this scheme by ascribing almost the whole Talmud to the older
Jews, and only rejecting the use which the modern Jews made of the
ancient material. His stance in the conflict between Reuchlin and the
Cologne dominicans over the question whether the Talmud should be
burned, a debate in which Galatinus took the part of Reuchlin, is in
accordance with this interpretation of the Talmud. The book follows, for

---

confessional fronts of the mid-century, he sent a number of presentation copies to Buxtorf
II, to distribute in Germany (Carpzov, "Praefatio" in Martini, *Pugio*, 123).
The Leipzig edition by J. B. Carpzov II (1639-99), a theologian: Herzog 3, 727-9.

[320] Cf. Cohen, *Friars*, 170-99. Above all via the works of Nicholas of Lyra, *Quodlibetum
de adventu Christi* and *Responsia ad quendam Iudaeum*, mostly included in the *Postilla*. See also
the survey in Carpzov, "praefatio", 102 of followers of Raymundus: Nicholas of Lyra,
Riccius, Hieronymus a Sancta Fide, Porchetus, Galatinus, Philippis Mornaeus et al.
Large parts of Thomas' *Summa contra Gentiles* are also taken from the *Pugio*: Berthier,
"Maître orientaliste," 300.

[321] For Galatinus (or Pietro Colonna): *DBDI* 27, 402-4; Kleinhans, *Vita*.

[322] Sec Scal, 529: "Beroaldus habebat *pugionem Raymundi Sebondi* contra Judaeos. Est
alterum exemplar Tholosae, au college de Foix; sunt duo maxima volumina. Ille
Raymundus erat Hispanus, Jacobin, bene versatus in Philosophia, Theologia & in
Thalmud. Scripsit librum illum ante 250 annos; est cum judicio legendus. Petrus
Galatinus, honeste Cordelier, fecit Epitomen, & non meminit sui benefactoris." Cf. also
Scaliger, *Epistolae*, 516-7, (no. ccxli). It is possible that he had himself seen Martini's
book: his formulation of the way in which the Talmud ought to be used against the Jews
(*Sec Scal*, 496-7: "ils (les Pères) devoient apprendre des Juifs, pour avoir puis apres
dequoy les battre, & leur couper la gorge de leur propre espée.") reminds us of Martini's
own description of his work (note 317).

[323] To make the plagiarism entirely clear, Carpzov even included in his edition of the
*Pugio* an "Index capitum libri Petri Galatini de Arcanis Catholicae Veritatis (..) cum
locus, quae in iis ex Pugione fidei desumpta sunt" (*Pugio*, 961-6).

[324] Galatinus, *De Arcanis*, 14: The Talmud contains "innumerabilia fere de Messia,
ac nostrae fidei admodum consentanea, arcana continentes, per multa annorum cur-
ricula, longe antequam Talmud confectus esset, a priscis Judaeorum traditae atque con-
scriptae". Cf. also 26-7.

the rest, the argument of Raymundus and uses his quotations. Galatinus' work, which was often reprinted in the 16th and 17th centuries, was exceptionally influential.[325]

The second great source of Martini's influence was Philippe Du Plessis Mornay's *De Veritate Religionis Christianae* of 1583.[326] Du Plessis Mornay (1549-1623) possessed a MS. of Raymundus' work, which he also lent to Buxtorf I.[327] He did not use the *Pugio* as a source for his whole work, but only for that part which concerned the Jews. His *De Veritate* is a general defence of the truth of Christianity against pagans and unbelievers and refrains from interconfessional polemic. Even so, the work is of an unmistakeably calvinist stamp. It begins with a philosophical discussion in which the existence of God is proved, and goes on to show the short-comings of man and his need for a revelation. It is then demonstrated that the Old Testament is a reliable source of revelation, which meets this need. Only where Du Plessis Mornay wishes to show that the Old Testament promises spiritual salvation—and by that stage he had reached the twenty-seventh chapter of his book—does he turn against the Jews. Here, he followed Martini entirely. He makes the methodological distinction between ancient and modern Jews,[328] and develops with the aid of rabbinical citations borrowed from Martini, the proof that a God-man is the necessary mediator for a spiritual salvation, that He has already come, and that He can be identified with Christ.[329] In the last chapter of his book, he proves the trustworthiness of the New Testament on the grounds of the foregoing. Du Plessis Mornay's *De Veritate* was frequently reprinted at the end of the 16th century[330] until it was driven out of the market by an even more successful work of the same name: Grotius' *De Veritate Religionis Christianae*.[331]

Part of the greater popularity of Grotius' work is undoubtedly the result of the fact that it was much shorter than that of Du Mornay. Another reason, which is associated with the content, can be found in the much more general and less scripturally based train of Grotius' argu-

[325] Editions: 1518, 1550, 1561, 1602, 1603, 1612, 1672.
[326] For du Plessis-Mornay (1549-1623), the "pope of the huguenots": *Haag* 7, 512-42.
[327] Du Plessis-Mornay to Buxtorf I; 23.7.1615, J. J. Buxtorf, *Catalecta*, 473-4. He gave it to him for publication. In 1627 Cappel, on behalf of the church and academy of Saumur, to which Du Mornay had bequeathed his library, requested its return. Cappel to Buxtorf II, 11.1627; J. J. Buxtorf, *Catalecta*, 480-3.
[328] Du Mornay, *De Veritate*, praefatio, 13-4.
[329] In chapter 27 (*De Veritate*, 596-628), in which he argues that the O.T. promises a spiritual salvation, Du Mornay disputes against the Jews from page 608. Chapter 28 then argues that this salvation must be brought by a God-man, 29 that this God-man has already come, and 30 that He can be identified with Christ.
[330] French: 1581, 1582, 1583, 1589. Latin: 1581, 1583 (2x) 1590, 1592, 1602, 1605.
[331] Ter Meulen/Diermanse, *Bibliographie*, no. 994-1090.

ment. His work too begins with a philosophical proof of the existence of God, but the second chapter proceeds directly to a proof of the reliability of Christ's teaching on the grounds of the miracles and resurrection of Jesus and the exalted character and great success of His doctrine. Only in the third chapter does the New Testament appear as a reliable source from which this doctrine can be derived. The reliability of the Old Testament is proved, as if in a footnote, at the end of the chapter by means of the use to which it is put in the New. This basis for the argument in the *De Veritate* can be harmonised with Grotius' exegetical practice. That is not the case in the last part of the book, in which the heathens, Jews and Muslims are refuted in three successive chapters. In the fifth chapter we find Grotius' use of the *Pugio Fidei*, which he had become acquainted with through Du Plessis Mornay.[332] After a discussion, typical of Grotius as a jurist, of the legality of Jesus' actions, there follows the by now familiar classical argument. In this chapter Grotius makes use of exegetical arguments which sometimes are not in accordance with the insights in his *Annotationes*. These inconsistencies can be explained in part by Grotius' dependence on his sources, but above all by the purpose of the work, which was not intended to be disseminated among those of other faiths, but for internal use within Christianity,[333] and which in any case attempted to present a modern message to a modern public. In 1640 Grotius yielded to years of pressure from his friends and was persuaded to publish scholarly notes on the work. In the notes to chapter five he displays an impressive rabbinical knowledge, employed according to the martinian scheme. Meijer has shown[334] that for a great many of these notes he was dependent on the works of L'Empereur. It is probable, from a note in L'Empereur's register of acquisitions, that Grotius also made use of his services directly. The list of acquisitions in 16mo mentions the Elzevier edition with notes, of the *De Veritate*, and comments "*donum pro opera praestita*".

Thanks to the works of Mornay and Grotius, both of whom published their works first in the vernacular, the martinian scheme for anti-Jewish polemic became widely known. In the world of the Christian hebraists it had been self-evident since the time of Galatinus. Yet the complete

---

[332] For the use of du Mornay: Spaans, "Bewijs".

[333] Grotius' attitude, as it appeared from his correspondence with Peter Heijling, was lukewarm (*Briefwisseling* VI, 132; VIII, 234). Heijling went to Ethiopia as a missionary, fulfilling a promise. Grotius admired this, but thought that such work was more necessary in Europe. Only when Christian unity had been re-established there, would it be time to think of missionary work elsewhere. For Grotius' intention in his *Bewijs*; Spaans, "Bewijs".

[334] Meijer, *Remonstrantie*, 57-63.

dependence of the protestant hebraists on mediaeval catholic works in this field continues to astonish us. In 1651 Buxtorf II, in a letter to Cocceius, gave a summary of the works which the latter could use to carry out his new function of writing against the Jews:[335]

> "you must yourself acquire, to use alongside Raymundus: Porchetus, the *Fortalitium Fidei*, *Stella Messiae*, Hieronymus de Sancta Fide, the book that is called *Zelus Christi*, published at Venice, Paulus de St Maria..."

All these are catholic works.[336]

After this survey we may return to L'Empereur's theological argument against Judaism. The use of the distinction between the ancient and modern Jews was self-evident for him, and it appears from a letter to Barbio (Appendix VI),[337] that in his eyes it already had its place in the teaching of rabbinica. Scattered through his works we find the classical, centuries-old arguments, which he sometimes provided with a new reference to rabbinical literature. Thus on the grounds of Gen. 49:10 and the seventy weeks of Daniel, he argued that the Messiah has already come,[338] that the ceremonial law is abolished,[339] and that man needs a reconciler for his original sin.[340]

Besides this wholly traditional theological method of attacking Judaism we find in his edition of Bava Kamma, another and much more modern argument.

L'Empereur's edition of *Bava Kamma* takes the same form as that of *Middot*; the work gives the Hebrew text, a parallel Latin translation and a commentary. *Bava Kamma* is a purely legal work. Developing Exodus 21 and 22 it contains the legal rules concerning damage to another's property or injury to his person. In the commentary L'Empereur compared these rules of the Mishna in detail with the legislation of the Roman Law. In his commentary we find about 140 references to the *Corpus Iuris Civilis*, largely to the *Digests*, but also dozens to the *Institutiones* and the *Codex*. The citations are drawn from the most various parts of the *Corpus Iuris*; at a rough estimate L'Empereur cites thirty different titles from the *Digests*. For virtually every separate mishna he mentions the corresponding passage in the Roman Law. On *Bava Kamma* vii,7, which deals with the capture of doves, for example, he cites D 41,1,5 where the same problem is discussed. Because the Roman Law has a fairly systematic

---

335 Buxtorf II to Cocceius, 3.9.1651; Cocceius, *Opera ANEKDOTA* II, 688.
336 For the identification of these works: Staehelin, ''Briefwechsel'', 379-80.
337 *Middot*, 101-2; *ComJes*, 69-70; the themes of *ItinBen* and *ParaDan*.
338 *Middot*, 87; *ParaDan*, 187.
339 *ParaDan*, 176. The theme of *ComJes*.
340 Appendix IX.

arrangement, most of the passages cited are drawn from a few titles: D
9,1 (*Actio de pauperie*), D 9,2 (*ad legem Aquilae*) and D 49,10 (*De injuriis*),
a restriction which Grotius, who had expected a full description of the
Jewish civil law, observed with some disappointment.[341]
There is a general purpose underlying the comparison. L'Empereur
regarded the Mishna and the Roman Law as the product of the work of
jurists, who developed an original law in order to apply it to concrete
cases and altered circumstances. The goal of this juridical work is the
preservation of the original justice.[342] L'Empereur's detailed comparison
investigated whether the rabbinical legal scholars had preserved the
original justice, as it had been laid down in the Word of God. In his opinion, that was not the case. In the Mishna, God's law had been twisted
and distorted.[343] The comparison with the *Corpus Iuris* shows the injustice
and the inhumanity of the Jewish legal scholars.[344] Whenever
L'Empereur compares the justice of the two systems of law, his verdict
is to the disadvantage of the Mishna,[345] and insofar as the laws of the
Mishna are just, then in his view they can be derived from Roman Law.
Thus on BK viii,7 L'Empereur cites D 27,1,11-13 and concludes:[346]

> "Through this (sc. Roman) law the preceding parts of the Mishna can be
> tested either immediately or by deduction (...) as to how far any equity
> (*aequitas*) is found in them; for it will be the judgment of sensible readers
> too that the Jews have gone further in this than right reason (*recta ratio*)
> requires."

L'Empereur considered Roman Law as an expression of natural justice
and equity, essentially in agreement with the Word of God. Such a view
of Roman Law as a law of nature is in harmony with his theological
background. Calvin and Melanchthon judged the *Corpus Iuris* in a like
manner, in the case of the latter under the influence of fear of the social
unrest which had arisen as a result of the reformation.[347] Comparisons
of Roman Law with the decalogue were a popular juridical genre in the
16th and 17th centuries, their most famous precursor and example being

---

[341] See the verdict in his letter to Vossius, 28.5.1638 (note 140).
[342] *Bava Kamma*, 7-9.
[343] "detorquent" (23)," in arctum cogere" (66), "coarctant" (158).
[344] *Bava Kamma*, 260: "Judaeorum inhumanitatem"; 280, "Judaeorum injustitia".
[345] *Bava Kamma*, 93, 123, 160, 184-5, 203, 227, 260, 280.
[346] *Bava Kamma*, 184-85: "Hac lege vel expresse praecedentia Misnae membra; vel
deducendo aliud ex alio *kat' akolouthian* probari possent, quatenus in iis aequitas quaedam
invenitur; longius enim in iis Judaeos progredi, quam recta ratio suadet, saniores lectores
judicabunt." For the concept of equity among the humanists: Kisch, "Summum ius
summa iniuria"; Grotius too, on Joh. 18:23 calls the Roman laws "aequiores" than
those of the Jews.
[347] For Melanchthon: Troje, "Literatur", 703 ff; Kisch, *Rechtslehre*, 116-26; for
Calvin, Bohatec, *Calvins Lehre*, 31-3.

the work of the pseudo-Ambrose, the *Collatio Legum Mosaicarum et Romanorum*.[348] Such works were intended to demonstrate the justice of the *Corpus Iuris*. It is not possible to point directly to any previous model for L'Empereur's use of the *Corpus Iuris* to test the justice of rabbinical literature, but nor is it necessary. The idea was more or less in the air. The Mishna and Talmud had been described as 'pandects' incidentally on earlier occasions,[349] and the comparison of legal systems had become common in the 17th century under the influence of the widely spread concept of the law of nations and nature.[350]

The nearest parallel to L'Empereur's comparison is to be found in Selden's work on the Jewish law. John Selden (1584-1654) was an English jurist who moved in the circles of such historians as Camden, Johnston and Cotton. He used his wide historical and legal learning to make it impossible to appeal to a divine or natural law against the positive law. He regarded all positive law in different societies as permissible modifications of à natural law, and could therefore argue in his *History of Tithes* that the ecclesiastical tax of tithes did not belong to the law of nature since there were societies in which they were not levied. For that reason the decision on the levy of such an ecclesiastical impost belonged, in his opinion, to the positive law, and thus to the State. The erastian Selden believed that the church could never appeal to a higher law than the positive. It was part of his argument that even the law of nature had had to be proclaimed by God, so that it too had a certain positive character. He dated this proclamation from the deluge, thereby following a rabbinical tradition. His rather incomprehensible works, written in a deliberately obscure style, aim to describe this law of nature, as it is to be found in the bible and in rabbinical tradition.[351] Selden had close contacts with the University of Leiden. He corresponded with de Laet, and Heinsius and de Dieu republished his *De Diis Syris* in 1629.

---

[348] Published by Pierre Pithou; for the nature and popularity of this book: Kelley, *Foundations*, 253; Troje, "Literatur", 659; Scaliger thought it a good book: *Sec Scal*, 272.

[349] Scaliger refers to a Talmud tractate as a "digest", e.g. *De Emendatione*, 536; in his *Arcanum* (I, 5, 4 ff), Cappel states that the Talmud, like Justinian's Codex, was composed of older "placita et decreta".

[350] Cf. the correspondence between Grotius and M. Ruarus, on a friend of the latter who had married his deceased wife's sister, and had got into difficulties as a result. They search through legal history to find precedents which could justify this second marriage. Among others, Maimonides is cited ("quem tu ( = Grotius) recte censes Hebraeorum veterum omnia legisse summoque judicio digessisse".) Grotius, *Briefwisseling* V, 171-5; 176-8. There is an amusing letter from Popellinière to Scaliger, 4.1.1604, *Epistres françoises*, 303-7, in which he proposes a kind of juridical voyage of discovery, to determine the civil and international law among the various savage tribes.

[351] Tuck, *Natural Right Theories*, 82-101. A criticism of his general thesis in Sommerville, "John Selden".

Other works by him were also published in Leiden.[352] But although his work was addressed, like that of no other Christian hebraist, to Jewish legal thought, it has another character and offers a quite different judgment of the rabbinical law, from that of L'Empereur's work in *Bava Kamma*.

All in all, L'Empereur's argument in *Bava Kamma*, which contains a social rather than a theological attack on Judaism, makes a rather unpleasantly modern impression. L'Empereur gave no sign of the outcome of his comparison either in his foreword or in his title, so that the nature of his anti-Jewish polemic only appears from an analysis of the commentary. Nor is his edition of *Bava Kamma* mentioned in later literature as an example of an anti-semitic work. But it was this book, written in the spirit of a humanist interest in the comparison of legal systems, that contained L'Empereur's potentially most dangerous attack on Judaism.

Following this survey of L'Empereur's most scholarly work it is worth returning to his appointment as professor with the duty of writing against the Jews. This appointment has been seen as a direct reaction by the University and the States of Holland to the negative judgment of the Leiden theology faculty on Menasseh's *Conciliator*. The authorities are supposed to have been alarmed by this Jewish publication, and to have appointed L'Empereur two days after the faculty's advice.[353] This explanation rests on two errors. In the first place, the initiative in no way came from the Mayors and Curators, although L'Empereur suggests this in the dedication of *Halikhot Olam*. So too in the appointment of Cocceius in 1651 to the post which L'Empereur had occupied, the initiative in fact came from the professor who then placed the responsibility with the Mayors and Curators.[354] Secondly, L'Empereur's appointment must not

---

[352] For Selden: *DNB* LI, 212-24. His knowledge of rabbinical literature: Herzog, "Selden". The edition of *De Diis Syriis*; Sellin, *Heinsius*, 104.

[353] Prijs, "Drukpersvrijheid", 156-7; Baron, *History* XV, 63-4; Blok, "Barlaeus", 98.

[354] Cocceius to Buxtorf II, 4.7.1651; *Opera Omnia* VIII, 87; the Curators of Leiden, "qui me ad scribendum contra Judaeos obligarunt", stimulate him: "ut ista potissimum edam, quibus patescat, doctrinam Novum Testamenti ubique in Veteri inculcari ejusque scopum unicum esse, Christi personam, adventum, dicta, facta, passiones, *doxas*, regnum, Ecclesiam redemtam, ejusque varios status describere; Quod si praestare possimus per divinam gratiam, nescio an ullum efficacius medium ad convertendos Judaeos esse possit." Now it seems unlikely that the Mayors and Curators were such thoroughgoing Cocceians in 1651. Moreover we know that in his negotiations with Mayors and Curators, who originally offered him a theologian's usual salary of f.1700, Cocceius asked for a higher salary, because otherwise he would not come. The Mayors and Curators agreed to this and minuted "that by this committee it shall also be more fully deliberated and resolved, concerning the cause or reasons, on which the aforesaid supplement shall be based." (*Molh.* III, 40-41). When he was finally appointed, he

be seen in the context of the affair of the condemnation of the *Conciliator*—there were not two days but three months between the two events—but in that of the struggle which surrounded the succession of Rivet and L'Empereur's ambition to become a professor in the faculty of theology. When L'Empereur at last achieved this professorship in 1646 the Mayors and Curators promptly withdrew his salary as professor *Controversiarum Judaicarum*.[355]

Nevertheless it would be unjust to dismiss his appointment as a purely personal matter. It has, it is true, nothing to do with the history of the Jewish community in the society of the Republic, but it is an important symbol in the history of the study of rabbinica in the 17th century. L'Empereur's activities as a hebraist were mainly directed towards making rabbinica accessible. The distinction between three aspects of his scholarly work, which is made in this chapter, may not lead us to forget that the first was the most important. This was how L'Empereur himself understood it, and how he set his work in the scholarly development which unlocked rabbinical literature. In a letter to Ussher he wrote, on the occasion of the appearance of Buxtorf's great dictionary to the Talmud:[356]

> "A work which is truly worthy of eternity. If a large number of translated texts from the Talmud were further to be added to it as a manual, we should finally be able to penetrate everywhere into it without the aid of the Jews. And, if God grants it, I shall shortly publish some of them."

The scholarly tradition by which rabbinica were made accessible was in the course of the 17th century to be largely the work of theologians. In this sense L'Empereur's appointment as *Professor Controversiarum Judaicarum*, intended to give him a post as close as possible to the faculty of theology, was a symbolically fitting reward for his work. We have seen how L'Empereur himself looked to rabbinical literature, despite the other goals which could be sought in it, chiefly for the satisfaction of his theological interests. In that too he was a sign of the further development of his subject.

---

received f.300 extra for the reason which had been thought of in the meantime: to write against the Jews (*Molh.* III, 43). On a further salary increase, seven months later, this salary was raised, but the position was then described as "writing against the Jews and others, who corrupt the truth of the Christian religion" (*Molh.* III, 54).

[355] *Molh.* II, 307: Mayors and Curators appoint L'Empereur as a theologian at the same salary as the other theologians, "with which he shall have to content himself, without being able to retain over and above it any of his present salaries, including also the additional salary which was granted to him to write against the Jews".

[356] L'Empereur to Ussher, 1.3.1641. Th 164, 6.

CHAPTER FIVE

POSTPONEMENT AND FULFILMENT.
MANDARIN IN THE REPUBLIC OF LETTERS (1634-1648)

> "Lipsius a escrit à Monsieur de Thou que ce n'est pas icy le
> siecle où il faille parler avec liberté. (..) Monsieur de Thou est
> fasché contre luy, & dit que nous ne vivons pas sous l'Inquisi-
> tion.(..) Je dedieray mon Eusebe à mon bon amy Monsieur
> de Thou, qui m'a fait avoir des livres du Roy: ny à Roy, ny
> à Prince, ny à Republique."
>
> (*Secunda Scaligerana*, 595)

On 27 August 1647 L'Empereur was called before the Mayors and
Curators. Six months before, he had—finally—been appointed to the
faculty of theology, and now the administrators wished to hear his opinion on a suitable successor to the Chair of Hebrew. L'Empereur summed
up a number of the qualities which were necessary in his eyes. As a successor, he wanted an "orthodoxus theologus, well experienced in the
Hebrew tongue, and also in Rabbinicis et Thalmudicis".[1] This is a not
inappropriate description of his own scholarly qualities in the years
1634-48.

In this chapter we shall describe the life and academic work of
L'Empereur in the last fourteen years of his life. During this period he
moved in the international community of scholars of his day: the
Republic of Letters. In this chapter, we shall study his place in this community and the manners and values to which it adhered.

The first section deals with L'Empereur's teaching and two different
groups of his pupils. Then follows a description of the Republic of Letters
and the typical activities which L'Empereur undertook as a member of
it, such as assisting other scholars in an extensive correspondence,
arranging the publication of the work of others, providing introductions
for young students, and his services to prince and state.

The period of his life described in this chapter began with an application for a chair in the faculty of Theology and ended with the fulfilment
of this ambition in 1647. Within the Republic of Letters too,
L'Empereur's conduct was that of an orthodox theologian. That is evident from his reissue of the work *De Republica Hebraeorum* by the Genevan
hebraist Cornelis Bertramus, from the attitude he took in various con-

---

[1] *Molh.* III, 7-8.

flicts, such as that on the philosophy of Descartes, and above all from his involvement in the publication of Cappel's *Critica Sacra*. This aspect of his activity will be analysed in the third and last section of this chapter.

## 5.1 *The teacher*

We can form a good impression of L'Empereur's teaching of Hebrew. In the first place it was intended for theologians. The University of Leiden owed its fame to the philological studies pursued there in the first half of the 17th century, but as an educational institution the academy was really a seminary for ministers. The theologians made up one third of the student body.[2] Since Amama's campaign a theology student had had to provide a testimonial from the professor of Hebrew, to be accepted for the ministry. This rule appears to have been fairly well observed in the second half of the 17th century. Carolus Schaaf, a rather insignificant lecturer in the subject towards the end of the century, could observe in a work written in his own defence, that his testimonials had always been accepted by the churches.[3] The bond with the faculty of theology was so close, that in the second half of the century the teaching of Hebrew was even to be undertaken for a time by a professor of theology.[4] It is, however, unclear whether every student of theology in L'Empereur's time really followed a course in Hebrew. There are a few remarks on the small number of students at his lectures, and soon after his death his successor complained that a blind eye was being turned to the rules of the synod.[5] In any case L'Empereur proceeded from the assumption, as he stated in the foreword to his edition of the grammar of Moses Kimḥi, published for educational purposes, that his teaching had to be directed in the first place to the needs of students of theology. Such a view of his teaching duties was in accordance with his self-image, and also determined the content of his lectures. We are in a position to get a clear idea of his teaching method, since a set of lecture notes has been preserved in his archives, forming the beginning of a course of lectures on the Hebrew text of Exodus.[6]

L'Empereur began these lectures with a quotation from Porphyry, expressing the truism that it is impossible to know things without a grasp of the words. Grammar is necessary to understand the connection of the

---

[2] Frijhoff, *Société*, 264. In the second quarter of the 18th century theologians, after a slow progression, formed 40% of the student body: Frijhoff, *ibid.*, 41.

[3] C. Schaaf, *Noodsaekelijk Teegen-Berigt, Op het Lasterschrift van Emanuel Vieira*, Leiden 1727 (Knuttel no. 16736).

[4] By A. Hulsius: *BL* 2, 266-9.

[5] *Molh.* III, 58, 66, 22*-23*; cf. de Jonge "Study", 68.

[6] In Th 164, 6.

words, because otherwise the words, and thus the things, would be wrongly understood. By 'things' L'Empereur meant the dogmas of Christian doctrine, as the examples he gave of heterodox interpretations of the Old Testament by catholics, Jews and socinians, make clear. All these errors, in L'Empereur's view, were based on mistaken grammatical readings. This does not mean, however, that he was an upholder of thorough grammatical knowledge. Not only in the lecture notes, but also elsewhere, he emphasised that grammatical knowledge had to be acquired through use,[7] since other methods only led to boredom among the students. After the introduction, L'Empereur made a short prayer for God's assistance to the teacher and the students in the study of Hebrew. After surveying various grammars by Jewish and Christian authors, and giving the preference to the works of Moses Kimḥi and Buxtorf, he dealt with the question of whether a Latin or a Hebrew grammar was to be used for the teaching of Hebrew. He chose the Hebrew grammar of Moses Kimḥi, because it was possible to learn from it not only the rules but also the use of words and the whole mode of expression, while from a Latin grammar one learned only prescribed rules, which, as was well known, led to boredom. As an introductory text, he read Exodus with the students in his lectures. The choice of this book of the bible was not motivated, as it had been by Amama, on the grounds that it was written in a simple Hebrew, but by a theological argument. He praised Exodus as the shortest introduction to the Old Testament.[8]

> "for in this little book of forty chapters, the whole theology of the ancients is to be found, and not obscurely, but clearly brought forward and explained. Do we not find here a clear description and prefiguring of the moral and political laws which are necessary to determine the best form for a republic?"

L'Empereur observed that ceremonial laws were also found in Exodus, but in his opinion they were brought to the fore, so that the Israelites could derive the gospel from them. The importance of Exodus for the theology of the Old Testament—a theology which was in essence identical with that of the New—was developed in a long argument by L'Empereur. Because of its theological importance he saw it as his task not "to expound (the second book of Moses) at length, so that we cause boredom and distaste, but briefly and concisely so that the literal sense,

---

[7] *HalOl*, **2b; L'Empereur to Barbio (Appendix 6).

[8] "quandoquidem hoc exiguo libello capitum 40 totam veterum Theologiam est invenire, non obscure, sed perspicue propositam ac explicatam. Nonne hic accurate descriptos ac delineatos habemus leges cum morales, tum Politicas ad constituendum optimam Reipublicae formam?"

as they call it, can be deduced from it''.[9] After this introduction it causes no surprise to find that his treatment of Exodus, besides grammatical comments, offers numerous theological observations, largely of a polemical nature, and intended to drive away the *taedium* which, in L'Empereur's eyes, inevitably oppresses the student of theology in learning Hebrew.

This pedagogical character also characterises his edition of Moses Kimḥi's grammar. Moses Kimḥi, the brother of David, was a 12th century Jewish grammarian. His grammar had been provided with a commentary by Elias Levita, and translated into Latin, with Levita's commentary, and published by Sebastian Münster in 1531 and 1536.[10] The parallel translation is omitted from L'Empereur's edition of 1631, and the work is only equipped with Latin notes by him. These notes, as L'Empereur states in the dedication, are intended to make the work attractive.

Thanks to the lecture notes in the *Bibliotheca Thysiana*, we know that L'Empereur in fact used this grammar in his teaching. The notes to the book have the same theological character as the comments in the lecture, and are typical of L'Empereur's personal interest in rabbinica. Moreover, they also give us an insight into the use that a theologian could make of rabbinical literature. The notes include polemical remarks against catholics, Jews and socinians, and defences of Old Testament citations in the New Testament. Others try to illustrate the importance of the Talmud. L'Empereur cited haggadic passages to show the untenableness of the Jewish religion, and quoted several texts on Jesus. Finally rabbinical literature is used to explain remarkable passages in the Old Testament, and to clarify customs, assumptions and things such as the Sons of God in Gen. 6:2.

L'Empereur's introductory teaching of Hebrew, which was based on the reading of a biblical book and a grammar, thus displayed pronounced theological traits. Because of his theological interests he was himself not a proponent of teaching theologians through cursory reading, as is clear from a letter to David de Wilhem. In 1646 L'Empereur was often consulted by this counsellor of Frederick Henry on the setting up of the High School at Breda. In a comment on the article in its statutes which dealt with the lectures on the bible, L'Empereur allowed his preference for a particular method of education to appear:[11]

---

[9] ''non prolixe ut nauseam ac taedium pariam, sed presse ac concise ita tamen ut literale (ut vocant) senso ex hax expositione hauriri possit.''

[10] Burmeister, *Münster*, no. 160, 161; Moses Kimḥi: *EJ* 10, 1007-8; Elias' edition: Weil, *Lévita*, 43-4.

[11] L'Empereur to de Wilhem, 11.7.1646, LB BPL 293A. Cf. also L'Empereur to Wilhem, 20.4.1646, LB BPL 293A: ''Primo Theologus occurrit, cujus partes esse

"in the same article the analysis of the whole scriptures is prescribed, although there are many historical books written in a chronological order. It is a waste of effort to treat them all. The experience of 27 years teaches me that, since the scriptures are very extensive, nothing is more useful in achieving more, than the discussion of difficult passages. They are difficult because of the connection, where a close analysis must be carried out, or passages are difficult because of the obscurity of the words and sentences, which in this case must be clarified, or finally, because of the malignity of the opponents, who strive to corrupt and distort these passages. These opponents must be answered from the text. It should be added, that passages sometimes seem to contradict each other; these must be reconciled."

This is a method of approaching the text which serves the purpose of theological instruction. The "more" which L'Empereur wanted to attain, refers to dogmatics, and the method he proposed consists in dealing with the texts which offer an opportunity for theological digressions in the style of his notes to Kimḥi's grammar and his lecture notes. In these digressions L'Empereur showed the theological usefulness of his rabbinical knowledge.

The combination of the two aspects in his own teaching brought him into conflict with his colleagues in the faculty of theology, who wanted him to provide a simple and short introduction to biblical Hebrew. On 12 August 1636 Polyander and Walaeus were summoned before the Mayors and Curators.[12] The College expressed its fears that students of theology might leave the University "since (as it is understood) the public lectures in the Hebrew tongue are not directed in such a way as is necessary for the furtherance of the said students". The two theologians replied to this, that L'Empereur in his public lectures:

"was also accustomed to teach from the rabbis, which was neither agreeable nor serviceable to the aforesaid students as it would otherwise have been, if he had exercised the youth in grammaticis of the aforesaid tongue, the better to make them understand the Holy Scriptures from the original text."

The faculty of theology, according to the two professors, had complained to L'Empereur about this and was confident that he would change his lectures. For safety's sake the Mayors and Curators, who feared the competition of the recently founded University of Utrecht,[13] also sent a representative to L'Empereur to encourage him to change his teaching

---

deberent, meo judicio et D. Salmasii (quicum ea de re serio contuli) locos communes explicare, et loca utriusque T. difficilia, a prandio vero Ebraeum contextum breviter enarrare."

[12] *Molh.* II, 205.
[13] Posthumus Meyjes, *Waalse College*, 85-6.

methods. In their conversation with the Mayors and Curators Polyander and Walaeus opposed teaching from the rabbis to the teaching of grammar. The latter was the introductory teaching of the original languages from the text of the bible, which must be distinguished from dogmatic instruction with the aid of the same text. They must have taken exception to L'Empereur's teaching from Moses Kimḥi's grammar, and their objections will have been directed above all against the difficult language of this work and its many digressions, which the theologians themselves could amply provide for. In a letter to Ussher L'Empereur complained of this belittling of rabbinical studies,[14] but there is no doubt that he will have changed his method of teaching.

Besides his public lectures, L'Empereur, like all Leiden lecturers, also gave private tuition. The nature of this teaching has left its traces in the books he possessed. He owned four copies of Mercerus' translation of the rabbinical commentaries on the minor prophets, probably to be used in accordance with the method recommended by Amama and Buxtorf for teaching rabbinica. In the second quarter of the 17th century, when the University was the most important centre of oriental studies in Europe, many students who were interested in such learning came to Leiden. References to recommendations for the benefit of such students to Golius, L'Empereur and de Dieu occur regularly in the correspondence of the period.[15] A brief description of these students who followed L'Empereur's courses for a time, and acquired a certain fame either by publishing themselves in the field of rabbinica, or by later occupying a university position, allows us to see how many groups were able to make use of rabbinical literature. Virtually all Christian authors of works in the field of rabbinica, which appeared in the Republic in the second quarter of the 17th century, spent some time studying under L'Empereur. The further career of these students thus sheds light on the position of rabbinical studies within the university world.

One of L'Empereur's first real students was Dionysius Vossius, the son of Gerard Johannes.[16] Dionysius matriculated as a student at Leiden in late 1628, at the age of fifteen, and followed lectures mainly on oriental languages. He had learned Hebrew at a very early age, probably from his father, who also lectured in Hebrew at the Athenaeum in Amsterdam in the thirties. L'Empereur, with whom Dionysius was on very friendly

---

[14] L'Empereur to Ussher, 25.12.1636; Ussher, *Works* XVI, 32: "Hoc tempore si quis abstrusiora tractet, vel invidia, vel pravo imperitorum judicio saepe laborat."

[15] Cf. for example Vossius, *Epistolae*, 174-5; from L. Crocius, 8.4.1638.

[16] For Dionysius: Rademaker, *Vossius*, 156. For his works: Katchen, *Christian Hebraists*, 161-235.

terms, discussed with him the works which he intended to publish.[17] In the 1630's Dionysius also studied with Menasseh ben Israel, whose services he repaid by translating into Latin various works of his, including the *Conciliator*. In December 1632 he began to translate the section of Maimonides' *Mishneh Torah* which deals with idolatry. The translation was completed in 1636[18] but Dionysius' *R. Mosis Maimonidae De Idolatria Liber* only appeared in 1642, posthumously, with his father's work *De Theologia Gentili*. The agreement between the two works was the reason which Vossius gave in a letter to Cocceius, for the long delay in publication.[19] In fact the two works show the same character and the origin of Dionysius' edition must be looked for in the stimulus and interest of his father. True, in the foreword to the *De Idolatria* in which he described the life and studies of his dead son,[20] Gerard Johannes named another reason. In this foreword he emphasised above all the desire of Dionysius to serve the church through his rabbinical studies. In letters to friends too, Vossius wrote that Dionysius had wished to write against the Jews.[21] That is not impossible, but little of such a goal appears in the work itself. Dionysius' *De Idolatria* is closely related to the great book of his father on the religion of paganism. Vossius had shown how the wealth of creation in which God had expressed himself, was the occasion for the pagan myths and ritual.[22] Such a neo-platonist view of God's inexhaustible power of creation is also found in Barlaeus.[23] The work of Dionysius bears witness to an astonishing classical and patristic erudition, much more extensive than L'Empereur's knowledge in this field, but citations from rabbinical literature and linguistic remarks are relatively scarce. Dionysius made use of Maimonides' attack on paganism in order to give his own description of it in his notes. In spite of the fact that the form would suggest otherwise, the book actually gives little information on Judaism or rabbinical literature. The work is a bilingual edition with notes, and thus betrays the influence of the editions of Mishna tractates by Cocceius and L'Empereur, the only Christian hebraists who are mentioned by name in the book. All in all the work is founded on a general

---

[17] L'Empereur mentions such contacts in his letter of condolence to Gerard Johannes on the death of Dionysius. (Draft in Th 164, 6). There is an exceptionally friendly letter from L'Empereur to Dionysisus (May 1633) in Vossius, *Epistolae*, 109.

[18] Vossius to Laud, 25.11.1632; Vossius, *Epistolae*, 208-10: Dionysius has begun; Vossius to Meursius, 6.10.1633, *Epistolae*, 224-5: the work is making good progress: Vossius to Cocceius, 28.6.1641, *Epistolae*, 376: the work was completed five years ago.

[19] In the letter to Cocceius of 1641 (note 18).

[20] The foreword, signed by Isaac Vossius, was in reality by Gerard Johannes: Blok "Barlaeus", 192, n. 58.

[21] E.g. to de Dieu, 13.3.1642; Vossius, *Epistolae*, 393.

[22] Rademaker, *Vossius*, 249-50.

[23] Blok, "Barlaeus", 196, n. 66.

Christian humanist interest in classical antiquity, for which rabbinica
were only a means. The intended dedication to Laud would not have
been out of place.

Dionysius Vossius was the son of an important scholar and leading
member of the humanist elite. If he had lived, then, like his brother Isaac
and the son of Daniel Heinsius, he would undoubtedly have made a
prominent career as a humanist scholar. Of the three pupils of
L'Empereur whom we shall discuss next and who were all of humble or
suspect origin, only one, Levinus Warner, was to attain a considerable
position. The social and religious barriers which could obstruct access to
the Republic of Letters may not be underestimated.

G. H. Vorstius, another pupil of L'Empereur from the thirties, has
been mentioned in the previous chapter. In the work of this sympathiser
with the dissident Christian groups in the Republic, polemic against
Judaism, as we have seen, played an important role. His first work, like
that of Dionysius Vossius a bilingual edition, appeared in 1638 from the
press of Blaeu in Amsterdam and consisted of the descriptions of the
Jewish faith by Maimonides—the first part of his *Mishneh Torah*—and
Abrabanel.[24] The form of the work is interesting. Only Maimonides'
treatise is provided with a parallel Hebrew text, in order, as Vorstius says
in the foreword, to prevent the printer's costs mounting too high. The
goal of the bilingual edition—the teaching of and practice in rabbinical
literature—can in his opinion also be achieved by printing only the text
of Maimonides in Hebrew. That Vorstius published both confessions of
faith was the result of his desire to demonstrate the inconsistency of his
religious opponent. The notes to both texts reveal a mainly theological
interest. Vorstius goes into detail on Maimonides' remark that the
miracles of Moses were not the reason why the Israelites accepted his doctrine.[25] He takes the necessary trouble to refute this opinion, because in
his eyes the miracles of Christ were in fact one of the most important
guarantees of the truth of his message. Theological preoccupations are
also evident from his notes to Abrabanel. Vorstius discusses at length his
views concerning the eternity of the law, and the coming of the
Messiah.[26]

His translation of the *Zemah David* of David Gans and of the *Pirkei de-
Rabbi Eliezer*, which was published by Maire at Leiden in 1644, is of the
same character. In this edition the Hebrew text is missing. In the
foreword Vorstius states that he had been occupied on the translation for

[24] For Vorstius: *NNBW* X, 1136. For his works: Katchen, *Christian Hebraists*, 235-60.
[25] *Constitutiones*, 109-14.
[26] *De fidei capite*, 57-62, 65-71.

some years, and only continued the work thanks to the encouragement of Gerbrand Anslo, to whom he had dedicated his first publication. He deeply regretted the death of his protector and friend. This Gerbrand Anslo (1612-43), a merchant and the son of a mennonite teacher, who himself also moved in heterodox circles—Vondel composed a poem for his wedding—was, as its patron, at the centre of an Amsterdam circle interested in oriental studies.[27] Anslo studied with Menasseh ben Israel, who dedicated his *De fragilitate humana* (1642) to him. In his turn Anslo wrote a Hebrew poem for Menasseh's *De Resurrectione Mortuorum*. Vorstius probably made Menasseh's acquaintance through Anslo. He also translated a number of works into Latin for Menasseh, after the death of Dionysius Vossius, as appears from a remark in the *Sorberiana*.[28] This personal friendship with Jews had no influence on his literary polemic against Judaism.

In the notes on his translation of David Gans' history Vorstius is interested above all in Gans' description of the false messiahs, who had managed to arouse the belief of the Jews. The notes to his translation of the *Pirkei de-Rabbi Eliezer* emphasise the absurdity of haggadic exegesis. In his argument for the truth of the Christian religion, the appeal to the Old Testament prophets is lacking, but he too follows the classical scheme of anti-Jewish polemic. He promised an edition of Abrabanel's commentary on Daniel in which he would show how the older rabbis agreed with the Christians.[29] The reference to this work could be a sign of his studies under L'Empereur. In the previous chapter we have seen how difficult it was around 1640 to acquire a copy of Abrabanel's commentary on Daniel. There is another indication which points to a close contact with L'Empereur. In his work Vorstius cites various passages from the Sefer Niẓẓaḥon,[30] and it is natural to assume that he had seen L'Empereur's copy of this work. At the time of the publication of Vorstius' translation of the *Zemaḥ David* his relationship with L'Empereur had been broken off. Unlike his first publication L'Empereur did not receive a presentation copy of this work.

---

[27] For Anslo: *NNBW* IX, 26-7.

[28] Sorbière remarked of Menasseh: "Latinae linguae non ita peritus erat ut aut scribere aut ex tempore loqui posset expedite, sed editos lusitanice, Consiliatorem, de Resurrectione, et de Creatione verterant Dionysius Vossius, Vorstius et alii amici." (Cited in Méchoulan, "Problème du Latin", 9 n. 12). Méchoulan identified Vorstius, in our opinion wrongly, with the Leiden medical professor A. Vorstius.

[29] Vorstius, *Animadversiones in Pirke*, 207: "Consensum veterum Rabbinorum cum Christianis acerbissimus hic doctrinae D. Iesu insectator constituit in sex Messiae signis, quae singula iam non expendemus, sed divino adspirante favore a nobis fiet, ubi integrum hunc Abarbinelis Commentarium publici fecerimus iuris." Another reference to Abrabanel's commentary: *Chronologia*, 286-7.

[30] Vorstius, *Chronologia*, 269-70, 291, *Pirkei*, 189.

Another of L'Empereur's pupils, Georgius Gentius (1611-87), also moved in the same circles as Vorstius. This German had studied oriental languages at Hamburg and Bremen. From Hamburg he received a letter of recommendation from Crocius for Vossius, who in turn recommended him to L'Empereur.[31] From 1638 to 1641 he was a student at Leiden. Isaac Aboab da Fonseca and Mozes d'Aquilar wrote Hebrew poems for his first work, an edition of Maimonides' *Hilkhot De'ot* with Hebrew text, parallel Latin translation and notes, dedicated to Gerbrand Anslo. In the foreword to this book, Gentius lavished praise on Anslo, as the phenomenon, so rare in that time, of a *mercator sapiens*. He praised his oriental library and mentioned that Anslo had translated a tractate from the *Mishneh Torah. Hilkhot De'ot* is mainly devoted to ethics, and in his notes Gentius analyses Maimonides' theory of virtue. He is also interested in the medical knowledge of Maimonides and the Talmud.[32] Anslo and de Wilhem provided financial support for Gentius so that he could undertake a journey to the east. L'Empereur, who received a presentation copy of Gentius' translation of *Hilkhot De'ot* gave him a letter of introduction to a high official, when he wished to pay a visit to England before his voyage to the east.[33] From 1642 to 1648 Gentius remained at Constantinople, where like so many students of orientalia, he stayed at the embassy of the Republic, and tried to compete with the regular though temporarily appointed ambassador, Caps, in writing long letters to Huygens. The death of Anslo was a heavy blow to him, because he had to abandon his plans for a journey through the middle east. Through the mediation of Vossius he tried to obtain a subsidy from the United East India Company for a journey through Persia.[34] In 1648 he returned to the Republic, where he again moved in the same circles as before his departure. In 1651 he was staying in the house of the mennonite teacher and doctor J. Verlaen, who had married Anslo's widow

---

[31] For Gentius: *NNBW* IX, 277; Juynboll, *Beoefenaars*, 215 ff; Meijer, *Remonstrantie*, 60, n. 20; Katchen, *Christian Hebraists*, 261-80. Vossius' letter of introduction to L'Empereur: Vossius, *Epistolae*, 221-2.

[32] Gentius, *Canones ethici*, \*\*2: "Notas generales & speciales, quarum illae exhibent fusiorem Moralium tractationem, (...) hae nonnullas continent observationes in auctoris nostri tractatum, in quibus etiam ex Talmude Babylonico medicamenta ibidem passim disjecta digessimus." pages 61-128 give general notes on the nature of the various virtues, etc. from the text of Maimonides; pages 129-60 special notes mainly concerned with Jewish theology and customs, with many medical observations on food and sexual practice.

[33] In Th 164, 6 the draft of a letter of recommendation for Gentius, dated 12.6.1640, without an addressee, but for an Englishman. In view of the language (Latin) and the humble conclusion (Excellentiam vestram), a letter to a very important person.

[34] Gentius to Vossius 7.5.1645; Vossius, *Epistolae*, 270-1.

and was also interested in oriental studies.[35] He had contacts with the rector of the Amsterdam Latin School, Adriaan Junius, and was a friend of the restless orientalist Christiaan Ravius.[36]

In 1651 Gentius published two works, which were intended to help him on the path to a further career. The first was a Latin translation without notes or Hebrew text, of Solomon ibn Verga's history of the Jews. This work, which contained principally a description of the persecutions of the Spanish Jews, was popular in the Jewish community of Amsterdam.[37] In the dedication to the city of Hamburg, Gentius describes the differences between the Jews, who are nationalist and inhumane, and the Christians who are hospitable to all mankind. He also sees this Christian hospitality in Hamburg, which had kindly received the Jews. In the foreword to the reader he uses the miserable history of the Jewish people as a proof of the falsehood of the Jewish faith. He emphasises how Verga's work shows the hope of the Jewish people for a messiah, as it describes the many impostors who have played this role. Gentius' second work, an edition of a Persian political treatise with translation and notes, was dedicated to John George II of Saxony, the prince in whose service he was to wear out his life, finally dying in poverty.

A similar journey to Constantinople was undertaken, with brilliant success, by the best known of L'Empereur's pupils: Levinus Warner (1619-65). This German student was in Leiden at the beginning of the forties, where he followed the lectures of Golius and L'Empereur. That he was also acquainted with Anslo cannot be ruled out. At least one of the manuscripts which he was later to bequeath to the University of Leiden, had been in the possession of the Amsterdam merchant.[38] Warner presented L'Empereur with books, which were the products of the group of students of rabbinica centred on Anslo, such as publications of Menasseh and Rittangel's translation of the *Sefer Yeẓirah*.[39] L'Empereur too—perhaps through the mediation of Warner—came into contact with this circle. In the *Bibliotheca Thysiana* a Hebrew letter in his hand to Rittangel has been preserved,[40] in which he declines Rittangel's

[35] *NNBW* IX, 1196-7.

[36] Ravius calls him his friend: Ravius to Ussher, 3.5.1650; Ussher, *Works* XVI, 146-7.

[37] For a description of this work: Waxman, *History* II, 470-3. For the interest in it among the Amsterdam community: Fuks, nos. 168, 242, 256.

[38] *Levinus Warner and his Legacy*, 16-7, 69.

[39] In the quarto section of L'Empereur's book list, around 1642, these titles follow each other: "Liber Jetsira, donum Warneri binden 12 st". and "Menasseh ben Israel de la fragilidad humana donum Warneri."

[40] In Th 164, 6. The letter is published and translated in Van Rooden/Wesselius, "Rittangel".

request to assist him in the publication of his works. In 1642 L'Empereur was even mentioned as a possible translator into Hebrew of the *Janua Linguarum* of Comenius,[41] with whom Rittangel associated at this time.[42] Warner published nothing in the field of rabbinica, but L'Empereur was a not unimportant influence on his career. He provided Warner with a scholarship from a fund which he adminstered,[43] and also arranged for his further support by procuring for him an appointment as tutor to the two counts of Chimitz and Tettau, who were students at Leiden. Warner was especially grateful for this.[44]

In the forties, Warner published a number of works to draw attention to himself and to make a name. He carefully chose subjects whose attractiveness was guaranteed. Thus his first work followed one of the greatest publication successes of the thirties: van Beverwijck's question whether the human lifespan could be influenced by medical science.[45] In 1642 Warner published a book on Arab and Persian views of longevity.

In 1644 he published a work on Muslim opinions of Christ, the *Compendium Historicum*. Such works, as we have repeatedly seen above were not well received in church circles, and thus there will have been a large market for them. Warner's work ran into the expected difficulties. Vorstius defended his publication of passages from the Talmud directed against Christ with a disparaging reference to Warner's edition.[46] From a letter from Warner to G. J. Vossius it appears that there were some who felt that his work would be better left unpublished. The Leiden theology faculty had even refused to write a foreword for it. L'Empereur, on the other hand, so Warner wrote, had written such a foreword at his request.[47] In his letter to Warner, which precedes the book L'Empereur

---

[41] H. Bruno to Huygens, 25.8.1642; Huygens, *Briefwisseling* III, 338: "Ejus ( = Comenius') *Ostium linguarum aureum* brevi, ut audio, opera clarissimi nobilisque domini l'Empereur sive Constantini Imperatoris, et loquetur ore sancto, et rotundo jam loquitur. Explicatius fabulabor: *Ianua* brevi et Hebraice patebit, et Graece jam patet, interprete Theol. quodam Simonio Hulsato, Heusdanae juventutis rectore."

[42] Blekastad, *Comenius*, 313-4, 333.

[43] Cf. Th 167. It appears from L'Empereur's account book (Th 108) that in 1644 he paid f.160 to Warner.

[44] Warner's *Proverbiorum et Sententiarum Persicarum centuria* is dedicated to C. Thysius. He states that he is known to the family, and praises L'Empereur enthusiastically, because he has won him the "favor" of others, who have become his patrons.

[45] Baumann, *Johan van Beverwijck*, 62-68.

[46] Vorstius, *Pirkei R. Eliezer*, ***3a: "non detractarunt alii vanissima Mahumedis deliria magno molimine in lucem proferre."

[47] Warner to G. J. Vossius, 20.7.1643; Vossius, *Epistolae*, 254: "Libellus hicce, quem transmitto, lucem videre vix ausus est; fuerunt enim, qui supprimendum eum esse dicerent, quod pessime consultum foret Religioni Christianae, si ejusmodi de Christo opiniones vulgarentur. Certe Theologica facultas religioni habuit, ut testimonio aliquo librum munirent. Cordatior fuit Dominus L'Empereur qui quod pretii, lubens volensque praestitit. Sed haec coram malo."

praised it highly. Yet the service which he rendered to his pupil must not
be interpreted as coming to the defence of Warner's intention. In his letter L'Empereur emphasises the involuntary support which such heathen
testimony about Christ gives to orthodoxy; in his foreword Warner is
thinking of its usefulness for missionary work and sees in the flowering
of Arabic studies a possibility of the conversion of the Muslims. Later in
his life Warner, wholly in the tradition of Arabic studies at Leiden, was
to show an interest in missionary endeavour, and with Comenius and
Golius to make a translation of the bible into Turkish, which however
was never published.[48] Finally in 1644, Warner issued a collection of Persian proverbs, in the style of Erpenius. Warner enjoyed considerable success with his published works: whereas in the dedication of *De termino vitae*
he still called himself *obscurus et ignotus*, his second work was dedicated to
Boswell, the influential English ambassador in the Republic, and for the
collection of Persian proverbs no less a person than Salmasius wrote a
laudatory letter.[49]

In 1644, with financial support from David de Wilhem, Warner left
for Constantinople, in order as Vossius wrote in a letter of introduction
to Grotius, to become better acquainted with oriental literature and to
see the cities and customs of men.[50] In Constantinople things went well
for him. More successfully than Gentius he provided the States General
with information at a time when a temporary deputy was filling the post
of ambassador after the departure of Haga. In 1655 he succeeded Caps
as the Republic's ambassador to the Sublime Porte. Thanks to the high
salary (fl. 7500 a year) and the numerous emoluments, he was able to
maintain a princely style of life and indulge his passion for collecting
oriental MSS. After L'Empereur's departure from the chair of Hebrew
in 1647 the Mayors and Curators wanted to invite Warner as the successor, even when L'Empereur, though pressed to do so, would not name
him as a suitable candidate, because he was working for Buxtorf II.
L'Empereur's profile of a successor as an *orthodoxus theologus* was probably
intended to exclude Warner, who had not studied theology. Warner was
invited by the Mayors and Curators, but after giving an undertaking, he
declined the offer.[51] That turned out in the end to be best for himself and

---

[48] Mout, "Calvinoturcicisme", 599-603.
[49] Salmasius to Warner, 9.8.1644, in *Proverbiorum et Sententiarum Persicarum centuria*.
[50] G. J. Vossius to Grotius, 5.9.1644; Vossius, *Epistolae*, 432-3.
[51] The Mayors and Curators asked Golius explicitly about the suitability of Warner
(*Molh.* III, 7) and made Warner grants on several occasions to allow him to remain in
Constantinople. On 8.6.1648 they resolved in the same meeting to appoint Uchtmannus
as extraordinary professor and to invite Warner in order to use him for the honour of
the university.

for the University of Leiden, to which he left his extensive collection of MSS.

Dionysius Vossius, G. H. Vorstius, Georgius Gentius and Levinus Warner were the most important pupils of L'Empereur in the field of oriental languages. The turbulent C. Ravius, who wandered all over Europe, also studied with him for a short time but can hardly be called a true pupil.[52] L'Empereur and Golius also had some students who concerned themselves with philosophy as well as eastern languages, like Antonius Deusing[53] a German who studied oriental languages, medicine and physics at Leiden from 1631. In 1636 Golius allowed him to prepare the new edition of the *Grammatica Arabica* of Erpenius.[54] In 1639 Deusing succeeded Pontanus at Harderwijk, where he became involved in a conflict with Cloppenburg. We shall meet him again in this connection in the last section of this chapter. Johan Elichman, a remarkable Silesian (1600-39) also studied oriental languages in Leiden at about this time.[55] He was a close friend of Salmasius,[56] very interested in philosophy, and an associate of both Descartes and Isaac Beeckman.[57]

But the most important group of students of L'Empereur were theologians who were interested in oriental languages and rabbinica. They spent several months at Leiden rounding off their theological studies by attending the lectures of Golius, L'Empereur and de Dieu. It is characteristic of the academic place of Hebrew in the 17th century that it was these men, and not the students with more literary interests whom we have discussed above, who all became professors of Hebrew.

In 1639 Jacobus Alting (1618-1679), the son of the Groningen professor, spent eight months at Leiden.[58] He had studied theology at Groningen, rabbinica under Rabbi Gumprecht ben Abraham in Hamburg, and after his stay at Leiden, he left for England, where he followed Pococke's lectures in oriental languages at Oxford. He later sent his *Chaldaei & Syriaci sermonis Synopsis* to L'Empereur for his appraisal, and L'Empereur encouraged him to publish.[59] In 1643 he succeeded Gomarus in his teaching duties in oriental languages, Gomarus' successor in theology being Maresius. In 1667 he became professor of

---

[52] For Rau: *ADB* 27, 396-7; Kernkamp, *Utrechtse Universiteit*, I, 127-8.
[53] De Haan, *Wijsgerig onderwijs*, 22-37.
[54] Juynboll, *Beoefenaars*, 147 f.
[55] *NNBW* I, 801; Juynboll, *Beoefenaars*, 191 ff.
[56] Leroy, *Dernier Voyage*, 41, 58, 59 n. 16.
[57] Van Berkel, *Beeckman*, 113, n. 34.
[58] *BL* 2, 24-5.
[59] Cf. the "Vita Altingii" in his *Opera Omnia* I.

theology at Groningen. This career, in which the professorship of
theology crowned that in Hebrew, was that of L'Empereur, Hackspan
and Buxtorf II and also the career of the two students whom we shall now
mention.

During his stay at Leiden Alting had met J. H. Hottinger. Hottinger
(1620-67) who was born at Zürich, studied theology in his native place,
and from 1638-42 made an academic tour through Europe.[60] In Groningen he became acquainted with the Moroccan Jew Saadiah ben Levi
and was encouraged by ben Levi's exceptional knowledge of Hebrew to
immerse himself in oriental languages. In 1640 he was at Leiden, and
worked on the Samaritan Pentateuch.[61] In 1641 L'Empereur gave him
letters of recommendation to archbishop Laud and Ussher and acquired,
through the mediation of his protege, the annotations on the Pentateuch
of Kilbye, the Regius professor of Hebrew at the time of his stay in
Oxford.[62] In England Hottinger also attended Pococke's lectures. On his
return to Zürich, he became a professor and lectured on the most various
subjects: from church history, catechism, and polemic to oriental
languages, logic and rhetoric. He gained his doctor's degree at Basle.
From 1655 to 1661 he was professor of Old Testament and oriental
languages at Heidelberg and in 1666, after his return to the university
of his native city, he was invited to Leiden as successor of Hoornbeek.
He was drowned on his journey to Leiden.

A third theologian on whose life L'Empereur even had a decisive influence, was Johan Braun (1628-1708).[63] He first met L'Empereur when
quite young. L'Empereur encouraged him to study and took him into his
house. After a study journey he became Walloon preacher and professor
of Hebrew at Nijmegen, and in 1680 succeeded Alting as professor of
theology at Groningen.

We have seen how L'Empereur used his influence to promote the
publication of works by his students, furnished them with letters of introduction, and tried to help them to appointments. This support was part
of the pattern of values of the scholarly community, the Republic of Letters. L'Empereur was a recognised member of this community and we
now turn to his place in it and the values which were upheld by it.

---

[60] *ADB* 13, 192-3; Herzog 8, 399-401.
[61] J. H. Hottinger, *Exercitationes Anti-Morianae,* \*\*2a. See Lebram, "Streit", 31, 59 n.
154.
[62] *BL* 2, 187. Draft of a letter of introduction to Ussher, 1.3.1641, in Th 164, 6.
[63] *BWPGN* I, 588-93.

5.2 *The mandarin*

The concept of the Republic of Letters was developed by Dibon and his pupil Bots.[64] They apply this concept to describe the nature of the scholarly community during the 17th century. The idea of the Republic of Letters, which was also used in the time, represented, according to Dibon and Bots, an ideal that was not utopian but which was not in fact realised within the community of scholars. That is nothing out of the ordinary, and the fate of all ideals but in the case of the Republic of Letters one may ask oneself whether the ideal as the two modern authors sketch it, was understood in that sense at the time. In this section we shall describe L'Empereur's academic and social activities within the community of scholars and find out how he realised the values upheld within it.

What were the characteristic features of the Republic of Letters? The most important was the feeling of being involved with each other, of all the scholars concerned, whether they were theologians or jurists, philologists or experimental researchers in the natural sciences. Their solidarity was founded on the experience of belonging to an intellectual and spiritual community, which transcended confessional and political differences of opinion, even personal rivalry and natural and social inequality. The homogeneity of their intellectual efforts went beyond the bounds of the various disciplines, directed itself towards practice, and stood at the service of the City, the social and political community.

This common effort, solidarity and equality, in short this feeling of being bound to the Republic of Letters as to an ideal that was greater and more important than their own convictions, is the core of the concept developed by Dibon and Bots. The goal and essence of the Republic of Letters was the duty of communication and mutual scholarly aid. On the grounds of this general description, the history of the Republic of Letters in the 17th century can be divided into periods. In the first half of the century, the intellectual community consisted mainly of producers, of scholars who made an independent contribution to the development of knowledge. They communicated by means of an extensive correspondence mainly carried on in Latin, in which famous scholars or the administrators of great libraries formed the nodal points of various networks. In the second half of the 17th century the greater part of the Republic of Letters consisted of consumers. New forms of communica-

---

[64] Bots, *Universitaire gemeenschap*; *Republiek der Letteren*; Dibon, "Université"; "Echanges épistolaires".

tion emerged—the learned periodicals, in which the use of Latin was abandoned and replaced by the vernaculars. The meeting at the home of a famous scholar developed into a new form of scholarly sociability: the learned academies.

This transformation of the *Respublica litteraria* into the *République des Lettres* went hand in hand with an intellectual reorientation. Increasingly scholars set themselves to investigate reality directly, without making use of classical literature. The members of the Republic in the second half of the century were less philologically erudite and more oriented to modern philosophy and natural science.[65] In spire of these differences, there was a clear continuity between the two forms of the Republic of Letters. Gradually a new intellectual climate arose inside this international community, which was the result of the discussions which took place on intellectual developments, such as the new philosophy and natural science, the geographical discoveries and the familiarity with exotic civilisations. This development was reinforced by the long term effects of the political, religious and economic polemics.

The concept of the Republic of Letters, with its social and intellectual component, is heuristically exceptionally fertile and grateful use of it will be made in the following sections. But Dibon and Bots' picture of the ideal of communication, solidarity and equality appears too rose-tinted, not because of the human shortcomings of the 17th century scholars, but because a number of its members knew of higher and in their eyes more important, values than the Republic itself. Moreover, it could not exist independently of the apparatus of the state, and such autonomy was never an ideal in the eyes of the majority of its members. This ambiguity can be illustrated from L'Empereur's life and ambitions in the years 1634-48.

L'Empereur belonged to a generation of the Republic of Letters which can be clearly identified: that of, to name only its most famous representatives, Mersenne, Gassendi, Descartes, Ussher, Selden, Grotius, G. J. Vossius, D. Heinsius, Rivet, Salmasius, the Dupuys and Sarrau, all of whom died around the middle of the century. It was the time when the community still consisted largely of scholarly producers, and was in its initial phase. The age of heavy and merciless interconfessional polemic, in which Scaliger and Casaubon had had to take part was hardly over. L'Empereur won his membership by his publications in the field of rabbinical literature, a rare scholarly specialism. Thus he regarded it

---

[65] Classically expressed in the title of the book by Mandrou, *Des humanistes aux hommes de science.*

himself, and it was as a specialist that he was considered by others. For the still largely philologically oriented interest of this period, such an expansion of textual knowledge was a welcome gain. In the previous chapter we have seen how much the content and form of his work was determined by his immediate surroundings.

These surroundings, the milieu of late humanism at the University of Leiden, certainly formed an important secondary factor which furthered his international recognition. The University of Leiden in the first half of the 17th century was a nodal point within the European intellectual community.[66] The university owed this position above all to its great tradition in philology, begun with Lipsius and reaching its full flowering under Scaliger. The young University of Leiden sought its teachers all over Europe, and whenever they accepted an invitation they brought all their international contacts with them. The most important group of foreign scholars belonged to the Franco-Walloon tradition, which had been the strongest since the founding of the University. The Leiden presses of Elzevier and Maire, which accepted commissions from all parts of Europe, strengthened the attractiveness of the city and contributed to make Leiden one of the intellectual centres of Europe.

We can find all these elements in L'Empereur's correspondence and the books he received. We have seen above, how around 1634 he had been fully accepted in the Leiden academic community. By the mediation of his colleagues at the university and through his students he came into contact with a great many foreigners. De Dieu introduced him to Ussher, and later L'Empereur in his turn was able to provide letters of introduction to the bishop for Hottinger and Gentius. From Ussher he borrowed manuscripts not only for himself but also for Thysius,[67] as well as mediating for others in contact with Ussher.[68] His relations were conducted partly through the English ambassador to the Republic, Boswell, who was interested in orientalia, and who also lent books himself to L'Empereur.[69] Young Englishmen from Ussher's circle, such as S. Johnson and A. Boate, made L'Empereur's acquaintance when they

---

[66] Dibon, "Université".

[67] L'Empereur to Ussher, 30.12.1633; Ussher, *Works* XV, 585-6.

[68] L'Empereur to Ussher, 21.12.1634; Ussher, *Works* XV, 589-90; He asks Ussher for a copy of the Scottish confession of faith, on behalf of a "vir nobilis et doctissimus qui omnium reformatarum ecclesiarum confessiones editurus".

[69] W. Boswell: *DNB* V, 440; Tyacke, "Arminianism", 109 ff. As early as 1634 L'Empereur sent his regards to Boswell in a letter to Rivet: L'Empereur to Rivet, 29.7.1634, LB BPL 285; Cf. L'Empereur to Ussher, 25.12.1636; Ussher, *Works* XVI, 32-3. In Th 164, 4 there is a note dated 2.10.1640 of books borrowed from Boswell and since returned.

studied at Leiden,[70] and in their turn renewed his contact with his old teacher at Oxford, Prideaux.[71]

L'Empereur's relationships went back in part to the beginning of the thirties. Cocceius sent L'Empereur his publications to be distributed among the Leiden professors.[72] Other contacts from this period which had their roots in earlier acquaintances, were those with Pontanus,[73] Engelerus,[74] and the Vossii, both Gerard Johannes and his sons Dionysius and Isaac.[75] In 1646 Isaac felt obliged to send L'Empereur his first work, a new edition of Ignatius of Antioch by which he hoped to make a name.[76] As a theologian L'Empereur came into contact in 1648 with the court preacher of the Great Elector, the somewhat eirenic Johan Bergius, whose son had defended in a disputation under L'Empereur.[77] The reverential tone in which Bergius, himself not an unimportant figure, wrote to L'Empereur is an indication of the leading position which the latter had won by the end of his life. Through Rivet L'Empereur had contact with Rivet's nephew Samuel Bochart in Caen, whose first work in Hebrew studies he received for appraisal and with whom he corresponded on Bochart's comparisons of Arabic and Hebrew.[78]

---

[70] Grotius to S. Johnson, 11.5.1635; *Briefwisseling* V, 468; letter from Boate, see note 85; for Boate, a physician: *DNB* V, 745-6; *C. I. Rivet/Sarrau* III, 509, n. 6. He wrote against Cappel's *Critica Sacra*. In 1645 Comenius was associating with him, his brother and one Johnson: Blekastad, *Comenius*, 316.

[71] S. Johnson to L'Empereur, 12/22.7.1634, Th 170, a letter of thanks to L'Empereur for a letter of introduction to Prideaux.

[72] Cf. N. M. Schneider to Cocceius, 23.1.1639, Spanheim to Cocceius, 16.4.1644. Rivet to Cocceius, 15.5.1644; Cocceius, *Opera ANEKDOTA* II, 643, 656-7.

[73] L'Empereur to Pontanus, 17.7.1631, draft in Th 164, 6.

[74] J. H. Engelerus to L'Empereur, Tiguri 5.9.1633, Th 171.

[75] See notes 17, 31, 76; L'Empereur to Vossius, 18.4.1642, 13.7.1642, 25.2.1644; Vossius, *Epistolae*, 234, 242-3, 259. In the last letter he ranks Vossius with Scaliger and Salmasius.

[76] L'Empereur to I. Vossius, 7.8.1646, UB Amsterdam, in which he reacts to Vossius' edition of Ignatius, which he had received as a present. L'Empereur doubted its authenticity, because of dogmatic objections concerning christology and the description of the episcopal office. He continued: "Tamen hujusmodi me ita moverunt, ut eruditissimo Salmasio in istiusmodi, ut et aliis omnibus, exercitatissimo dubia mea exponerem, quod mihi non fiderem. Is vero, ut sincere loqui solet aperte significavit, istud scriptum tantam antiquitatem non spirare: quod praeter alia isthic haereseos fieret mentio, quae quarto demum seculo invaluerit, vel exorta etiam fuerit." For Salmasius' involvement in the various editions of Ignatius: Leroy, *Dernier voyage*, 73, n. 64.

[77] J. Bergius to L'Empereur, 13/3.5.1648, Th 170; Bergius gave L'Empereur detailed information on the difficult relations with the lutherans in Brandenburg. For the disputation by his son: L'Empereur, *Disputationes*, no. 10, 21.12.1647: "De Providentia". For Bergius: *Herzog*, 2, 613-4.

[78] In his *Hierozoicon*, Bochart refers to a correspondence with an anonymous "vir doctus" on some derivations of Hebrew words from Arabic. According to the index in Bochart's *Opera Omnia* I, this was L'Empereur (the passage involved, *ibid.*, 675);

Rivet, a representative par excellence of the Franco-Walloon tradition at the University of Leiden, was very important for L'Empereur, particularly since he had been at Court. Thus, he intervened at L'Empereur's recommendation with prince Radziwill on behalf of a student.[79] In turn, Rivet, like many others, used L'Empereur because of his position and abilities as a contact person and corrector with the Leiden printers. That happened for example in the publication of Bochart's work on the origin of peoples,[80] and it should also have been the case in the publication of Louis Cappel's *Critica Sacra*, to be discussed in the next section. Many young scholars, including the young Alting,[81] Ledebuhr,[82] Paschatius,[83] Datior[84] and Boate[85] sent their MSS. to L'Empereur for appraisal and possible management and correction at the Leiden printers. L'Empereur also performed a similar work on the request of the printers themselves. In 1638 he made an agreement with Elzevier that he should receive six extra copies of his *Bava Kamma* in addition to the thirty he had been promised, and in exchange would correct the Hebrew portions of the work by Selden which Elzevier was to print.[86] In publishing another's work, besides special talents and access to a publisher, contact with the authorities could also be important. This brings us to the complicated question of the relationship of the Republic of Letters to the apparatus of the state.[87]

This relationship and the curious way in which the values of the state were duplicated within the Republic of Letters, reveal the limits to the

---

L'Empereur to Rivet, 29.3.1642; LB BPL 285 criticises Bochart's work on the mandrakes of Gen. 30: 14-7; cf. *C. I. Rivet/Sarrau*, I, 691.

[79] Rivet to L'Empereur, 25.4., Th 170.

[80] Rivet to G. J. Vossius, n.d. Vossius, *Epistolae*, 266-7 on the publication of Bochart's work: "Tentabimus (nempe quia Cl. Viri L'Empereur & Golius possent emendationi praeesse) Le Maire, quod se facturum suscepit D. Salmasius."

[81] See note 59.

[82] C. Ledebuhr to L'Empereur, n.d., Th 170 on his *Tractatulus de duplici decalogi accentuatione*. This letter also contains the remark "Quaesivo hanc rem nuper Amstelodami a R. Menasseh sed frustra." For Ledebuhr: Jöcher II, 2330-1.

[83] P. Paschatius to L'Empereur, Geneva, 27/17.10., Th 170. He offers a work against Socinus for publication.

[84] L'Empereur to F. Datior, 14.5.1639, draft in Th 164,6. His book and that of Boate are to be published by Le Maire. L'Empereur thinks Datior's translation of *Cosri* not good enough for publication.

[85] A. Boate to L'Empereur, 30.11.1636, Th 170. Deals with the publication of a book by Boate, to be arranged by Heinsius and L'Empereur. The book contains an attack on Morinus; he copied the two chapters of a Syriac MS. of Ussher for Thysius' benefit (see note 67).

[86] In Th 164, 4 a note, dated 15.2.1638, that he had agreed with Elzevier that he should receive six extra copies of *Bava Kamma*, in addition to the thirty promised him "provided that I should correct Selden's little book in Hebrew."

[87] Cf. Kühlmann, *Gelehrtenrepublik und Fürstenstaat*, 319-30.

ideal which inspired it, and to the freedom which it enjoyed. In 1637
Buxtorf II was looking for a patron to whom he could dedicate his
father's lexicon to the Talmud. He thought of the Netherlands, where he
had previously, in 1632, sought support from Heinsius and L'Empereur
for a possible publication by one of the Leiden houses.[88] He revealed to
Gomarus his intention to dedicate the work to the States of Zeeland and
those of Groningen. Gomarus in his reply approved the intention,
because such a dedication would cause the two bodies to vie with each
other in *liberalitas*. He advised Buxtorf on the best way to obtain a
substantial financial reward for the dedication and named the politicians
in both provinces who were elegible to be approached. In a second letter,
of 1638, Gomarus described the plan of campaign to be followed. He
himself and Alting would use their influence with the States of Groningen. Buxtorf must induce L'Empereur to approach the Zeeland
representatives in the States General at The Hague, Beaumont and
Vosbergen. Further Buxtorf must ask L'Empereur if he would ask his
colleague Walaeus to exert his great influence in the States of Zeeland
and the church council of Middelburg. In his letter Gomarus used a
technical term for having influence over a politician: *gratia pollere apud*.[89]
This lobbying yielded the desired results and Buxtorf received a not
inconsiderable recompense for his dedication.[90]

This connection with the state, or better, with patrons in the various
organs which exercised the functions we should as a whole call the state,
was an important part of the life of a scholar. A patron's favour was
necessary for a dedication, publication, an appointment at a university,
protection against enemies and the obtaining of an honourable position.[91] In return, princes and states had an interest in their glory and
their presence in all forms of social activity which was displayed by their
patronage,[92] and they demanded gratitude and recognition in return for

---

[88] Heinsius to Buxtorf II, 9.8.1632; J. J. Buxtorf, *Catalecta*, 471-2. The lexicon can be
printed in Leiden. There are good correctors there and the quality of the printers is high.
L'Empereur will send some sample types. In 1610 Heinsius had already acted as an
intermediary between Buxtorf I and Wtenbogaert when the former wished to offer his
*Thesaurus Grammaticus* to the States General: J. J. Buxtorf, *Catalecta*, 464.

[89] Gomarus to Buxtorf II, 17/27.1.1637, 27.8.1638, Van Itterzon, "Nog twintig
brieven", 423 ff. Cf. Tacitus, *Historiae*, 2, 92.

[90] The work was ultimately dedicated to the States of Groningen: Prijs no. 237.

[91] A good summary of the activities of a patron by Salmasius to Sarrau 18.1.1642;
Leroy, *Dernier Voyage*, 165: "J'ai été sensiblement touché de la mort de Mr. Aerssens,
j'y ai perdu en mon particulier, sans compter la perte qu'y fait l'Etat, plus qu'on ne
scauroit dire. Il a été l'aucteur et le promoteur de ma vocation en ce pays là, il m'a tou-
jours porté contre mes ennemis desquels il connaissoit mieux que personne la malice et
l'envie et tous leurs artifices."

[92] For a brilliant description of the reasons why authorities sometimes take an interest
in culture: Veyne, *Le Pain et le Cirque*, 676-81. It could of course also be a matter of simply

their gifts. There is a remarkable passage in the *Scaligerana*, in which Scaliger praises Maurice as a "tres gentil Prince". He need only wait on him three times a year, while other princes insisted on it much more often.[93] And this was the scholar who had won the place of honour at the University of Leiden, and was regarded as the greatest humanist in Europe! Frederick Henry took a similar interest in Salmasius and reminded the scholar of his duties.[94]

This dependence led, among the late humanists, to involved and ambiguous intellectual reactions. A distaste for such obligations and a yearning for freedom were certainly present. An important factor in the much vaunted freedom of the Republic of the United Netherlands in the 17th century was certainly the absence of too burdensome obligations to a patron. The expression of Scaliger chosen as the motto of this chapter finds a parallel in the behaviour of Salmasius, who also refused to dedicate his books to a patron.[95] On the other hand, the world of the great men was the only source of real status, even in the minds of the princes in the Republic of Letters. With some self-mockery Salmasius described his feelings before a meeting with Richelieu as those of a virgin before her wedding night.[96] But there was no self-mockery at all about Salmasius when it was a matter of his prestige and the honour shown to him at the University of Leiden. He erupted into the most violent rage when he was addressed as "professor", and even after it had been explained to him that "professor" in the Republic was a more honourable title than in France, he insisted that he was not a professor,

---

taking an interest. L'Empereur was involved in the translation of the New Testament into modern Greek, for the benefit of the reform project of Lucaris: *C. I. Rivet/Sarrau* III, 105; Sepp, "Nieuw-Grieksche Testament", 231. For the political aims behind this: Hering, *Oekumenisches Patriarchat*.

[93] *Sec Scal*, 447: "Maurice n'est point glorieux, je ne le vay saluer que deux ou trois fois l'année, il n'y prend plus garde, & ne s'en soucie pas; s'il estoit comme les autres, il m'y faudroit aller souvent. (...) La Religion des Princes est nulle." Cf. *Sec Scal*, 556: "Il y a dix mois que je n'ay salué Son Excellence."

[94] *C. I. Rivet/Sarrau* II, 181. Cf. the explanation of Morus, cited with approval by Leroy (*Dernier Voyage*, 99) concerning Salmasius' non-intervention in the conflict over Amyrault: "Il est certain qui'il suivit plustost sa prudence que son inclination en ce qu'il ne pût jamais estre induit, quoy que fit M. Sarrau pour cet effet, à prendre le parti de Saumur. S'il l'eust fait, il eut donné trop de prise sur lui .... et il vouloit se mettre bien dans la maison d'Orange, directement opposée aux Arminiens."

[95] Leroy, *Dernier Voyage*, 68. The ambiguous attitude towards a patron is brilliantly expressed in the citations chosen by Leroy on p. 199 of his book. For the relations of the "hommes de lettres" with their patrons in France: Martin, *Livre* I, 430 ff.

[96] Salmasius to Sarrau, 16.11.1640; Leroy, *Dernier Voyage*, 130-2. Cf. also Salmasius to Sarrau, 22.11.1640; Leroy, *Dernier Voyage*, 133-4; "Mais laissons les Hauteurs et les Eminences, qui nous regardent comme du ciel en terre, pour descendre en bas où les hommes marchent au même rang que nous".

but a member of the *Conseil d'Etat*.[97] Salmasius, who was celebrated as the greatest scholar of his age, and ultimately chose exile in Leiden over a life of intellectual servitude in France, nevertheless continued to see the highest form of life in service to a prince. His sons were, with the full approval of their parents, brought up for military service.[98] This remarkable combination of the desire for freedom and service, also determined the life of Hugo Grotius, who like Salmasius destined a son for service to the real Republic, not that of Letters. Grotius had the same highly developed sense of the honour which he derived from his non-literary position. In 1641 he reacted fiercely when correspondents from the Republic began to omit to give him the titles which were due to a Swedish ambassador. The first to commit this offence against Grotius' honour was L'Empereur, who wrote *Illustrissimus* on the outside of a letter, and *Amplissimus* only on the inside. Grotius smelt a plot behind this and proposed in future to burn such letters unread.[99] The careful use of titles was so common, that a friendship which did not trouble itself about it, was reason for comment.[100]

The values of honour and glory were even duplicated within the Republic of Letters itself. The most notorious scholarly quarrel in the second quarter of the 17th century was that between Heinsius and Salmasius.[101] L'Empereur succeeded for most of the time in retaining the friendship of both sides.[102] Around 1640 he spent many a Sunday afternoon in the circle that gathered at Salmasius' house, while he also passed for one of the best friends of Heinsius, who had seen the coming of his rival with displeasure and tried in every possible way to make life unpleasant for him. When the two titans succeeded in giving their quarrel the form of a scholarly conflict over the question whether the Greek of the New Testament was a language that was really spoken, and not just a

---

[97] Leroy, *Dernier Voyage*, 96, 213-4.

[98] Leroy, *Dernier Voyage*, 110-4. *Sec Scal*, 551: Si j'avois dix enfans, je n'en ferois estudier pas un, je les avancerois aux Cours des Princes.'', and *Sec Scal*, 553: ''J'honore les Grands mais je n'ayme point les Grandeurs.''

[99] Grotius to W. de Groot, 13.4.1641 and 27.4.1641, Grotius, *Epistolae*, 918-9.

[100] *C. I. Rivet/Sarrau* II, 155: ''Monsieur de Laët son bon ami ne met jamais pour suscription a celles qu'il luy escrit que: 'A Monsieur, Monsieur de Saumaise', et il ne le trouve pas mauvais.''

[101] The most recent account of the conflict: Leroy, *Dernier Voyage*, 37-42.

[102] *Sorberiana*, 192-3 (cited in Cohen, *Ecrivains français*, 331): ''J'ay eu le bonheur de converser deux ans assez familierement avec feu Monsieur de Saumaise de que j'étois voisin à Leyden (...) Je me rendois chez lui particulierement le Dimanche au sortir du diner; parce qu'il n'alloit pas au Preche du soir, & qu'ainsi nous demeurions seuls deux ou trois heures, après quoi j'étois bien aise de voir la compagnie qui y arrivoit. Il s'y formait un cercle de quinze ou vingt personnes de remarque, telles qu'étoient Messieurs L'Empereur, de Laët, Golius etc. Et il y avoit beaucoup de plaisir & de profit en ces conversations.'' For L'Empereur's friendship with Heinsius, see note 104.

phenomenon created on one occasion by translation from semitic languages,[103] L'Empereur was convinced by Salmasius' arguments.[104] What decided the question for L'Empereur was Salmasius' recognition that for a good understanding of the New Testament, a knowledge of Greek alone was inadequate, and that the oriental languages were also necessary. Although the dispute was not destitute of scholarly importance, many correspondents saw it as a purely verbal quarrel. Sarrau observed that both opponents naturally abused each other in brilliant Latin, but that they could better use this talent for something more useful.[105] Elisabeth the Winter Queen concluded that it was apparently not only theologians who could seek out quarrels on trivial points.[106] In fact the conflict lends itself to an explanation which appeals to minor human sins. But it also has another and more interesting aspect. Both Heinsius and Salmasius were princes in the Republic of Letters, such as few others were, and both were outstandingly aware of their position, to which they attached great importance. Salmasius could say with pride: "je ne fais rien pour le gain, mais je la fais pour la gloire".[107] In essence the conflict was based on 17th century society's system of values which was upheld in the Republic of Letters also.

It was not only his erudition, but also his position, that decided a scholar's name, honour and prestige. In 1642 Rivet wanted to bring Samuel Petit, a professor at Nîmes, to Leiden. The mechanism which he devised for this hinged on the idea that L'Empereur should first be appointed to the faculty of theology, so that Petit could then be appointed to the place vacated by L'Empereur. The only problem in Rivet's eyes was the low status of the faculty of letters. He let himself be assured by Sorbière that Petit took a stoical view with regard to his honour.[108] L'Empereur's continual efforts to win an appointment to the theology faculty thus rested not only on a personal preference and inclination, but were also the consequence of a desire for a higher social position.

L'Empereur used his friendship with Rivet to satisfy this desire by becoming Rector Magnificus. The Rector was appointed each year by

---

[103] For a description of the scholarly aspects of the dispute: de Jonge, *Bestudering*, 32-5.

[104] Cf. Rivet to Sarrau, 27.4.1643; *C. I. Rivet/Sarrau* I, 453: "Je vi ces jours Mons. l'Empereur, qui dit qu'il a tousjours entendu ce que dit Mons. de Saumaise, et que Mr. Heins a tort de faire une langue d'une version. Voila ce qu'a gagné le *Funus*, sur un des principaux fauteurs." Cf. Rivet to Sarrau, 9.5.1644, *C. I. Rivet/Sarrau* II, 267.

[105] Sarrau to Rivet, 4.2.1645; *C. I. Rivet/Sarrau* III, 38, "Ils recommenceront à se dechirer et se dire des iniures en beau Latin. J'aimerois mieux qu'ils l'employassent plus utilement."

[106] A. Colvius to G. J. Vossius, 10.9.1643; Vossius, *Epistolae*, 252.

[107] Cited in Bots, *Republiek der Letteren*, 16. Cf. the account of the controversy in Leroy, *Dernier Voyage*, 42.

[108] Rivet to Sarrau, 1.9.1642; *C. I. Rivet/Sarrau* I, 253.

the prince, from a list submitted by the Senate, and the intrigues which were associated with the nominations for this mainly ceremonial office, reveal how fiercely desired such a position was.[109] L'Empereur became Rector in 1638 and was able to deliver an address before the mother of the king of France, Marie de Medici, who was then on a tour in the Republic.[110] In a letter to Rivet of 1647 L'Empereur wrote that because of a conflict with Polyander on the filling of the Rector's post, he was afraid of being slandered before the court by Polyander's parvenu son, the lord of Heenvliet. He requested Rivet to use his influence with Elisabeth, the princess Palatine, and counter any such reflections on his name.[111] This correspondence is full of concepts which are associated with "fame".

Given such a desire for honour, glory and service to a prince, a grand lifestyle was fitting, and in L'Empereur's case we know that he kept up such a mode of living.[112] He owned a country house in the neighbourhood of Valkenburg, and in 1631 he bought from the widow of Amelis van Hoogeveen, a large house on the Papengracht in Leiden, where he had rebuilding works costing thousands of guilders carried out. Some years later he bought a garden in Leiden, between the Witte Poort, and the Koepoort, next to Heinsius' garden. In a word he was wealthy. In 1635 he had a capital of forty thousand guilders, and thus fell within the same well to do class as the more prosperous theology professors.[113] His cash was invested in loans to individuals, and, very shrewdly, to a great extent in shares of the United East India Company. Thanks to these investments he was able, in spite of a lifestyle in which he spent more than he earned in salary, to leave a capital of sixty thousand

---

[109] L'Empereur to Rivet, 4.2.1638, LB BPL 285, asks Rivet to use his influence with van Aarssen, describes how the Prince can best have his attention drawn to him by two friends, one in the morning and the other in the afternoon, and gives a good insight into university politics. A letter full of such concepts as "dedecorus" and "honor".

[110] For the politically delicate visit: Poelhekke, *Frederik Hendrik*, 520-2; naturally Trigland mentions this event in his funeral address as one of the great moments in L'Empereur's life.

[111] L'Empereur to Rivet 1.8.1645, LB BPL 285. The mediator with the Winter Queen must be Boswell. Key concepts: "fama, gloria." In 1648 L'Empereur was assessor for the theological faculty and apparently deputised for the Rector Magnificus on some occasions. Schoneveld, *Intertraffic of the Mind*, 148, n. 31.

[112] Thanks to his financial records for the years 1628-48, almost completely preserved in Th 108 and Th 163.

[113] De Lind van Wijngaarden, *Walaeus*, 92 n.1 gives the following estimate of the wealth of several Leiden professors: Walaeus: f.32,000; Thysius: f.45,000; Hommius: f.25,000, Vorstius: f.4000. This estimate based on the levy of the 150th penny tax only gives a very rough indication. On both the occasions when L'Empereur paid the 200th penny (in 1632 and 1637), he was assessed for 150 guilders. His estate in those years amounted, not to thirty thousand, but respectively forty and fifty thousand guilders.

guilders at his death. The pomp in which he lived gradually increased and in the forties he was spending more than twice his salary of fifteen hundred guilders.

Besides his own estate, he also administered the capital of a nephew of his second wife, Johannes Thysius, over whom he was joint guardian with A. Thysius sr.[114] He complained occasionally of this responsibility for Thysius, whom he took into his houses and brought up.[115] The way in which Thysius was educated was one befitting his descent and L'Empereur's way of life. Naturally, he studied law and at the end of his student years L'Empereur chose a private tutor for him, such as aristocratic students had. This was Job Ludolph (1624-1704) the great researcher into Ethiopian. Ludolph had been interested in this language as early as his student years, and on L'Empereur's recommendation he was permitted by Heinsius to look into Scaliger's Ethiopian MSS. With Johannes Thysius he made a Grand Tour, which, much more than L'Empereur's own study tour of thirty years before, was intended as a preparation for Thysius' role in society.[116] Johannes Thysius was devoted to the L'Empereurs, and on his death in 1652 he left a considerable part of his estate to his cousin Sara, the daughter of L'Empereur. With the remaining money, he had a library built by Sara's husband, Marcus Baron du Tour. Du Tour bought land on the Rapenburg and had a building designed by Arent Van 's Gravezande, the architect of the Lakenhal and Marekerk in Leiden. Three paintings were hung in the building: of Johannes Thysius himself and of his two guardians, A. Thysius sr. and L'Empereur.[117] The prestigious marriage of Sara with a real baron and councillor of Brabant makes it probable that if L'Empereur had had a son, he, like the son of Polyander, would have made his way into the administrative elite of the Republic.

An agreeable source of extra income for L'Empereur in these years came from his share in a trading partnership, the Halewijn company, which traded with Brazil in the sugar produced by the new colony there. His brother Theodosius, destined by his father for commerce, and probably bankrupt in 1621,[118] was in Pernambuco in the thirties. With Isaac Bernard at Amsterdam they formed a partnership which was active from 1634, when the sugar trade was opened up to private individuals,[119] to

---

[114] Van Roijen, "Inleiding".
[115] For example in the foreword to *RepHeb*.
[116] De Jonge, "Grand Tour".
[117] Van Oerle, "Bouwgeschiedenis"; Blok, "Bibliotheca".
[118] Gijswijt-Hofstra, *Wijkplaatsen*, 227, mentions an asylum-seeking Theodorus L'Empereur and his wife in Culemborg in 1625.
[119] Boxer, *Nederlanders*, 99 ff.

1641 when the war situation in Brazil began to put an end to this highly
lucrative trade.[120] Although it was only a small partnership in comparison with the total Brazilian trade, the earnings for L'Empereur were
very substantial. Each year he made a profit of at least a thousand
guilders from this sideline, and in the best year 1639 he even earned more
than three thousand guilders. The sugar trade was to an important extent
in the hands of Jews, and the names of some of them appear regularly
in L'Empereur's cash books.[121] More important even than these profits
for L'Empereur was the contact with Johan Maurits of Nassau-Siegen
that he acquired by means of this commerce. There is no contradiction
between his participation in trade, and the feeling of honour and the
aristocratic ethos which is revealed in the correspondence with Maurits,
discussed below. L'Empereur saw himself as a professor, who carried on
commerce on the side, not as a merchant who lived from his trade.[122]

Johan Maurits (1604-79) a younger son from a cadet branch of the
house of Nassau, received a thorough modern education, based on neostoicism, and made a career in the armies of the Republic.[123] In 1636 he
was sought out by the West India Company to become governor of the
newly conquered Brazil, and there he remained until 1644. His government of the colony was efficient, effective and ephemeral. He reminds us
in this of no one as much as Wallenstein, the commander of the imperial
armies in the Thirty Years' War. Like Wallenstein in Friedland, Maurits
in Brazil was above all a creator of order. He cared for economic growth,
allowed freedom of religion, was a great patron of artists, had palaces
built and gardens laid out. Both Maurits and Wallenstein ultimately
remained dependent on others, and after their departures, their creations
were overwhelmed by war. The great impression which Maurits' striving
for fame made on the humanists of the Republic is clear from one of
Barlaeus' letters.[124] With enthusiasm he described how the work on the
Mauritshuis in The Hague was proceeding, the palace which the
Brazilian had built in the east to preserve the glory he had won in the

---

[120] Israel, "Economic Contribution", 519-21.

[121] Isaac Seraiva Coronel: Loys Nunes.

[122] For the way in which a value system that looked down on trade and manual work
could be combined with the accumulation of capital by capitalist activities, see Veyne,
*Le Pain et la Cirque*, 127-40.

[123] Van den Boogaart, *Johan Maurits*. For his upbringing, the fine article of Mout,
"The Youth of Johan Maurits", *ibid*. 10-38.

[124] Barlaeus to Vicofortius, 13.6.1639; Barlaeus, *Epistolae*, 758-60: "Etiam cum isthic
( = Den Haag, PvR) essem, conspexi surgentia culmina Comitis Mauritii, qui dum in
Occidente militat, in Septentrione aedificat, & gloriae suae commodisque receptaculum
parat illustre."

west. In 1647 Johan Maurits entered the service of the Great Elector as governor of the Cleves-Brandenburg territories and collaborated in building up an absolutist state.

L'Empereur made Maurits' acquaintance either through the mediation of Rivet, who corresponded with Soller, a preacher at Pernambuco, whose daughter was Maurits' mistress,[125] or thanks to the Brazil trade of the firm of Halewijn. After some small services he received the honorific title of Counsellor to the Prince.[126] The way in which he thanked Maurits for this honour is typical of the view he held of service to a prince:[127]

> "I have meanwhile received an act of authorisation; wherein the honour is done me, to be accepted and recognised as a Counsellor of your Excellency. Through which honour I am all the more bound, and owe your grace gratitude, since it has been pronounced from pure goodwill and favourable opinion. It has always been considered as a great good fortune, to enjoy the favour and esteem of illustrious persons and even more to be held capable in their opinion of serving them. Finding both these now in me, I cannot omit to acknowledge in this my missive, your Excellency's regard and favourable opinion, as singular kindnesses. For which, being asked, I shall always be ready zealously to employ myself in your Excellency's service."

L'Empereur's services, which he was glad to devise, offer and perform with great zeal, were those of what would today be called a "lobbyist". He regularly went to The Hague and Amsterdam to effect something for Maurits. Thus he was involved in the legal finesses of one or other madcap scheme of an old Jew in Brazil, who for a share in the revenues was willing to reveal a secret which would make a great treasure accessible.[128] He used his influence with the directors of the West India Company, in his eyes small minded men who thought only of profit and not of glory,[129] to improve the conditions of Maurits' appointment. When the Polish general Arciszewski returned from Brazil after a great dispute with Maurits in 1639, L'Empereur kept his prince informed of the Pole's activities and the political opinion concerning this affair.[130] He arranged Maurits' contacts with artists in the Netherlands who produced works

---

[125] Van Opstal, *Rivet*, 97.

[126] For a description of this "rather vague" function: Poelhekke, *Frederik Hendrik*, 134.

[127] L'Empereur to Johan Maurits, 10.12.1639, draft in Th 164,6.

[128] Benito Henriques. The affair is most clearly described in L'Empereur to Johan Maurits 26.8.1639, draft in Th 164, 6. The activities of L'Empereur in the matter were chiefly concerned with the distribution of the chickens before the eggs were hatched. He enquired whether Maurits was empowered to make an arrangement with Henriques, in which Maurits himself would also receive a share of the proceeds.

[129] The letters of L'Empereur to Maurits in draft in Th 164,6.

[130] Description of this affair: Boxer, *Nederlanders*, 115; Literature, *ibid.*, 88, n. 37.

describing Brazil.[131] His relations with Maurits passed through his brother Theodosius in Brazil, and partly also through the mediation of Isaac Palache. Palache was a member of a Moroccan Jewish family, which had been involved in diplomatic relations between the Republic and Morocco since the early years of the century. Isaac had converted to Christianity, and received in return a subsidy from the Particular Synod of South Holland, which was paid to him by the Leiden professors. In 1639 he intervened in the contacts between the Republic and a rebel Moroccan prince, for which purpose L'Empereur wrote several letters. The handling of the mission appears not to have been wholly satisfactory, and there was a rupture between L'Empereur and Isaac.[132]

Maurits made a great impression on L'Empereur and he described him in 1642 as a perfect patron and a possible successor to Frederick Henry,[133] an opinion which he claimed was shared by many. His appointment as a Counsellor of the Prince was of great value for L'Empereur's self-esteem. On his portrait and funeral monument he had himself described as "Professor Sacro-Sanctae Theologiae" and "Counsellor of Prince Maurits".[134] In his funeral oration Trigland naturally paid much attention to the office.

---

[131] E.g. with Plante: cf. Maurits to L'Empereur, 12.11.1645; an undated letter of Plante to L'Empereur in Th 170. For Plante: R. A. Eekhout, "The Mauritius. A Neolatin Epic", in: Van den Boogaart, *Johan Maurits*.

[132] Two drafts of a letter to Seid Ali in Th 164,6. For the confused political situation in Morocco at this time: Caillé, "Ambassades", 7-8. When Palache arrived at the prince's court the prince had just received a letter from Isaac's brother David Palache in which Isaac was slandered. L'Empereur attributed this to the hate of this brother who had remained a Jew, for the convert (to Hendrik Casimir, 18.5.1640, draft in Th 164,6), but the various members of this fairly entrepreneurial family often competed among themselves in such a hard fashion: De Groot, *Ottoman Empire*, 295, n. 86. For the Palaches as agents of Morocco: Caillé, "Ambassades". It appears that L'Empereur too went back on his verdict about the reasons for the failure of Isaac's mission. In 1634 Isaac "for the last time" asked for a subsidy from the churches (*Acta* 1634 a.52). In 1637 all the professors of theology recommended him to the synod (*Acta* 1637, a.38). In 1639 he left for the Barbary Coast (apparently on his mission to Seid Ali), but left his family behind him in needy circumstances (*Acta* 1639, a.34). Form 1640 there were unpleasant rumours about Palache circulating, and many classes stopped their subsidy to him (*Acta* 1640, a.54; 1641, a.6); they wished him first to clear himself of the charges before the States General, the West India Company and the Leiden church council. Apparently something went fundamentally wrong with the mission to Morocco. L'Empereur also complains of Palache in his letter to Theodosius cited below, note 133.

[133] L'Empereur to Theodose L'Empereur, 20.8.1640, Th 164,6: "Car comme je dis tousjours aupres grands et petits, Maurice est un patron d'une Prince parfait. Il n'y ast personne plus capable que luy pour gouverner ces pais, s'il arriva quelque cas humain a son Altesse."

[134] Prentenkabinet LB, sign. 7920. Around the portrait in a ring: Constantinus L'Empereur Ab Oppyck S.S. Theologiae Professor et Illustrissimi Com. Mauritii Nassovii Ind. Occ. Gubernatoris consiliarus." Trigland, *Oratio*, 17. Trigland's oration is preceded by a picture of his funeral monument.

Thanks to his appointment as a Counsellor of the Brazilian, L'Empereur came into contact with further members of the house of Nassau. He must have known Frederick Henry since his appointment at Leiden, and must also have thanked him in 1637 when chosen as Rector Magnificus. After he was made a Counsellor, he became acquainted with the high functionaries at The Hague, and often spoke to Hendrik Casimir, the Stadhouder of Friesland. He served other members of the house of Nassau in the last years of his life, when employed in the re-establishment of the higher educational institution of Nassau, the High School of Herborn.[135] This had fallen into decay as a result of the Thirty Years' War and in the years after 1645 attempts were made to restore it to its old renown. Johan Maurits too was involved, and requested the Emperor to reinstate the High School in the rank of a university.[136] Money was collected in the Republic and a subsidy was attempted. L'Empereur played a part in this. He gave an important address on this matter before the States of Holland, and administered the money collected by the Synod of South Holland.[137]

We have already referred briefly to his concern for the High School of Breda. After the reconquest of Breda in 1637 van Renesse was appointed to reform the city and bailiwick of Breda. He was eager to found a high school, which was finally opened in 1646. It was financed entirely by the house of Orange and bore the arms of Frederick Henry.[138] The High School had some aspects of a military academy, and was chiefly intended for the sons of the nobility who served in the States' army, who were to complete their education there outside the campaigning season. At the time of the foundation L'Empereur was several times consulted by de Wilhem and Rivet (who was its curator) on aspects of the establishment.[139] It was in this way that he came into contact with Huygens.[140]

These contacts with the court built up at the end of the thirties most probably assured him the fulfilment of his most cherished ambition. L'Empereur still wanted to become a professor of theology, even after his

---

[135] For the university: Grün, "Geist and Gestalt". Documents on this in Th 169; accounts of this and other attempts: Steubing, *Herborn*, 98 ff.

[136] Steubing, *Herborn*, 151.

[137] In Th 169, with letters of recommendation of Johan Maurits for L'Empereur, who had praised him for his aid to the high school in a letter of 12.11.1645 (Th 169). L'Empereur also sought support from the Synod of South Holland: *Acta*, 1647 a.15; 1648 a.36.

[138] Van Alphen, "Illustre School"; Lindeboom, "Illustere School".

[139] The correspondence between de Wilhem and L'Empereur from the years 1646-7 in LB BPL 298A is virtually all devoted to this theme.

[140] L'Empereur to Huygens, 13.3.1645; Huygens, *Briefwisseling* IV, 133.

fruitless application for the post of Rivet in 1634. In 1642, when the succession to A. Thysius sr. was open, he was considered as a candidate but passed over in favour of Spanheim.[141] In 1646, Polyander died. There were two candidates to succeed him: Abraham Heidanus and L.'Empereur. The former had been recommended as his successor by the deceased Polyander, but L'Empereur was able to count on more sympathy within the university.[142] On 12 February 1647, his wishes were fulfilled and he was appointed professor of theology. The influence of the Court will have been decisive, for Heidanus was a strong candidate. After L'Empereur's death, he became his successor, in spite of the theology faculty's objections to his cartesian views.

The only work published by L'Empereur as the result of this appointment as professor of theology, was a posthumous collection of disputations. A comparison between this and the *Synopsis Purioris Theologiae* yields an unsurprising result. L'Empereur differs in no respect from the moderate orthodoxy of Dordt. Even references to more modern views, if only to attack them are not to be found. The citations of Hebrew words in the disputations are wholly traditional, and do not appeal to any deeper knowledge of Hebrew he had acquired in the meantime. If occasional use is made of rabbinical knowledge, it is to support traditional dogmas.[143] In favour of the disputations it can be said that they do not suffer from the "five article mania". They are treatments of traditional dogmatic *loci*, not the reflection of teaching based on the bible, but they do not all consist of a polemic refutation of dissidents. That was an improvement on the existing programme, for in 1648 each of the three professors at the Leiden theology faculty presented a disputation against

---

[141] In the letter to Rivet cited in note 111, L'Empereur complains that he has been passed over several times for appointments. That must also refer to the succession to the post vacated by A. Thysius sr. Cf. Rivet's plan, described above, to bring about the appointment of Petit.

[142] Cf. Rivet to Sarrau, 26.3.1646; *C. I. Rivet/Sarrau* III, 367. In a letter to de Wilhem of 30.11.1646 (LB BPL 293A) L'Empereur speaks in hopeful terms. The whole city is for him.

[143] E.g. the use of the meaning of *htsdiq* for the support of a forensic doctrine of justification, which we saw already in his *Oratio* and which also appears in the *Synopsis*, 331. The difficult passage, James 2:20-1 (justification by works), was explained by L'Empereur with an appeal to Ibn Ezra as a frequently occurring case of the omission of the *nomen regens*; what James wanted to say was "justification by the works of faith". In various reference books there is mention of a theological system by L'Empereur, published at Harderwijk. The fullest title is given by Nauta, in BL: *Disputationes theologicae Hardervicenae sive systema theologicum*, Hard. 1626; LB 1648. It appears that some confusion has arisen, caused by the printer's foreword to the disputations discussed here, which states that if L'Empereur had lived longer, he would certainly have issued a "Theologiae systema".

his favourite heresy: respectively against the arminians, catholics and anabaptists.[144]

L'Empereur's late appointment does not mean that he had not applied himself to the theological field after 1634. We have already observed that he felt himself a theologian above all else, and as early as 1634 had succeeded in having his chair of Hebrew set as close to the faculty of theology as possible. We now turn to his activities as an orthodox theologian.

### 5.3 *The theologian*

L'Empereur felt himself to be a theologian above all, but the intellectual climate of late humanism, the prevailing cultural force at the University of Leiden, determined to a great extent the form and content of his works. Through them he was able, in spite of a theological self-awareness and his explicit support of orthodoxy, to become a fully fledged member of the Republic of Letters. L'Empereur's philological and grammatical publications, by which he unlocked rabbinical literature for Christian readers, had won him this place and could be regarded by the intellectual community as useful, albeit slightly eccentric contributions.

L'Empereur's generation was the last in which an orthodox theologian could become a member of the Republic of Letters in such a way, and even in his lifetime the development which was to make it impossible to belong to these two worlds at the same time, was already heralded. We shall devote some attention to the symptoms of the approaching breach in this last section. The study of rabbinical literature, which in L'Empereur's work still formed part of the implicit programme of this intellectual community, was gradually to acquire another basis and another public as a result of this development.

But even during the period 1634-47, before his appointment to the faculty of theology, L'Empereur was not regarded purely as a philologist, but was involved in various questions in the field of philosophy and theology. Whenever the Mayors and Curators had a need for specialist knowledge they were accustomed to consult the experts in their own university. Thus L'Empereur and Golius gave advice on the acquisition of oriental MSS.[145] In 1641 the Mayors and Curators asked the advice of a committee on the best way to regulate the teaching of philosophy. Although it has been assumed that this was the first round in the conflict over the philosophy of Descartes, the advice only concerned the question

---

[144] Rivet to Sarrau, 20.6.1644; *C. I. Rivet/Sarrau* II, 304-5: "On a longtemps dit ici, que nos Escholiers *laborabant morbo quinquarticulari*". He proceeds to describe the teaching of Polyander, Trigland and Spanheim.

[145] *Molh.* II, 194.

whether Aristotle should be treated directly from the texts or more systematically.[146] Heerebord, the proponent of the second method, had no objection to faithfulness to Aristotle in itself. Be that as it may, what is important for us is that L'Empereur was one of the experts consulted by the Mayors and Curators. He had had a thorough philosophical training in his youth, and as we have seen could have become a professor of philosophy on the grounds of his achievements in that field, and was still apparently considered as a specialist in it. He continued to acquire philosophical works during his professorship of Hebrew. Thus, in 1644 he bought Descartes' *Discours de la Méthode*, published by Maire in 1637. L'Empereur undoubtedly knew the name of the French philosopher before that. As early as 1631 Golius was on friendly terms with Descartes[147] and de Dieu also knew the philosopher. The purchase of the *Discours* in 1644 will have been connected with the conflict over cartesianism which was raging at that time in the University of Utrecht. When problems over the new philosophy also arose at the University of Leiden in 1647, L'Empereur was to take a negative attitude towards Descartes' opinions. Trigland, who had begun the struggle against cartesian philosophy in a disputation against Golius, states in his funeral address on L'Empereur that the faculty of theology had been delighted by his appointment, because they knew that he was averse to the new philosophy which taught men to doubt everything.[148] Such an attitude was not shared by the authoritative circles in the Republic of Letters. Descartes could count on considerable support at court, as appeared from the assistance which was given him in 1643, in his conflict with Schoeck and Voetius. One of Descartes' most important allies was L'Empereur's relative, friend and patron, David de Wilhem,[149] and when Trigland began his campaign, Descartes sent de Wilhem a letter with a request for support. In this letter he mentions that Trigland had said that his colleagues in the faculty of theology supported him, but that he did not believe this:[150]

---

[146] Dibon, *Philosophie*, 109.

[147] Thijssen-Schoute, *Cartesianisme*, 78.

[148] Thijssen-Schoute, *Cartesianisme*, 101-3. The letter from Descartes to the Mayors and Curators, in which he complains of Trigland and Revius, 4.5.1647, is in *Molh.* III, 1*-6*. The resolution of the Mayors and Curators, 20.5.1647: *Molh.* III, 4-6. In his *Oratio*, 18, Trigland mentions that the faculty was delighted by L'Empereur's appointment: "quandoquidem de ipsius Orthodoxia in omnibus Theologiae capitibus certissime nobis constaret, quem etiam alienissimum esse sciremus a nova quadam Philosophia, qua de omnibus dubitandum esse statuitur, omniaque ex animo eliminanda praejudicia, quo proinde subvertitur argumentum ab Apostolo ad convincendos gentiles usurpatum in Epist. ad Romanos Cap. 1, adeoque via sternitur ad Atheismum." This was certainly also a dig at Heidanus, the most likely candidate to succeed L'Empereur.

[149] Thijssen-Schoute, *Cartesianisme*, 476-8; Duker, *Voetius* II, 197.

[150] Descartes, *Oeuvres* V, 32-4; to de Wilhem, 24.5.1647.

"...pource que ie les estime l'un et l'autre trop honestes gens pour cela. Outre que Mr. Spanheim a, des le commencement, declaré vouloir estre neutre; &, pour Mr l'Empereur, ie ne me souviens point d'avoir iamais parlé a luy qu'une seule fois, qui fut au logis de Mr. Vorstius, ou nous disnions ensemble; mais il parloit alors si avantageusement & avec tant de franchise, pour la liberté de philosopher & contre la malignité des pedans, que ie ne me puis imaginer qu'il ait tant changé depuis."

Yet, to be absolutely safe he asked de Wilhem, whom he knew as a relative and friend of L'Empereur, to use his influence with L'Empereur to persuade him to refrain from taking up a position in the conflict. No great weight is to be attached to L'Empereur's statements in the conversation to which Descartes refers in the passage quoted above. In conversation, he was accustomed to be friendly and sympathetic.[151]

Descartes' philosophy and method of thinking were to prevail in the future, but in the second half of the 17th century this development did not create difficulties for calvinist orthodoxy, which was founded on aristotelian scholasticism. Rather, it inflicted serious damage on late humanism. Orthodoxy in the Dutch Republic managed to immunise itself against cartesianism for a long time, while it was the Republic of Letters which was particularly exposed and open to the new philosophy. There is a well known story how Descartes, when residing with the sons of the great Dutch humanist families at the court of Christina of Sweden, tried to convince the queen of the futility of learning Greek.[152] Descartes' way of thinking was characterised by an aversion to old rules, as laid down in books, and was based on the desire for new knowledge, which had to be logical, clear and simple, and which had to permit itself to be discovered "en moi même, ou bien dans le grand livre du monde".[153] These aspects of his thought were in harmony with other new trends, and were most suitable to acquire influence in wide circles. They were in sharp contrast with erudite late humanism, which was still striving for a synthesis of classical antiquity, Christianity and oriental history, and saw philology as the mother of all sciences. The progress of cartesian philosophy and the new natural science was not to result in the end of philological studies, but it was to rob them of their place of the highest prestige in scholarly life.

On at least two occasions L'Empereur helped the faculty of theology to prepare an official statement of position. In 1637 he and Louis de Dieu signed a testimonial for the theology faculty on behalf of Samuel

---

[151] L'Empereur to Vossius, 13.7.1642; Vossius, *Epistolae*, 242-3: "Nosti indolem meam, omnibus placere studeo; inprimis viris probis, doctis ac piis."

[152] Gerretzen, *Schola Hemsterhusiana*, 6.

[153] The whole "Première partie" of the *Discours de la Méthode* illustrates the slight value which Descartes attached to the study of classical literature.

Heucherius, a German. The testimonial explained that the lexicographical activities of Heucherius in the field of Hebrew were of great importance, and that he was therefore eligible for financial support. The recommendation was supported by a reference to the nature of New Testament Greek, which in the opinion of the faculty contained numerous hebraisms.[154] Undoubtedly, in this case L'Empereur and de Dieu had been asked because of their linguistic abilities.

In 1643 L'Empereur and Golius signed a *judicium* of the faculty of theology. It concerned a conflict between two friends of L'Empereur, the theologian Cloppenburg and L'Empereur's former student Anthonius Deusing, who had both become professors at Harderwijk. The conflict had arisen over the accusation of Cloppenburg, that Deusing's philosophical work *Naturae Theatrum*, in which he posited the existence of a world-soul was heterodox. The faculty refrained from condemning it, and in this case L'Empereur and Golius must have been called in to sign the verdict on the grounds of their philosophical knowledge.[155]

Another conflict at Harderwijk was the occasion for the only stance taken by L'Empereur in which he distanced himself from his fellow theologians. It concerned the fiercely contested intended appointment at Harderwijk of Salmasius' friend and pupil Alexander Morus in 1647. Morus, a theologian and the successor of Spanheim at Geneva, was suspected of heterodoxy and of sympathy for the theology of Saumur.[156] Salmasius campaigned actively for his appointment during 1647—and of course Heinsius worked against it,—and thus incurred the hostility of Spanheim. In December 1647 L'Empereur had not yet dared to take sides,[157] but in the spring of 1648 he chose the party of Salmasius and Morus, which earned him an angry letter from Rivet.[158] L'Empereur's choice in this contest was probably determined by his friendship for Salmasius. His essential orthodoxy is evident from his involvement in a number of publications of these years.

In 1641 L'Empereur prepared an edition of C. Bertramus' *De Republica Hebraeorum*, for the Leiden printer Maire. The edition, in 16mo, offered the text of Bertramus' work to which L'Empereur added some explanatory notes. In the foreword he states how, because of his many

---

[154] De Jonge, *Bestudering*, 82-3.
[155] De Haan, *Wijsgerig Onderwijs*, 22-37.
[156] For Morus: Haag 7, 543-8; *NNBW* X, 652-3.
[157] Ter Horst, *Isaac Vossius*, 17-8, 45-6; Isaac Vossius to Salmasius, 30.12.1647: "Imperatori vero Constantino aqua haeret, neque enim vel in hanc vel in illam partem aliquid audet pronuntiare."
[158] Rivet to L'Empereur, 25. 4. ⟨1648⟩, Th 170. An undated letter of L'Empereur to Salmasius ("Le neuviesme de ce moy") in UB Leiden, Pap 7, in which L'Empereur writes as an ally. A letter of C. Follius, 21.4.1648 on the same affair, Th 170.

activities, he had only been able to meet Maire's request for a book on the state institutions of Israel by preparing this new edition. He also explains that he chose Bertramus' work although two others on the subject existed, the publication of which appeared less opportune to him.[159] This edition by Maire was part of a large project of the Leiden printers. In the twenties, Elzevier had begun to publish a series of 16mo volumes, in which the political institutions of all the European and a great many ancient and foreign states were described.[160] The series, which formed a kind of encyclopaedia of history and political science, was exceptionally successful and other printers, including Maire, imitated this project and published various "Republics".[161] In his series Elzevier had also included a Hebrew Republic, a new edition of the work of Cunaeus, dating from 1617.

This work by Cunaeus, his *De Republica Hebraeorum*, is one of those which L'Empereur rejected for possible republication without naming it. The reason given by him—that Cunaeus had only wished to collect what others had omitted—is not the true one.[162] Undoubtedly L'Empereur was repelled by the odour of heterodoxy which clung to Cunaeus' work. As early as 1620, at the time of the purging of the University, the book had caused its author the inevitable difficulties. Petrus Cunaeus (1586-1638) was a Zeelander by descent and related to a number of the magistrates of that province, who in the first half of the 17th century showed more interest in oriental languages than the rulers of the other provinces. A copy of Maimonides' *Mishneh Torah*, the most important rabbinical source of his *Republica*, had been given to Cunaeus by Boreel.[163] He studied at Leiden, where he was a member of the circle of young, gifted students which Scaliger gathered around himself, made a career there, and ultimately became a professor in the faculty of law.[164]

---

[159] *RepHeb*, *7: "Nam aliorum unus linguae Rabbinicae non ita gnarus subsidia, quae ad istiusmodi commentationem merito requiruntur, pariter non habuit, alter tantum ab aliis praetermissa *liberrima scriptione*, uti testatur ipse, *congerere* voluit. qui tamen praeclara quam plurima nobis e tenebris eruit." The first is C. Sigonius, whose *De Republica Hebraeorum* was long popular. The second is P. Cunaeus, see note 162.

[160] Frick, *Elzevir'schen Republiken*.

[161] The Leiden University Library possesses a series which is outwardly uniform of seventy-seven volumes (shelf numbers 274 G15 1/- 276 G 28), and which includes besides the thirty works published by Elzevier and summarised in Frick, books from the presses of Maire, Janssonius, Blaeu and a number of smaller printers.

[162] The expressions italicised in the passage cited in note 159 occur in the foreword to Cunaeus' *De Republica*, where he compares his work with those of Sigonius and Bertramus. For Cunaeus' knowledge of Hebrew: Katchen, *Christian Hebraists*, 37-55. The data which Katchen supplies on the politico-religious background to the work are incorrect.

[163] Cunaeus, *De Republica*, praefatio.

[164] *NNBW* I, 658-60. Scaliger described him (*Sec Scal*, 287) as "bene doctus sed melancholicus."

In his youth he took a rather irreverent position in theology. His name was mentioned in connection with a serious incident at the University of Leiden in 1614, when several young students cast doubt on the revelatory character of the bible in a radical way.[165] During the remonstrant disputes, in 1612, he published a satire inspired by Erasmus' *Praise of Folly*, abusing the quarrelling divines. He was not a theologian nor a convinced remonstrant partisan, but an erasmian humanist with little interest in the subtler details of dogmatics. He was even on such good terms with Sibrandus Lubbertus that he could send him a copy of the satire and of his *De Republica*.[166] After the remonstrant disputes, so it appears from the correspondence which the South Holland Synod had with him on his satire and description of the Republic of Israel, he became a member of the reformed church.[167] The Synod took offence above all at his depiction of the preachers in his *Satyra Menippea*, but was also disturbed by the picture of the faith of the simple Israelites in his *De Republica Hebraeorum*, who according to Cunaeus, knew nothing of Christ. Some other points in this last work were also considered as less successful,[168] while another stumbling block for more orthodox circles was provided by the way in which Cunaeus described the relationship of church and state in Israel.

How sensitive this subject was, is evident from a letter of Cunaeus to Barlaeus from the early thirties.[169] Barlaeus had enquired if the title page of the *De Republica*, in which Moses is portrayed on the left and Aaron on the right, had been deliberately so composed. Cunaeus replied that this order of precedence was an accident, and that he had run into difficulties because he had suggested a subordination of the church in his book.[170] In the 17th century the opinion held on the institutions of Israel was still of immediate relevance for the forming of political theory. In his *De Republica emendanda*, Grotius felt obliged to go deeply into the social institutions of the Hebrews and Israelites as they were described in the Old Testament. Spinoza in his *Tractatus Theologico-Politicus* and Hobbes in his *Leviathan* also devoted chapters to the state of Israel, and in one of his letters to Rivet L'Empereur assured his patron that the Jews had never acknowledged a particular religious order.[171]

---

[165] *Molh.* II, 51-4. They praised Lucian and said that Christ and Moses were sorcerers.

[166] Cunaeus to Lubbertus, 9.5.1617, Cunaeus, *Epistolae*, 91.

[167] Cunaeus to the Particular Synod of South Holland, Cunaeus, *Epistolae*, 61-74.

[168] Balthasar Lydius on behalf of the Synod to Cunaeus, 6.7.1620; Cunaeus, *Epistolae*, 50-61.

[169] Cunaeus to Barlaeus, 12.1.1632; *Praestantium ac Eruditorum virorum Epistolae*, 765.

[170] Especially in book I, chapter 14. He had even omitted the clearest references to his views on the relationship of church and state: Cunaeus to Grotius, 25.8.1615; Cunaeus, *Epistolae*, 96-7.

[171] L'Empereur to Rivet, 1.2.1646; LB BPL 285.

L'Empereur's choice of Bertramus' work as the one to be reissued can, in view of this background, only be regarded as the adoption of a calvinist position. Cornelis Bertramus (1531-94) the successor of Chevalier as professor of Hebrew at Geneva, was of unimpeached orthodoxy.[172] The structure of his work was determined by the idea of the separation of church and state, of which he found the beginnings in Paradise.[173] In his notes L'Empereur maintains this distinction. In this view he was of course a good calvinist[174] but rather out of tune with the Republic of Letters, the members of which inclined to a more erastian standpoint such as that of Cunaeus. The roots of the latter point of view were very various and rested on theological convictions inspired by Zwingli and Melanchthon, political experiences, especially in the wars of religion, and the social composition of the Republic of Letters which had a great many legally trained state officials among its members. This intelligentsia, so closely linked with the apparatus of the state, was the upholder of a certain incipient nationalism and longed for peace and order. They supported a state which would embrace all its citizens both in the spiritual and the physical sphere and impose order on them. The Church of England, ideologically polished up by the work of a number of humanists at the turn of the century, was the great example of the true church for these circles.[175] L'Empereur in his edition followed the calvinism of the Republic, which in its political theory carefully maintained the essential independence of the church.[176] In spite of his position at the University of Leiden and his close links with the Republic of Letters, the church remained decisive for L'Empereur on this point.

The development within the Republic of Letters by which humanism—originally a general cultural striving to achieve a synthesis of classical and Christian antiquity in order to improve the individual and thus society—was gradually transformed into a technical discipline, philology, whose results could no longer be absorbed by calvinist orthodoxy, can be illustrated from L'Empereur's involvement in the publication of two others works.

In 1636 and 1637 L'Empereur prepared an edition of Gomarus' *Lyra Davidis*. Entirely in accordance with the humanist ideology of *eruditio trilinguis* Gomarus attempted to show in this work that Greek poetry derived from Hebrew. Like all wisdom, art was supposed to derive originally

---

[172] *Haag* 3, 229-31; *DBF* VI, 260.
[173] Chapter 2 is entitled "Politia Ecclesiae ab orbe condito"; chapter 3 "Politia Civilis ab orbe condito". This twofold division recurs in all the chapters of the book.
[174] Weber, "Compétence de l'Eglise".
[175] Cf. Posthumus Meyjes, "Hotman", 74-7.
[176] Conring, *Kirche und Staat*.

from Moses, and for that reason biblical poetry, inspired by the Holy Spirit, was the highest of all forms of art.[177] In the foreword to the Latin translation of the bible made by himself and Tremellius, Junius had proclaimed a similar view.[178] The aged Gomarus left it to L'Empereur to translate into Latin the fragments of Sophocles and Pindar which he had collected and compared with Hebrew poetry. Occasionally L'Empereur's Latin translation differed from that of Junius and Tremellius, whom he criticised with remarkable severity in an afterword.[179] The orientalists and theologians of the Republic, brought up in the humanist ideology that Hebrew was the source of all culture, received the book enthusiastically.[180] Yet Gomarus' work was an elaboration of an ideology which was in fact no longer entirely current. In the course of the century it was mocked in such puns as *Lyra Davidis delirat*, while in 1643 there appeared the *Ad novam Davidis Lyram animadversiones*, an attack on the work of Gomarus by the professor of Hebrew at Saumur, Louis Cappel.

In this attack, Cappel revealed himself for the first time as the author of the *Arcanum Punctationis Revelatum*, published by Erpenius, in which he had demonstrated that the vocalisation signs in the Masoretic text were a later accretion. It was with the aid of this hypothesis that he made his *Animadversiones* on Gomarus. His argument is very simple. Since the original form of the Hebrew words is not certain, the metre of the poetry written in this language cannot be reconstructed. Cappel's work and his whole approach breath a new spirit. He is not the omniscient erudite, but a critical specialist. This characteristic comes most clearly to the fore in his great work, the *Critica Sacra*.

L'Empereur's part in the history of this work was important. The book had been completed in 1634, and in 1639 Cappel had sought support from Grotius to have it published at Leiden.[181] This attempt was unsuccessful, and in 1645 L'Empereur became involved with Cappel when Sarrau offered the *Critica Sacra* to the Leiden printers for publication, through Rivet. Publication by Janssonius at Amsterdam was also considered, but he did not have a good corrector for Hebrew. He used

---

[177] Brief description of the works: Van Itterzon, *Gomarus*, 371-3.

[178] Van Dorsten, "Sidney and Junius".

[179] The conclusion of *Davidis Lyra* contains an *Epikrisis* by L'Empereur, justifying his translation which often differs from that of Junius and Tremellius. "Hoc enim in ista bibliorum versione saepe observavi, conceptam animo analysin veluti normam statui, ad quam in vertendo respiceretur, cum hoc modo a vero sensu saepe recedatur." Simon, by a traditional polemical artifice, recurred to this in his judgment of this translation, in his *Histoire Critique du Vieux Textament* II, 236.

[180] Cf. Gomarus to Buxtorf II, 17/27.1.1637, Van Itterzon, "Nog twintig brieven", 442-3; even the Jews thought it a fine work: Vossius to Gomarus, 10.3.1638; *Epistolae*, 317.

[181] Cappel to Grotius, 10.10.1639; *Briefwisseling* X, 659.

Menasseh ben Israel, but Sarrau had heard from Grotius that Menasseh had been unreliable and careless in the correction of his annotations on the Gospels.[182] Since the *Critica Sacra* contained a great deal of Hebrew, it had to be corrected thoroughly. The advantage of Leiden over Amsterdam was that good correctors were available in Leiden, L'Empereur and Golius. Once a first fascicle had been sent Rivet submitted it to both professors for reading through. L'Empereur's verdict was unambiguous and strictly negative. In May 1645 Rivet wrote to Sarrau that he had little hope that the edition would be carried out[183]

> "Car il n'y a que trois jours que j'avoy'icy Mons. l'Empereur, qui me dit ouvertement qu'en bonne conscience il ne le pouvoit recommander aux Imprimeurs, qu'il estoit obligé au contraire par conscience de declarer que cette Critique est dangereuse, et que si on la suit, il n'y aura rien de certain en l'Escriture, qu'on se donnera licence de contester les lieux les plus claires."

We recognise in this verdict, passed on by Rivet, two earlier statements of L'Empereur,[184] so that it is not impossible that Rivet, who clearly had doubts of his own about the edition, was repeating L'Empereur's actual words. What were the aspects of the *Critica Sacra* which so disturbed L'Empereur?

Like the *Arcanum*, the *Critica Sacra* was in essence a work of textual criticism. Cappel argued that in the transmission of the text of the Old Testament, corruptions have taken place at a great many places, which concern not only the vocalisation signs, but also the consonants and sometimes even whole words. The work is one of overwhelming thoroughness. In six books Cappel hunts down textual corruptions by comparing all the parallel texts on which he could lay hands. He investigates parallels within the Old Testament, compares the Masoretic text with the LXX, Vulgate and Samaritanus, and deals with the citations from the Old Testament in the New. The great force of Cappel's argument lies in his classification of the various errors in the transmission of the text, on the grounds of the way in which they originated. He

---

[182] Rivet to Sarrau, 12.9.1644: "Janssonius nous donne esperance d'imprimer la Critique. Mais je ne sçay s'il aura un bon Hebrieu pour le corriger, car je ne croy pas qu'il s'en falle fier en Manasseh Ben Israel Juif." Sarrau to Rivet, 23.9.1644: "Pour la correction de l'Hebreu par Manasseh Ben Israel elle n'est pas excellente et me souviens d'avoir oui Mr Grotius se plaindre qu'il avoit esté mal servi de lui en l'Hebreu de ses Evangiles, si tant estoit que Blaew l'y eust employé comme il le disoit."; *C. I. Rivet/Sarrau* II, 376, 390.

[183] Rivet to Sarrau, 8.5.1645; *C. I. Rivet/Sarrau* III, 114.

[184] With reference to the promotion of Episcopius (Appendix IV) and Heinsius' textual criticism (chapter 5, note 170).

illustrated every possible cause of textual corruption with so many examples that the usual practice of harmonisation becomes not impossible, but unworthy of belief.

Thus, the contradiction, mentioned in the previous chapter, between the number of horsemen of Hadadezer whom David defeated according to II Sam. 8:4 and I Chron. 18:4, explained by L'Empereur, following Abrabanel, with the aid of an historical hypothesis, occurs in the *Critica Sacra* in a short paragraph discussing textual corruptions caused by the omission of a word. In the same paragraph Cappel gives three other examples of such omissions. The passage in question contains only a few lines of the hundreds of pages which make up the work.[185] Cappel was well aware that he was in fact applying to the Old Testament the textual criticism developed by humanism for the study of classical literature. The last section of the sixth book of the *Critica Sacra* is entitled: "Confirmation and illustration of our criticism, by means of the like phenomenon of variant readings in all sorts of ancient literature". In this section he describes how, after completing his work, he had read H. Stephanus' *Castigationes in Marci Tulli Ciceronis locos quamplurimos* (155), and realised that the same causes of error which he had described in his work also occurred in the classics.[186] Sarrau who was irritated and surprised by the rejection from the men he disparagingly referred to as "Messieurs vos Rabbins de Leyde", also understood that it was this humanist-philological aspect of the book which had provoked such aversion. In his correspondence with Rivet he often recurs to the fact that Erpenius, if he had still been alive, would have welcomed the book, published and defended it.[187]

L'Empereur did not do so. The theological situation had changed since 1625. As early as the publication of the *Arcanum* a correspondent had told Buxtorf I that he was the appropriate scholar to refute this work, which would have the result that nothing in the Scriptures would be certain any longer.[188] Buxtorf had in fact rejected the *Arcanum*, which he had read in

---

[185] Cappel, *Critica Sacra*, 34.

[186] Book VI, caput xii: "Criticae huius nostrae confirmatio & illustratio, ex simili variarum lectionum, in omni genere antiquorum librorum, observatione." After the discussion of Stephanus' work he concludes (*Critica Sacra*, 439): "Ex quibus manifestum est illum eosdem plane hic errorum, sive mendorum in Graecis & Latinis auctoribus fontes designare atque aperire, quos ego statim initio huius Criticae proposui, multis ante annis priusquam in hunc viri illius docti locum incidissem." From this it appears that Diestel's opinion (*Geschichte*, 347), in which he has been followed by several learned men, that Cappel had been inspired by Stephanus, is incorrect.

[187] A survey of what Sarrau did for his friend Cappel: *C. I. Rivet/Sarrau* II, 379, n. 3; for Sarrau's amazement at L'Empereur's refusal: *ibid.* III, 123, 125.

[188] L. Fabricius to J. Buxtorf I, 24.8.1625; J. J. Buxtorf, *Catalecta*, 434-6.

MS. before its publication in 1622, but he had not attacked it.[189] Two
developments in France were responsible for the greater difficulties Cappel experienced twenty years later in the publication of his *Critica*.

In 1631 Jean Morin, a calvinist who had gone over to catholicism and
become a member of the Oratory, issued a great work of textual criticism
in which he impugned the reliability of the Masoretic text and defended
the accuracy of the LXX and the Samaritanus. This had caused great
indignation in protestant circles and called forth a number of refutations,
because Morin deliberately attacked the principle of the reliability of the
Scriptures in the original languages.[190] Cappel's book did not support
Morin's judgment—ultimately determined by confessional considerations—of the Hebrew text. Unlike Morin, who had compared whole
forms of text with each other, Cappel believed that one had to consider
what the correct reading was case by case. Yet his work was regarded as
a contribution to catholic polemic, and this explains L'Empereur's
refusal—shocking in the light of the norms of the Republic of Letters—to
sponsor its printing and his verdict that it would be best if it were not
published at all.[191] In the end such censorship was unreasonable. When
the work could not be published in Leiden, the publication of the *Critica
Sacra* was promoted by catholic members of the circle around Dupuy,
especially Mersenne and Morin. The last named made alterations to the
text, to bring the work into greater harmony with his own thesis. The
motives for this edition are a remarkable mixture of the services which
one was bound to perform for a fellow member of the Republic of Letters
and the desire for interconfessional polemic. They ran into several difficulties, because such works were also regarded with suspicion from the
catholic side. Twenty years afterwards Simon had the greatest difficulty
in gaining permission for the publication of his *Histoire Critique du Vieux
Testament*, a work of a similar critical tendency.[192]

The second factor behind the resistance to Cappel's work was the
result of a trend within French protestantism. The theological academy
of Saumur where Cappel taught with Amyrault and de la Place,
developed a more moderate calvinism which threatened to overstep the
bounds set at Dordt.[193] This development was most explicit in the
theology of Amyrault, who even dared to touch on the prolegomena of
double predestination. In spite of great difficulties his doctrine was never

---

[189] Cf. Cappel to J. Buxtorf I, 10.7.1622, J. J. Buxtorf, *Catalecta*, 476-9.
[190] Lebram, "Streit", 31-2.
[191] Rivet to Sarrau, 19.6.1645; *C. I. Rivet/Sarrau* III, 143: "Mons. l'Empereur dit
ouvertement que cela ne sera jamais publié de son consentement."
[192] Auvray, "Jean Morin", 404; Auvray, *Simon*; Steinmann, *Simon*.
[193] Laplanche, *Orthodoxie*; Armstrong, *Calvinism*.

condemned by the French churches, because the high protestant nobility
put an end to the discussions in 1650. His view did encounter fierce
opposition abroad, and in the Republic Amyrault was bitterly attacked
by Rivet and Spanheim.[194] Cappel was personally concerned in this
dogmatic trend at Saumur—he published the works of Cameron, the
spiritual father of Amyrault[195]—and the various projects of Saumur in
the field of dogma and philology were regarded by their supporters and
opponents as the work of a single school. Sarrau, who was a supporter
of Saumur, could write in a letter to Rivet that he had heard to his
amazement that there were still scholars at Leiden, who upheld the antiquity of the vowel signs. This opinion had been given up by French protestantism under the influence of Cappel's *Arcanum* and was regarded as
hopelessly antiquated by Sarrau.[196] From another letter it is evident how
far Sarrau saw Amyrault and Cappel as belonging to one and the same
school. At the same time that Sarrau was working for the publication of
Cappel's *Critica*, the two correspondents began a discussion on Amyrault
which was ultimately to lead to a rupture between them. When Sarrau
wanted to tell Rivet that Rivet's nephew Samuel Bochart agreed with
Cappel's approach, he simply wrote: "Monsieur votre Neveu de Caen
favorise Saumur".[197]

The discussion which arose in Switzerland about Saumur, makes it
clear that this link between Cappel and Amyrault was also self-evident
for opponents of the school. There, the outcome of the conflict was the
*Consensus Helvetica* of 1675, in which Cappel and Amyrault were equally
condemned and the antiquity of the vowel signs elevated to an article of
faith.[198] One of the driving forces behind this condemnation was Buxtorf
II, who took up his pen against Cappel at the end of the forties, to defend
his father's opinion on the antiquity of the vocalisation signs. In a series
of charges and counter-charges both adversaries defended their views
time and again.[199] While Buxtorf attacked his opponent on philological
grounds, he condemned Cappel's opinion in a series of disputations as
a heresy of the same rank as catholicism,[200] although, as had been the

---

[194] The intervention of the nobles: Armstrong, *Calvinism*, 114. The conflict with
Spanheim and Rivet: *ibid.*, 102 ff. Laplanche, *Orthodoxie*, 127-30; 189-93; 197-218.
[195] Cappel to Buxtorf I, 27.6.1628; J. J. Buxtorf, *Catalecta*, 484-6. For Cameron,
Laplanche, *Orthodoxie*, 50-5.
[196] Sarrau to Rivet, 22.7.1642; *C. I. Rivet/Sarrau* II, 332-3.
[197] Sarrau to Rivet, 8.12.1645; *C. I. Rivet/Sarrau* III, 281. Another example, *ibid.* III,
507.
[198] For the Formula Consensus: Pfister, *Kirchengeschichte* II, 490-8.
[199] Cf. Schnederman, *Controverse*; Muller, "Debate". The writings of Buxtorf: Prijs
nos. 250, 252, 257.
[200] Cf. the work of the theologians of Basel, including Buxtorf II, *Syllabus Controversiarum Religionis*, Basel 1663, in which disputations 5, 14, 15, 16 of the chapter on the

case over Grotius' *Annotationes*, he also appealed to the verdict of those catholics who condemned Cappel's work.[201] The controversy between Buxtorf and Cappel has often been related and for our argument it suffices to mention two aspects.

First of all, the way in which Buxtorf II argued in this discussion was an indication of the theological nature of his opinion. He did not try, as Cappel did in his *Critica Sacra*, to make the probability of his view acceptable, but was satisfied if he had shown that it was possible that the vowel signs indeed went back to Moses. In his eyes the bible was a special text, which needed only to be protected against slanders. Such an approach was inadequate against the method of disputing adopted by Cappel in his *Critica Sacra*, that of adducing a great many passages to demonstrate the likelihood of his hypothesis.[202]

The second aspect of the conflict which interests us is the use that both parties made of rabbinical literature. Here Buxtorf II undoubtedly had the better of it, for his knowledge and mastery of that literature were far greater than his opponent's. He employed his knowledge to support his point of view with a superabundance of rabbinical citations. Just as L'Empereur used the rabbis as an authority for the use of the Old Testament citations in the New Testament, so Buxtorf appealed to the rabbis as a reliable authority fit to be produced as an argument against the opinions of his adversary. This appeal to the rabbis to shore up the authority of the bible, endangered by the development of humanist critical exegesis, was to gain steadily in importance during the second half of the 17th century.

Thus in his person and in his work L'Empereur appears to reflect the most important aspects of the development of rabbinical studies. He owed his place in the Republic of Letters to the interest that late humanism took in rabbinical literature, a part of its wider interest in history and biblical exposition. This interest determined the form and content of most of the works from L'Empereur's pen. But those circles which set the tone in the Republic of Letters were to turn away from philology and above all from rabbinica after the middle of the century. That can be illustrated from the appointments policy of the University of Leiden, which betrayed little interest in oriental studies in the second

---

scriptures are explicitly directed against Cappel (the others attack Jews, catholics, socinians and remonstrants).

[201] Buxtorf to Cocceius, 3.9.1651, Cocceius, *Opera ANEKDOTA* II, 688: "Commune sibi hoc libro conflavit odium omnium Evangelicorum & saniorum Pontificiorum. Si haec Crisis valet, actum est de Thesauro hoc, quem ex Dei singulari providentia nacti sumus: actum est de studio Hebraico, imo de omni eruditione Hebraica."

[202] Cf. Schnederman, *Controverse*, 34-5.

half of the century. After L'Empereur's promotion to a professorship of theology, the Mayors and Curators allowed him to continue teaching Hebrew for a time while they tried to invite Warner or Buxtorf. In April 1647 they resolved that if Buxtorf declined their invitation, L'Empereur would have to carry on teaching Hebrew.[203] Just before his death a teacher was appointed, an extraordinary professor—the lowest rank that the Mayors and Curators could award him—and although this man in the end acquired an ordinary professorship, for the rest of the century the teaching of Hebrew was in the hands of a mere lecturer.[204]

On the other hand, L'Empereur showed at decisive moments that his highest loyalty was not to the Republic of Letters but to the Church. He was not alone in this. The theologican Rivet for example could only remark on the death of Grotius, that this death was a great gain for the church.[205]. L'Empereur too was a theologian above all else, who found in rabbinical literature a confirmation of the special character of the bible, which had gradually come under attack through the development of that very biblical scholarship to which he owed his position. In the second half of the century, the way in which Buxtorf and L'Empereur applied their rabbinical knowledge was to find imitators.

L'Empereur died on 1 July 1648. His death and obsequies were quite an event. L'Empereur's symptoms and utterances in his last hours are described in great detail by Trigland in his funeral oration. The age took

---

[203] C. Ravius to Ussher, 8.4.1647: Ussher *Works* XVI, 80-1: "L'Empereurius est professor theologiae, isque locus vacat, et si Cl. Buxtorfium Basilae nancisci potuissent, vocatum magno gaudio suscepissent, cum desistat, locum illum pariter supplere perget L'Empereurius."

[204] On 8 June 1648 Uchtmannus was appointed as extraordinary professor of Hebrew (*Molh.* III, 20) while at the same time an invitation was made to Warner. In 1654 Uchtmannus gave lectures on the grammar of Moses Kimḥi, in 1655 on a rabbinical work (*Molh.* III, 26*-27*, 47*-48*). In 1668 his teaching of Hebrew was taken away from him, that in Greek given to him, and his former duties given to Hulsius (*Molh.* III, 221). Only then was he made an ordinary professor. In 1672 he resumed his Hebrew responsibilities, (*Molh.* III, 263), but six years later he was no longer doing anything even when given a considerable salary reduction (*Molh.* III, 338, 345). In 1680 a Jew gave lessons in talmudica, (Molh. III, 351) and in the same year C. Schaaf was appointed. He was to remain a lecturer for forty years. The teaching of oriental languages was also entrusted to him, and for twenty years was not mentioned against in the minutes of the Mayors and Curators (Juynboll, *Beoefenaars*, 234 ff.).

[205] Rivet to Sarrau, 19.9.1654; *C. I. Rivet/Sarrau* II, 218: "On ne pourra pas dire que je l'ay craind quand il vivoit, et je voudray encore qu'il vescust tant pource que d'ailleurs il avoit de grandes parties que pource que je luy pourroy faire voir ses beveües; encore que l'Eglise ait gagné en la perte d'un homme qui se monstra ennemi passioné ..." The contrasts with Sarrau could not be greater: Sarrau to Rivet, 4.11.1645; *C. I. Rivet/Sarrau* III, 254; "Le nom de Grotius sera grand tant que dureront les livres et pour moy je n'y pense jamais sans veneration."

a great interest in such elaborate accounts of deathbeds.[206] The funeral was a great social occasion, as was customary at the time. At the interment of a young daughter of Salmasius, the whole university—apart from Heinsius—had attended,[207] and at the funeral of Polyander, which was attended by William II, the throng was so great that the cortège took two hours to pass, in spite of the presence of armed men to clear a path.[208] Such a funeral reveals the very prominent social position occupied by a professor of theology in the Republic, and something similar must have been seen at L'Empereur's funeral. The total costs amounted to nearly the annual salary of a professor, more than twelve hundred guilders, of which two hundred and fifty were spent on drink alone.[209] The University of Leiden took a fitting leave of one of her most important professors, in a style which matched the position which this son of a stateless immigrant from the South had succeeded in winning for himself.

---

[206] Trigland, *Oratio*, 19 ff. Cf. the "Novissimae horae seu ultima vitae clausula Andreae Riveti", an extremely detailed account, in several folios, of the deathbed of Rivet, in his *Opera* III, (1282)-(1292). Sarrau asked Rivet for the account of the last moments of Grotius, which had appeared almost immediately, "estant utile de scavoir la fin aussi bien que la vie des grands hommes" (7.10.1645, *C. I. Rivet/Sarrau* III, 237).

[207] Rivet to Sarrau, 19.9.1644; *C. I. Rivet/Sarrau* II, 386.

[208] Rivet to Sarrau, 18.2.1646; *C. I. Rivet/Sarrau* III, 336.

[209] The account of the funeral expenses for L'Empereur in Th 108.

# CONCLUSION

L'Empereur's self-awareness and ambitions as a theologian determined his life, and were the foundation of his own view of his scholarly work. The actual nature of this work, however, was closely connected with the customary forms of the scholarly community in which he moved. Thus, there was a gap between L'Empereur's own opinion of what he ought to do, and his actual scholarly practice, of which he was never fully aware.

L'Empereur's father was a calvinist merchant and exile from the southern Netherlands. His life was inspired by a typical reformed piety, related to neostoicism, with at its core a belief in providence. His son Constantijn was born at Bremen. Intended for theology by his father, he studied in that faculty at Leiden and Franeker. At an early stage, his ambitions were directed to a chair of theology. In 1617 he took his doctorate under Lubbertus. Two years later he became a lecturer in theology and Hebrew at the High School of Harderwijk, from where he was called to Leiden in 1627 to succeed Erpenius as professor of Hebrew.

In these years his intellectual interests lay in scholastic calvinist theology, largely of Franco-Walloon origin, and aristotelian philosophy. Neo-scholastic dogma was directed towards religious truth, which was unfolded in a system of principles and theses highly dependent on the method and philosophy of Aristotle. The importance of reason and logic was emphasised. The Scriptures were to a great extent understood as a collection of proof texts for a dogmatic system. Views which deviated from the mainstream of calvinist orthodoxy, such as the German federal-theological and the English puritan traditions, played no part in L'Empereur's intellectual development. There are no indications that for L'Empereur, religion was closely involved with a personal piety.

The humanist erudition which he had acquired during his education was slight. Among his books we find only those classical authors from whom he had gained his earliest knowledge of Greek and Latin. His knowledge of Hebrew was reasonable for a theologian, but not exceptional. Following the tradition of university teaching in the Republic, it was based on the works of French hebraists and concerned biblical Hebrew only. Before his appointment at Leiden, there was no question of a particular interest in this language or in rabbinica.

The appointment of the theologian L'Empereur as professor of Hebrew reflected the ambiguous position of the subject at the University of Leiden. Hebrew was taught in the Faculty of Letters, but much more than Greek it was purely a propaedeusis for the dogmatic instruction given in the Faculty of Theology from the Old and New Testaments. In their programme for the university study of theology, the Leiden professors after the Synod of Dordt saw the value of Hebrew only in such a propaedeusis. The professors of Hebrew in the Republic also saw it as their chief task to teach students of theology. This position of their subject can be explained by the simple fact that the study of Hebrew, unlike that of Greek, was based purely on a collection of texts, the Old Testament, which also formed the subject of the lectures given to the theologians.

Thomas Erpenius, who provided teaching in Hebrew at Leiden in the early 1620's, in spite of his lip service to the humanist ideal, in fact reconciled himself to the dependent status of the subject, which had been entrusted to him alongside his actual teaching duties in Arabic. The Franeker professor Sixtinus Amama did not do so. He upheld a highly personal combination of radicalised humanism with pietist elements. He led a successful campaign to make a knowledge of Hebrew compulsory for ministers. In accordance with his ideal of humanist *eruditio trilinguis* he saw in Hebrew a means to promote personal piety and social unity, rather than an aid to the defence of orthodox doctrine, which in his eyes, when it was overstressed, was in fact a cause of division and disunity. But Amama's campaign for Hebrew was also aimed at the church and the university study of theology. The independence of the subject which L'Empereur was invited to teach from the Faculty of Theology was very limited.

In his inaugural lecture L'Empereur described the usefulness of Hebrew in terms of dogma. The knowledge of the language was in his view of importance because of the contribution it could make to preserving the purity of doctrine and refuting heterodox opinions. He regarded his task as identical with that of the dogmatist, although he had to defend orthodox truth with other means.

L'Empereur's scholarly work was produced for the most part during the early years of his Leiden professorship. He himself regarded his chair of Hebrew as a possible means to acquire an appointment in the Faculty of Theology. Nonetheless, he won recognition in these years in the international community of the Republic of Letters. This recognition—a rarity in the case of theologians of his origin and education—he owed to his publications.

In fact the content of these works was not based on the view of his subject which L'Empereur had expressed in his inaugural lecture. His publications were of importance because they made rabbinical literature accessible, especially the Mishna and the Talmud. He produced text editions with parallel Latin translations, mostly provided with notes, chiefly of an explanatory and grammatical nature. He was induced to undertake these publications, with their humanistic form, by Daniel Heinsius. L'Empereur's editions were among the earliest aids to the study of rabbinica. He stood at the beginning of the great flowering of rabbinical studies, which in the course of the 17th century was to result in a comprehensive technical apparatus.

In spite of the fact that the performance of his scholarly work was only to a limited extent theological, L'Empereur himself, as appears from the forewords to his publications, saw its usefulness above all in its interest for a theological exegesis of the bible, and the refutation of Judaism. Yet by their nature his publications, characterised by the norms and values of the Republic of Letters, lent themselves to use as aids to the philological exegesis of the bible. Heinsius made use of L'Empereur's special talents for his grammatical-historical research into the New Testament. Grotius too used L'Empereur's works for his historicising exposition. That took place partly to the dissatisfaction of the author who himself preferred to use the rabbis in the service of a harmonising exegesis. In L'Empereur's own rather scanty, theological exegesis, he attached himself to the rabbinical view of the bible as revealed divine truth, and used their exegesis to defend the integrity of the biblical text.

L'Empereur's refutation of Judaism was of a purely intellectual character and devoid of any special emotion. Despite his personal contacts with the very mixed Jewish community of Amsterdam, he regarded Judaism not as another form of life, but as an intellectual heresy, which wrongly appealed to the Old Testament. He considered it as his task, to refute what he saw as the monolithic Jewish doctrine. He was only slightly interested in the conversion of the Jews. His refutation was, like that of all the protestant Christian hebraists, both in its approach and in its components, dependent on medieval catholic polemic. He judged Judaism no differently from any heterodox Christian tendency. In this he differed from the Christian humanism of the Republic of Letters, which preferred to seek its opponents outside Christendom, in order to be able to circumvent its own internal divisions, by refuting external opponents. L'Empereur's attachment to the interests of the church explains his refusal to publish Jewish anti-Christian works. He feared that such editions, even if they were provided with a refutation, could be used by heterodox Christian groups in their struggle against the church of the Republic. He approached a judgment of Judaism which inclined to anti-semitism in his edition of *Bava Kamma*. This judgment was however not of a theological nature, and was based on a humanistically inspired comparison between Roman law and the work of the Jewish legal scholars.

Besides the philological interest which the Republic of Letters took in his editions of rabbinical literature, L'Empereur was also able to satisfy his own theological interests. In Jewish exegesis and religious philosophy theologians could find a view of the revelatory character of the bible which was akin to their own. The undeniable differences did not form a problem for theologians who had been trained in attacking differing opinions. On the contrary, in rabbinica L'Empereur and Johan Buxtorf II, who were the leading practitioners of these studies in the second quarter of the 17th century, found an ally against what they saw as the unwelcome developments in humanist biblical exegesis, through which the bible was gradually coming to be treated as an ordinary text.

L'Empereur's activities during the last fourteen years of his life revealed the increasing tension between the values of the scholarly community in which he moved, the environment of late humanism at the University of Leiden and the Republic of Letters, and his own theological convictions. The teaching which he gave in Hebrew in these years was essentially of a theological nature. His most important pupils fell into two groups. A number of them, like himself, attained an appointment in a faculty of theology after holding a chair of Hebrew. A second group used his teaching to acquire the knowledge of rabbinical literature which was valued in the Republic of Letters, because it concerned an unknown aspect of antiquity, only accessible to specialists. L'Empereur belonged to the last generation in which an orthodox theologian, on the grounds of his special knowledge and abilities, could also become a fully fledged member of the Republic of Letters. In many ways he performed the services to fellow scholars, pupils and princes, which were expected from a member of this community. In the verdicts on new developments and publications which he expressed, partly on the grounds of his close ties with the faculty of theology, he placed his dependence on the church above his duties as a citizen of the Republic of Letters. He had already objected to certain results of philological exegesis in the *Exercitationes sacrae*, the work of his friend Heinsius. He decidedly disapproved of the exegetical results of Grotius. He prevented the publication at Leiden of the researches in the textual criticism of the Old Testament of Louis Cappel. L'Empereur himself had contributed in his own publications to humanist exegesis. Now however it began to yield results, thanks to its highly developed technique, which could no longer be incorporated by protestant orthodoxy.

L'Empereur's tendency to use rabbinical literature to impugn the critical results of this exegesis of the bible, as they had been achieved by Heinsius and Grotius, was to find imitators in the 17th century, when rabbinical studies were carried on by circles outside the Republic of Letters. This development was connected with a fundamental change in the

European scholarly community, in which the most important positions were no longer occupied by philology and history but by the natural sciences and the new philosophy. This caused a profound shift in the interest of the scholarly community, in which L'Empereur's work was used for the benefit of philological exegesis. The most important publications in the field of humanist biblical scholarship in the second half of the 17th century were reprints of earlier works.

Through this development the study of rabbinica in the generations after L'Empereur came to be separated from the philological exegesis of the bible. The dependent position of Hebrew, closely linked to the teaching of theology, could have led to such a development during his lifetime. This was prevented by the strength of late humanism at the University of Leiden, which put its scholarly work at the service of a grammatical understanding of the biblical text. Thus in the end the nature of L'Empereur's scholarly work proves to be best understood as a part of the striving, rooted in the Netherlands universities to discover "the simple meaning of things in their time".

# APPENDIX I

*Bibliotheca Thysiana* 204. Anthoine L'Empereur to his nephew Hans L'Empereur, January 1597.

Copy

Il fault aussy que celuy qui veult venir a cest estat, soit aucunement ancxieus, et que les occasions que Dieu donne pour se resjouir, affin de passer nostre vie plus alegrement, ne nous facent oublier nousmesme au milieu d'icelle. Au contraire que l'ancxion soit tellement modere, que la providence de Dieu nous soit devant les jeux et que nous n'ignorons point qu'il ne tient le gouvernail de ce monde, que rien ne se faict sans sa volonte et commandement, non a la legiere, mais une sagesse infini, le tout a sa gloire et au bien de ses enfants, pour laquell il a cree toute chose. Et d'autant que ses conseils nous sont incomprehensible, avisons de ni vouloir entrer plus avant que nostre capacite ne peult porter, et comme nous sommes asses prudent de ne regarder ce soleil en face quant il est en sa pleine clarte, pour ce que cognoissons la debilite de nostre veue, ne soyons moins advises en ceci, de vouloir par nostre debile entendement comprendre et regarder en face les secrets jugements de Dieu, et contentons nous de ce qu'il luy a pleu nous donner a cognoistre, ce qu'il convient de savoir pour nostre salut. Du reste, Saint Augustin dit, atendons jusques a ce que soions venus en la chambre celeste ou que tout ces secrets sont cachez; la nous aurons contentement de ce qu'a present nous donnons peine par curiosite.[1]

La consideration doncques de la providence de Dieu est fort profitable, a ce qu'elle nous console que apres avoir fait toute chose avec prudence, nous nous consolons en adversites, sachant que le Seigneur l'a faict autrement que ne l'avons desires, pour nostre bien, et que fortune n'a point ici de lieu, comme s'il estoit venu a l'adventure. Mettons en avant l'histoire de Joseph, lequel dict a ses freres, vous aves pensse mal et le Seigneur l'a tourne en bien. Tel sont les considerations de la providence de Dieu.

Cependant sachons que ce que dit Salomon doibt aussi avoir lieu, et n'est point contraire a ce que dessus: "le cœur de l'homme doibt penser a sa voye, et le Seigneur gouvernera ses pas".[2] Voila le debvoir que doibt estre vers nous.

---

[1] Cf. Calvin, *Institutions* III, 21, 2 (CR XXXII, 456-7): "Nous sommes parvenues en la voye de la foy, dit Sainct Augustin, tenons-nous y constamment: icelle nous menera iusques en la chambre du Roy celeste, ou tous les thresors de science et sagesse sont cachez." L'Empereur's linking of the citation with *curiosité* is understandable, because the passage is embedded in warnings against idle curiosity. For Calvin's thoughts on election and curiosity, E. P. Meijering, *Calvin wider die Neugierde. Ein Beitrag zum Vergleich zwischen reformatorischem und patristischen Denken*, Nieuwkoop 1980, 55-66.

[2] Prov. 16:9: "le cœur de l'homme delibere de sa voye; mais le Seigneur dresse ses pas" (sic!). The form of L'Empereur's citation is not to be found in biblical translations of the 16th century, while elsewhere he cites very accurately (cf. notes 4-5). He has taken this form of Prov. 16:9 from the *Institutions* of Calvin (I,17,4; CR XXXI 254-5): "Aussi en un autre lieu il parle ainsi, 'le cœur de l'homme doit penser a sa voye, et le Seigneur gouvernera ses pas' (...) Maintenant il appert quel est nostre devoir. Si le Seigneur nous a baille nostre vie en garde, que nous le conservions; s'il nous donne les moyens de ce

Dieu nous a mis nostre vie en garde; de la vient le proverbe "helpt u selven soo helpt u Godt".[3] Au reste, c'est le Seigneur qui le faict tout en tout. C'est comme dit Jeremie, "la voye de l'homme n'est pas en sa liberte et comment pouldra il gouverner ses pas".[4] Salomon dict, "les pas de l'homme sont de par le Seigneur, et comment l'homme pouldra il dresser sa voye".[5]

En somme, la providence de Dieu est un emplastre fort bonne en nostre siecle tant miserable. Mais la mal entente est qu'icelle est souvent mal applicque, comme souvent nous voulons mectre le jugement de Dieu et sa justice devant l'afflige, et les promesses, graces et misericorde de Dieu et nostre Seigneur Jesu Christ devant les desbordes, et qu'esse autre chose que faire comme les amis de Job pour engrever le mal, combien qu'il parloint bien et disoint vray, mais l'application estoit mauvais, comme le Seigneur le reprent en la fin.

Et pour conclusion, tout ce que est reqiert cognoissance affin d'estre applicque a ce qu'il puisse profiter, a la gloire de Dieu et de nostre salut. Je ne vous penssoy pas vous faire ce discours, commencant ceste lettre, mais a la verite ma plume s'est escoulle en ceci, esperant que ne sera sans fruict envers vous pour vous instruire a toute diligenge, et vous asseurant que faysant tout ce qui sera en vous possible, que le Seigneur accomplira le surplus a vostre bien et salut a sa gloire.

---

faire, que nous en usions ...". L'Empereur gives the content of the passage accurately. The letter even contains literal reminiscences.

    [3] Cf. note 16 of chapter 2.

    [4] Jer. 10:23: "Seigneur, je cognoy que la voye de l'homme n'est pas en luy, & n'est pas en l'homme de cheminer et d'adresser ses pas."

    [5] Prov. 20:24: "les pas de l'homme sont de par le Seigneur, comment donc l'homme entendra il sa voye."

# APPENDIX II

*Bibliotheca Thysiana* 231. Anthoine L'Empereur to H. Isselborgh, 8 August 1602.

Copy (fragment)

Je voy par deca peu de discipline par la liberté trop grande, de maniere que rien ne nous advient que par un juste jugement de Dieu, et nous aurions matiere de craindre davantage les verges du Seigneur, voyans les desbordemens voloptueus, ne fut que cognoissons en partie la misericorde de nostre Dieu, pour autant qu'il luy plait nous esluminer par son esprit. Sur laquel nous mettons nostre confiance, Esaye cha 48. v 9, ou il dit "Pour l'amour de mon nom J'ay differé mon ire, et pour ma louange Je t'ay suporté, afin que Je ne te exterminasse". Ce sont vrayement des paroles doree, le Seigneur nous face grace de les bien savoir comprendre a sa gloire et a nostre salut. Le Seigneur doncques est de bon vouloir pour l'amour de sa justice, pour magnifier et anoblir sa loy, car ainsi il sera exalte en nous pardonnant.

Pour conclusion, j'espere que Dieu nous fera estre de ceux, desquels il dict par son prophete: "J'ay forme pour moy un peuple", Esaye 43 v 21, "afin qu'il racontast ma louange", et que par sa grace il me fera jouir de ses promesses, s'il est a sa gloire et a mon salut. Ainsi qu'il est dit Esaye 65: "mes esleus jouiront en viel age de l'œuvre de leur mains et leur enfans seront avecq eux. Je les exauceray et les escouterey".[1] Or n'est ce point petit tesmoignage de veoir a l'oeul les marques evidentes de l'aliance de Dieu tel qu'il la nous declare en sa parole. Ainsi que nostre Seigneur nous declare par ses evangelistes, d'une facon de parler, "les roys ont desiré de veoir ce que vous voyes, et ne l'ont point veu".[2] Ainsi Esaye cha 59 v 21 dit: "Voyci mon aliance acecq eux, dit le Seigneur, mon esprit qui est en toy et mes paroles que J'ay mise en ta bouche, ne bougeront point de ta bouche, ni de la bouche de ta semence a jamais, dit le Seigneur." Ainsi nos peres ont eu la Parole de Dieu en leur bouche, et par la grace de Dieu ceste grace est parvenu a nous. Si par sa faveur paternel elle soyt de mesme en la bouche de nos enfants, faysant croistre la semence d'icelle, laquelle journellement nous plantons en eux, lors nous jouirons, ainsi que j'entens de la parolle, de ceste alliance duquelle le prophete nous fait mention. Je say que cela peust ausi estre deduit plus generalement, mais ce qui est general, requiert aussy bien que chacun l'aplique a soy. Ma plume ne pensoit s'escouler jusqu'a ce point, mais estant pousse, et me playsant au riches promesses et graces de nostre Dieu, qu'il nous daigne de faire en sa parole, j'ay laissé courir ma plume jusques a la fin. C'est maintenant que je prie le Seigneur qu'il vous benisse et nous tous des ses benedictions, et nous face la grace de nous aquiter de nostre debvoir, et au deffaut de nostre debvoir nous faire misericorde et nous donner un heur fort heureuse de vivre et de mourir et qu'il ne nous delaisse jamais, affin que ne le delaissons. Aus surplus je me recommande a vos graces et plus saintes prieres, ainsi que j'ay eu memoire de vous, le Seigneur le sait.

Votre amys, anthoyne Lempereur

---

[1] Is. 65: 22-3.
[2] Luke 10:24.

# APPENDIX III

*Bibliotheca Thysiana* 271. Constantijn L'Empereur to his mother Sara van der Meulen, 25 February 1617.

Original (fragment)

Alors je parloy au magnificus Rector qu'il assembleroit le Senat Academice. Lequel estant assemble, je fis une oration par laquelle je requerois qu'ils feroyent un decret, selon la coustume, pour m'examiner. Apres me commanderent de sortir et ayant deliberé ensemble, m'ayant rappellé, le mag. Rector disoit, que encores que j'avoye vecquu louablement entre eux, toutesfois pour faire tout avec ordre, qu'ils desiroient un tesmognage, lequel je leur donnois à savoir de Festus. Apres ils ordonnerent que je serois examiné; lequel examen commença le 27 de Janvier et dura deux semeines, en aucuns jours d'icelles. Et cest examen m'est fort bien succedé. Car comme les professeur y vindrent pour escouter, apres l'examen par diverses fois je receu grande louange; et mesme aux prieres qu'on fait devant et apres l'examen Sibrandus rendoit graces à Dieu d'avoir excité un tel que moy etc. pour le bien de l'Esglise. Apres l'examen, quelques jours passé, les Theologiens me donnerent un text à exposer. Car cela est la coustume, que devant la promotion on faςe une leςon en la Theologie, laquelle j'ay faict devant le senat de l'Academie le 10 de Febvrier, avec grande aprobation de tous. Pour faire la leςon me donnerent deux jours, pour la composer et dire par coeur. Elle duroit un heure et demi. En cela aussi Dieu m'a donné ses benedictions. Maintenant reste la dispute de laquelle vous voyez les Theses ausquelles j'ay adjousté la copie de ma leςon pour faire lire à mes freres, car pource que je ne sςay si celuy qui l'a copié, a bien descrist, je ne desire pas qu'on la montre à d'autres devant que je l'aye releu. Or la dispute sera, moyenant la grace de Dieu de Lundi en huict jours qui sera le 10 de Marts stil vieu. Mais pource que c'est ici une mauvaise coustume, qu'on ne peut pas disputer sans moderateur ou praeses, je ne desire pas qu'on fait encore grande mention de ma dispute. Quand je seray docteur, il peut avenir que je sois moy mesme preses des aultres, lequel me sera plus agré et honneur. Pour la promotion j'estime de la faire 8 ou douze jours apres la dispute, et pour garder mon honneur il me faudra faire une robbe de doctorat.

# APPENDIX IV

A) *UB Leiden*, BPL 1886. J. Polyander to C. L'Empereur, 9 October 1617.
Original.

Domine Doctor Constantine, Quoniam hic S.S. Theologiae candidatus a D. D.
Curatoribus summopere petiit ut a me possit promoveri, D. D. Curatores consultum indicarunt ut ad vitandam aemulationem, non minus Collega meus,
quam ego ab aliquo tertio prius promoveatur. Id si praestare non graveris,
quamprimum id D. D. Curatoribus indicabo. Promotio nostra fiet privatim in
nostro Senatu. Si hac in re D. D. Curatorum petitioni satisfeceris, eos tibi
devincies. Bene vale in Domine, quem precor ut piis tuis conatibus abunde e
caelo benedicat. Raptim. 9 Octob. 1617
    Tui Studiosus J. Polyander
    Per hunc amicum responsum expecto.

B) *Bibliotheca Thysiana* 271. C. L'Empereur to his mother, Sara van der Meulen,
4 October 1617.

Original (fragment)

Or j'ay par letres respondu à Poliander et aussi escrist à Festus pour entendre
leur deliberation en cecy. Car j'ay dit que je suis prest pour promover Poliander, mais point Episcopius, ou il me fauldroit avoir aultres raisons de cela, tant
de Poliander que de Festus. Car je ne voy pas comment je pourroye faire cela
avec bonne conscience.

C) *UB Leiden*, BPL 1886. J. Polyander to C. L'Empereur, 26 October 1617.

Original

Gratiam tibi habeo pro benevolo tuo erga me affectu. Pietatem tuam laudo. Ut
alterum quoque promoveas auctor esse nequeo. Reliqua intelliges ex D. Kelle-
nario qui Franekeram proficiscitur, ut isthic promoveatur. Commenda ipsum
de nota meliori D. D. Lubberto et Maccovio. Est juvenis pereruditus et ortho-
doxae doctrinae studiossisimus. Vale intime amice ac frater in Christo. Raptim
Leydae 26 Octob. 1617. Saluta meis verbis salutatos (sic) inprimis matrem piam
matronam.
    Tui amantissimus J. Polyander.

# APPENDIX V

*Archief Gabbema.* S. Amama to J. Saeckma, n.d.

Copy

Magnifice D. Curator, superiori die Dominico domum meam cum familia universa reversus sum, ac die hesterno, qui Lunae erat, reversus sum ad operas tot jam septimanis intermissas. Neque nam ego illis meum addo calculum, qui mali ominis notam isti diei inurunt, quod tamen a quibusdam vestrae Curiae statutis aut consuetudine aliquando defendi memini. Filium Theodorum post tot mensium fastidia et languorem convaluisse non nolenti mihi fuit audire. Deum veneror ut quamdiutissime illum sospitet. Auguror nam fore, ut uterque filius in aetatis vere maturam & non inutilibus curis parem autumnitatem exhibeant atque in parentis sui vestigia pedes ponant.

Intellexi ex D. Amesio, qui Lugduni Batavorum Reverendum nostrum compellavit, illos jam absolvisse v libros Mosis. Ipse quoque Amsterodami de concionibus N.N. idem judicat et intellexit quod ego. Si coram adessem, possem T. A. commemorare integrum filum concionis Smoutianae. Profecto si ad ejus & alterius exemplum caeteri se componerent, jam non erubescerem Stentoria voce proclamare, ecclesiasticam cathedram vertisse in ludum & arenam bestiariorum.

Unus eorum graviter mihi conquerebatur de D. Festo, duplici nomine. Primo nam miscuerat ille se causae cujusdam Bocardi, collegae olim Lydii Dordraceni, qui pacis causa in pagum aliquem secesserat. Is jam a Roterodamensibus vocatus amplexari illam conditionem voluit, antequam sibi a caeteris collegis cautum esset de vi articulis, qui concernebant receptionem moderatiorum Remonstrantium in Ecclesiam. Affulgebat nam magna spes, si ille Roterodamum venisset, fore uti Ecclesi⟨.......⟩ci brevi coalesceret. Hanc gloriam illi invidere fratre⟨.......⟩indignum rati unius Presbyterii vel Presbyteri arbitrio tantae molis negotium permittere, Nationali Synodo aut saltem ad provisionem provinciali synodo, tantae rei arbitrium competere. Hic tamen a caeteris dissensit Festus & nihil intentatum reliquit quod faceret ad pacem istius ecclesiae. Sed frustra fuit. Vicit nam adversa pars, jussusque est Bocardus ad pagum suum redire, addito mandato, ne quid in Controversiis istis suo solius arbitrio ageret. Alterum erat, quod coram Consulibus Amsterodamensibus, qui Hagae Comitis in Comitiis aliquando liberum gemitum adversus quosdam ministros suae urbis ediderunt, liberius in ipsorum vehementiam aliquoties dixerit illosque consiliis quibusdam instruxerit. Ea res percrebuit & dimanavit ad ministros Amsterodamensos, non sine invidia Consiliarii. Haec habeo ex ore ministri cujusdam Amsterodamensis & quia bonus ille vir communis amicus nostrum est, nolui T. A. illud ignorare.

Mitto Paraenesin meam, non nimis nitide descriptam. Aliud exemplar non est ad manum. Quid Patres Conscripti ad eam in Synodo decreverint, necdum intellexi. Non dubito autem quin bene successerit. Misi singulis Classibus specimen Grammaticae Belgicae. Intellexi nam ex uno et altero, meum institutum pigris quibusdam displicuisse. Audebant nam profiteri metum suum, fore ut

---

* the passages enclosed in ⟨...⟩ are so damaged in the copy that the text has disappeared.

laici aliquam Ebraismi notitam consecuti, adversus Ministros, qui ejus omnino ignari sunt, insolescant, illisque aliquando insultent & imperitiam objectent. Et certe illud apud T. A. non diffitebor, hunc non fuisse postremum meum scopum. Si nam vel mediocriter successerit meum propositum, audebo spondere multis fucis incubituram necessitatem, his quoque musis litandi. Et fortassis multos zelotas a spinosarum quaestionum vorticibus haec quoque studia abstrahent. Quicquid sit, nunc jacta est alea.

De dedicatione quid cogitaverim T.A. non celabo. Decreveram ego primo hanc Grammaticam tuo nomini inscribere, atque in ea praefatione Belgas docere, quantum tibi Academia & Literae debeant, quot item nomininibus ego T.A. obnoxius sim. Postea subiit haec cogitatio, tua in Remp. Acad. & literas & me merita longe majora esse, quam ut Belgii septis includi debeat eorum praedicatio. Itaque T. Amplitudini destinavi meum Synedrium seu tractatum de Concilio magno & judiciis criminalibus Ebraeorum, quem hac hyeme, si otium & valetudinem summus ille rerum arbiter dederit, horis subsecivis, ad umbilicum perducam. Cogitavi ergo hanc Gramm. Dominis Deputatis solis vel una cum DD. Curatoribus inscribere. Si placebit T.A. argumentum dedicatoriae, quam hic addo non displicebat, credo, & hoc consilium. At si illud intempestivum videbitur, non video causam cur ipsis hoc opusculum debeam inscribere Dictionarium meum, quod jam jam quoque edetur, T.A. filio Theodoro, juniori Aylvae & Hanjae (nam & hunc habebo discipulum in hebraïcis) inscribam. Ubi otium erit T.A. heac obiter lustrabit & ubi lubebit, remittet cum censura. Neque enim opus est magna festinatione. Vale Ampliss. Dne & me ama, qui

Tm. Am. Colo & veneror<br>
S. Amama

Uxori lectissimae & filiis salutem dico, nominatim D. Theodoro, cui quo minus respondeam ad eruditam & humanissimam epistolam, alia negotia obstant. Jam nam domum redux ultra xv epistolas inveni, ad quas hac septimana respondendum erit. Redibo tamen Die saturni, si Deus volet, ad lectiones Historicas.

# APPENDIX VI

*Bibliotheca Thysiana* 164,6, 11$^v$-13$^v$. C. L'Empereur to B. Barbius, 4 March 1639.

Draft

Viro doctissimo, omnique virtutum genere ornatissimo D. Benedicto Barbio amico singulari.

Vir doctissime

Litterae tuae fuere gratissimae, quod in iis animum discendi cupidum perspicerem; non modo res ipsas, sed etiam methodum ad rerum cognitionem perveniendi. Cum alii in discendi modo semper sibi sapere videantur: quum saepe hic prae reliquis omnibus aberrent: adeoque id tandem experti: quod inceperant, pertaesi, derelinquant. Caeterum in linguis addiscendis id agere videntur mihi plurimi, ut non absimiles sint illis, qui voluptates saepenumero per ea quaerunt, quibus vel maxime impediuntur. Ea plerumque methodus discipulis praescribitur, qua efficacius medium excogitari non posset, ad creandum taedium, quo plurimi tandem in studio incepto abhorrent. Grammatica praecepta ad nauseam usque ab ipsis inculcantur, eaque ferme innumera. Deinde vocabula memoriae mandari volunt, denique omnia in authore quodam legendo ad grammaticam examinari, tam operose, ut non tantum quam plurimum temporis amittatur, sed mens etiam istis minutiis perturbetur. Et hac quidem omnia, antequam discipulus quid sit, cujus its satagit, cognoscat. Eo modo hic proceditur, ac si faber, ligni vel metalli alicujus massam coelo suo prius expolire aggrederetur, in imagine quadam conficienda, quam rudem formam induxisset. Non aliter illi, qui de expolienda linguae cognitione prius sunt solliciti; quam vel rudem et superficiariam cognitionem discipulus adeptus est. Ego aliam hic desidero rationem ac modum; ut linguae studiosus generalissimis grammaticae imbutus praeceptis, statim sibi praestantissimos authores comparet, eosque versos, ne versando logica (sic) tempus nimium perdat; authores istos deligat, qui verbotenus sunt versi, alioqui vix quid cui respondeat, linguae adhuc ignarus percipere poterit. Istos authores legat ac relegat donec sibi mediocrem paraverit cognitionem linguae quam tractat. Tum demum pleniorem quaerat Grammaticam, cujus Cynosyra textum paulo accuratius examinet. Ita fiet, ut examen istud minus sit taediosum, et longe majori cum profectu instituatur; legendo etiam istos authores, voluptatem ex rebus ipsis prius percipiet, quam minutiae Grammaticales creent taedium. Deniuqe illud in examine volupe erit, quod de re, quam tractat, jam judicare poterit.

In Ebraea lingua, seligi poterit brevis institutio, vel tabellae D. de Dieu. In Chaldaea ac Syra Grammatica Chaldaea et Syra D. Erpenii, Amstelodami apud Henricum Laurentii. In Graecis legantur sacrae litterae; pariter in Chaldaicis et Syriacis. Verum id observa, vocales in paraphrasi Chaldaica saepissime male ascriptas fuisse: ideoque parum ad eas vocales attendendum esse. In Novo testamento Syro eam editionem sequendam, quae literis Syriacis expressa est. In qua olim quaedam deerant, jam a D. de Dieu et Eidwardo Pococke veteri editioni addita et hic excusa. Syriacum etiam Psalterium excusum jam pridem Romae cum punctis.

Rabbinica si quis addere cupiat, id facili negotio facere poterit, et tandem ad Talmudica assurgere. Nam Grammaticam quod concernit, Ebraea, Chaldaea et Syra hic sufficiunt, et si quae sint diversa in Talmuda, attentus lector ea usu facile observabit. Verum in particulis summa difficultas: ideoque hic compendium fieri velim libelli, quem Drusius de istis particulis conscripsit, illudque compendium memoriae infigi. Tandem legat authores accurate versos: cujusmodi plures edidi adjectis notis necessariis. Profuturum etiam est, ut antequam Talmudica tractentur, authores legantur, qui de Ebraeorum ritibus scripsere. Alioqui cum et ipsa phrasis satis difficilis sit, vix authoris mens liquebit, si difficultas rerum et vocum sine praecognitis conjugatur. Quia vero rabbinica non adeo multa sunt translata, pauciora Talmudica; omnia conquiri debent, quo ad solidam cognitionem pervenire queat istorum studiosus.

Mercerus transtulit Rabbinos in minores quosdam Prophetas. Cocceus (sic) transtulit Sanedrin et Maccoth et commentariis illustravit. Gerson judaeus conversus olim transtulit Gemaram Babylonicam ex Sanedrin in linguam Germanicam. verti Jachjadem in Danielem, Benjaminis itinerarium, Clavem Talmudicam, Codicem Middoth, codicem primum nezikim. notis illustravi Grammaticam M. Kimchi et Abrabanielem in Esaiam. Alia multa verti et illustravi, sed nondum edita. Adjici vis catalogum eorum authorum qui propter rem ipsam legendi sint, quaeque ex iis notanda indicavi. De sacris jam tibi constat; Chaldaicas Paraphrases eo etiam nomine diligenter legendas arbitror, quod infinita ferme de Messia illic legantur. Excerpi et notari inprimis in istis debet, quae loca Veteris Testamenti ad Christum applicata in novo testamento a chaldaeo paraphrases eo etiam referantur, quod fit saepissime; et N. testamentum a sarcasmis Judaeorum vindicat; qui loca male citata esse a scriptoribus n. foederis ogganniunt. Liber Zohar etiam utilissimus lectu, quia ex eo multa Christiana dogmata annotari possunt et debent; ubi semper attendendum, an non applicetur locus aliquis ad Messiam, qui vel in novo Testamento citatur, vel facit ad probandum aliquod dogma Christianum, si ad Messiam referatur; quae duo passim in omni (sic) Judaeorum scriptis attendi debent, cujusmodi etiam sunt Rabboth et Midrashim in V. Testamentum. Ad Antiquitates Judaicas quod attinet, unus Maimonides hic sufficit, qui in Jad Chazaka congessit ritus omnes. Ad Scripturam Sacram intelligendam, nemo praeferendus Abrabanieli, cujus scripta diligenter conquisivi. Haec sunt quae ad epistolam tuam raptim respondenda videbantur. Vale vir praestantissime et Episcopo tuo viro illustrissima stirpe oriundo, et quod in ducibus rarum, omnis literaturae non tantum amantissimo, sed etiam peritissimo, viro undique magno, omnia officia mea et humilima obsequia meo offeras nomine quaeso, si quando occasio sese offerat. Iterum vale, et diu reipublicae vivas exopto qui

Eruditionis tuique sum observantissimus

CLE ab oppyck

Lugd Batav. 4 Ma anno
partae salutis 1639

## APPENDIX VII

*UB Leiden*, BPL 285. C. L'Empereur to A. Rivet, 26 January 1639.
Original.

Vir amplissime,
   Quum ad Judaeum doctissimum Fonsecam scribere cogitarem, ipse me convenit. Itaque cum ex ipso rogassem, an ullius loci in antiquis scriptis meminisset, ubi annuli tanquam pignoris in sponsalibus fieret mentio, negavit tale quid extare, atque caput, quod nuper coram citavi, produxit. Ubi tria illa, quibus sponsalia confirmantur, quae recensebam in nupero colloquio, juris semper fuisse, manifeste confirmatur. Addebam quaestionem de more hodierno: cui respondebat, annulum quidem ex more gentis hujus adhiberi; verum perinde jam esse, sive annulus, sive nummus ex veteri ritu, daretur. Prout nuper promisi, textum, id est Misnam ex primo capite, codicis Talmudici de sponsalibus, ascribo, una cum versione mea:

> "mulier desponsatur tribus modis; et vindicat seipsam duobus modis. Despondetur argento, instrumento dotali, congressu. De argento secta Schammaei ait, denario, aut eo quod aequivalet. Familia Hillelis ait, minuto, eoque quod minuto aequivalet. At quanti est minutum? Octava pars assari Italici. Vindicat autem seipsam libello repudii, et morte mariti."

Quod hic de vindiciis uxoris dicitur, eo pertinet, ut quomodo sese liberam a viro censere queat, distincte constet. Aequivalentia hic dicuntur, quae numo isto aestimantur et emi possunt. De minuto et assaro nihil addo; quia ista explicantur Cod. de legibus pag. edit. meae 217. 238. 245. Vale Vir venerande.
   Deus te tuosque incolumes servet, exopto
      D. tuae observantissimus CL'E Lugd Bat 1639 26 Jan.

---

\* The original also includes the Hebrew text of *Qidduschin* 1,1.

# APPENDIX VIII

*Bibliotheca Thysiana*, 170. J. Buxtorf II to C. L'Empereur, 12 March 1648.
Original.

S. P. Praeteritis nundinis, Vir Reverende et Clarissime, Amice pl. honorande, una cum literis meis, transmisi tibi exemplar Tractatus mei de Punctorum Vocalium Origine et Antiquitate. Spero illum recte tibi esse redditum. Judicium tuum avide de eo exspecto. Nihil hactenus inaudire possum de Antagonista meo, aliquid novi moliente vel tentante. Forte manus dabit. Hac vice mitto exemplar Florilegii mei Hebraici recenter excusi. Tale illud est, quale in privatos meos usus collectum erat. Non licuit hac vice per alias graviores occupationes illud ornatius expolire et augere. Spero tamen gratum fore, et simul utile, Linguae Hebraeae studiosis. Tu id aeque bonique consules.

Quid verum agas, quibusque in studiis verseris scire desidero. An nova Professio exprimet vel supprimet foetum Controversiarum Judaicarum, in quibus scio te multum laborasse? Ego inposterum non tantum in Hebraicis praestare, potero, sicut hactenus, ob novae Professionis onus. Non enim lectiones tantum sunt habendae, sed et exercitia subinde habenda et instituenda. Hac vero ratione video Dei voluntatem fuisse, ut in nostra Academia exercitia Theologica, fori intermortua exsuscitarentur.

Inter scripta mea Hebraica confecta, habeo integrum Commentarium Abarbenelis in Danielem, Latine a me versum, ante aliquot annos, eo quidem animo, ut ederetur. Posteaquam, cum vidi, illum plura illis laborare contra Christianos, dubitavi, an e re sit, ut edantur, et adhuc haerer. Quid tibi de eo videtur? Scio enim Tibi quoque eum lectum est.

Plura nunc non licet. Itaque Vale Vir Clarissime, et in eo amore quo me hactenus complexus es, constanter, persevera

Datam Basileae 12 Martii Ann. 1648.

R. T. Addictissimus
Johannes Buxtorfius

# APPENDIX IX

*UB Leiden*, BPL 293A. C. L'Empereur to D. de Wilhem, 5 October 1632.
Original.

Dilectissime cognate,

Quum saepissime antehac de Abrabanielis operibus te sollicitarem, quo ista mihi alicunde comparare non gravaveris, lubens hoc pro tuo ad mea studia promovenda affectu ac studio in te recepisti; scriptis etiam in eum finem literis, quas in orientem quoque (uti literae tuae quondam continebant) misisti. Quocirca ubi ex D. Eligmanno percepisssem, D. Borelii catalogum librarium in tuas incidisse manus; quin etiam quosdam illic libros notatos fuisse, quos ab isto viro emi velles: coepi mecum cogitare, te procul dubio mei adhuc memorem fortasse eidem in mandatis dedisse vel daturum esse, ut Abrabanielem mihi coemat. Ideoque cum jam amico cuidam injunxerim ut reliqua Abrabanielis, quae mihi desunt, meo nomine emeret; mei officii esse autumavi, hac de re cognatum certiorem facerem, ne ipsius benignus in me animus et studiorum meorum studiosus mihi mea culpa et negligentia obesset: ubi haberem qui pro me contra me liceretur; quod amicum non monuissem. Inter commentaria Abrabanielis nihil accuratius commentario in Pentateuchum: nam magna cura et diligentia Mosis libros, utpote omnium legum fundamentum, exposuit; deinde Danielem pari fere *akribeiai* enarravit, et alia quaedam eaque praecipua Scripturae loca in suo Matsmiah Jeschoua. Hos libros mihi comparavi: restant commentarii in historicos libros et Prophetas posteriores, quos ex Borelii auctione emendos curavi. Voti me fore coemptorem spero: ita enim omnia istius opera habebo; siquidem polemica et historica ipsius opera antehac mihi comparavi, unico atque altero opusculo excepto. haec paucis tibi, mi cognate, significanda existimavi. Tu porro mihi favere peragite. ego vicissim me ad quaevis obsequia offero, ut tuo favori respondeam.

Datam Lugduni Bat 3 non Oct a. 1632 partae salutis.

Tuus cognatus, tuique observantissimus

Constantinus L'Empereur

# BIBLIOGRAPHY

1. *Unpublished sources*

*Bibliotheca Thysiana*, now in the Leiden University Library: numbers 108, 163, 164,3, 164,4, 164,6, 169, 170, 171, 172, 178, 203, 204, 206, 216, 231, 234, 238, 245, 271, 284.

*Archief Gabbema*, now in the Provincial Library of Friesland: the letters to and from Sixtinus Amama.

*University Library, Leiden*
BPL 285 (letters of S. Amama, J. Buxtorf II and C. L'Empereur to A. Rivet).
BPL 293A (letters of C. L'Empereur to D. de Wilhem).
BPL 1886 (letters of C. L'Empereur to J. Polyander)
Pap 2 (a letter of C. L'Empereur to A. Pauw).
Pap 7 (a letter of C. L'Empereur to C. Salmasius).


2. *Published sources and literature.*

G. van Alphen, "De Illustre School te Breda en haar boekerij", *TvG* 64 (1951), 277-314.
J. Alting, *Opera omnia theologica*: analytica, exegetica, practica, problematica et philologica, 5 vols., Amstelaedami 1687.
A. Altmann, "Eternality of Punishment: A Theological Controversy within the Amsterdam Rabbinate in the thirties of the Seventeenth Century", *Proceedings of the American Academy for Jewish Research* XL (1973), 1-88.
S. Amama, *Dissertatiuncula*, qua ostenditur praecipuos papismi errores ex ignorantia ebraismi et Vulgata versione partim ortum, partim incrementum sumpsisse..., Franekerae 1618.
——, *Censura Vulgatae* atque a Tridentinis canonizatae versionis quinque librorum Mosis, Franekerae 1620.
——, *Oratio de Ebrietate*, Franekerae 1621.
——, *Bybelsche Conferentie*. In welcke de Nederlandtsche Oversettinghe des Bybels (..) van Capittel tot Capittel aen de Hebreusche waerheyt beproeft, ende met de beste Oversettinghen vergheleken wort. (..) Tot aenwysinghe van de noodtwendicheyt der verbeteringhe dezer Oversettinghe, ende tot verclaringhe van vele duystere plaetsen, t'Amsterdam 1623.
—— *Cort Vertoogh*, Waer inne alle ghetrouwe Dienaers ende Opsienders der Ghereformeerde Gemeynten van Vrieslant worden ghebeden, omme de behulplycke handt te bieden tot de hoochnoodighe opweckinghe der vervallende studien der heylighe Talen, in welcke de H. Schriftuyre oorspronckelyck gheschreven is, Franeker 1624.
——, *Sermo Academicus ad locum Eccles. 12, 1,* Holmiae 1625.
——, *Anti-Barbarus biblicus* in vi libros distributus, quorum primus ostendit vii fontes omnis barbariei, quae superioribus seculis sacras literas foedavit: reliqui v non solum exhibent centurias aliquot crassissimorum errorum, qui circa particularium locorum interpretationem ex istis fontibus emanarunt, sed & compluribus locis Scripturae facem allucent, Amstelrodami 1628.
——, *Grammatica Ebraea Martino-Buxtorfiana*, seu grammatica Pt. Martinii quam ex aliorum grammaticis, praecipue Buxtorfii, suisque etiam observationibus, Sixtinus Amama auxit, Amstelrodami 1634.
——, *Coronis ad Grammaticam Martinio-Buxtorfianam*, Amstelaedami 1635.
G. Amesius, *Opera Omnia*, 5 vols., Amstelaedami 1658.
C. Andresen (Hrsgb.), *Handbuch der Dogmen- und Theologiegeschichte* 2. Die Lehrentwicklung im Rahmen der Konfessionalität, Göttingen 1980.

B. G. Armstrong, *Calvinism and the Amyraut Heresy*. Protestant scholasticism and humanism in seventeenth century France, Madison and London, 1969.

E. Armstrong, *Robert Estienne, royal printer*. An historical study of the elder Stephanus, Cambridge 1954.

P. Auvray, "Jean Morin (1591-1659)", *Revue Biblique* 66 (1959), 397-414.

——, "Richard Simon et Spinoza", in: *Religion, érudition et critique à la fin du XVII<sup>e</sup> siècle et au début du XVIII<sup>e</sup>*, Paris 1968, 201-214.

——, *Richard Simon (1638-1712)*. Etude bio-bibliographique avec des textes inédits, Paris 1974.

A. G. H. Bachrach, "The foundation of the Bodleian library and 17th century Holland", *Neophilologus* 36 (1952), 101-114.

C. Barlaeus, *Epistolarum liber*, Amstelaedami 1667.

S. W. Baron, *A social and religious history of the Jews*, 14 vols., Philadelphia 1952-1969.

V. Baroni, *La Contre-Réforme devant la Bible*. La question biblique, Lausanne 1943.

——, *La Bible dans la vie catholique depuis la Réforme*, Lausanne 1955.

H. J. Bashuysen, *Observationum sacrarum* Liber I, agens de Integritate Sacrae Scripturae, imprimis Veteris testamenti, Francofurti ad Moenum 1708.

——, *Clavis talmudica maxima*, Hannoviae 1714.

E. D. Baumann, *Johan van Beverwijck in leven en werken geschetst*, Dordrecht 1910.

W. Baumgartner, "Eine alttestamentliche Forschungsgeschichte", *Theologische Rundschau* N.F. 25 (1959), 93-110.

B. Becker-Cantarino, *Daniel Heinsius*, Boston 1978.

J. A. F. Bekker, *Correspondence of John Morris with Johannes de Laet (1634-1649)*, z.p. 1970.

J. van den Berg, *Joden en christenen in Nederland gedurende de zeventiende eeuw*, Kampen 1969.

——, "Eschatological Expectations concerning the Conversion of the Jews in the Netherlands during the Seventeenth Century", in: P. Toon, *Puritans, the Millennium and the Future of Israel*, Cambridge and London 1970, 137-153.

K. van Berkel, *Isaac Beeckman (1588-1637) en de mechanisering van het wereldbeeld*, Amsterdam 1983.

A. Berthier, "Un Maître orientaliste du XIII<sup>e</sup> siècle: Raymond Martin O.P.", *Archivum Fratrum Praedicatorum* 6 (1936), 267-311.

E. Bischoff, *Kritische Geschichte der Thalmud-Uebersetzungen aller Zeiten und Zungen*, Frankfurt 1899.

E. Bizer (Hrsgb.)/H. Heppe, *Die Dogmatik der evangelisch-reformierten Kirche*, Neukirchen 1958.

J. L. Blau, *The Christian interpretation of the cabala in the Renaissance*, New York 1944.

M. Blekastad, *Comenius*. Versuch eines Umrisses von Leben, Werk und Schicksal des Jan Amos Komensky, Oslo/Praag 1969.

F. F. Blok, *Contributions to the history of Isaac Vossius's library*, Amsterdam/London 1974.

——, "Caspar Barlaeus en de Joden. De geschiedenis van een epigram", *Nederlands Archief voor Kerkgeschiedenis* 57 (1976/77), 179-209; 58 (1977/78), 85-108.

P. J. Blok, "De Bibliotheca Thysiana te Leiden", *Tijdschrift voor boek- en bibliotheekwezen* 5 (1907), 53-61.

S. Bochart, *Opera Omnia* I. Hierozoicon sive bipertitum opus de animalibus S. Scripturae. ed. III ex recensione J. Leusden, Lugduni Batavorum 1692.

J. T. Bodel Nyenhuis, "Levensbijzonderheden van den Nederlandschen geschiedschrijver Joh. Isacius Pontanus, meest geput uit deszelfs Album", *Bijdragen voor Vaderlandsche Geschiedenis en Oudheidkunde* 2 (1840), 81-110.

W. B. S. Boeles, "Levenschetsen der Groninger Hoogleeraren", in: *Gedenkboek der Hoogeschool te Groningen* ter gelegenheid van haar vijfde halve eeuwfeest (..) uitgegeven door W. J. A. Jonckbloet, Groningen 1864, Bijlage I, 1-167.

——, *Frieslands Hoogeschool en het Rijks Athenaeum te Franeker*, 2 delen, Leeuwarden 1878-1889.

J. Bohatec, *Calvins Lehre von Staat und Kirche mit besonderer Berücksichtigung des Organismusgedankens*, Breslau 1937.

E. van den Boogaart (red.), *Johan Maurits van Nassau-Siegen*. 1604-1697: a humanist prince in Europe and Brazil, Den Haag 1979.

L. J. M. Bosch, *Petrus Bertius (1565-1629)*, Meppel 1979.

P. N. M. Bot, *Humanisme en onderwijs in Nederland*, Utrecht/Antwerpen 1955.

J. A. H. G. M. Bots, "André Rivet en zijn positie in de Republiek der Letteren", *TvG* 84 (1971), 24-35.

——, "Cultuurgeschiedenis. Het intellectuele leven in Gelderland gedurende de 16de, 17de en 18de eeuw", in: J. J. Poelhekke e.a. (redd.), *Geschiedenis van Gelderland* II (1492-1795), Zutphen 1975, 385-428.

——, *Van universitaire gemeenschap tot academische kring*. Enige aspecten met betrekking tot de opkomst en ontwikkeling van geleerde academies en genootschappen in West-Europa, Amsterdam 1976.

——, *Republiek der letteren. Ideaal en werkelijkheid*, Amsterdam 1977.

H. Bouman, *Geschiedenis van de voormalige Geldersche Hoogeschool en hare hoogleeraren*, 2 vols., Utrecht 1844-1847.

C. R. Boxer, *De Nederlanders in Brazilië, 1624-1654*, Alphen aan den Rijn [1977].

J. C. Boyajian, "The New Christians reconsidered: evidence from Lisbon's portuguese bankers, 1497-1647", *SR* 13 (1979), 129-156.

J. G. C. A. Briels, *Zuidnederlandse boekdrukkers en boekverkopers in de Republiek der Verenigde Nederlanden omstreeks 1570-1630*, Nieuwkoop 1974.

F. G. M. Broeyer, *William Whitaker (1548-1595)*. Leven en werk van een anglocalvinistisch theoloog, Utrecht 1982.

E. Bronchorst, *Diarium Everardi Brochorstii* Uitgegeven door J. C. van Slee. Werken Historisch Genootschap, 3e serie, no. 12, 's-Gravenhage 1898.

J. Brugman, "Arabic Scholarship", in: Th. H. Lunsingh Scheurleer/G. H. M. Posthumus Meyjes (edd.), *Leiden University in the Seventeenth Century*. An Exchange of Learning, Leiden 1975, 202-215.

——, /F. Schröder, *Arabic Studies in the Netherlands*, Leiden 1979.

H. Brugmans/A. Frank (redd.), *Geschiedenis der Joden in Nederland* I, Amsterdam 1940.

C. C. de Bruin, *De Statenbijbel en zijn voorgangers*, Leiden 1937.

K. H. Burmeister, *Sebastian Münster*. Eine Bibliographie mit 22 Abbildungen, Wiesbaden 1964.

J. Buxtorf (I), *De Abbreviaturis Hebraicis* (..) cui access. Operis Talmudici brevis recensio cum ejusdem librorum et capitum indice. Item *Bibliotheca Rabbinica* nova, ordine alphabetico dispositae, Basilae 1613.

——, *Synagoga Judaica*, hoc est Schola judaeorum, in qua nativitas, instituto, religio, vita, mors: sepulturaque ipsorum e libris eorundem, Hanoviae 1614.

——, *Biblia rabbinica*, Basileae 1618-1619.

——, *Lexicon Hebraicum et Chaldaicum*. Acc. *Lexicon breve Rabbinico-philosophicum*, ed. III recogn., Basileae 1621.

J. Buxtorf (II), *Rabbi Mosis Majemonidis Liber* (..) *Doctor Perplexorum*, Basilae 1629.

——, "Epistola de recte instituendo studio Rabbinico", *Museum Helveticum ad juvandas Literas in publicos usus apertum* viii, Turici 1748, 122-127.

——, *Liber Cosri*, continens Colloquium seu Disputationem de religione, Basilae 1660.

J. J. Buxtorf, *Catalecta Philologico-theologica*. Accedunt Mantissae loco Virorum celeberrimorum Epistolae ad Joh. Buxtorfium Patrem & Filium nunc primum in lucem editae, Basilae 1707.

D. Buxtorf-Falkeissen, *Johannes Buxtorf Vater*, erkannt aus seinem Briefwechsel, Basel 1860.

J. Cabeljavius, *Epistolarum centuria I*. Adjuncto libro adoptivo, in quo ad auctorem doctorum virorum aliquot Epistolae, Holmiae 1626.

——, *Liber Adoptivus*, in quo insignium aliquot doctorum virorum ad auctorem & epistolae, & testimoniae, Holmiae 1626.

J. Caillé, "Ambassades et missions marocaines aux Pays-Bas à l'epoque des sultans saadiens", *Hespéris Tamuda* 4 (1963), 5-67; 9 (1968), 171-207.

[L. Cappel], *Arcanum Punctuationis revelatum* sive de punctorum vocalium et accentuum

apud Hebraeos vera et germana antiquitate, diatriba. In lucem edita a Thoma
    Erpenio, Lugduni Batavorum 1624.
——, *Ad novam Davidis lyram animadversiones*, Salmurii 1643.
——, *Critica sacra*, sive de variis quae in sacris Vet. Testam. libris occurrunt lectionibus
    libri sex. Cui subj. est ejusdem Criticae adversus injustum censorem justa defensio:
    cum appendicibus. Edita in lucem stud. et op. Joa. Cappelli, auct. filii, Parisiis
    1650.
J. B. Carpzov, "Introductio", in R. Martini, *Pugio Fidei*, Lipsiae 1687, 1-126.
C. Cartwright, *Electa Thargumico-Rabbinica*, sive annotationes in Genesin, Londoni 1648.
I. Casaubonus, *Epistolae*, insertis ad easdem responsionibus (..) curante Th. Janss. ab
    Almeloveen, ed. III, Roterodami 1709.
*Censura in Confessionem* sive declarationem sententiae eorum qui in foed. Belgio
    Remonstrantes vocantur, super praecipuis articulis christianae religionis, a Theolo-
    giae professoribus Academiae Leidensis instituta, Lugduni Batavorum 1626.
P. Chaunu, *Le temps des Réformes*. Histoire religieuse et système de civilisation, 2 parties,
    Paris 1975.
M. D. Chenu, *La théologie au douzième siècle*, Paris 1957.
J. Cocceius, *Duo tituli Thalmudici: Sanhedrin et Maccoth* (..) cum excerptis ex utriusque
    Gemara, versa et annotationibus depromtis maximam partem ex Ebraeorum com-
    mentariis, illustrata a Joanne Coch Bremensi, Amsterodami 1629.
——, *Opera omnia* theologica, exegetica, didactica, polemica, philologica. Ed 3a, auctior
    emendatior, 10 vols., Amstelodami 1701.
——, *Opera ANEKDOTA* theologica et philologica, 2 vols., Amstelodami 1706.
G. Coddaeus, *Oratio funebris*, in obitum (..) Rud. Snellii, Lugduni Batavorum 1613.
G. Cohen, *Ecrivains Français en Hollande dans la première moitié du XVIIᵉ siècle*, Paris 1920.
J. Cohen, *The friars and the Jews: the evolution of medieval anti-Judaism*, Ithaca 1982.
E. Conring, *Kirche und Staat nach der Lehre der niederländischen Calvinisten in der ersten Hälfte
    des 17. Jahrhunderts*, Neukirchen 1965.
J. Coppens, "De geschiedkundige ontwikkelingsgang van de Oudtestamentische exegese
    vanaf de Renaissance tot en met de Aufklärung", *Mededeelingen van de Koninklijke
    Vlaamsche Academie voor Wetenschappen, Letteren, en Schoone Kunsten van België* 5,4 (1943).
J. Cost Budde, "Johannes Leusden", *Nederlands Archief voor Kerkgeschiedenis* 34 (1944-45),
    163-186.
*Critici sacri* sive annotata doctissimorum virorum in Vetus ac Novum Testamentum. Qui-
    bus accedunt tractatus varii theologico-philologici. Editio nova aucta, 8 vols.,
    Amstelaedami 1698.
P. Cunaeus, *De Republica Hebraeorum libri III*, Lugduni Batavorum 1617.
——, *Petri Cunaei & doctorum virorum ad eumdem Epistolae*. (..) Nunc primum editae cura
    Petri Burmanni, Leidae 1725.
A. Curiander, *Vitae, Operumque Ioh. Drusii editorum et nondum editorum delineatio et tituli*, Fra-
    nekerae 1616.
M. H. Curtis, *Oxford and Cambridge in transition, 1558-1642*. An essay on changing relati-
    ons between the English universities and English society, Oxford 1959.
R. Descartes, *Oeuvres*, 11 vols., publ. par C. Adam et P. Tannery. Nouv. prés, Paris
    1964-1974.
P. A. G. Dibon, *La philosophie néerlandaise au siècle d'or* I: L'enseignement philosophique
    dans les universités à l'époque précartésienne (1575-1650), Paris 1954.
——, "Une famille noble du Refuge Wallon; les Polyander à Kerckhoven", *Bulletin de
    la Commission de l'histoire des Eglises Wallonnes*, (1967-68), 101-124.
——, "L'Université de Leyde et la République des Lettres au XVIIᵉ siècle", *Quaerendo*
    5 (1975), 5-38.
——, "Les échanges épistolaires dans l'Europe savante du 17e siècle", *Revue de Synthèse*
    97 (1976), 31-50.
F. Dickmann, "Das Judenmissionsprogramm Johann Christoph Wagenseils", *Neue Zeit-
    schrift für systematische Theologie und Religionsphilosophie* 16 (1974), 75-92.
J. I. Dienstag, "Christian Translators of Maimonides' Mishneh Torah into Latin. A

Bio-Bibliographical Survey'', in S. Lieberman/A. Hyman (edd.), *Salo Wittmayer Baron Jubilee Volume*, Jerusalem 1974, 287-309.

L. Diestel, *Geschichte des Alten Testamentes in der christlichen Kirche*, Jena 1869.

L. de Dieu, *Critica sacra* sive animadversiones in loca quaedam difficiliora Veteris et Novi Testamenti. Ed. nova aucta. Amstelaedami 1693.

J. G. van Dillen, ''Vreemdelingen te Amsterdam in de eerste helft der zeventiende eeuw. I. De Portugeesche Joden'', *TvG* 50 (1935), 4-35.

J. A. van Dorsten, ''Sidney and Franciscus Junius the Elder'', *Huntington Library Quarterly* XLII (1978), 1-13.

J. Drusius, *Miscellanea locutionum sacrarum*, Franekerae 1586.

——, *Alphabetum ebraicum vetus* (..) C. Sententiae veterum Sapientium triplici charactere, Ebraico, Latino et Graeco, Franekerae 1587.

——, *Proverbiorum classes duae* (..) Item Sententiae Salomonis, allegoriae etc., Franekerae, 1590.

——, *Proverbia Ben-Sirae* (..) Opera I. Drusii, in Latinam linguam conversa scholiis aut potius commentario illustrata. Accesserunt Adagiorum Ebraicorum Decuriae aliquot nunquam antehac editae, Franekerae 1597.

——, *Quaestionum Ebraicarum libri tres*. In quibus innumera Scripturae loca explicantur aut emendantur. Editio secunda melior et auctior, Franekerae 1599.

——, *De Hasidaeis*, quorum mentio in libris Machabaeorum libellus, Franekerae 1603.

——, *Tetragrammaton*, sive de nomine Dei proprio, quod Tetragrammaton vocant, Franekerae 1604.

——, *Responsio ad Serarium de tribus sectis Judaeorum*, Franekerae 1605.

——, *Ad Minerval Serarii Responsio*, libris duo comprehensa cum appendice, Franekerae 1606.

——, *Annotationum in totum Jesu Christi Testamentum*, sive praeteritorum libri decem. In quibus (..) consensu ostenditur synagoge Israelitice cum ecclesia Christiana, Franekerae 1612.

——, *Apophthegmata Ebraeorum ac Arabum*, Franekerae 1612.

——, *Henoch*, sive de patriarcha Henoch, ejusque raptu & libro e quo Judas Apostola testimonium profert; ubi & de libris in scriptura memoratis, qui nunc interciderunt, Franekerae 1615.

——, *Ad voces ebraicas Novi Testamenti commentarius duplex* (..) item *Annotationum in N. Testamentum pars altera*, Franekerae 1616.

——, *Ad Loca difficiliora Pentateuchi id est Quinque librorum Mosis Commentarius*, Franekerae 1617.

——, *De sectis Judaicis* commentarii, Trihaeresio et Minervali Nic. Serarii oppositi (..) Sixtinus Amama hanc editionem accuravit, Arnhemiae 1619.

A. C. Duker, *Gisbertus Voetius*, 3 vols., Leiden [1893]-1914.

G. Ebeling, ''Die Bedeutung der historisch-kritischen Methode für die protestantische Theologie und Kirche'', *Zeitschrift für Theologie und Kirche* 47 (1950), 1-46.

A. Eekhof, *De theologische faculteit te Leiden in de 17e eeuw*, Utrecht 1921.

J. E. Elias, *De Vroedschap van Amsterdam, 1578-1795*, 2 vols., Amsterdam 1963.

*Epistolae celeberrimorum virorum*, nempe H. Grotii, G. J. Vossii, cet., antehac ineditae. Ex scriniis literariis Jani Brantii, Amstelaedami 1715.

D. Erasmus, *Opera Omnia*, recognovit Joannes Clericus, 10 vols., Lugduni Batavorum 1703-1706.

——, *Opus Epistolarum* Desiderii Erasmi Roterodami, denuo recognitum et auctum per P. S. Allen, 12 vols., Oxonii 1906-1958.

Th. Erpenius, *Grammatica Arabica*, Leidae 1613.

——, *Proverbiorum Arabicorum centuriae duae*, Leidae 1614.

——, *Rudimenta linguae Arabicae*, Leidae 1620.

——, *Samuelis libri duo* Ebraice et Latine ad usus Academiarum, Leidae 1621.

——, *Orationes tres de linguarum ebraeae atque arabicae dignitate*, Leidae 1621.

——, *Grammatica Ebraea generalis*, Lugduni Batavorum 1621.

L. van der Essen, ''Les progrès du lutheranisme et du calvinisme dans le monde commercial d'Anvers et l'espionnage politique du marchand Philippe Dauxy, agent secret de Marguerite de Parme, en 1566-1567'', *Vierteljahrschrift für Sozial- und Wirtschaftsgeschichte* XII (1914), 152-234.

P. Fagius, *Sententiae* vere elegantes, piae, mireque, cum ad linguam discendam, tum animum pietate excolendum utiles, veterum sapientum Hebraeorum, quas PIRKE AVOT, id est Capitula, aut si mavis, Apophthegmata Patrum nominant: in Latinum versae, scholiisque illustratae, Isnae 1541.

——, *Sententiae morales Ben Syrae*, vetustissimi Authoris Hebraei, qui a Iudaeis nepos Hieremiae prophetae fuisse creditur, cum succincto commentario, Isnae 1541.

O. Fatio/P. Fraenkel, *Histoire de l'exégèse au XVIe siècle*. Textes du Colloque international tenu à Genève en 1976, Genève 1978.

M. Flacius Illyricus, *Clavis Scripturae Sacrae* seu de sermone sacrarum literarum, Basilae 1609.

J. Flemming, ''Hiob Ludolph. Ein Beitrag zur Geschichte der orientalischen Philologie'', *Beiträge zur Assyriologie und vergleichende semitische Sprachwissenschaft* 1 (1890), 537-582.

J. Foster, *Alumni Oxonienses 1500-1714*, 2 vols., Oxford 1891.

A. Frank-Van Westrienen, *De Groote Tour*. Tekening van de educatiereis der Nederlanders in de zeventiende eeuw, Amsterdam 1983.

G. Frick, *Die Elzevir'schen Republiken*, Halle a.S. 1892.

W. Th. M. Frijhoff, *La société néerlandaise et ses gradués, 1575-1814*, une récherche sérielle sur le statut des intellectuels, Amsterdam 1981.

H. Fuhrmann, ''Die Sorge um den rechten Text'', *Deutsches Archiv für Erforschung des Mittelalters* 25 (1969), 1-16.

L. Fuks, ''Het Hebreeuwse brievenboek van Johannes Drusius jr. Hebreeuws en hebraïsten in Nederland rondom 1600'', *SR* 3 (1969), 1-52.

L. Fuks/R. G. Fuks-Mansfeld, *Hebrew and Judaic manuscripts in Amsterdam public collections*, 2 vols., Leiden 1973-1975.

——, ''Jewish Historiography in the Netherlands in the 17th and 18th Centuries'', in: S. Lieberman/A. Hyman (edd.), *Salo Wittmayer Baron Jubilee Volume*, Jerusalem 1974, 433-466.

——, ''Menasseh ben Israel as a Bookseller in the light of new data'', *Quaerendo* 11 (1981), 34-45.

——, *Hebrew Typography in the Northern Netherlands 1585-1815*. Historical Evaluation and descriptive Bibliography I, Leiden 1984.

P. Galatinus, *Opus de arcanis catholicae veritatis*: hoc est in omnia difficilia loca Veteris Testamenti ex Talmud aliisque Hebraicis libris contra obstinatam Judaeorum perfidiam commentarius, Basileae 1561.

H. A. E. van Gelder, *Getemperde Vrijheid:* een verhandeling over de verhouding van Kerk en Staat in de Republiek der Verenigde Nederlanden en de vrijheid van meningsuiting in zake godsdienst, drukpers en onderwijs, gedurende de 17e eeuw, Groningen 1972.

G. Gentius, *Canones Ethici* R. Moseh Meimonidis (sic!) Hebraeorum sapientissimi, ex Hebraeo in Latinum versi, uberioribusque notis illustrati, Amstelodami 1640.

——, *Historia Judaica*, res Judaeorum ab eversa aede Hierosolymitana ad haec fere tempora usque complexa. De Hebraeo in Latinum versa, Amstelodami 1651.

——, *Musladini Sadi Rosarium politicum*, sive Amoenum sortis humanae Theatrum, de Persico in Latinum versum, necessariisque notis illustratum, Amstelodami 1651.

J. G. Gerretzen, *Schola Hemsterhusiana*. De herleving der Grieksche studiën aan de Nederlandsche universiteiten in de achttiende eeuw van Perizonius tot en met Valckenaer, Nijmegen/Utrecht, 1940.

A. Godin, ''Fonction d'Origène dans la pratique exégétique d'Erasme: les Annotations sur l'épître aux Romains'', in: O. Fatio/P. Fraenkel, *Histoire de l'exégèse au XVIe siècle*, Genève 1978, 17-44.

F. Gomarus, *Davidis lyra*, seu Nova hebraea S. Scripturae ars poetica, canonibus suis descripta, et exemplis sacris, et Pindari ac Sophoclis, parallelis demonstrata, cum selectorum Davidis, Salomonis, Jeremiae, Mosis et Jobi poëmatum analysi poëtica, Lugduni Batavorum 1637.

M. H. Goshen-Gottstein, "The Textual Criticism of the Old Testament: Rise, Decline, Rebirth", *Journal of Biblical Literature* 102 (1983), 365-399.

A. T. Grafton, *Joseph Scaliger. A Study in the History of Classical Scholarship*. I. Textual Criticism and Exegesis, Oxford 1983.

——, "Protestant versus Prophet: Isaac Casaubon on Hermes Trismegistus", *Journal of the Warburg and Courtauld Institutes* XLVI (1983), 78-94.

V. H. H. Green, *A History of Oxford University*, London [1974].

G. Groenhuis, "Calvinism and National Consciousness: the Dutch Republic as the New Israel", in: A. C. Duke/C. A. Tamse (edd.) *Britain and the Netherlands* 7. Church and State since the Reformation, The Hague 1981, 118-133.

A. H. de Groot, *The Ottoman Empire and the Dutch Republic. A History of the Earliest Diplomatic Relations, 1610-1630*, Leiden/Istanbul 1978.

——, *De betekenis van de Nederlandse ambassade bij de verheven Porte voor de studie van het Turks in de 17e en 18e eeuw*, Leiden 1979.

H. de Groot, *De veritate religionis Christianae*. Editio tertia, prioribus auctior et emendatior, Lugduni Batavorum 1633.

——, *Annotationes ad Libros de veritate religionis Christianae*, Lugduni Batavorum 1640.

——, *Annotationes in libros Evangeliorum* cum tribus tractatibus et appendice eo spectantibus, Amstelodami 1641.

——, *Annotata ad Vetus Testamentum*, 3 vols., Lutetia 1644.

——, *Annotationum in Novum Testamentum tomus II*, Parisiis [1646].

—— *Annotationum in Novum Testamentum pars III*, Parisiis 1650.

——, *Epistolae quotquot reperiri potuerunt*, Amstelodami 1687.

——, *Briefwisseling*, uitgegeven door P. C. Molhuysen, B. L. Meulenbroek, P. P. Witkam. Rijksgeschiedkundige publicatiën, G. S. 64, 82, 105, 113, 119, 124, 130, 136, 142, 154, 179, 11 vols., 's-Gravenhage 1928-1984.

H. Grün, "Geist und Gestalt der Hohen Schule Herborn", *Nassauische Annalen* 65 (1954), 130-147.

E. van Gulik/H. D. L. Vervliet, *Een gedenksteen voor Plantijn en Van Raphelingen te Leiden*, Leiden 1965.

M. F. Gijswijt-Hofstra, *Wijkplaatsen voor vervolgden*. Asielverlening in Culemborg, Vianen, Buren, Leerdam en IJsselstein van de 16e tot de 18e eeuw, z.p. 1984.

A. A. M. de Haan, *Het wijsgerig onderwijs aan het Gymnasium Illustre en de Hogeschool te Harderwijk, 1599-1811*, Harderwijk 1960.

Th. Hackspan, *Liber Nizachon* oppositus Christianis, Sadducaeis atque aliis. Curante Th. Hackspan. Acc. Tractatus de usu librorum Rabbinicorum, Noribergae 1644.

A. von Harnack, *Lehrbuch der Dogmengeschichte*, 4. neu durchgearb. und verm. Aufl., 3 vols., Tübingen 1909-1920.

D. Heinsius, *Sacrarum exercitationum ad Novum Testamentum libri viginti* quibus Aristarchus sacer, emendatior nec paulo auctior, cet. accedunt, Lugduni Batavorum 1639.

G. Hering, *Oekumenisches Patriarchat und europäische Politik, 1620-1638*, Wiesbaden 1968.

I. Herzog, "John Selden and Jewish Law", *Journal of Comparative Legislation and International Law* XIII (1931), 236-245.

L. Hirschel, "Johannes Leusden als hebraist". Postuum uitgegeven, van noten en inleiding voorzien door A. K. Offenberg, *SR* 1 (1967), 23-50.

R. Hooykaas, *Humanisme, science et réforme. Pierre de la Ramée (1515-1572)*, Leyde 1958.

W. Horbury, "The Basle Nizzahon", *The Journal of Theological Studies* N.S. XXXIV (1983), 497-514.

D. J. H. ter Horst, *Isaac Vossius en Salmasius*. Een episode uit de 17e eeuwsche geleerdengeschiedenis, '-Gravenhage 1938.

J. H. Hottinger, *Exercitationes Anti-Morinianae de Pentateucho Samaritano*, Tiguri 1644.

W. J. A. Huberts, *De geschiedenis der oude Zutfensche Latijnsche School*, Zutfen 1863.

C. Huygens, *De briefwisseling van Constantijn Huygens (1608-1687)* uitgegeven door J. A. Worp, 6 vols., 's-Gravenhage 1911-1917, Rijksgeschiedkundige Publicatiën G.S. 15, 19, 21, 24, 28, 32.

J. I. Israel, "Spain and the Dutch Sephardim, 1609-1660", *SR* 12 (1978), 1-61.
——, *The Dutch Republic and the Hispanic World 1606-1661*, Oxford 1982.
——, "The Economic Contribution of Dutch Sephardi Jewry to Holland's Golden Age, 1595-1713", *TvG* 96 (1983), 505-535.
G. P. van Itterzon, *Franciscus Gomarus*, 's-Gravenhage 1929.
——, "De 'Synopsis Purioris Theologiae'. Gereformeerd leerboek der 17de eeuw", *Nederlands Archief voor Kerkgeschiedenis* 33 (1930), 161-213; 225-59.
——, "Nog twintig brieven van Gomarus", *Nederlands Archief voor Kerkgeschiedenis* 56 (1976), 413-49.
C. de Jonge, "De Grand Tour van Johannes Thysius" [onuitgegeven doctoraalscriptie; Leiden 1975].
H. J. de Jonge, *Daniel Heinsius and the textus receptus of the New Testament*. A study of his contributions to the editions of the Greek Testament printed by the Elzeviers at Leiden in 1624 and 1633, Leiden 1971.
——, "J. J. Scaliger's de LXXXV Canonibus Apostolorum diatribe", *Lias* 2 (1975), 115-124.
——, "The Latin Testament of Joseph Scaliger, 1607", *Lias* 2 (1975), 249-263.
——, "The Study of the New Testament", in: Th. H. Lunsingh Scheurleer, G. H. M. Posthumus Meyjes (edd.), *Leiden University in the Seventeenth Century*. An Exchange of Learning, Leiden 1975, 64-109.
——, "Jeremias Hoelzlin: editor of the 'Textus receptus' printed by the Elzeviers Leiden 1633", in: T. Baarda, A. F. J. Klijn, W. C. van Unnik (edd.), *Miscellanea Neotestamentica* I, Leiden 1978, 105-128.
—— *De bestudering van het Nieuwe Testament aan de Noordnederlandse universiteiten en het Remonstrants Seminarie van 1575 tot 1700*, Amsterdam/Oxford/New York, 1980.
——, "Hugo Grotius: exégète du Nouveau Testament", in: *The World of Hugo Grotius (1583-1645)*. Proceedings of the International Colloquium (..) Rotterdam 6-9 April 1983, Amsterdam/Maarssen 1984, 97-115.
F. Junius, *Opera theologica*, quorum nonnulla nunc primum publicantur. Praefixa est Vita auctoris, 2 vols., [Heidelbergae] 1608.
W. M. C. Juynboll, *Zeventiende-eeuwsche beoefenaars van het Arabisch in Nederland*, Utrecht 1931.
Y. Kaplan, "The Portuguese Jews in Amsterdam. From forced Conversion to a Return to Judaism", *SR* 15 (1981), 37-51.
H. Karpp, "Zur Geschichte der Bibel in der Kirche des 16. und 17. Jahrhunderts", *Theologische Rundschau* N.F. 48 (1983), 129-155.
A. L. Katchen, *Christian Hebraists and Dutch Rabbis:* Seventeenth Century Apologetics and the Study of Maimonides' *Mishneh Torah*, Cambridge (Mass.) & London 1984.
E. Kautzsch, *Johannes Buxtorf der Aeltere*, Basel 1879.
H. F. Kearney, *Scholars and Gentlemen*. Universities and Society in pre-industrial Britain, 1500-1700, London [1970].
D. R. Kelley, *Foundations of Modern Historical Scholarship:* Language, Law and History in the French Renaissance, New York 1970.
G. W. Kernkamp e.a., *De Utrechtsche Universiteit 1636-1936*, 2 vols., Utrecht 1936.
J. H. Kernkamp, "Rondom het huwelijk van Marnix' dochter Amelie", in: *Marnix van Sinte Aldegonde*. Officieel gedenkboek, Amsterdam z.j., 281-301.
G. Kisch, "Summum ius summa iniuria", in: *Aequitas und bona fides*. Festgabe zum 70. Geburtstag von August Simonis, Basel 1955, 195-213.
——, *Melanchthons Rechts- und Soziallehre*, Berlin 1967.
W. Klatt, *Hermann Gunkel*. Zu seiner Theologie der Religionsgeschichte und zur Entstehung der formgeschichtlichen Methode, Göttingen 1969.
A. Kleinhans, "De vita et operibus Petri Galatini O. F. M. scientiarum biblicarum cultoris (c. 1460-1540)", *Antonianum* 1 (1926), 145-179, 327-356.
E. G. Kraeling, *The Old Testament since the Reformation*, London [1955].
H. J. Kraus, *Geschichte der historisch-kritischen Erforschung des Alten Testaments*, 2. Aufl. Neukirchen/Vluyn 1969.

W. J. Kühler, *Het Socinianisme in Nederland*, Leiden 1912.

W. Kühlmann, *Gelehrtenrepublik und Fürstenstaat.* Entwicklung und Kritik des deutschen Späthumanismus in der Literatur des Barockzeitalters, Tübingen 1982.

A. Kuenen, "Hugo de Groot als uitlegger van het Oude Verbond", *Verslagen en Mededeelingen der Koninklijke Akademie van wetenschappen; Afdeling Letterkunde*; 2e Reeks 12 (1883), 319-333.

E. T. Kuiper, *Het Geuzenliedboek naar de oude drukken*, 2 vols., Zutfen 1924-1925.

G. C. Kuiper/C. S. M. Rademaker, "The Collegium Theologicum at Leiden in 1615. Correspondence between P. Bertius and G. J. Vossius, the resigning regent and his successor", *Lias* 2 (1975), 125-176.

A. Kuyper jr., *Johannes Maccovius*, Leiden 1899.

H. H. Kuyper, *De opleiding tot den Dienst des Woords bij de Gereformeerden* Deel I, 's-Gravenhage 1891.

——, *De Post-acta* of Nahandelingen van de Nationale Synode van Dordrecht, Amsterdam [1899].

E. Labrousse, *Pierre Bayle*, 2 vols., La Haye 1963-1964.

P. S. Lachs, "Hugo Grotius' Use of Jewish sources in 'On the Law of War and Peace'", *Renaissance Quarterly* 30 (1977), 181-200.

A. J. Lamping, *Johannes Polyander.* Een dienaar van Kerk en Universiteit, Leiden 1980.

F. Laplanche, *Orthodoxie et Prédication.* L'œuvre d'Amyraut et la querelle de la grace universelle, Paris 1965.

H. Lausberg, *Handbuch der literarischen Rhetorik.* Eine Grundlegung der Literaturwissenschaft, 2 vols., München 1960.

J. Le Brun, "Das Entstehen der historischen Kritik im Bereich der religiösen Wissenschaften im 17. Jahrhundert", *Trierer Theologische Zeitschrift* 89 (1980), 100-117.

J. C. H. Lebram, "Ein Streit um die Hebräische Bibel und die Septuaginta", in: Th. H. Lunsingh Scheurleer/G. H. M. Posthumus Meyjes (edd.), *Leiden University in the Seventeenth Century.* An Exchange of Learning, Leiden 1975, 21-63.

——, "Hebräische Studien zwischen Ideal und Wirklichkeit an der Universität Leiden in den Jahren 1575-1619", *Nederlands Archief voor Kerkgeschiedenis* 56 (1975/1976), 317-357.

——, "De Hasidaeis. Over Joodse studiën in het oude Leiden", *Voordrachten Faculteitendag 1980*, Leiden 1981, 21-31.

C. L'Empereur, *Oratio inauguralis (..) de linguae hebraeae dignitate et utilitate*, Lugduni Batavorum 1627.

——, *Talmudis Babylonici codex Middoth* sive de mensuris Templi. una cum versione Latina (..) Additis commentariis, Lugduni Batavorum 1630 ( = *Middot*).

——, *D. Isaaci Abrabanielis et R. Mosis Alschechi Comment. in Esaiae prophetiam*, cum additamento eorum quae R. Simeon e veterum dictis collegit. Subiuncta (..) refutatione et textua nova versione ac paraphrasi, Lugduni Batavorum 1631 ( = *ComJes*).

——, *Mosis Kimchi HODOIPORIA ad scientiam*, cum expositione Doctoris Eliae. Item Introductio D. Binjamin F. D. Judae Omnia...annotationibus illustrata, Lugduni Batavorum 1631 ( = *Moskim*).

——, *Paraphrasis Iosephi Iachiadae in Danielem* cum versione, et annotationibus, Amstelodami 1633 ( = *ParaDan*).

——, *Itinerarium D. Benjaminis*, cum versione et notis, Lugduni Batavorum 1633 ( = *ItinBen*).

——, *Halichoth Olam* sive Clavis Talmudica, complectens Formulas, Loca Dialecta et Rhetorica priscorum Judaeorum, Lugduni Batavorum 1634 ( = *HalOl*).

——, *De Legibus Ebraeorum forensibus Liber singularis.* Ex Ebraeorum pandectis versus et commentariis illustratus, Lugduni Batavorum 1637 ( = *Bava Kamma*).

——, C. B. Bertramus, *De Republica Ebraeorum*, rec. commentarioque ill. opera Constantini L'Empereur ab Oppyck, Lugduni Batavorum 1641 ( = *RepHeb*).

——, *Disputationes theologicae* XVIII, Lugduni Batavorum 1648.

P. Leroy, *Le dernier voyage en France d'un intellectuel d'opposition au XVIIᵉ siècle: Claude Saumaise en Bourgogne (1640-1643)*, Amsterdam 1983.

*Levinus Warner and his Legacy*. Three centuries Legatum Warnerianum in the Leiden University Library. Catalogue of the commemorative exhibition held in the Bibliotheca Thysiana from April 27th till May 15th 1970, Leiden 1970.

J. Lightfoot, *Opera omnia*, Roterodami 1686.

J. D. de Lind van Wijngaarden, *Antonius Waleus*, Leiden 1891.

G. A. Lindeboom, "De Illustere School in Breda", *Spiegel Historiael* 6 (1971), 88-94.

*Livre Synodal contenant les articles résolus dans les Synodes des Eglises Wallonnes des Pays-Bas*, publié par la Commission de l'histoire des Eglises wallonnes, tome premier 1563-1685, La Haye 1896.

H. de Lubac, *Exégèse médiévale*, les quatres sens de l'Écriture, 4 vols., Paris 1959-1964.

J. H. Majus, *Vita Abrabanelis*, [Giessen 1707].

C. E. Mallet, *A History of the University of Oxford* II. The Sixteenth and Seventeenth Centuries, London 1924.

R. Mandrou, *Des humanistes aux hommes des science* (XVI$^e$ et XVII$^e$ siècles), Paris 1973.

G. Mann, *Wallenstein*, Frankfurt a.M. 1971.

[P. van Marnix van Sint-Aldegonde], *Catalogue of the Library of Philips van Marnix van St-Aldegonde*. Sold by auction (July 6th), Leiden, Christophorus Guyot, 1599 [Repr. Intr. by G. J. Brouwer], Nieuwkoop 1964.

E. Marsch, *Biblische Prophetie und chronographische Dichtung*. Stoff- und Wirkungsgeschichte der Vision des Propheten Daniel nach Dan. VII, Berlin 1972.

H.-J. Martin, *Livre, Pouvoirs et Société à Paris au XVII$^e$ siècle* (1598-1701), 2 vols., Genève 1969.

R. Martini, *Pugio Fidei adversus Mauros et Judaeos*, cum observationibus Jos. de Voisin et introductione Jo. Ben. Carpzovii, Lipsiae 1687.

H. Méchoulan, "A propos de la visite de Frédéric-Henri, Prince d'Orange, à la synogogue d'Amsterdam. Une lettre inédite de Menasseh ben Israel à David de Wilhem, suivie de la traduction française du discours de bienvenue", *Lias* 5 (1978), 82-86.

——, "Lorsque Saumaise consultait Menasseh ben Israel: deux lettres inédites du rabbin d'Amsterdam à l'humaniste de Leyde", *SR* 13 (1979), 1-17.

——, "Le problème du latin chez Menasseh ben Israel et quelques implications religieuses et politiques à propos d'une lettre inédite à Beverovicius", *SR* 14 (1980), 1-7.

——, "Menasseh ben Israel au centre des rapports judéo-chrétiens en Hollande au XVII$^e$ siècle dans une lettre inédite d'Isaac Coymans a André Colvius", *SR* 16 (1982), 21-24.

P. Melanchthon, *Opera quae supersunt omnia* edidit C. G. Bretschneider XI-XII, Halis Saxonium 1843-44.

R. Melnick, *From Polemics to Apologetics*. Jewish-Christian Rapprochement in 17th Century Amsterdam, Assen 1981.

Menasseh ben Israel, *Conciliator*, sive de convenientia locorum S. Scripturae, quae pugnare inter se videntur, Francofurti [ = Amstelodami] 1633.

——, *Espérance d'Israel*. Introduction, traduction et notes par H. Méchoulan et G. Nahon, Paris 1979.

J. Mercerus, *In Genesin Commentarius*, [Genevae] 1598.

J. ter Meulen/P. J. J. Diermanse, *Bibliographie des écrits imprimés de Hugo Grotius*, La Haye 1950.

J. Meijer, *Hugo de Groot. Remonstrantie nopende de ordre dije in de landen van Hollandt ende Westvrieslandt dijent gestelt op de Joden*. Naar het manuscript in de Livraria D. Montezinos uitgegeven en ingeleid door J. Meijer, Amsterdam 1949.

Th. J. Meijer, *Album Promotorum Academiae Franekerensis* (1591-1811), Franeker [1973].

G. Moeckli/P. Chaix/A. Dufour, *Les livres imprimés à Genève de 1550 à 1600*, Genève 1959.

J. Moltmann, "Zur Bedeutung des Petrus Ramus für Philosophie und Theologie im Calvinismus", *Zeitschrift für Kirchengeschichte* 68 (1957), 295-318.

Th. Mommsen/P. Krueger (edd.), *Corpus iuris civilis*, 3 vols., Berolini 1918-1919.

G. Moreau, *Histoire du protestantisme à Tournai jusqu'à la veille de la Révolution des Pays-Bas*, Paris 1962.

Ph. de Mornay, *De veritate religionis Christianae liber*; adversus atheos, Epicureos, ethnicos, Judaeos, Mahumedistas et caeteros infideles, Lugduni Batavorum 1587.

M. E. H. N. Mout, "Calvinoturcisme in de zeventiende eeuw. Comenius, Leidse oriëntalisten en de Turkse bijbel", *TvG* 91 (1978), 576-607.

G. Müller, "Christlich-Jüdisches Religionsgespräch im Zeitalter der protestantischen Orthodoxie; Die Auseinandersetzung Johann Muellers mit Rabbi Isaak Troki's 'Hizzuq Emunah' ", in: *Glaube-Geist-Geschichte*. Festschrift Ernst Benz, Leiden 1967, 513-524.

R. A. Muller, "The debate over the vowel points and the crisis in orthodox hermeneutics", *Journal of Medieval and Renaissance Studies* 10 (1980), 53-72.

G. Nahon, "Les Marranes espagnols et portugais et les communautés juives issues du marranisme dans l'historiographie récente (1960-1975)", *Revue des Etudes juives* 136 (1977), 297-367.

——, "Les rapports des communautés judeo-portugaises de France avec celle d'Amsterdam au XVIIᵉ et au XVIIIᵉ siècles", *SR* 10 (1976), 37-78, 151-188.

D. Nauta, *Samuel Maresius*, Amsterdam 1935.

B. Netanyahu, *Don Isaac Abravanel, Statesman and Philosopher*, Philadelphia 1953.

F. Nettesheim, *Geschichte der Schulen im alten Herzogthum Geldern*. Ein Beitrag zur Geschichte des Unterrichtswesen Deutschlands und der Niederlandse, Düsseldorf [1880-1881].

H. F. K. van Nierop, *Van Ridders tot Regenten*. De Hollandse adel in de zestiende en de eerste helft van de zeventiende eeuw, z.p. 1984.

H. A. Oberman, *Wurzeln des Antisemitismus*: Christenangst und Judenplage im Zeitalter von Humanismus und Reformation, Berlin 1981.

H. van Oerle, "De bouwgeschiedenis van de Thysius' bibliotheek aan het Rapenburg", *Leidsch Jaarboekje* 35 (1943), 170-179.

W. J. Ong, *Ramus. Method and the Decay of Dialogue*. From the art of discours to the art of reason, Cambridge, Mass. 1958.

A. G. van Opstal, *André Rivet*, een invloedrijk Hugenoot aan het hof van Frederik Hendrik, Harderwijk 1937.

*Orationes inaugurales* a SS Theologiae Professoribus & Collegii Illust. Ordinum Hollandiae & West-Frisiae Moderatoribus habitae cum facultas Theologiae & Collegium Ill. Ord. ab Amplissibus D. Curatoribus solemniter instaurarentur, Lugduni Batavorum 1620.

M. Pattison, *Isaac Casaubon (1559-1614)*, London 1875.

F. Petri/G. Droege, *Rheinische Geschichte* II, Düsseldorf 1976.

R. Pfister, *Kirchengeschichte der Schweiz*, 2 vols., Zürich 1964-1974.

J. Pistorius, *Artis Cabalisticae*, hoc est, reconditae theologiae et philosophiae, scriptorum, tomus I. Basilae [1587].

J. E. Platt, "Sixtinus Amama. Citizen of the Republic of Letters", in: G. Th. Jensma, F. R. H. Smit, F. Westra (edd.), *Universiteit te Franeker 1585-1811: bijdragen tot de geschiedenis van de Friese Hogeschool*, Leeuwarden 1985, 236-48.

J. J. Poelhekke, *Frederik Hendrik, Prins van Oranje:* een biografisch drieluik, Zutphen [1978].

P. Polman, *L'élément historique dans la controverse religieuse du XVIᵉ siècle*, Gembloux 1932.

J. I. Pontanus, *Brieven van en aan Jo. Is. Pontanus*, 1595-1639, uitgegeven door P. N. van Doorninck en P. C. Molhuysen, Haarlem 1909.

G. H. M. Posthumus Meyjes, *Geschiedenis van het Waalse College te Leiden*, 1606-1699, tevens een bijdrage tot de vroegste geschiedenis van het fonds Hallet, Leiden 1975.

——, "Jean Hotman en het calvinisme in Frankrijk", *Nederlands Archief voor Kerkgeschiedenis* 64 (1984), 42-77.

*Praestantium ac eruditorum virorum epistolae ecclesiasticae et theologicae varii argumenti*, ed. III novo augmento locupletata, Amstelodami 1704.

I. Prins, "De oud-Hollandse drukpersvrijheid ten opzichte van het Joodsche boek", *Bijdragen en Mededelingen van het Genootschap voor de Joodsche wetenschap in Nederland* 5 (1933), 147-176.

M. E. Pronk-Bosch, "Bertrand Theophile de Banos en zijn stipendium", *Kerkhistorische studiën*, uitgegeven ter gelegenheid van het 75-jarig bestaan van het kerkhistorisch gezelschap S.S.S., Leiden 1977, 97-113.

B. Prijs, *Die Basler hebräischen Drucke (1492-1866)*, bearb. von J. Prijs, ergänzt und hrsg. von B. Prijs, Olten/Freiburg i. Br. 1964.

C. S. M. Rademaker, *Gerardus Joannes Vossius* (1577-1649), Zwolle 1967.

J. Rainoldus, *Censura librorum apocryphorum Vet. Testamenti adversus pontificios, inprimis Rob. Bellarminum* 2 vols., Oppenheim 1611.

A. Reeland, *Analecta Rabbinica*, Ultrajecti 1702.

*Hermann Samuel Reimarus* (1694-1768); ein "bekannter Unbekannter" der Aufklärung in Hamburg. Vorträge gehalten auf der Tagung der Joachim Jungius-Gesellschaft der Wissenschaften Hamburg am 12. und 13. Oktober 1972, Göttingen 1973.

H. S. Reimarus, *Vindicatio dictorum Veteris Testamenti in Novo allegatorum*, Hrsgb. von P. Stemmer, Göttingen 1983.

B. Rekers, *Benito Arias Montano*, 1527-1598, London/Leiden 1972.

I. S. Revah, *Spinoza et le Dr. Juan de Prado*, Paris/La Haye 1959.

H. Reventlow, "Richard Simon und seine Bedeutung für die kritische Erforschung der Bibel", in: G. Schwaiger (Hrsgb.), *Historische Kritik in der Theologie*. Beiträge zu ihrer Geschichte, Göttingen 1980, 11-37.

——, *Bibelautorität und Geist der Moderne:* die Bedeutung des Bibelverständnisses für die geistesgeschichtliche und politische Entwicklung in England von der Reformation bis zur Aufklärung, Göttingen 1980.

F. A. Ridder van Rappard, *Ernst Brinck*, Utrecht [1867].

O. Ritschl, *Dogmengeschichte des Protestantismus*, 3. Band; Die reformierte Theologie im 16. und 17. Jahrhunderts in ihrer Entstehung und Entwicklung, Göttingen 1926.

J. S. Rittangelius, *Liber Iezirah*, qui Abrahamo Patriarchae adscribitur, una cum commentario Rabi Abraham (..) super 32 Semitis Sapientiae, a quibus liber Iezirah incipit, Amstelodami 1642.

A. Rivet, *Isagoge*, sive Introductio generalis ad Scripturam sacram Veteris et Novi Testamenti, Lugduni Batavorum 1627.

——, *Commentarii in librum secundum Mosis*, qui Exodus apud Graecos inscribitur, in quibus praeter scholia, analysim, explicationem, & observationes doctrinarum in usum Concionatorum, variae quaestiones Theoreticae & practicae discutiuntur, & solvuntur. Ex publicis ejus praelectionibus in celeberrima Batavorum Academia, Lugduni Batavorum 1634.

——, *Opera theologica quae latine edidit*, 3 vols., Roterodami 1651-1660.

H. C. Rogge, *Johannes Wtenbogaert en zijn tijd*, 3 vols., Amsterdam 1874-1876.

P. T. van Rooden, "Spinoza's bijbeluitleg", *SR* 18 (1984), 120-133.

——, "Willem Surenhuis' opvatting van de Misjna", in: J. de Roos, A. Schippers & J. W. Wesselius, *Driehonderd jaar oosterse talen in Amsterdam*, Amsterdam 1986, 43-54.

P. T. van Rooden & J. W. Wesselius, "J. S. Rittangel in Amsterdam", *Nederlands Archief voor Kerkgeschiedenis* 65 (1985), 131-152.

——, "Two early cases of publication by subscription in Holland and Germany: Jacob Abendana's *Mikhlal Yophi* (1661) and David Cohen de Lara's *Keter Kehunna* (1668)", *Quaerendo* 16 (1986), 110-130.

——, "The early Enlightenment and Judaism: The 'civil dispute' between Philippus van Limborch and Isaac Orobio de Castro (1687)", *SR* 21 (1987), 140-153.

J. Ros, *De studie van het Bijbelgrieksch van Hugo Grotius tot Adolf Deissmann*, Nijmegen 1940.

A. W. Rosenberg, "Hugo Grotius as Hebraist", *SR* 12 (1978), 62-90.

G. B. de Rossi, *Bibliotheca Judaica antichristiana*, qua editi et inediti Judaeorum adversus christianam religionem libri recensentur, Parmae 1800.

H. W. Rotermund, *Lexikon aller Gelehrten die seit der Reformation im Bremen gelebt haben*, nebst Nachrichten von gebornen Bremern, die in andern Ländern Ehrenstellen bekleideten, 2 vols., Bremen 1818.

B. Roussel, "Histoire de l'Eglise et histoire de l'exégèse au XVI<sup>e</sup> siècle", *Bibliothèque d'Humanisme et Renaissance* 37 (1975), 181-192.

R. van Roijen, "Inleiding", in: *Bibliotheca Thysiana*. Catalogus archief, familiepapieren en koopmansboeken [ongedrukt; Leiden oktober 1941].

H. P. Salomon, "The 'De Pinto' Manuscript. A 17th century Marrano family history", *SR* 9 (1975), 1-62.

——, "Haham Saul Levi Morteira en de portugese nieuw-christenen", *SR* 10 (1976), 127-141.

J. J. Scaliger, *Opus de Emendatione Temporum*; castigatus et auctius. cum Notis ejusdem Scaligeri, Lugduni Batavorum 1598.

——, *Elenchus Trihaeresii Nicolai Seraii*, Franekerae 1605.

——, *Epistres Françoises des personnages illustres et doctes à M. Joseph Juste de la Scala*. Mises en lumière par Jacques de Rèves, Harderwijck 1624.

——, *Epistolae omnes quae reperiri potuerunt nunc primae collectae et editae*, Lugduni Batavorum 1627.

——, *Lettres Françaises inédites*, publiées et annotées par P. T. de Larroque, Agen/Paris 1879.

W. Schickard, *Jus Regium Hebraeorum*, e tenebris Rabbinorum erutum, Argentae 1625.

H. Schilling, *Niederländische Exulanten im 16. Jahrhundert. Ihre Stellung im Sozialgefüge und im religiösen Leben deutscher und englischer Städte*, [Gütersloh 1971].

G. Schnedermann, *Die Controverse des Ludovicus Cappellus mit den Buxtorfen über das Aelter der hebräischen Punctation*, Leipzig 1879.

H. J. Schoeps, *Philosemitismus im Barock*. Religions- und geistesgeschichtliche Untersuchungen, Tübingen 1952.

K. Scholder, *Ursprünge und Probleme der Bibelkritik im 17. Jahrhundert*. Ein Beitrag zur Entstehung der historisch-kritischen Theologie, München 1966.

G. G. Scholem, *Sabbatai Sevi, the mystical Messiah, 1626-1676*, London 1973.

——, e.a., *Kabbalistes chrétiens*, Paris 1979.

C. W. Schoneveld, *Intertraffic of the Mind*. Studies in seventeenth-century Anglo-Dutch translation with a checklist of books translated from English into Dutch 1600-1700, Leiden 1983.

O. Schutte, *Repertorium der Nederlandse vertegenwoordigers residerende in het buitenland 1584-1810*, 's-Gravenhage 1976.

A. Schweitzer, *Geschichte der Leben-Jesu-Forschung*. 2. neu bearb. und verm. Aufl. des Werkes "Von Reimarus zu Wrede", Tübingen 1913.

F. Seck (Hrsgb.), *Wilhelm Schickard*, 1592-1635. Astronom, Geograph, Orientalist, Erfinder der Rechenmaschine, Tübingen 1978.

F. Secret, *Le Zohar chez les Kabbalistes chrétiens de la Renaissance*, Paris 1958.

J. Selden, *Opera omnia*, tam edita quam inedita. collegit ac recensuit D. Wilkins, 3 vols., Londini 1726.

P. R. Sellin, *Daniel Heinsius and Stuart England*, Leiden 1968.

——, "Daniel Heinsius and the genesis of the medal commemorating the Synod of Dort, 1618-1619", *Lias* 2 (1975), 177-185.

C. Sepp, *Het godgeleerd Onderwijs in Nederland gedurende de 16e en 17e eeuw*, 2 delen, Leiden 1873-1874.

——, "Het Nieuw-Grieksche Testament van 1638", *Bibliographische Mededeelingen*, Leiden 1883, 188-256.

R. Simon, *Histoire Critique du Vieux Testament*. Nouv. édition, augmentée d'une apologie générale, de plusieurs remarques critiques et d'une réponse par un théologien protestant, Rotterdam 1685.

——, *Histoire Critique des principaux Commentateurs du Nouveau Testament*, Rotterdam 1693.

F. Socinus, *De auctoritate Sacrae Scripturae*, in: *Bibliotheca Fratrum Polonorum* I, Irenopoli 1656, 265-280.

H. Soly, "Het 'verraad' der 16e eeuwse burgerij: een mythe?", *TvG* 86 (1973), 262-280.

J. P. Sommerville, "John Selden, the Law of Nature and the Origins of Government", *The Historical Journal* 27 (1948), 437-447.

J. W. Spaans, "Het bewijs van de waarheid der christelijke religie. Hugo de Groot 'teghen de Mahumetisterije", [onuitgegeven doctoraalscriptie, Leiden 1982].

T. Sprat, *The History of the Royal Society of London for the improving of Natural Knowledge*, London 1667.
K. L. Sprunger, *The learned doctor William Ames.* Dutch backgrounds of English and American Puritanism, Urbana [1972].
E. Staehelin, "Der Briefwechsel zwischen Johannes Buxtorf II und Johannes Cocceius", *Theologische Zeitschrift* 4 (1948), 372-391.
*De Statenvertaling* 1637-1937, Haarlem 1937.
J. Steinmann, *Richard Simon et les origines de l'exégèse biblique*, [Paris 1960].
M. Steinschneider, *Bibliographisches Handbuch über die theoretische und praktische Literatur für hebräische Sprachkunde*, Leipzig 1859.
——, *Catalogus librorum hebraeorum in Bibliotheca Bodleiana*, Berolini 1852-1860.
J. H. Steubing, *Geschichte der hohen Schule Herborn*, Hadamar 1823.
W. Surenhuis, *Mischna* sive totius Hebraeorum juris, rituum, antiquitatum ac legum oralium systema, cum Maimonidis et Bartenorae commentariis integris. Quibus acc. variorum auctorum notae (..) Latinitate donavit ac notis illustravit Guill. Surenhusius, 6 vols., Amstelaedami 1698-1703.
——, *Biblos Katallages* in quo secundum veterum theologorum hebraeorum formulas allegandi et modos interpretandi conciliantur loca ex V. in N.T. allegata, Amstelaedami 1713.
*Syllabus Controversiarum Religionis*, quae Ecclesiis Orthodoxis cum quibuscumque Adversariis intercedunt, Basilae 1663.
*Synopsis Purioris Theologiae* (ed. H. Bavinck), Lugduni Batavorum 1881.
J. den Tex, *Oldenbarnevelt*, 5 vols., Haarlem 1960-1972.
C. L. Thijssen-Schoute, *Nederlands Cartesianisme*, Amsterdam 1954.
M. Todd, "Seneca and the Protestant Mind: The Influence of Stoicism on Puritan Ethics", *Archiv für Reformationsgeschichte* 74 (1983), 182-200.
P. Toon (ed.), *Puritans, the Millennium and the Future of Israel:* Puritan Eschatology 1600-1660, Cambridge/London 1970.
D. Tossanus, "Oratio de vita & obitu Johannis Buxtorfii", in: *Memoriae philosophorum, oratorum, poetarum, historicorum, et philologorum nostri saeculi*, curante M. Henningo, Francofurti 1667, 306-324.
J. Trigland, *Oratio funebris in obitum Nobilissimi, Clarissimi, Doctissimique Viri, D. Constantini L'Empereur Ab Opwiick*, S.S. Theologiae Doctoris, & dum viveret, Professoris in Academia Lugduno-Batavae. Habita in Auditorio Theologico nonis Iulii 1648, Lugduni Batavorum 1648.
H. E. Troje, *Graeca leguntur.* Die Aneignung des byzantinischen Rechts und die Entstehung eines humanistischen Corpus Iuris Civilis in der Jurisprudenz des 16. Jahrhundert, Köln 1971.
——, "Die Literatur des gemeinen Rechts unter dem Einfluss des Humanismus", in: H. Coing (ed.), *Handbuch der Quellen und Literatur der neueren Privatrechtsgeschichte* II/1, München 1977, 615-788.
R. Tuck, *Natural right theories. Their origin and development*, Cambridge 1979.
N. Tyacke, "Arminianism and English Culture", in: A. C. Duke/C. A. Tamse (edd.), *Britain and the Netherlands* 7. Church and State since the Reformation, The Hague 1981, 94-117.
B. Ugolino, *Thesaurus antiquitatum sacrarum* complectens selectissima clarissimorum virorum opuscula, in quibus veterum Hebraeorum mores, leges, instituta, ritus sacri et civiles illustrantur, 34 vols., Venetiis 1744-1769.
J. Ussher, *The whole Works of James Ussher*, 17 vols., Dublin 1847-1864.
A. L. E. Verheyden, *Le Conseil des troubles.* Liste des condamnés (1567-1573), Bruxelles 1961.
A. Versprille, "De geschiedenis van het huis van Daniël van der Meulen (Rapenburg 19)", *Leidsch Jaarboekje* 35 (1943), 158-169.
P. Veyne, *Le Pain et le Cirque.* Sociologie historique d'un pluralisme politique, [Paris] 1976.

L. Voet, *The Golden Compasses*. A history and evaluation of the printing and publishing activities of the Officina Plantiniana at Antwerp, 2 vols., Amsterdam 1969-1972.

G. H. Vorstius, *Constitutiones de fundamentis legis Rabbi Mosis F. Maiiemon*, Latine redditae (..) additis quibusdam notulis, & Abravanelis scripto *De Fidei Capite*, Amstelodami 1638.

——, *Chronologia sacra-profana*, a mundi conditu ad annum M. 5352 vel C. 1592, dicta (..) Germen Davidis. Auctore R. David Ganz. Cui addita sunt *Pirke* vel Capitula *R. Elieser*. Utraque ex Hebraeo in Latinum versa, & observationibus illustrata; quibus etiam inserta sunt Hebraeorum tam veterum quam recentiorum testimonia de D. Iesu, nec non de Pseudochristis Judaeorum, Lugduni Batavorum 1644.

D. Vossius, *R. Mosis Maimonidae De Idolatria Liber*, cum interpretatione latina et notis, Amsterdami 1642.

G. J. Vossius, *Doctissimi clarissimique Gerardi Joannis Vossii et ad eum virorum eruditione celeberrimorum epistolae* (..) Ex autographis mss. collegit et ordine secundum singula tempora digessit Paulus Colomesius. iterata ed., Londini 1693.

J. C. Wagenseil, *Tela ignea satanae*. Hoc est arcani et horribiles Judaeorum adversus Christum Deum et christianam religionem libri *ANEKDOTOI*, Altdorfi 1681.

A. Walaeus, *Opera*, 2 vols., Lugduni Batavorum 1647-1648.

L. Warner, *Dissertatio* qua de vitae termino, utrum fixus sit, an mobilis, disquiritur ex Arabum & Persarum scriptis, Amsterdami 1642.

——, *Compendium historicum* eorum quae Mohammedani de Christo et praecipuis aliquot religionis Christianae capitibus tradiderunt, Lugduni Batavorum 1643.

——, *Proverbiorum et Sententiarum Persicarum centuria*, collecta & versione notisque adornata, Lugduni Batavorum 1644.

M. Warner, *Joan of Arc*. The Image of Female Heroism, London 1981.

M. Waxman, *A History of Jewish Literature*, 4 vols., New York 1930-1933.

O. Weber, "Compétence de l'Eglise et compétence de l'Etat d'après les ordonnances ecclésiastiques de 1561", in: *Regards contemporains sur Jean Calvin*. Actes du Colloque Calvin, Strassbourg 1964, Paris 1965, 74-85.

G. E. Weil, *Elie Lévita, humaniste et massorète* 1469-1549, Leiden 1963.

T. Willi, "Christliche Hebraisten der Renaissance und Reformation", *Judaica* 30 (1974), 78-85, 100-125.

I. Willi-Plein/T. Willi, *Glaubensdolch und Messiasbeweis*. Die Begegnung von Judentum, Christentum und Islam in 13. Jahrhundert in Spanien, Neukirchen 1980.

H. H. Wolf, *Die Einheit des Bundes*. Das Verhältnis von Altem und Neuem Testament bei Calvin, Neukirchen 1958.

J. C. Wolfius, *Bibliotheca hebraea*, sive notitia tum auctorum Hebraeorum cujuscunque aetatis, tum scriptorum quae vel Hebraice primum exarata vel ab aliis conversa sunt, 4 vols., Hamburgi et Lipsiae, 1715-1733.

H. F. Wijnman, "De Hebraicus Jan Theunisz Barbarossius alias Johannes Antonides als lector in het Arabisch aan de Leidse Universiteit (1612-1613). Een hoofdstuk Amsterdamse geleerdengeschiedenis", *SR* 2 (1968), 1-30, 149-178.

C. van der Woude, *Sibrandus Lubbertus*. Leven en werken in het bijzonder naar zijn correspondentie, Kampen 1963.

——, "Amesius' afscheid van Franeker", *Nederlands Archief voor Kerkgeschiedenis* 52 (1971-1972), 153-177.

E. Zimmer, "Jewish and Christian Hebraist Collaboration in Sixteenth Century Germany", *Jewish Quarterly Review* 71 (1980-1981), 69-88.

R. Zuber, "De Scaliger à Saumaise: Leyde et les grands 'Critiques' français", *Bulletin. Société de l'histoire du Protestantisme Français* 126 (1980), 461-88.

# INDEX OF SUBJECTS

# INDEX OF NAMES

Heinsius, D.   37, 40, 44, 54, 57, 59, 82, 106, 108, 117, 125-6, 127, 134, 135-42, 147, 151, 152, 153, 181, 200, 203, 204, 206-7, 208, 209, 218, 223, 229, 232, 233
Helles, C.   20
Helwicus, C.   113-14
Hendrik Casimir   212*
Henriques, B.   211
Herera, A. Cohen de   159
Heringius, J.   122
Hesiod   143
Heucherius, S.   218
Heurnius, O.   162
Hieronymus a Sancta Fide   176, 179
Hobbes, T.   220
Holbein, H.   58
Hommius, F.   26, 32, 66, 86, 94, 208, 238, 239, 240
Honert, R. van der   84
Hoogeveen, A. van   208
Hooker, R.   39
Hoornbeek, J.   198
Horowitz, S.   123
Hottinger, J. H.   198, 201
Hulsatus, S.   195
Hulsius, A.   185, 228
Huygens, C.   193, 213*
Hyperius, A.   38

Isaac ben Abraham of Troki   171
Isselborg, H.   19, 20, 237

Jacchaeus, G.   31, 37-8, 40
Jacob ben Asher   98, 128
Jehuda ha-Levi   118
Jerome   141
Jeshua ben Joseph ha-Levi   128
Johan Maurits of Nassau-Siegen   210, 211*, 212*, 213
Johan Willem of Nassau   23
Johnson, S.   201*
Johnston, J.   181
Joseph ibn Jahya   126, 154-8
Josephus   156
Josephus ben Gorion   157
Julian   141
Junius, A.   194
Junius, F.   38, 52-3, 56, 58, 79, 86, 87, 90, 112, 139, 146, 156, 222
Justo, J.   101

Keckermann, B.   40
Kellenarius   239
Key, L. de   15
Kilbye, R.   27, 198

Kimḥi, D.   43, 44, 45, 85, 96, 115, 118, 142, 187
Kimḥi, J.   45
Kimḥi, M.   45, 95, 185-9

Laet, J. de   109, 153-4, 181, 206
Langton, W.   64, 78
Lara, David Cohen de   170
Lasco, J.à   38
Laud, W.   28, 191, 198
Ledebuhr, C.   203*
Leidekker, M.   119
L'Empereur, Alexander   19, 20, 21, 30
L'Empereur, Anthoine jr.   19, 20, 25, 30
L'Empereur, Anthoine sr.   15-21, 22*, 23*, 24*, 26*, 31, 135, 235-7
L'Empereur, Constantijn, family, 14-20, 26, 33-4, 209; study, 20-5, 37-47; defective humanist training, 40-1, 156-7; library, 36-7, 84-5, 96-101; promotion, 29-30; noble pretentions, 14, 24; social status, 28, 33-4, 202, 207-13, 228-9; place in Republic of Letters, 106-10, 131, 200-4, 205-8; involvement with Heinsius' *Exercitationes Sacrae*, 135-42; participation in Brazilian sugar-trade, 165, 209-10; appointment at Leiden, 35, 83-4; sollicitations to theological faculty, 33, 94, 104-5, 184, 207, 213-4; appointment as *professor controversiarum judaicarum*, 95, 105-6, 107, 182-3; philosophical interests, 27, 30-1, 32, 40, 215-7, 218; theological bias, 29, 38-40, 47, 103, 129, 154, 214-5, 221, 228; views on the development of exegetical practice, 148, 222-3; views on mystical sense, 149-52; contacts with Jews, 88, 101, 163-5, 170, 210; views on Judaism, 90, 102, 165-68; views on the use of Hebrew, 85-90; views on the use of rabbinical literature, 127, 129, 151-2; interest in rabbinics, 92-3, 100, 102, 158; use of rabbinics, 88, 148-53, 153-58, 179; knowledge of Hebrew and rabbinical literature, 27, 41-5, 91-2, 127-8; teaching of Hebrew, 185-89; teaching of rabbinics, 130, 179, 189; works: *Oratio*, 85-93; *HalOl*, 95, 105, 107, 128-9, 151-2, 163, 166, 182; *Middot*, 102-3, 108, 110, 124-7, 149-50; *ItinBen*, 105, 153-4; *Bava Kamma*, 107, 110, 127-8, 167, 179-82, 203; *RepHeb*, 107, 218-21; *ParaDan*, 154-8, 167; *ComJes*, 168-9, 174; *MosKim*, 185, 186-7; edition of *Lyra Davidis*, 221-2; unpublished works, 107, 131
L'Empereur, H.   17, 235-6

Valera, C. de   79
Valla, L.   133
Vatablus, F.   44, 45, 112, 113, 145
Vedelius, N.   166
Vere, H.   71
Verhel, A.   33
Verlaen, J.   193
Voetius, G.   22, 42, 94, 164, 216
Voisin, J. du   99, 175-6
Vondel, J. van den   192
Vorstius, A.   208
Vorstius, C.   22, 26, 32, 173
Vorstius, G. H.   173-4, 191-2, 195, 197
Vosbergen, C. van   127, 167, 204
Vossius, D.   108, 163, 164, 189, 190*,
   191, 192, 197, 202
Vossius, G. J.   15, 50, 59, 108, 110, 125,
   135, 145, 162-4, 190, 193*, 195, 196,
   200, 202*, 203, 217*
Vossius, I.   190, 191, 202*
Vranckhemius, M.   21
Vulcanius, B.   36

Wagenseil, J. C.   171-3
Walaeus, A.   32, 42, 54-7, 89, 103, 110,
   188-9, 204, 208
Wallenstein, A. W. E.   210
Warner, L.   194-7, 228
Weber, M.   17
Whitaker, W.   39, 78
Wilhem, D. de   99, 108, 109, 162, 169,
   187*, 196, 213*, 214*, 216-7, 246*
Willet, A.   39
Witt, J. L. & W. J. de   33-4
Wolfius, J. C.   97-8
Wtenbogaert, J.   104, 204

Xenophon   47, 157

Zacuto, A.   153, 162
Zanchius, H.   39
Zarnovechius   39
Zwingli, H.   38, 221